NEW YORK CITY

FODOR'S TRAVEL PUBLICATIONS, INC.

NEW YORK • TORONTO • LONDON • SYDNEY • AUCKLAND

WWW.FODORS.COM

Important Note
Time inevitably brings changes, so always confirm
prices, travel facts, and other perishable information
when it matters. Although Fodor's cannot accept
responsibility for errors, you can use this guide in the
confidence that we have taken every care to ensure its
accuracy.

Copyright © The Automobile Association 2000
Maps copyright © The Automobile Association 2000

All rights reserved under International and Pan-
American Copyright conventions. Distributed by
Random House, Inc., New York. No maps, illustrations,
or other portions of this book may be reproduced in any
form without written permission from the publishers.

Published in the United States by Fodor's Travel
Publications, Inc.
Published in the United Kingdom by A.A. Publishing.

Fodor's is a registered trademark of Random House, Inc.

ISBN 0-679-00479-3
Fourth Edition

Fodor's Exploring New York

Author: **Mick Sinclair with additional "Hotels and
Restaurants" material by Mitchell Davis and Jane Miller**
Series Adviser: **Ingrid Morgan**
Joint Series Editor: **Susi Bailey**
Revisions Editor: **Grapevine Publishing Services**
Cartography: **The Automobile Association**
Cover Design: **Tigist Getachew, Fabrizio La Rocca**
Front Cover Silhouette: **Robert Kristofik/Image Bank**

Special Sales
Fodor's Travel Publications are available at special
discounts for bulk purchases for sales promotions or
premiums. Special editions, including personalized
covers, excerpts of existing guides, and corporate
imprints, can be created in large quantities for special
needs, For more information, contact your local
bookseller or write to Special Markets, Fodor's
Travel Publications, 201 East 50th Street, New
York, NY 10022. Inquiries from Canada should
be directed to your local Canadian bookseller
or sent to Random House of Canada, Ltd.,
Marketing Department, 2775 Matheson
Blvd. East, Mississauga, Ontario L4W 4P7.

Printed and bound in Italy by Printer Trento srl
10 9 8 7 6 5 4 3 2 1

How to use this book

ORGANIZATION

New York Is, New York Was
Discusses aspects of life and culture in contemporary New York and explores significant periods in its history.

A–Z
Breaks down the city into regional chapters, and covers places to visit, including walks and drives. Within this section fall the Focus On articles, which consider a variety of subjects in greater detail.

Travel Facts
Contains the strictly practical information vital for a successful trip.

Accommodations & Restaurants
Lists recommended establishments throughout New York, giving a brief summary of their attractions.

ABOUT THE RATINGS
Most places described in this book have been given a separate rating. These are as follows:

▶▶▶   **Do not miss**

▶▶   **Highly recommended**

▶   **Worth seeing**

MAP REFERENCES
To make each particular location easier to find, every main entry in this book has a map reference to the right of its name. This comprises a number, followed by a letter, followed by another number, such as 176B3. The first number (176) refers to the page on which the map can be found, the letter (B) and the second number (3) pinpoint the square in which the main entry is located. The maps on the inside front cover and inside back cover are referred to as IFC and IBC respectively.

Contents

How to use this book 4

Contents pages 5–7

My New York 8

NEW YORK IS 9–28
On the street 10–11
Opportunity 12–13
Films 14–15
Music 16–17
Transformation 18–19
Art 20–21
Literature 22–23
Architecture 24–25
Festivals and events
26–28

NEW YORK WAS 29–47
Early settlers 30–31
Colonial to independent
32–33
Immigration 34–35

Entrepreneurs 36–37
Expansion 38–39
The Depression 40–41
Corruption 42–43
The port 44–45
Bankrupt 46–47

Sign-cleaning on the corner of Seventh Avenue and Broadway

A–Z

Areas of New York 48–53
Itineraries 56–57
A–Z 60–193
Excursions 194–211
Accommodations 212–215
Food and drink 216–225
Shopping 226–231
Nightlife 232–241
New York for children 242–243
New York for free 244

Focus On

Survival guide 54–55
Views 58–59
Boat trips 67
African-Americans 73
Brooklyn-by-the-Sea 75
The Chelsea Hotel 85
The Chinese 88
Sports 90
East Europeans 105

Luxurious restaurants 108–109
Bars 114–115
Gay life 117
The Beats 119
Places of worship 120–121
Guggenheim architecture 124
Puerto Ricans 127
Abstract expressionism 128–129
The media 132–133
The Italians 136
The Jewish community 139
Secondhand shopping 140–141
Egyptian art 143
Islamic art 145
The Lehman Collection 147
The Irish 154
MoMA's third floor 160
Art deco 162–163
Grand Central Terminal 166–167
Art galleries 176–177
Statue of Liberty 181
The U.N. in New York 185
Woody Allen 188

Statue of Liberty

Walks
Chinatown streetlife 87
The East Village stores and sights
99
Financial District architecture
104
The heart of Greenwich Village
113
Midtown Manhattan landmarks
150
Midtown churches and
museums 150
Art and elegance 187

Midtown Manhattan 151
Upper East Side 187
Catskill Mountains 196
Hudson Valley 201
Long Island 206–207
New York Subway 286–287

Excursions
Catskill Mountains 196–199
Hudson Valley 200–205
Long Island 206–211

TRAVEL FACTS 245–260

**ACCOMMODATIONS AND
RESTAURANTS** 261–279

Index 280–285

Acknowledgments 288

Maps and Plans
Manhattan's 3-star sights
IFC–IBC
New York's boroughs
48–49
Brooklyn 77
Central Park 82
Chinatown 87
The East Village 99
Financial District 104
Greenwich Village 113

New York fire engine

My New York

Mick Sinclair has made a career out of homing in on the nooks and crannies of America's major cities. The author of guidebooks to Chicago, Miami, and San Francisco, he has contributed travel articles and features on culture and the arts to magazines and newspapers all over the world.

Whether they love it or loathe it, few can deny that New York is the most stimulating city in the world, and the only one where so much is so familiar even at first sight. The Statue of Liberty, the Empire State Building, and Central Park are just three New York landmarks well known to visitors before they set eyes on them. Equally familiar are the New York sights—such as bagels with cream cheese, and yellow cabs—that could exist anywhere but which the media has made iconographic images of the city.

It could be said that there is nothing new for an author to say about the city, but writing about New York provides the challenge to make the familiar suddenly seem less familiar. It means pounding the streets and combing the archives to dig up the inside stories that swiftly make visitors realize that, for all their preconceptions, they never really knew New York at all.

A closer look at New York opens up a great metropolis built on madness and mayhem, energy and imagination, fortuitously coupled to sufficient money to buy it the kind of things rival cities can only dream about. New York museums are vast, and reflect the achievements of every culture. New York buildings might be places in which to live and work, but are frequently also groundbreaking architecture. New York's stores hold everything anyone could ever want to buy.

Everyone recognizes the Statue of Liberty, but how many know it was originally intended for the Suez Canal? Who can name the hard-headed 19th-century financier who consulted an astrologist for assistance with decision-making? And how many visitors can explain how profits from the notorious slum tenements of the Lower East Side were instrumental in giving New York one of the world's greatest reference libraries?

In finding the answers, I was able to steadily peel back the layers to reach the city beneath. New York stripped naked is not always a pretty sight, but it is one that is ultimately much more believable than the city of myth. If only to encourage others to find something new in this seemingly familiar, but also strange and mysterious, place, the undertaking was a worthwhile one.
Mick Sinclair

New York Is

Great museums, fantastic architecture, luxurious hotels, and every imaginable kind of restaurant—New York has them all. But it is only by stepping out among the sights, smells, and sounds that fill its streets that you will begin to feel the true pulse of the mighty city.

NONSTOP STREETS A New York street can be a lonely place but seldom is it an empty one. Around 5 AM, the first batches of briefcase-carrying commuters emerge from the city's subway stations, just in time to see the nightclubbers heading for home. A few hours later, young people make their way to school; soon after, the first lunch-seeking office workers begin filing onto the sidewalks. By early afternoon, some commuters are already making for the stations and by dusk Midtown Manhattan is buzzing with pre-theater diners. In Greenwich Village and the East Village, bars and clubs prepare for another long, busy night.

Despite the zero tolerance policy in New York, graffiti is still visible on some city streets

10

❏ The 12,000 yellow taxis that cruise New York's streets are much more than merely a quick (traffic permitting) way of traveling from A to B. Enshrined in city mythology, taxis have inspired a T.V. series (*Taxi*, which made a star of Danny DeVito), been represented as small yellow rectangles in a major painting—Mondrian's *Broadway Boogie-Woogie* (displayed at New York's Museum of Modern Art)—and, like taxis the world over, are infamously hard to find when it rains. Why are they yellow? Because John Hertz, who founded the Yellow Cab Company in 1907, read a survey carried out by the University of Chicago which found that yellow was the color most people found easiest to spot. ❏

OFF THE STREET One contributory factor to the round-the-clock hubbub on New York's streets is the size and price of the apartments that rise above them. Most Manhattan apartments are small and, except for a few rent-controlled properties, extremely expensive. Rather than stay indoors cooking in a tiny kitchen, New Yorkers will welcome any opportunity to eat, drink, and socialize outside their apartments.

STREET DEALS Free enterprise rules the New York streets. An abundance of foodstands can be found all around the city, and appetites can be satisfied—often surprisingly well—without ever venturing inside a restaurant. Bookworms can shop at makeshift outdoor tables, which offer for sale all kinds of reading material ranging from brand-new discounted hardbacks to used paperbacks. Many New York apartments have been furnished by various purchases from street markets, where the merchandise ranges from eccentric junk to valuable pieces of matching furniture.

Even if it rains, there is no need to duck inside for shelter. As the first drops start to fall, street-corner traders appear, seemingly from nowhere, bearing armfuls of inexpensive umbrellas.

STREET TRAFFIC Listen to bike riders and truck drivers locked in verbal combat at traffic lights, after jostling for prime position the length of the last block. Careful eavesdropping may even provide you with useful ammunition if *you* ever find it necessary to exchange insults with a New Yorker.

Watch out for rollerbladers who tempt death by weaving through Fifth Avenue's frantic rush-hour traffic—sometimes they will even grab hold of passing vehicles for a free tug.

IMPROVING STREETS After decades of cost-cutting in city services had left some city streets potholed and socially unsafe, New York's Times Square and the area around Grand Central Terminal underwent dramatic changes during the 1990s. Designated as Business Improvement Districts (BID) under a nationwide scheme funded by a tax on local businesses, both neighborhoods now employ unarmed security forces to heighten safety and provide visitor-friendly services such as information desks and street maps. Both New York BIDs offer free walking tours to highlight their success.

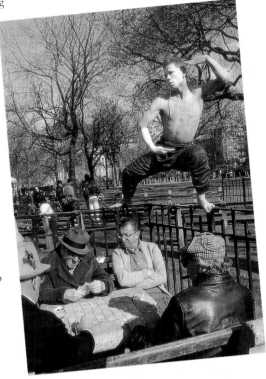

Tompkins Square Park. Street culture comes in many guises

11

❏ Everyone knows New York is nicknamed the Big Apple but nobody is sure of the origins of the term. Musicians, gangsters, and horse-racing devotees have all been cited as its source, but the phrase's recent popularity stems from a tourism campaign launched in 1971. ❏

SAFER STREETS Through the 1990s, levels of crime in New York fell sharply. Between 1993 and 1995 there was a 27.4 percent drop in reported crime and a further 7 percent drop between 1996 and 1997. Subway offences declined by 64.3 percent in five years. As in most of the world's big cities, it is wise to be cautious, but New York is not particularly unsafe. Nonetheless, visitors should heed the Survival Guide on pages 54–55.

For anyone, anywhere, with aspirations and dreams, New York is the place to be. Whether you want to sing and dance your way to fame, make a mint on Wall Street, or start a new life in a new land, New York is—as it has always been—the beacon of opportunity.

HIGH FINANCE For those who can stand the stresses and strains, the heady world of New York high finance offers rewards unimagined and a level of power that few outside the realms of international politics ever experience.

Take one look at the glass-and-steel high-rise towers of the Manhattan skyline, and it should be no surprise that New York provides 3–3.5 million people with jobs, 80 percent of them in the private sector. New York annually also hosts around 1.7 million convention delegates, bringing over a billion dollars to the city economy.

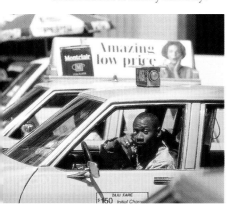

Cab driving: a steady living

Industrial giants such as international oil companies may have blue-collar work forces around the globe but their companies are driven by decisions made in the penthouse boardrooms of their Manhattan headquarters. These decisions not only directly affect the livelihoods of millions but indirectly influence the well-being of the country's—and the world's—economy.

❏ During the 1980s, a surging New York Stock Exchange helped create the yuppie and the junk-bond millionaire. Following the stock-market crashes of 1987 and 1989, overnight fortunes have been harder to find. Nonetheless, the New York Stock Exchange was at the heart of the "bull market" of the mid-1990s, when stock prices soared and workers' performance bonuses, estimated to average $54,000 per person in 1996, created a knock-on effect across the city as money was lavished on goods and services. Financial collapses in Asia, Russia, and South America during the late 1990s, however, emphasized the downside of a global economy, bringing uncertainty and major falls on the New York financial markets, and wiping out many paper fortunes despite the fast-rising value of Internet-related stocks. ❏

TAXI DRIVERS Shortly after the internal combustion engine replaced the horse on the New York streets, driving a taxi became the staple first job of arriving immigrants.

Less than 11 percent of applications for cab-driving jobs are from native-born New Yorkers. More noticeable in some instances is a cab driver's less than fluent command of English.

Many of these newly arrived taxi-drivers may have a university degree or years of experience in some profession in their native land. Being a cabbie in New York means steady wages and a chance to provide their children with a standard of education not available back home.

UNCONVENTIONAL LIFESTYLES

Many come to New York simply for the opportunity to live as they want to. Multicolored hair and bizarre attire seldom raise eyebrows on Manhattan's seen-it-all-before streets. Avid night clubbers can go out and enjoy themselves all night every night, stay in bed all day and never feel that New York life is passing them by in this city that never sleeps.

ambitious news-gatherers across the country. Some New York-based magazines enjoy worldwide esteem. In recent years, the *New Yorker*, *Vanity Fair*, and *Vogue* have had little trouble in luring overseas talent and in the past have raised some eyebrows by appointing British editors to their most coveted jobs.

Most of the country's major publishers are based in New York, which attracts writers—both American and émigré—to the city and gives agents and editors the chance to work with some of the world's most celebrated literary names.

13

New Yorkers have learned to take the eccentric in stride

New York also promises a supportive infrastructure for gays and lesbians, many of whom come to escape discrimination in jobs and housing elsewhere.

PUBLISHING The New York-based *Wall Street Journal* and *The New York Times* lead the country for quality reporting and carry journalism's most prestigious jobs—coveted by

❏ An estimated 770,000 college graduates move to New York annually. ❏

THE STAGE

Those intent upon a career in the performing arts ignore New York at their peril. A major early boost is to be one of the thousand students accepted every year into the city's highly rated Juilliard School of Music and Performing Arts.

For thespians, New York's place is clearly at the heart of U.S. theater, whether it is Broadway blockbusters or the dozens of Off-Off-Broadway productions. New York also offers acting opportunities away from live audiences: the majority of T.V. soap operas and commercials are cast in Manhattan, although most T.V. and film work is centered in Los Angeles.

New York's ballet, orchestras, and opera companies, are among the world's most highly rated.

Everybody knows, or thinks they know, New York long before they actually arrive there, having seen the city depicted—be it lovingly or with loathing—in innumerable movies. Here is a highly selective list of the most revealing, famous, or simply the most enjoyable, films set in New York. (Woody Allen's New York films are detailed on page 188.)

Breakfast at Tiffany's (1961). On screen New York has never appeared more romantic than in this adaptation of the Truman Capote novella; Audrey Hepburn stars as the free-spirited Holly Golightly who—dressed in a chic black evening gown—drinks coffee shortly after dawn as she admires the jewels in the shop window of Fifth Avenue's Tiffany and Company.

The Crowd (1928). Two years after Fritz Lang's futuristic *Metropolis*, inspired by the Manhattan skyline, came King Vidor's expressionistic study of the ordinary man's struggle in the seething city: memorable New York scenes abound.

Do The Right Thing (1989). In what might be Spike Lee's best film, the director uses the setting of a New York ethnically mixed community—such as the Korean grocer and Italian pizzeria owner who operate in a predominantly African-American neighborhood—in a witty and provocative exploration of complex racial issues.

❏ Thomas Edison may have electrified the city but a combination of factors—royalties due on Edison-patented cinematic equipment, the demands of actors' unions, and inclement weather—encouraged fledgling filmmakers to leave New York (where movies were a natural offshoot of Broadway theaters) in the early 1900s for the sunshine of southern California. ❏

I Shot Andy Warhol (1996). Fact-based evocation of Warhol's Factory and the insularity of the 1960s New York art world as seen through the eyes of Valerie Solanas, played in marvelously intense style by Lili Taylor, whose rising anger culminates in her shooting of Andy Warhol.

King Kong (1933). The conflict between man and nature reaches its climax as the giant ape swats planes while flirting with Fay Wray beside the Empire State Building.

The Lost Weekend (1945).The bar in which Billy Wilder's alcoholic weekend began still exists—P. J. Clarke's, Third Avenue at 55th Street.

Mean Streets (1973). Martin Scorsese had a bigger hit in 1976 with *Taxi Driver*, but this contrasts the New York of hippies and flower-power with the macho traditions of young Italian-Americans on the make.

Metropolitan (1990). This witty comedy focuses on the alternately comic and poignant adventures of a West Side intellectual who befriends a group of Upper East Side young people who are attending Manhattan debutante balls at Christmas time.

On the Town (1949). One of the first MGM musicals shot on location, this fast-paced film follows three sailors (Gene Kelly, Frank Sinatra, and Jules Munshin) on a 24-hour pass as they dash around the city, stopping at Rockefeller Center, the Statue of Liberty, the Bronx Zoo, the Brooklyn Bridge, and other key sights.

14

The city's best-known screen moment: King Kong and Fay Wray in 1933

Portrait of Jennie (1948). A lovely and appropriately haunting film in which a troubled artist is enchanted by a young girl in Central Park and later discovers that she is a ghost.

Q—The Winged Serpent (1982). Witty, low-budget piece in which a giant bird flies out of Aztec mythology to terrorize New Yorkers. It lays an egg inside the Chrysler Building, only to be discovered by a hoodlum who tries to cash in on his amazing find.

Saturday Night Fever (1977). A product of 1970s disco mania that gives a taste of the culture of young Italian-Americans in Brooklyn's Bensonhurst neighborhood.

Serpico (1973). In real life, Frank Serpico was an honest cop whose efforts to stamp out corruption in the New York police force met with intimidation and violence. Serpico's stand eventually led to a massive clean-up campaign—and to Al Pacino playing him in this highly charged thriller, which has great location shots.

Seven Year Itch (1955). Probably Marilyn Monroe's finest screen moment, this film is known for one of her most enduring images: her skirt is lifted by air rising from the subway grate at the junction of 52nd Street and Lexington Avenue.

Sweet Smell of Success (1957). A brilliant Tony Curtis as the sleazy press agent currying favor with Broadway gossip columnist, Burt Lancaster.

❏ An unknown 18-year-old actress called Lauren Bacall was crowned Miss Greenwich Village in 1942. ❏

Saturday Night Fever *in Brooklyn*

From Broadway shows to live bands in Bowery basements, New York resonates with music and has frequently attracted the composers, lyricists, musicians, and those simply seeking stardom, who have reshaped popular music and created some of the world's most memorable songs.

TIN PAN ALLEY The sound of pianos resembling the rattling of tin pans earned a section of 28th Street the nickname Tin Pan Alley from the 1890s. George Gershwin began his career as a Tin Pan Alley composer with the song "Swanee" (1918). The pianos belonged to music publishing companies, many of which later moved to the Brill Building (1619 Broadway; see below).

RHAPSODIES IN BLUE African-American migration to New York underpinned the city's emergence as a jazz center during the 1920s when emerging talents took jazz far beyond its roots. Among the innovators were Duke Ellington, pianist, composer, and band leader in Harlem's Cotton Club; and jazz-influenced classical composers such as Gershwin, whose *Rhapsody in Blue* became synonymous with New York. The city also provided a launch pad in the 1940s for bebop, a new improvisational style with the glorious Charlie Parker, Thelonious Monk,and Dizzy Gillespie among its practitioners.

LULLABIES ON BROADWAY In the early 1900s, Broadway's vaudeville shows beckoned aspiring songwriters. After working in Chinatown as a 'singing waiter,' Irving Berlin found success with the Ziegfeld Follies and composed classics such as *White Christmas, There's No Business Like Show Business,* and *Everybody's Doin' It.* George M. Cohan's *Give My Regards to Broadway* and *I'm a Yankee Doodle Dandy* both originated in Broadway shows. Howard Arlen penned reviews for Harlem's Cotton Club, including the song *Stormy Weather,* before heading for Hollywood and *Somewhere Over The Rainbow.*

❏ Penned during the 1950s and 1960s were: *The Locomotion, One Fine Day, Da Wah Diddy, Baby I Love You, Hound Dog, You've Lost That Loving Feeling, Da Doo Ron Ron* and *Oh Caroll.* ❏

Irving Berlin at his piano

16

FOLK AND ROCK Through the late 1950s and early 1960s, Greenwich Village coffee houses and folk clubs provided the breeding ground for a new batch of young folk singers, often dealing with topical issues and inspired by luminaries such as Woody Guthrie and Pete Seeger. Those who emerged to wide success included Judy Collins and Bob Dylan.

Dylan's switch from folk to rock music pre-empted the psychedelic era. The streetwise cynicism charac-teristic of New York was at odds with the sensibilities of psychedelia, however, but provided a perfect set-ting for the Velvet Underground. Using violas alongside guitars, cymbal-less drumming and songs about the seedier side of urban life, the Velvet Underground (and their main singer and songwriter Lou Reed) become one of the city's most enduring influences on rock music, despite being commercially unsuc-cessful during their short life.

BRILL The Brill Building was home to song-writers Carole King, Jerry Goffin, Neil Sedaka, Neil Diamond, Barry Mann, and Cynthia Weill, who created some of the famous hits of the 1950s and 1960s (see panel).

NEW WAVE A Bowery basement club, CBGBs, became a venue for nascent bands of the New Wave movement from the mid-1970s.

Mr. Tambourine Man, Bob Dylan

Musically diverse but sharing an attitude, Blondie, The Ramones, and Talking Heads all regularly appeared here, as did other seminal figures such as Patti Smith and Richard Hell. Blondie evolved into the biggest-sell-ing band in the world, reforming in the 1990s to still more success.

RAP AND HIP-HOP Also in the mid-1970s, DJs in the predominantly African-American-populated South Bronx began forging the turntable style known as "scratching", often adding beats from their own drum machine and sometimes joined by an MC providing an improvized vocal "rap" over the music.

Scratching, rap, and the associated break dancing and graffiti art (collec-tively known as hip-hop) evolved into a worldwide phenomenon dur-ing the 1980s, with first hits from the Sugarhill Gang, and Grandmaster Flash and the Furious Five, and then by the Beastie Boys and Run-DMC. By the late 1990s, rap-related music had a global audience, and, in the U.S., was outselling the commercially dominant country music.

Run DMC in concert

17

Few areas of New York stay the same for long. Not only do entire districts undergo staggering transformations—socially, architecturally, and commercially—within a few years, but sometimes a whole new neighborhood can suddenly rise up where previously there was nothing but a hole in the ground.

TIMES SQUARE AND 42ND STREET

The 1970s saw Times Square and the adjacent stretch of 42nd Street—on the borders of Broadway—being taken over by porno theaters, massage parlors and adult bookstores. Drug dealers and prostitutes plied their trade; homeless people were a common sight, and the pedestrian congestion was ideal for pickpockets.

18

A major program of regeneration and development got underway in the mid-1980s, under the banner of the Times Square Business Improvement District. The now considerably transformed area—patrolled by its own security force and kept clean with frequent garbage collection—succeeds in its intention of being a safe and welcoming part of the city to shoppers, tourists, and legitimate businesses alike.

New construction work over recent years has seen high-rise hotels, shopping complexes, and office buildings appear and a number of the area's historic theaters have received much-needed renovations.

Nonetheless, the new-look square has drawn a mixed response from New Yorkers. While most are happy to see crime levels reduced and relish a much-improved subway station, many fear Times Square's "Disneyfication," its character buried beneath theme restaurants and major retail franchises.

BATTERY PARK CITY The sleekest testament to New York's powers of metamorphosis is Battery Park City, a $4-billion project combining commercial, residential, and recreational areas on a 92-acre landfill site situated on the western edge of the Financial District (see pages 102–104).

Conceived in the 1970s, Battery Park City gave a new lease of life to an abandoned stretch of Hudson River waterfront, while finding a use for the thousands of tons of earth and rock excavated during the building of the World Trade Center.

The redeveloped Times Square

The Esplanade along the Hudson

Like Rockefeller Center (to which it is frequently compared), Battery Park City is evolving through the labors of several prestigious architects who are working within a single master plan, which has the intention of re-creating the atmosphere of an elegant, traditional Manhattan neighborhood.

> ❏ "A sobering effect"—the architects' intended impact of Times Square Center on seething Times Square. ❏

The residential buildings hold luxury apartments, while the commercial architecture includes Cesar Pelli's World Financial Center, completed in 1986 and noted for its palm-decorated Winter Garden atrium. The mile-long Esplanade, with Victorian-style lamp-posts and wooden benches, has now restored public access to this section of the Hudson River for the first time in several decades.

CHELSEA Approximately bordered by 14th and 29th streets, and Sixth Avenue and the Hudson River, the Chelsea neighborhood began collecting the residential overspill from the increasingly upscale Greenwich Village through the 1980s. By the early 1990s, the neighborhood—a prominent shopping area during the 1890s and now a mixture of town houses and apartment buildings,

industry and commerce—was an increasingly important nightlife and restaurant area, with a strong gay contingent among its residents and business owners.

A growing number of galleries have made Chelsea a serious rival to the longer-established SoHo art scene and have encouraged more and more stores and restaurants to open up in the area. On Chelsea's western edge, four early-1900s cruise-ship docks have been redeveloped into what is now known as Chelsea Piers, offering a variety of sports activities, as well as dining and shopping, beside the Hudson River.

Many early landmarks remain, not least the Chelsea Hotel (page 85) and those of the Chelsea Historical District (page 153).

> ❏ The continuing eastward migration of New York's unknown and lesser-known artists from Greenwich Village, through SoHo and the East Village neighborhoods, now finds them located across the East River, creating loft studios in the former factories of Brooklyn's Williamsburg. Here they form a striking contrast to the area's concentration of orthodox Jews. ❏

Thanks to a unique combination of wealthy collectors and a wartime influx of modern European artists, New York has not only amassed some of the world's finest pieces of art—displaying them in several world-class museums—but has also evolved into a show-case for new artistic ideas and directions.

FIRST COLLECTIONS Founded in 1804, the **New-York Historical Society** became the city's first repository for art, acquiring a singular collection of Early American works, including many commissioned by Robert Lehman, a New Yorker who opened part of his town house as a gallery and brought American artists such as Thomas Cole to public attention.

The paintings collection of New York's **Metropolitan Museum of Art** (pages 142–148) began with a modest purchase of 174 Dutch and Flemish canvases in 1870 and grew—aided by bequests and donations—into a world-class stock, including many major pieces by Van Gogh, Turner, El Greco, and Vermeer.

BUSINESSMEN BECOME COLLECTORS Having amassed wealth through their control of the industrialization of the United States, and with newly built Fifth Avenue mansions in need of decoration, New York's 19th-century

millionaires began raiding the art collections of Europe. One such was Henry Clay Frick, who acquired the phenomenal hoard now known as the **Frick Collection** (see page 110).

PATRONS Many affluent New Yorkers indulged themselves by commissioning artists to paint their portraits, but one who did a great deal more to encourage the creativity of American artists was Gertrude Vanderbilt Whitney.

Displaying and promoting emergent artists such as Edward Hopper and John Sloan, Whitney also established an influential Parisian-style salon during the early 1900s. Her legacy, the **Whitney Museum of American Art** (page 191), continues to champion the country's unknown artists regardless of prevailing fashions, and has many of the finest, long-established American artists of

The Metropolitan Museum of Art

Art for Sale—a private SoHo gallery

❑ New York is said to be home to 90,000 artists and to hold over 1,000 art galleries. A new and controversial form of New York art emerged in the 1970s when complex and colorful graffiti began appearing in public places, such as subway trains and billboards, created with paint sprayed from cans and signed by its makers only with a distinctive symbol or "tag." ❑

the 20th century represented among its permanent stock.

As Gertrude Whitney was furthering appreciation of American art, wealthy industrialist Solomon R. Guggenheim was discovering the art and artists of modern Europe. Guggenheim's purchases of early Cubist and abstract canvases were displayed on the walls of his suite at the Plaza Hotel, and later became the basis of the **Guggenheim Museum** (pages 122–124). Frank Lloyd Wright designed the building, which is as remarkable as the innovative works of art it holds.

AN INTERNATIONAL ART CENTER As war loomed in Europe, New York found itself acquiring not only European art but European artists as well. By the 1940s, many of modern art's major names resided in the city. They were to have a colossal impact on the New York art scene.

New York surpassed Paris (then under Nazi occupation) as the center for international art dealing and the city's preeminence was confirmed by the emergence of abstract expressionism (see pages 128–129). Meanwhile, the **Museum of Modern Art** (see pages 158–160), founded in 1929, was evolving into the world's most prestigious and most popular modern art museum.

NEW YORK NOW New York spawned pop art, op art, and minimalist art during the 1960s, and by the late 1970s the shabby warehouses of SoHo (see page 175) had been transformed into pristine galleries showcasing new trends and new talents.

In the economically buoyant 1980s, New York art became big business. The artists in vogue then—Julian Schnabel, David Salle, and Eric Fischl—could expect poverty to be a thing of the past.

Today, artist-run galleries can be found in the East Village, Chelsea, and on the Lower East Side. While still energetically showcasing emerging New York artists, the larger galleries also reflect interest in the relatively underacknowledged art of Latin America, Africa, and Asia.

❑ Among the most remarkable of New York's many plaza sculptures is Jean Dubuffet's *Group of Four Trees*, located at the Chase Manhattan Bank in the Financial District. ❑

Not only is New York the center of U.S. publishing, it has also provided more material for 20th-century writers than perhaps any other city. Literary landmarks are liberally strewn about, and several New York neighborhoods have carved out special places for themselves in the annals of literary achievement.

22

A PUBLISHING CAPITAL Geography made New York the publishing capital of the U.S. in the 1850s. Before the U.S. recognized international copyright laws in 1891, any book could be copied, printed, and sold, earning its publisher fat profits as no royalties were due.

To maximize earnings, publishers vied with one another to be first with the latest foreign manuscripts. As New York became the nation's major seaport, the city's publishers could get their hands on new books and produce pirate versions of them faster than rivals elsewhere.

THE CITY OBSERVED New York has long provided rich pickings for observant writers. From a bar-stool vantage point in the early 1900s, O. Henry (the pen name of William Sydney Porter) produced short stories drawing on the seamy side of city life. In a similar vein a few decades later,

Damon Runyon

Damon Runyon described the characters on the fringes of Broadway theaterland. Truman Capote's *Breakfast at Tiffany's* was fine-tuned to 1950s New York high life, while J.D. Salinger's *Catcher in the Rye* followed its young narrator through a New York night and became a benchmark of adolescent angst.

The strains and stresses of 1980s New York underpinned Tom Wolfe's comic novel, *Bonfire of the Vanities*, and the same decade saw the emergence of writers such as Tama Janowitz and Jay McInerney, whose ambivalent prose dwelt on the selfishness and conceits of contemporary New York. Their cocaine-fueled tales were later followed in the 1990s by more introspective, if similarly drug-centred work, such as Elizabeth Wurtzel's *Prozac Nation* and Linda Jablonky's *The Story of Junk.*

❏ Born in Manhattan in 1783, Washington Irving might well be considered New York's first home-grown writer. His satirical *A History of New York* was written under the memorable pseudonym of Diedrich Knickerbocker. ❏

LITERARY NEIGHBORHOODS In the mid-1880s, New York literary life revolved around the fashionable drawing-rooms of Greenwich Village town houses, where heavyweights like James Fenimore Cooper rubbed shoulders with the publishers of literary journals. Such times were described in Edith Wharton's *The Age*

Washington Square and (below right) Henry James

of Innocence and by Henry James in *Washington Square.*

As Greenwich Village rents fell, it drew a host of talented but impoverished writers—as diverse as Willa Cather, John Reed, Theodore Drieser, John Dos Passos, Robert Frost, Eugene O'Neill, and Thomas Wolfe—who left the area filled with literary landmarks (see pages 112–118). The East Village and the Lower East Side began attracting impecunious scribes in the 1950s, when Beat writers like William Burroughs and Allen Ginsberg moved in alongside émigrés such as W.H. Auden. Another arrival was Norman Mailer, who formerly lived in Brooklyn Heights (and lives there now). Mass African-American migration into Harlem helped stimulate the Harlem Renaissance of the 1920s, bringing black writers such as Langston Hughes and Zora Neale Hurston to public notice. In the 1950s, Harlem-born James Baldwin created a stir with *Go Tell It on the Mountain* as did Ralph Ellison with *The Invisible Man.* More recently, Chester Himes used Harlem as the setting for a series of thrillers.

A history of New York's Jewish population can be found in *World of Our Fathers*, by Irving Howe; *Call It Sleep*, by Henry Roth; *The Promise*, by Chaim Potok; *The Assistant*, by Bernard Malamud and *Enemies, a Love Story*, by Isaac Bashevis Singer.

The Manhattan skyline is the stuff of dreams. The city's colonial structures may have almost vanished, but New York's existing buildings are a thrilling mixture, encompassing styles from the country's formative years to the contemporary adventures in postmodernism.

THE FEDERAL STYLE From 1760 to 1830, the Federal style became the first genuine American building style, though it drew heavily on British Georgian and treated public buildings to columns and domes reminiscent of ancient Rome: **City Hall** (see page 89) is a prime example.

Federal-style residential architecture was distinguished by semi-detached houses of brick and wood, with fanlights above the entrances and dormer windows. **Gracie Mansion** (see page 111) is one example. A grander specimen is the former James Watson residence, now the **Shrine of Elizabeth Ann Seton** (see page 66).

❏ The zoning law of 1916, which outlawed new buildings rising sheer from their plot to rob the streets of light, shaped the look of the Manhattan skyscraper. The law led to the widespread use of cutbacks (also called step-backs), a tapering effect that has been interpreted by architects in various ways, and perhaps most memorably demonstrated by the well-known profile of the Empire State Building. ❏

REVIVALS As New York enjoyed an economic surge during the 19th century, the Greek revival style—bringing porticoes and floral-patterned ironwork to the facades of the new rows of townhouses, such as those facing **Washington Square Park**—was the first of a spate of revivals, which included Italianate, Renaissance, and Gothic. Examples of all these are widely found.

BROWNSTONES A cheap form of sandstone quarried in New Jersey, brownstone was used to build swiftly and at low cost in the mid-1800s, and brownstone town houses became the main residences of the middle classes. Held in little affection at the time, brownstones enjoyed a surge of popularity from the 1950s and those that remain—especially in Midtown—are highly prized, both as residences and offices.

LUXURY APARTMENT HOUSES By the turn of the century, property prices in Midtown Manhattan had risen beyond the pockets of the middle classes, who began colonizing the new luxury apartments on the Upper West Side. Sumptuously appointed and with anything up to 10 rooms, the apartments also boasted futuristic extras such as built-in refrigerators and pneumatic mail-delivery systems. The still-standing **Dakota** (see page 96) was the first such building; several others remain near by.

EARLY SKYSCRAPERS The **Flatiron Building** (see page 106) was the city's first "world's-tallest" structure and was also the first to be supported by a steel frame—a technique that showed the way for creating even taller buildings. A 1920s building boom gave Manhattan the **Chrysler** and **Empire State buildings**, both of which not only reached record heights but bore the hallmarks of art deco (see pages 162–163).

THE INTERNATIONAL STYLE

The towers of steel and glass above Manhattan resulted from the arrival in New York of Europe's most creative architects, who fled Nazism and brought with them the antitraditional ideas of the International style.

The **Museum of Modern Art** (see pages 158–160), its original facade designed by Goodwin and Stone in 1939, gave New York a taste of the International style. Among later examples was Mies van der Rohe's 1958 **Seagram Building** (Park Avenue between 52nd and 53rd streets), which gave New York its first plaza. By the late 1970s, plazas were found in every high-rise plan, some enclosed to form atriums.

THE 1980S BOOM

With the 1980s construction boom, Manhattan

❏ The beaux-arts style arrived in New York in 1890 and is exemplified by Carrère and Hastings' **New York Public Library** (see page 168), Cass Gilbert's **U.S. Custom House** (see page 190), and works by the firm of McKim, Mead, & White, such as **Washington Memorial Arch** (see page 116). ❏

gained its first modern buildings not bearing the International-style stamp. Philip Johnson's **A.T. & T. Building** (on Madison Avenue between 55th and 56th streets) became known as the Chippendale skyscraper; **Trump Tower** (see page 183) rose as a shrine to vulgar consumerism, and the **World Financial Center** filled its atrium with palm trees. A key theme in the 1990s was the development of entire areas, notably Times Square.

The Chrysler Building and its futuristic neighbors

Rare is the visitor who manages to be in New York when there is not some kind of festival taking place, whether a traffic-stopping parade along Fifth Avenue or a low-key neighborhood get-together. These are just a few highlights from an exceptionally busy festivals and events calendar. For precise dates and details, check the local newspapers or contact the New York Convention and Visitors' Bureau (tel: 484-1222 or 800 NYC VISIT).

JANUARY
Chinese New Year (The exact date depends on the lunar cycle; sometimes this takes place in early February.) Celebrated by giant dragon and lion dances through the streets of Chinatown. Festive banquets are offered by the neighborhood's restaurants.

❑ With a 150-year history, the St. Patrick's Day Parade (along Fifth Avenue between 44th and 86th streets) is by far the biggest of New York's parades.
  Green proliferates in many of the city's bars, which often mark the day with a variety of special events, as do other institutions through the city.
  Tens of thousands take part in the parade itself, and many more join in other St. Patrick's Day-related activities. ❑

Winter Antiques Fair At Seventh Regiment Armory, Park Avenue at East 66th Street. Upscale antiques and their dealers; browsers are also welcome (see also page 226).

FEBRUARY
Black History Month Lectures and exhibitions on African-American themes are held throughout the city.
Empire State Building Run-Up Indoor joggers dash from the landmark building's lobby to its 86th floor by way of 1,575 stairs; the winner usually climbs all the steps in approximately 12 minutes.

MARCH
Greek Independence Day Parade On Fifth Avenue between 59th and 79th streets. Honors the regaining of Greek independence in 1821: a sea of blue and white as school bands and

Chinese New Year celebrations: the Lion Dance

Greek-Americans dressed in their national costume march jovially along the route.

Parade of Circus Animals
Creatures from the Ringling Bros. and Barnum & Bailey Circus trek from a railroad siding at Twelfth Avenue and 34th Street to Madison Square Garden.

St. Patrick's Day Parade (see previous page).

Check the daily papers for parade routes and arrive early for the best view

❑ The Puerto Rican Day Parade, along Fifth Avenue between 44th and 86th streets on the first Sunday in June, brings New York's huge Puerto Rican population onto the streets to celebrate their nation's Independence Day. Red, white, and blue Puerto Rican flags are everywhere, traditional foods are sold from stalls, and live bands playing on floats provide a nonstop soundtrack of salsa music to wildly appreciative audiences. ❑

APRIL
Easter Day Parade Participants stroll on Fifth Avenue near St. Patrick's Cathedral wearing extravagant Easter bonnets. On the Saturday before Easter a children's egg-rolling contest takes place on Central Park's Great Lawn. Check out Macy's ground floor the week before the holiday—it's wall-to-wall flowers.
Japanese Cherry Blossom Festival Highlights bloomtime in Central Park's Conservatory Garden and at the Brooklyn Botanic Garden.

MAY
Martin Luther King Memorial Day Parade Along Fifth Avenue from 44th to 86th streets. Marchers celebrate the life and achievements of the civil rights leader and highlight other African-American issues.
Ninth Avenue International Food Festival A two-day feast of the city's ethnic cuisines, on Ninth Avenue between 37th and 57th streets.
Ukrainian Festival In the East Village along 7th Street on the weekend closest to May 17: traditional foods, crafts and folk dancing.
Washington Square Outdoor Arts Show A gathering of local artists showing and selling their wares over three successive weekends.

JUNE
American Crafts Festival Lincoln Center. Over two successive weekends, exhibitors from all over the country show their skills.
Welcome to Brooklyn Festival Stalls and events along Eastern Parkway provide a focal-point while happenings throughout the borough mark local history and culture.
Feast of St. Anthony of Padua Little Italy. More restrained than the neighborhood's Feast of St. Gennaro (see September), with food stalls along Sullivan Street, the feast culminates with an image of the saint carried through the streets after dark.
Puerto Rican Day Parade See box.
Lesbian and Gay Pride Day Parade Along Fifth Avenue to Washington Square Park and around Greenwich Village. New York's gay and lesbian community stands together for this assertion of strength through unity.

27

Museum Mile Celebration The museums ranged along Fifth Avenue hold special events and stay open later than usual.

The Metropolitan Opera Free performances in city parks, including Central Park; continues all through the summer.

Shakespeare in the Park Staged for free at Central Park's Delacorte Theater, this continues all summer.

SummerStage Varied events at Central Park's Naumburg Bandshell during July and August.

JULY

Feast of O-Bon Japanese music and dance in the Upper West Side's Riverside Park, timed to mark the full moon.

Independence Day celebrations Including Macy's firework display, the site of which varies.

The horrors of Halloween

Mostly Mozart Festival At Lincoln Center's Avery Fisher Hall (see page 235); continues into August.

AUGUST

Harlem Week A two-week celebration of Harlem's history and culture.

New York Philharmonic Open-air concerts in city parks.

SEPTEMBER

New York Is Book Country Fifth Avenue between 48th and 59th streets. Major—and numerous minor—publishers are represented at stalls along the avenue and many well-known authors give readings and signings.

New York Film Festival At Lincoln Center (see page 234).

Feast of St. Gennaro Lasts ten days along Little Italy's Mulberry Street. Makeshift kitchens serve sausages and hunks of pizza; final night sees a shrine to the saint carried through the streets and showered with dollar bills. (See also page 135.)

Washington Square Outdoor Art Show Stands with locals' artworks and ethnic food sold from stalls.

OCTOBER

Columbus Day Parade Fifth Avenue between 44th and 72nd streets. As awareness of indigenous American cultures grows throughout the U.S., this parade to commemorate Christopher Columbus' "discovery" of the New World has become increasingly controversial. Many Native American and Hispanic groups—and others—actively oppose the event.

Halloween Parade Outrageous drag queens and others in freakish costumes parade through Greenwich Village to Washington Square Park Memorial Arch.

New York Marathon Run from Verrazano-Narrows Bridge to Central Park's Tavern on the Green (occasionally early November).

NOVEMBER

Macy's Thanksgiving Day Parade Along Central Park West and Broadway starring the famous helium-filled balloons—more spectacular than you can imagine. The area around the American Museum of Natural History is mobbed.

DECEMBER

Rockefeller Center The lighting of the Rockefeller Center Christmas Tree in early December begins NYC's festive season, when many stores mount magical window displays.

❏ Thousands of New Yorkers gather in Times Square to see in the New Year. As midnight approaches, an illuminated ball (disguised as a big apple) slides down Times Tower. ❏

New York Was

During the 16th century, the eastern seaboard of North America was steadily explored by European seafarers, not with the expectation of locating the site of the future world's greatest metropolis but in the hope of finding the North West Passage—a shortcut to the spice islands of the Pacific. Many years were to elapse between the European discovery of the land that now holds New York and its eventual settlement.

EARLY EXPLORERS The first European sighting of what became New York was made in 1524 by Giovanni da Verrazano, a Florentine merchant employed by the French. Verrazano described the land he found as having "commodiousness and beauty" and its native inhabitants uttering "loud cries of wonderment" as they spotted the vessels of the Europeans.

It was not until 1609 that a more thorough navigation of the area was made, this time by Henry Hudson, an Englishman working for the Dutch East India Company. Hudson's voyage was made along the river that now bears his name as far north as present-day Albany.

New Amsterdam (New York), 1673

❏ Before European settlement, the New York area was inhabited by several Native American groups, most being of the Algonquin tribe. The Native Americans, who lived by farming, hunting, and fishing, did not share the European concept of land ownership—the root of many future disputes—but they did share the European enthusiasm for trading, which helped keep early relations fairly cordial.

A sustained series of Dutch-led attacks eventually forced the natives away from the settled areas. European diseases, to which Native Americans lacked immunity, also took their toll. ❏

Like Verrazano, Hudson failed to find the fabled North West Passage, but he did note that the Native Americans were rich in beaver, mink, and otter pelts and were also eager to trade them.

THE FIRST NEW YORKERS Attracted by the prospect of commerce with the Native Americans, the Dutch West India Company was founded in Amsterdam and launched several North American settlements. In 1625, one such settlement—named

The arrival of Henry Hudson in 1609 at the mouth of what is now the Hudson River

New Amsterdam—was founded in what is now Lower Manhattan. It was made up of Dutch and French-speaking Walloon families and their African slaves. In 1626, the leader of the Dutch colony, Peter Minuit, bought Manhattan (a native term possibly meaning "Island of Hills") from a local tribe for a box of tools and trinkets worth the equivalent of $24.

Though established as a colonial trading base, Dutch New Amsterdam—soon to become British New York—quickly acquired a character of its own, partly through the ethnic and religious diversity of its inhabitants and partly through the fact that many of them came to share a desire to rid themselves of their Old World links for good.

NEW AMSTERDAM—SUCCESS AND FAILURE Much to the delight of the Dutch West India Company, New Amsterdam soon began to flourish as a trading center. New settlers arrived, taking advantage of the company's generous land grants. Some came to escape religious persecution, seeking the freedom of worship that the company had promised.

New Amsterdam was far from being the tranquil replica of a Dutch town that the company might have hoped for, however. Violence and lawlessness were rife, unmarried couples cohabited, pigs ran wild in the streets, and—with a tavern for every 12 adults—many of the population spent their spare time drinking to excess.

A NEW GOVERNOR In 1647, the corrupt governor was dismissed and the job of bringing order to bear on the wayward colony was given to Peter Stuyvesant, a noted disciplinarian. Under his iron rule, and with a new city charter providing for elected officials, New Amsterdam doubled in population and in size, gaining its first hospital, prison, school, and post office, and its first real commercial institutions.

The colony also gained a protective northern wall , which would later prove ineffectual at halting British advances but did give rise to the thoroughfare named Wall Street.

Peter Stuyvesant

THE BRITISH ARRIVE Stuyvesant's unpopularity, coupled with excessive tax demands by the Dutch West India Company, caused the population of New Amsterdam to offer no resistance when four British warships blockaded the harbor in 1664. Under British rule, the colony was renamed New York, after James, Duke of York, brother of King Charles II.

Set between the major British bases to the south and north, and at the mouth of the strategically important Hudson River, it is not surprising that New York became a prominent seaport. Nonetheless, the British proved no more able to stamp their authority on the everyday life of the colony than had the Dutch, and New York remained as socially robust as ever.

By 1700 New York had acquired a population numbering 20,000, composed of a mix of nationalities and a variety of religions.

THE AMERICAN REVOLUTION After the 1763 Treaty of Paris confirmed their dominance over the 13 American colonies, the British imposed a series of punitive taxes on the settlements. Previous anticolonial uprisings had been quashed by the British, but with the world entering a postcolonial age and the theories of republicanism being universally discussed, the idea of independence became increasingly attractive to the 13 economically thriving colonies.

Declaration of Independence

In Congress, July 4th, 1776.

The Unanimous Declaration of the Thirteen United States of America.

❏ When the Declaration of Independence was publicly read at New York's Bowling Green in July 1776, the excited crowd overturned the green's equestrian statue of King George III. Legend has it that the lead statue was melted down and turned into bullets, subsequently used against the British. ❏

Following the Declaration of Independence in 1776, General George Washington led the war against the British. Many British troops were billeted in New York, where they commandeered food supplies, terrorized locals, and imprisoned captured rebel prisoners on board ships in which hunger and disease were rife.

New York was to remain the last toehold of British rule in the New World. Although the 1783 Treaty of Paris formally ended the War of Independence, it was not until Washington's march from Harlem down to the Bowery in November of that same year that the last remnants of the British troops were finally withdrawn from the area.

The last act of defiance carried out by the British was to grease the flag-pole to hinder the raising of the Stars and Stripes.

As the country's major seaport, New York was the gateway to the New World. Through the 19th century it received the largest migration in human history: a mass movement of people which not only transformed the city but shaped the future of the entire nation.

34

New York's population had been markedly cosmopolitan from the earliest days of settlement, and a steady influx of immigrants continued after the Revolution.

Some new arrivals were attracted by the prospect of shaping the first democratic mixed-nationality society, others were radical intellectual rebels driven into exile by governments who feared them, and a few were simply adventurers or fortune-seekers.

In the mid-19th century, however, came the great waves of mass immigration into New York that were to change the city completely.

MASS MIGRATIONS There were three major factors all of which contributed to the mass waves of European migration into New York during the first half of the 19th century: the social upheaval which had been caused by the Napoleonic wars, the potato famines in Ireland and Germany, and the industrial revolution, which spread across Europe and robbed many skilled craftsmen and smallholding farmers of their livelihoods.

Arriving in the New World: an engraving of 1892

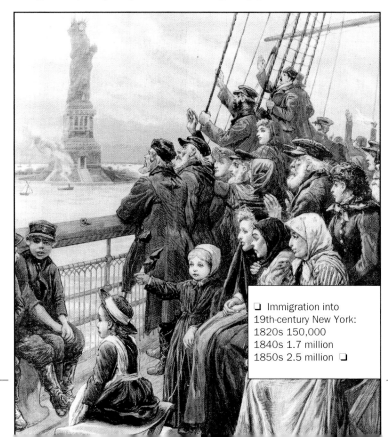

❏ Immigration into 19th-century New York:
1820s 150,000
1840s 1.7 million
1850s 2.5 million ❏

On the receiving end of a mass movement of people on a scale never before known, New York's overstretched Castle Garden (now called Castle Clinton) immigrant processing center was replaced in 1890 by the federally funded Ellis Island complex. The new receiving center, which was a pristine, state-of-the-art affair, was a far cry from the slums that awaited most new arrivals once they set foot in New York as American citizens.

While not all of the new arrivals stayed in New York, many did; and they placed a massive burden on the city's resources. The 1860s saw the creation of tenements in an effort to fit more people into small areas—five- or six-story buildings where an entire family would sometimes occupy a single windowless room. These tenements earned the nickname "lung blocks" due to the high incidence of tuberculosis among their inhabitants. Inadequate drainage and sewage systems made diseases such as yellow fever and cholera a constant threat.

In a city of immigrants, a mix of guile, initiative, and extremely hard work in appalling conditions usually bore rewards, and the major ethnic groups became assimilated and began climbing the city's social ladder comparatively swiftly (particularly as child immigrants reached adulthood fully conversant with the ways of the New World).

The northward spread of Manhattan's grid-style streets was matched by a steady northward flow of wealth. As the city's rich occupied the newest, most northerly homes, their previous dwellings were occupied by prospering ethnic groups while the poor—the latest immigrants—were housed in the south, usually in the tenements of the Lower East Side.

ANTI-IMMIGRATION LAWS

Established and powerful groups campaigned for tighter immigration controls. They feared loss of jobs, the spread of disease, and the decline of Anglo-Saxon supremacy (after the Revolution, 60 percent of Americans had been of English origin).

In 1882, the Chinese Exclusion Act banned further Chinese immigration into the U.S. The Act reflected an anti-Chinese feeling that also led to lurid stories about New York's Chinatown. The U.S. entered the 20th century as the world's richest industrial power, and the calls for protecting its economic well-being grew much stronger.

The outbreak of World War I encouraged the isolationist stance that paved the way for the immigration curbs of the 1920s (although the granting of U.S. citizenship to Puerto Ricans in 1917 was an exception). Mass immigration as seen in earlier decades came to an end.

35

❑ Immigration into New York is not a thing of the past. Easing of immigration restrictions in the 1960s caused a dramatic expansion of Chinatown (where many inhabitants are now actually Vietnamese or Cambodian). Indians, Koreans, West Indians, Filipinos, Latinos, Middle Eastern nationals, and Eastern Europeans from the former Iron Curtain countries are among the 90,000 people who still settle in New York every year. ❑

Seldom has the entrepreneur (or the rogue) had such opportunities to make a name and a fortune for himself as in 19th-century New York. At that time the city, rapidly evolving from an outpost to a great metropolis, was alive with speculation, sharp dealing, and money-making. From those heady times, a handful of names are remembered—fondly or otherwise—in the present day.

JOHN JACOB ASTOR (1763–1848) A fur-trade millionaire, John Jacob Astor switched his attentions to property in 1834, buying New York land while currying favor with city politicians and ingratiating himself into New York high society. Profits from slum housing helped Astor become the country's richest man by the time he died in 1848. In a rare act of generosity, however, Astor bequeathed $400,000 for the creation of the U.S.'s first public library, now the Public Theater in the East Village.

ANDREW CARNEGIE (1835–1919) Andrew Carnegie started in industry as a cotton-factory worker and rose to become a magnate with interests spanning iron, coal, steel, ships, and railroads. Believing in the motto "a man who dies rich, dies disgraced," Carnegie financed numerous trusts, some 2,000 libraries, and gave $2 million for the building of Carnegie Hall—yet still had $23 million when he died in 1919. The Carnegie mansion on Fifth Avenue is now the home of the Cooper-Hewitt Museum, (see page 95).

From mill-worker to multimillionaire: Andrew Carnegie

❑ When Caroline Schermerhorn married into the Astor family in 1853, she became the fabled "Mrs. Astor," a New York high-society legend whose annual balls were regarded as the city's definitive social barometer. The 400 people invited (the number of people in New York who, it was thought, fit into her ballroom) could consider themselves "in"; those not invited—which included anyone who worked for a living or who had made their millions through railroads—were definitely "out." ❑

HENRY CLAY FRICK (1849–1919) A partner of Andrew Carnegie in the Carnegie Steel Company, Henry Clay Frick was credited with few redeeming qualities. He instigated the blackest event in the history of U.S. labor relations: hiring a mob to bring a steel-mill strike to a violent and murderous end.

Some of Frick's fortunes went into acquiring the great stash of European art that now forms the Frick Collection, housed in his Fifth Avenue mansion (see page 110).

JAY GOULD (1836–1892) Robber baron, dealer, and socialite, Jay Gould made his first fortune at the age of 21. He would bet on the outcome of Civil War battles, having learned the result by tapping telegraph lines. In 1869 he manipulated the price of gold, made himself a profit of $11 million on the gold market, and incidentally brought about the calamitous "Black Friday" financial crash.

JOHN PIERPONT MORGAN

(1837–1913) Much of the European money invested in the U.S. during the 19th century was channeled through banker and financier John Pierpont Morgan. Able to wield influence on every new project that needed money, Morgan gained considerable wealth and importance. He had a finger in every entrepreneurial pie and oversaw the creation of the U.S. Steel Corporation, which became the world's first billion-dollar business in 1901.

Morgan spent $25 million buying gold to help save New York—and the nation—from bankruptcy in 1907. He also founded the Pierpont Morgan Library (see page 169).

CORNELIUS VANDERBILT

(1794–1877) Beginning with a ferry service between Staten Island and Manhattan in the early 1800s, Cornelius Vanderbilt built a steamship empire that dominated transportation across New York Bay and plied routes as far afield as Latin America and—at the height of the Gold Rush—to California. In 1864, Vanderbilt diverted some of his $20 million into railroads, laying the tracks that linked the steel-producing factories of Pittsburgh and the dairy farms of rural New York state to the city's docks—where his cargo ships awaited loading.

When he died in 1877, Vanderbilt was worth $105 million.

> ❏ J.P. Morgan fully deserved his reputation as a hard-headed businessman, but he regularly consulted society astrologist Evangeline Adams before making decisions. Evidence of the banker's interest in astrology is easy to find at the Pierpont Morgan Library, where symbols of the zodiac are incorporated into the lavish decoration. ❏

37

An early wheeler-dealer: investment banker John Pierpont Morgan

Unusually for a major city, the pattern of New York's expansion is easy to trace. The city's growth was a simple case of the long, narrow island of Manhattan being smothered with urban development, starting at one end and working systematically toward the other.

The European settlement of Manhattan began at the island's southern tip, the easiest place for ships to berth. Here the first businesses and homes became established. As the settlement grew, it could only expand northward. In the process, it acquired the haphazard street pattern which remains largely intact in today's Financial District.

THE GRID PLAN In 1811, the Board of Commissioners ratified a rectangular, grid-style street plan formulated by a surveyor, John Randel. Ignoring all existing streets except for Broadway—a track that followed an ancient Native American route—the design called for numbered streets (intended for residence) running east–west and numbered avenues (intended for commerce) running north–south.

The new Brooklyn Bridge must have seemed a miracle in its day

The grid plan provided a blueprint for Manhattan's development. In 1820, with a population of 123,000, New York was already the U.S.'s largest city, despite barely extending beyond Canal Street. North of Canal Street, a few villages had taken root in what are now Chelsea and Greenwich Village, and the areas now comprising the Upper East Side and the Upper West Side were a mixture of farms, wasteland, and squatters' camps.

When the Erie Canal opened in 1825, it linked New York to the Great Lakes and the agriculturally productive Midwest, and left the city unchallenged as the major American seaport—the gateway to lucrative international trade. This, coupled with the waves of mass immigration which began in the 1840s, set the scene for New York's rapid expansion throughout the 19th century.

Harlem was speedily developed by 19th-century speculators

MONEY MOVES NORTH Property developers wasted little time in moving northward through Manhattan, flattening hilly land and erecting new buildings. Around the mid-1800s, the first of the city's handsome brownstones appeared, providing comfortable accommodation for New York's expanding moneyed classes on the city's northerly fringes.

In the Lower East Side, meanwhile, the first tenement houses were erected, sheltering penniless immigrants and swiftly maturing into desperate slums.

As its poor toiled in sweatshops, New York generated incredible wealth for its already well-heeled élite. By the 1860s, several hundred millionaires were calling Manhattan home. Many of them occupied the luxury apartment houses recently erected along Fifth Avenue, facing the newly created Central Park—and the Upper East Side became the lasting domain of the rich.

A METROPOLIS IS BORN Steadily, the city gained an infrastructure worthy of the metropolis it was becoming. In 1868, the first "El" (or Elevated) train went into service. Two years later the first subway line was drilled. Work on the Brooklyn Bridge—the engineering miracle of its day—began in 1870 and was completed in 1883. Thomas Edison's company began the electrification of the city, opening its first generating station in 1882.

In 1898, the creation of Greater New York linked the five boroughs—Manhattan, Brooklyn, the Bronx, Queens, and Staten Island—under a single municipal government. New York City's population was now 3.8 million, making it the second largest city in the world.

❏ When work began on New York's City Hall in 1803, the building stood on what was then the city's northern edge. Marble was used for the building's front and sides, but the north-facing rear was made from cheap red sandstone in the expectation that nobody would ever see it. Such was the rate of New York's expansion, however, that by the time of its completion in 1812, City Hall was already ringed by new buildings. ❏

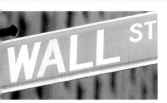

The U.S.'s early years were colored by frequent financial uncertainties, but none of the early banking troubles quite prepared the city for "Black Tuesday," the Wall Street crash of 1929, which dragged the country—and the world—into the Depression.

New York lasted only a year as the capital of the U.S., but the financial institutions on and around Wall Street—most notably the Stock Exchange, which began as a trading place for the $80 million-worth of bonds created to pay Revolutionary War debts—remained at the heart of the nation's monetary system.

As unscrupulous investors played on the insecurities and inexperience inherent in the new nation's financial systems, crashes were numerous. The panic of 1837 wiped $60 billion off the value of shares and left 50,000 people without jobs; 20 years later, another crash put 40,000 out of work. A further stock-market tumble occurred in 1873, and in 1907 New York's banks had to be saved from insolvency by the wealthy financier J.P. Morgan.

THE ROARING TWENTIES As the federal government came to replace independent financiers and the U.S. emerged from World War I as a rich and powerful nation, financial uncertainties seemed very much a thing of the past.

The economy boomed, and rumors of fortunes being made overnight caused the stock market to trade faster than ever before, its ticker-tape machines struggling to keep up with developments.

Even economically irrelevant events, such as Charles Lindbergh's successful first solo flight across the Atlantic in 1927, were enough to quicken dealing. Trading levels regularly broke new records during 1928.

THE CRASH OF 1929 Although the warning signals had been observed—industrial production was declining and the economy was beginning to stagnate— few people paid any heed until the third week of October 1929 when everyone began selling at once. Millions of shares were traded at a loss, causing 11 dealers to kill themselves and the date October 29, 1929, to go down in history as "Black Tuesday"—the day the Depression began.

> ❏ "Sooner or later a crash is coming, and it may be terrific"— financial expert Roger W. Babson, speaking in September 1929. ❏

By 1932, the Depression's bleakest year, more than a third of New York's 29,000 manufacturing firms had closed down, leaving a quarter of the city's work force idle. Many people, unable to afford rent, lived in the shanty towns that appeared in Central Park (dubbed "Hoovervilles" after the incumbent president, Herbert Hoover) and lined up for free food provided by soup kitchens.

Many of the city's most enduring skyscrapers had appeared through the buoyant 1920s, but now the building boom ground to a halt. The Empire State Building, opened in 1931, had to pay for its upkeep on the proceeds of tourist visits rather than office rents.

LA GUARDIA LEADS RECOVERY For New Yorkers, the woes of the Depression were made worse by the incompetence of their mayor, Jimmy Walker, better known for his songwriting skills than for his political abilities. Not the first—nor the last— city mayor to be embroiled in a corruption scandal, Walker departed from office in 1932 and fled to Europe. His replacement was Fiorello

La Guardia, a young, credible politician pledged to ending corruption and leading the city out of the Depression.

While La Guardia engineered the social policies which did lift New York from the Depression, it was Robert Moses who oversaw city planning and development from the 1930s to the 1960s, and gave New York a new look. Old neighborhoods were razed to make way for the expressways, tunnels, and bridges of the modern city, as well as for specific projects that included the creation of the Lincoln Center and Battery Park City.

Staged in Queens, the 1939 World's Fair was intended to symbolize New York's emergence from the Depression, but it was the country's entry into World War II in 1941 that really restored the city's finances, as tens of thousands of soldiers and streams of tanks, trucks, and planes passed through New York bound for the European theater.

❑ In 1940, the capital budget of New York City was $1. ❑

Below: the drama of the Wall Street crash, as illustrated by an Italian magazine of the day

Police being paid off by criminals and the mayor using public funds for private gain are enduring images of New York—and with good reason. Corruption was part of New York life from the city's earliest days and has proved hard to shake off, even in recent times.

THE TWEED RING A former volunteer fireman and street-gang member, William Marcy "Boss" Tweed got himself elected in 1851, age 21, as assistant alderman to a council body popularly nicknamed "the 40 Thieves."

Tweed quickly rose to the top of the thuggish faction of New York's Democratic Party (called Tammany after a Native American chief) by promising (and delivering) jobs and money to people—often freshly arrived immigrants—in return for votes. The city's administration was soon under the thumb of the "Tweed Ring," a coterie of corrupt officials who, during their brief reign, are estimated to have helped themselves to $300 million of public money.

As commissioner of public works, Tweed extracted fat commissions from construction companies as a reward for giving them lucrative contracts, and extorted large sums from businesses in return for providing essential services. A share of the ill-gotten gains was earmarked for bribes to the police and others, to dissuade them from speaking up.

Tweed's most spectacular swindle involved the construction of the New York County Courthouse (now known informally as the Tweed Courthouse). Having started in 1862 with a budget of $250,000, the courthouse eventually cost New York taxpayers $14 million, of which the Tweed Ring creamed off around $12 million.

Eventually, an angry City Hall clerk (said to have been offered a $500,000 bribe to keep quiet) passed incriminating documents to *The New York Times*. In jail, Tweed was allowed out each day for lunch and escaped to Chile before being recaptured. He died in 1878 in a jail which his corrupt regime had commissioned.

THE "BRAINS"

The secret of success: one 1871 cartoonist's view

❑ Since most of the people who voted for him were illiterate, Tweed claimed to have little interest in what newspapers wrote. He considered the satirical cartoons published in *Harper's Weekly*— which he called "them damn pictures"—to be more damaging to his career than reports on his dirty dealings documented in words. ❑

42

Mayor William O'Dwyer at his desk in City Hall (below)

MAYORS Quaker Fernando Wood was viewed as the man to end corruption at City Hall in 1844, despite previous accusations of fraud and the fact that he was elected mayor with more votes than there were voters. In fact, Wood sold the job of city commissioner for $50,000 and provided guarantees of naturalization to immigrants in return for their electoral favors.

A symbol of the booming 1920s, songwriter and playboy Jimmy Walker was elected mayor in 1925. Walker dressed in white suits, frequented nightclubs, and never arrived for work until the afternoon. After raising his own salary from $25,000 to $40,000, Walker skipped town in 1932 as the news broke that he had taken $1 million in payoffs for city contracts.

After the term of the admired mayor Fiorello La Guardia, it was dirty business as usual at City Hall. The subsequent incumbent, William O'Dwyer, made a swift exit to Mexico in 1951 as his links with organized crime were about to be exposed.

THE POLICE In a city corrupt from head to toe, it was little surprise that 19th-century New York police similarly veered off the straight and narrow. Patrolmen routinely acted as

paid lookouts for illegal gambling dens and brothels, while higher ranks improved their salaries with bribes and the proceeds of bank robberies. Crimes were liable to "disappear" in return for payments, and many robberies were investigated only if a reward was offered.

Actual arrests were usually intended to improve the appearance of the city for its affluent classes, removing any "lewd women," beggars, or homeless people from well-to-do areas.

Within the force, payments secured a popular beat and would bring promotion. According to a newspaper report of 1892, a fee of $300 was required to become a patrolman, while $14,000 was the asking price for a precinct captain's job.

It may be a bastion of big business, high finance, the media, and the arts, but New York's lofty position in the hierarchy of world cities is largely due to the simple matter of possessing an outstanding natural harbor. This stroke of geographical good fortune made possible its rise from an obscure colonial trading post to the world's greatest port.

44

EARLY DAYS New York's discovery by Europeans stemmed from the search for the North West Passage, a short-cut to the spice islands of the Pacific. Early explorers did not find the short-cut, but they did record that New York Bay provided a safe, sheltered anchorage in an area that enjoyed a comparatively mild climate and was relatively free of fog. With the Hudson River, the bay also provided access to a navigable route inland.

Even so, New York was but one of several moderately busy ports on the continent's east coast and was fortunate when the British—then ruling over the American colonies—chose it in preference to Boston as the main recipient of their exports.

THE ERIE CANAL The trigger of New York's phenomenal rise as a seaport—and its subsequent emergence as a major world city—was the building of the Erie Canal. The Hudson River provided a transportation route between the city and the

❏ New York's waterside streets were traditionally among the dirtiest, most dangerous, and crime-ridden in the city. The glamor accorded to Fifth Avenue partially derived from its geographical position: plumb in the center of Manhattan and as far from the rivers as it was possible to be. ❏

upstate farms (and the important towns of New England), but the Erie Canal—begun in 1817 and completed in 1825 at a cost of $7 million—connected the Hudson to Lake Erie and thereby opened a swift, direct line of communication between New York and, via the Great Lakes, the newly settled farmlands of the Midwest.

Using the canal, the 500-mile journey between Buffalo (on Lake Erie) and the city could be completed in

Manhattan and several of its numerous busy piers in the 1860s

The 20th-century port: South Street Seaport today (above) and (right) the Queen Mary *at 51st Street Pier*

10 days. With the American heartland opened up, ships from almost every nation converged on New York bearing products destined for the interior.

THE PORT EXPANDS By the turn of the 20th century, the southern end of Manhattan was lined by 22 miles of docks, with 270 piers extending along the East River and the Hudson River.

The advent of the railroads did more to improve New York's transportation links. Many freight lines ran directly to the docks, while Grand Central Station (now Grand Central Terminal) became the country's foremost rail passenger station.

By the 1930s, "the freighter, the river boat, the ferry and the soot-faced tug" plied the city's rivers—making the Hudson River itself barely viewable below 23rd Street. These craft were among the 3,500 vessels that berthed in New York each month.

OCEAN-GOING LUXURY Cargo may have been the bread and butter of the city's docks, but its place among the world's great ports was symbolized by the graceful ocean liners of the 1910s to the 1950s. Greeted by low-flying planes and water jets, the *Queen Mary* arrived in New York for

the first time in 1936 as one of several vessels regularly ferrying the rich and famous between Europe and the U.S., where New York welcomed them in a blaze of publicity.

GRADUAL DECLINE Changing patterns in international trade caused New York's port to lose its commercial importance. Also the rising popularity of air travel reduced the demand for ocean-going liners, and the great passenger ships made their last farewells to New York, although the *Q.E.2* (as well as modern cruise ships) is still a regular visitor. Nonetheless, the city's port is the third busiest in the U.S. (after New Orleans and Houston) and annually handles 116.7 million tons of freight. Meanwhile, the fall in passenger routes failed to deter the construction of a new passenger ship terminal on the Hudson River in 1974.

Three centuries of almost constant growth had made it one of the world's most affluent cities, so nobody could quite believe the news in 1975 that New York was almost bankrupt. Years of poor economic management, however, had left city finances in tatters.

The 1960s was a decade of turmoil and change throughout the country. In New York, violence erupted in the black ghettos of Brooklyn and Harlem, tens of thousands of Puerto Rican immigrants settled in East Harlem and the Lower East Side, and the so-called "White Flight"—the movement of around a million white middle-class families, and many businesses, out of New York—was in full swing.

STRAINED RESOURCES The exodus of the affluent white-collar workers and of many profitable companies (600,000 jobs disappeared in the six years from 1969) eroded one of the city's main sources of revenue at a time when the cost of its welfare policies, then among the most liberal in the country, was spiraling upward.

The incumbent mayor, John Lindsay, insisted that there would be no cuts in welfare services. Through Lindsay's intransigence, a strike by 34,000 transit workers, which brought the city to a standstill in 1966, ended up costing the city $70 million and gave the

❏ "Saving New York is like making love with a gorilla—you don't stop when you're tired, you stop when the gorilla's tired"—Felix Rohatyn, Chairman of M.A.C. ❏

green light to other unions to demand high pay increases.

Meanwhile, the number of people employed by the city had grown by nearly a third in five years, and their wages—plus increased pensions and other benefits—put further strain on the city's over-stretched finances.

The city administration resorted to ever more creative accounting in order to maintain its levels of expenditure, at one stage even creating a 364-day year to enable debts to be passed on to the next 12-month period. This short-term planning had the effect of increasing interest levels on city-borrowed money—and simply postponed an inevitable crisis.

BRINK OF DISASTER This state of financial disorder was inherited by Abe Beame, elected mayor in 1974. An accountant by profession, Beame was nonetheless unable to balance the city's books, and in 1975 New York was $2 billion in the red.

❏ "Ford to City: Drop Dead!"— *Daily News* headline encapsulating President Ford's attitude to New York's financial crisis. ❏

Strikes dogged 1960s New York

Lines at Grand Central Terminal in the 1966 transit workers' strike

As Wall Street financiers warned that municipal bonds would soon be worthless, Beame made cuts in public expenditure on a scale not seen since the Depression and labor unions agreed to wage freezes.

With no money to pay for garbage collection or water supplies—and with President Ford refusing federal aid—New York's entire infrastructure seemed about to collapse.

RESCUE The governor of New York injected state funds into the city and set up the Municipal Assistance Corporation (popularly known as the Big M.A.C.) to control expenditure at City Hall, but it took an eleventh-hour loan from the city's sanitation workers' union to finally pull New York back from the brink. Being advised that the future of the world economic system depended on New York's survival, the White House eventually agreed to a $2.3 billion federal loan.

In effect, the city came under the control of the M.A.C., whose primary concern was to retain the confidence of bankers. New York's underfunded services continued to decline, and welfare benefit levels were frozen for seven years.

RECOVERY AND ED KOCH Elected in 1978, Ed Koch had a style that made him a popular mayor, and he presided over years of steady recovery. Money was saved by laying off approximately 65,000 city workers, while others accepted wage freezes lasting several years, making further reductions in social services. A tight grip on public expenditure helped make Koch popular with big business and encouraged a Manhattan office building boom. Symbolically, in 1976 the World Trade Center leased all its office space and, by the mid-1980s, the stock market was booming.

However, as Wall Street buzzed, a 1985 survey found that more than 23 percent of New Yorkers were living below the poverty line.

Ed Koch

RIVERDALE
Mount Vernon
Pelham Manor
New Rochelle

Long Island Sound

Van Cortlandt Park
WOODLAWN
Bronx Hauptman House

Van Cortlandt Mansion
Woodlawn Cemetery
Pelham
EASTCHESTER

Prospect Point

KINGSBRIDGE

Edgar Allen Poe Cottage
BAYCHESTER
Barstow-Pell Mansion

Sands Point
Hunters Island

New York Botanical Garden

Sands Point

Bronx Zoo

95

Eastchester Bay
City Island

Hart Island

Port Washington

Manbasset Bay

BRONX
BRUCKNER

SOUNDVIEW
THROGS NECK

Kings Point

Bronx Museum of the Arts

HUNT'S POINT

678

East River
BRONX WHITESTONE BRIDGE
295

THROGS NECK BRIDGE

Throgs Point

Great Neck

Manhasset

CROSS ISLAND

Rikers Island

COLLEGE POINT

Little Neck Bay

Whitestone

La Guardia Airport

Flushing Bay

CLEARVIEW EXPRESSWAY

DOUGLASTON

LONG ISLAND EXPRESSWAY

ASTORIA

GRAND CENTRAL

WHITESTONE EXPRESSWAY

Bowne House

JACKSON HEIGHTS

New York Hall of Science

Shea Stadium
(New York Jets & New York Mets)

495

GRAND CENTRAL PARKWAY

Lake Success

GLEN OAKS

ELMHURST
REGO PARK
495

Flushing Meadows
Queens Museum
Corona Park

Golden Center for the Performing Arts, Queens College

Floral Park

Garden City

FOREST HILLS

GLENDALE

VAN WYCK EXPRESSWAY

JAMAICA

QUEENS VILLAGE

Belmont Park Race Track

KEW GARDENS

JACKIE ROBINSON PARKWAY

Forest Park

RICHMOND HILL

ST ALBANS

Elmont

WOODHAVEN
OZONE PARK
678

SOUTHERN STATE PARKWAY

EAST NEW YORK

Aqueduct Racetrack

SOUTHERN PARKWAY

Valley Stream

PARKWAY

HOWARD BEACH

ROSEDALE

Lynbrook

CANARSIE SHORE

Jamaica Bay

John F Kennedy International Airport

Gateway National

Cedarhurst

Jamaica Bay Wildlife Refuge

Inwood

Lawrence

Floyd Bennett Field

Recreation Center

Lawrence Marsh

Jacob Riis Park

Rockaway Beach

Atlantic Beach

Atlantic Beach

ROCKAWAY POINT

0   2   4   6   8   10 km
0   2   4   6 miles

4   5

49

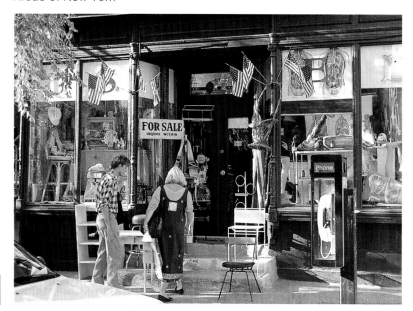

Browsing in Greenwich Village makes good entertainment: stores here range from the mildly quirky to the completely outlandish

▶▶▶ CITY HIGHLIGHTS

Brooklyn Museum
pages 78–79

Central Park
pages 82–84

Ellis Island page 100

Empire State Building
pages 100–102

Guggenheim Museum
pages 122–124

Metropolitan Museum of Art pages 142–148

Museum of Modern Art
pages 158–160

New York Public Library
page 168

Pierpont Morgan Library
page 169

Statue of Liberty
page 180

Not for nothing did they name New York twice. What most people think of as being New York is really Manhattan, a long, narrow island squeezed between two rivers. Manhattan is the kernel of New York life, home to much of the city's affluence and élan. Most New Yorkers live in the so-called Outer Boroughs which form the remainder of New York City: Brooklyn, the Bronx, Queens, and Staten Island.

MANHATTAN As far as the rest of the world is concerned, the island of Manhattan is everything that defines New York, with its towering skyscrapers, teeming streets, ceaseless noise, and giant neon advertisements that turn night into day. However, strangely enough, only a fraction of Manhattan—just over 12 miles long and for the most part 2½ miles wide—actually fits this image. The island is divided into a number of separate areas, and each has its own distinctive history, looks, atmosphere, and residents.

Lower Manhattan At Manhattan's southern extremity, the modern high-rise towers of the **Financial District** rise above the oldest part of New York. It was here that the first Dutch settlement took root and, while few markers of the colonial days remain, the entrepreneurial spirit with which the colony was founded remains very much alive—from the floor of the New York Stock Exchange to the street-side foodstands dispensing all kinds of ethnic food to power-dressed brokers.

Pressed hard against the Financial District's northern edge, the short busy streets of **Chinatown** make up one of New York's longest-established ethnic areas. Lately, Chinatown's banks, bakeries, and dim sum houses have spread across the traditional boundaries into **Little Italy**—a tiny area where freshly made cappuccino and creamy pastries can still be consumed at sidewalk tables.

To the west, the ethnic atmosphere gives way to artiness in compact **SoHo** and **TriBeCa**, trendy locations that, not long ago, were derelict industrial areas—prime examples of the neighborhood transformations that are a New York specialty, as is the thriving **Chelsea** further north.

By contrast, the elbow of land jutting toward the East River is consumed by the **Lower East Side**, a long-time first base of newly arrived immigrants, and now the home of cut-rate stores and street markets where the work-hard-and-prosper ethos that built the city remains strongly in evidence despite a substantial number of newer stores and bars.

Greenwich Village is packed with restaurants, cafés, bars, and clubs. This area also has some fine houses, intriguing narrow streets, and even today, a knack for attracting the writers and artists who, historically, have shaped American culture.

Across Broadway—which runs the length of Manhattan—the **East Village** provided a less costly alternative for those dispossessed by Greenwich Village's rising rents and gentrification during the 1980s. With offbeat stores and cafés, the area still has a modestly radical atmosphere, although the writers and artists who once colonized it are being replaced by trendy professionals.

H.G. WELLS ON NEW YORK
"To Europe, she was America, to America she was the gateway of the earth. But to tell the story of New York would be to write a social history of the world."

Choose from a few skyscraper viewing galleries to contemplate the almost unbelievable panorama of Manhattan and beyond

51

52

Midtown Manhattan Unlike Lower Manhattan, where the streets tend to have names and to be short and crooked, Midtown Manhattan is all numbered streets and avenues that fortunately make the visitor's life a simple one.

With the exception of the Statue of Liberty (which holds its flame aloft off Manhattan's southern tip), Midtown Manhattan includes many of New York's main attractions: the Empire State Building, the United Nations complex, Rockefeller Center, St. Patrick's Cathedral, the Chrysler Building, the Museum of Modern Art, Grand Central Terminal, Times Square and the Broadway theater district, and department stores such as Macy's and Bloomingdale's, as well as broad, busy thorough-fares packed with people and reverberating to the wail of police sirens.

Midtown Manhattan's northern border is defined by the southern perimeter of **Central Park**, an imposing and precisely rectangular chunk of greenery which re-creates a piece of the country in the heart of the city. At this, Central Park succeeds admirably.

Upper Manhattan To the east of Central Park, gaining much of its long-lasting prestige from the mansions and apartment houses erected to face the bucolic expanse, the **Upper East Side** is far and away Manhattan's wealthiest neighborhood, a fact borne out by its exclusive clothes stores, gourmet restaurants, and sizable gathering of upscale art galleries.

Three of the city's major art museums are located here: they are the Metropolitan Museum of Art, the Guggenheim Museum, and the Whitney Museum of American Art. To enjoy art in a luxurious setting, it is hard to beat the Frick Collection, still housed in Henry Clay Frick's 19th-century mansion.

Across Central Park, the **Upper West Side** offers Lincoln Center, the American Museum of Natural History, and the Cathedral of St. John the Divine as its major attractions. The neighborhood's tall apartment houses—among them the Dakota, which has been home to celebrities ranging from Judy Garland to Leonard

Little Italy—one of several ethnic areas that make up New York's complex cosmopolitan patchwork

Bernstein and John Lennon—were the height of luxury living at the turn of the century and are still coveted addresses in what has grown into a vibrant bastion of the upper middle class.

Stretching across the northern reaches of Upper Manhattan, **Harlem** has played a key role in the history and culture of black America from the turn of the century. The economic and social infrastructure that has traditionally held back African-Americans also contributed to Harlem spending many years in decline.

Similar problems derived from institutionalized racism have been experienced in **East Harlem**, above the Upper East Side, a major base for the city's enormous Hispanic population. Like Harlem, however, local initiatives as well as the passing of time have helped reduce long-held assumptions that the area is off-limits to, and has nothing to interest, those from outside the resident community.

THE OUTER BOROUGHS Locals would disagree but, unless your time is limitless, the Outer Boroughs probably merit only day-trip excursions from Manhattan.

Brooklyn, with the exceptional Brooklyn Museum, the enjoyable Brooklyn Heights neighborhood, and Prospect Park, has most in its favor. On the coast, Brooklyn also has Coney Island. Its glory days are gone, but the amusement area and boardwalk remain a curious piece of Americana. The latter leads to the New York Aquarium and to the lively Russian community of Brighton Beach.

Staten Island is also worth a visit, partly for the fun of the ferry ride to reach it, but also to enjoy the pastoral pace and the scattering of low-key museums.

In the **Bronx**, the Bronx Zoo (now called the Bronx Wildlife Conservation Park) is wonderful, as is the New York Botanical Garden next door. A more somber relic is the cottage in which author Edgar Allan Poe resided for two troubled years.

In **Queens** (named for the wife of England's King Charles II), features include thriving ethnic communities and the American Museum of the Moving Image.

The Wollman Memorial Rink in Central Park

LE CORBUSIER ON NEW YORK
"A hundred times I have thought New York is a catastrophe and fifty times: it is a beautiful catastrophe."

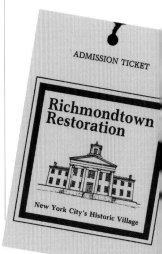

ADMISSION TICKET

Richmondtown Restoration

New York City's Historic Village

You may hear—or fear—that New York is a dangerous place. But for every visitor who gets mugged (or worse), there are many hundreds more who leave the Big Apple with nothing but good memories—and millions have lived there for years without becoming crime victims. Unless you are very unlucky, surviving New York simply means being prepared.

NIGHTTIME NO-GO AREAS

Wherever you go in Manhattan at night, you will need to be more cautious than by day. Several areas that you might visit with comparative nonchalance in daylight (most of which are described in the A to Z section of this book) should be regarded as off-limits at night: Alphabet City past Avenue C (Avenues A and B are fine), Central Park, the western edge of Greenwich Village along the Hudson River, Harlem, and most of Midtown Manhattan west of the theater district.

A native's rule of thumb: if the street is busy, you're okay; if deserted, make a beeline for the nearest avenue, or hail the first yellow cab you see.

Arriving Airports are comparatively safe havens, but be sure to check transportation routes into the city *before* leaving the terminal building.

If you take a taxi from the airport, look for the uniformed guide who will show you to the official taxi dispatch lines. Stick to official yellow-cab operators, and always check that the cab meter is on and make sure the driver is not quoting a price he has decided on. Official fares are those on the meter, with a few permitted exceptions which are clearly posted on the back of the front seat.

Arriving at Manhattan's train and bus terminals can be more problematic, especially late at night. Although taxis can usually be hailed immediately outside, it is worth taking the trouble to plan your route from the terminal in advance. Do not let a stranger carry your bags for you. If you are planning to walk to your hotel, make sure you know the route.

Walking in the city Stash your valuables in the hotel safe and carry only enough cash to get you through the day. Never carry a wad of cash. If you are embarking on a major shopping expedition, take credit cards or traveler's checks to pay for your purchases.

Walking is much the best way to explore Manhattan, but you should exercise common sense when doing so. Stick with the crowds, avoid deserted alleys, and do not flash expensive jewelry—even costume jewelry, since it might

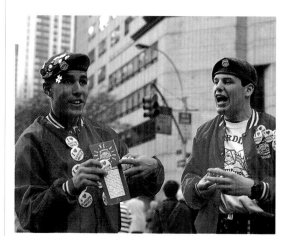

The city's self-styled (and controversial) "Guardian Angels" aim to keep the streets and subways free from crime and violence

not be recognized as such. Women should not hang bags on the backs of chairs in restaurants, and men should carry their wallets in their front pockets.

Plan your route before setting out. Manhattan's grid system makes navigation easy (though Lower Manhattan can be confusing). Even for lifelong New Yorkers, no street is perfectly safe, so never carry anything that can be easily snatched. Do not be taken in by anyone who approaches you with a hard luck story, and beware that if you buy watches or jewelry in the street, they are likely to be fakes. Videotapes bought on the street are likely to be defective or blank.

Riding the subway While some people still regard going down into New York's subway system as akin to a descent into hell, the system is by no means the Dante's Inferno that it once was. Certainly there is no speedier way to get around. By day your biggest problem is figuring out the subway system (see pages 252–253 for advice). If you find yourself at the wrong station in an unsavory neighborhood, simply take the next train back as soon as you can.

Late at night in the subway, you may well find a cheerful crowd in a partying mood along with people on the night shift headed to or from their jobs—or you may find the train empty. To be on the safe side, always board the middle cars, where there is usually a conductor, or look for occupied cars. If you are waiting on a near-deserted platform, look for the supervised "off-hours" waiting area. Once on board, stay alert and get off at the right station.

A farewell to crime? Visitors may be comforted by the fact that New York crime levels are at their lowest for years. One factor may be the "zero tolerance" policy introduced in the mid-1990s, based on the idea that stopping small crimes prevents bigger ones. After crackdowns on graffiti and unlicensed street vending came more random searches of individuals on the street. More police and a new system of police accountability for local crime have also made a significant difference.

Faster than walking, driving or taking the bus, the New York subway is usually crowded only during rush-hour periods

READY CASH
The odds are astronomical against your being mugged in New York, but should a figure leap from the shadows and demand money, it is a good idea to have some cash ready to hand over. Many New Yorkers have got into the habit of carrying a small sum (sometimes contained in a spare wallet), usually around $20, partly to avoid losing a larger amount and partly to save time. The longer a mugger has to wait, the more unstable he may become.

Itineraries

WALKING TOURS
A number of organizations run walking tours of various Manhattan neighborhoods (see Travel Facts). Historical walks led by Columbia University historians are run by Big Onion (439-1090), and walks through the Lower East Side are organized by the Lower East Side Tenement Museum (see page 138).

You could spend your entire life in New York and never feel you had seen the whole city. Nonetheless, these suggested itineraries will provide as balanced a view of New York as is possible within limited time periods.

Weekend itinerary
Day one In the morning, visit the Empire State Building and continue on foot to the New York Public Library, Rockefeller Center, and St. Patrick's Cathedral. Have lunch in Midtown Manhattan and spend the afternoon at the Museum of Modern Art.
Day two Take an early-morning ferry from Battery Park to the Statue of Liberty and Ellis Island. After returning, have lunch at the World Financial Center and spend the afternoon exploring Greenwich Village.

More than 20 years after losing its world-record status, the Empire State Building is still a magnet for visitors

One-week itinerary
Day one As day one of weekend itinerary.
Day two Take an early-morning ferry from Battery Park to the Statue of Liberty and Ellis Island. After returning, have lunch at the World Trade Center and spend the afternoon exploring the Financial District and South Street Seaport.
Day three Spend the whole day at the Metropolitan Museum of Art. If a whole day seems too long, spend part of it shopping for clothes in Midtown and along Madison Avenue, or in the discount outlets of Lower Manhattan.
Day four In the morning, you can explore Central Park. Travel to Greenwich Village for lunch and spend the afternoon exploring Greenwich Village, SoHo, Little Italy, and Chinatown.
Day five On the Upper East Side, tour the Frick Collection or the Cooper-Hewitt Museum. After lunch, continue to the Guggenheim Museum or the Whitney Museum of American Art.
Day six Travel by subway to the Brooklyn Museum. Spend the day at the museum, pausing to eat a picnic lunch in the Brooklyn Botanic Garden. Alternatively, spend the day exploring Brooklyn Heights, dropping into the Brooklyn Historical Society and continuing to the New York Transit Museum.
Day seven Tour the Lower East Side and the East Village. After lunch, explore the Gramercy Park area and conclude at the Pierpont Morgan Library.

Two-week itinerary

Day one As day one of weekend itinerary.

Day two As day two of week itinerary.

Day three As day three of week itinerary.

Day four In the morning, explore Central Park. Have lunch on the Upper West Side before visiting the American Museum of Natural History.

Day five Spend the whole day on Staten Island, visiting the Snug Harbor Cultural Center, the Richmondtown Historic Restoration, and the Jacques Marchais Center of Tibetan Art.

Day six Tour the Lower East Side and Chinatown. Have lunch in Chinatown and spend the afternoon exploring Greenwich Village.

Day seven As day six of week itinerary.

Day eight On the Upper East Side, zip through the Frick Collection or the Cooper-Hewitt Museum. After a late lunch, continue to the Museum of the City of New York.

Day nine Visit the Forbes Galleries and idle away the rest of the morning in Washington Square Park. Have lunch at a café in Greenwich Village and then continue on to the East Village, or explore the Gramercy Park area, and conclude your sightseeing at the Pierpont Morgan Library on 36th Street.

Day ten Explore Harlem and the museums of the Audubon complex on West 155th Street. After lunch, tour the Columbia University campus and the Cathedral of St. John the Divine.

Day eleven Make a visit to the Bronx Zoo and the New York Botanical Garden.

Day twelve Divide the day between the Whitney Museum of American Art and the Guggenheim Museum.

Day thirteen Travel by subway to Coney Island, tour the New York Aquarium and continue to Brighton Beach.

Day fourteen Spend the morning at the Cloisters, returning to Midtown Manhattan for lunch and to visit the Museum of T.V. and Radio, or the American Craft Museum—and any landmark building you have yet to view at close quarters.

The Statue of Liberty is essential viewing, even if you're on a flying visit to the Big Apple

GUIDED TOURS OF HARLEM
Harlem is one of New York's most celebrated areas but can be intimidating for the first-time visitor. One way to see Harlem without worries is with a guided tour. Harlem Spirituals, Inc (tel: 391-0900) offers a choice of several: a Sunday or weekday tour that combines a gospel church service with a tour of historic Harlem, another that offers a soul-food lunch and a local history commentary, and an evening fling based around several hours of jazz at a local venue.

From the top of the World Trade Center or the decks of the Staten Island Ferry, New York has views that no other city comes close to matching. Observation decks are a feature of a few Manhattan skyscrapers—a couple of which, in their day, were the tallest buildings in the world. The Empire State Building and the Woolworth Building are two that can now be viewed from the top of even taller towers— an angle their architects never imagined possible. Alternatively, leave Manhattan and view it from afar. Don't miss New York views as night falls; a panorama of Manhattan by night is a sight you will remember for years.

H.G. WELLS ON NEW YORK VIEWS, 1906
"Suddenly as I looked back at the skyscrapers of lower New York a queer fancy sprang into my head. They reminded me quite irresistibly of piled-up packing cases outside a warehouse. I was amazed I had not seen the resemblance before."

Empire State Building This is the star of virtually every Manhattan view except those from its own 86th-floor observation level. On a clear day, the eagle-eyed can see through the wire mesh into Massachusetts and Pennsylvania and peer down at jets swooping into New York's airports. Come after dusk to see nighttime Manhattan: the building is open until midnight.

World Trade Center The twin towers are only eight stories taller than the Empire State Building, but their sheer sides make them seem far higher. From the southernmost tower's observation level, the long-distance views are not significantly different from those of the Empire State Building. From the open-air rooftop level, however, the experience is quite different as a simple turn of the head brings a near-360 degree sweep of the New York area and beyond.

Rockefeller Center Look out from the 65th-floor windows of the Rainbow Room restaurant complex in the G.E. (formerly R.C.A.) Building and you will see the Empire State Building rising regally to the south as the World Trade Center looms to its rear. Look north, and the green rectangle of Central Park cuts between the stately apartment buildings of the Upper East Side and the Upper West Side toward Harlem.

Above the East River From its terminal at the junction of Second Avenue and 60th Street, the cable car that crosses the East River to Roosevelt Island gives clear views of the island's former lunatic asylums and hospitals. The memorable views, though, are in the other direction, taking in a lengthy swath of riverside Manhattan from Midtown's United Nations complex northward, far into the Upper East Side. A bonus is a bird's-eye view of any passing river traffic.

Fort Tryon Park Close to the northern tip of Manhattan, Fort Tryon Park offers not only the unexpected sight of a reassembled medieval European monastery (the Cloisters) but also, from the hilltop site of the fort itself, there are views across the Hudson River to New Jersey's Palisades Park and, on the other side of Manhattan, the Harlem River.

Brooklyn Some of the most rewarding views of Manhattan are found by leaving it. From Brooklyn Heights Promenade, the eastern edge of the Financial District—the so-called Water Street corridor, a heady mix of glass, steel, limestone, and marble—walls the East River. In the foreground are the tall ships of South Street Seaport. Behind Water Street's forest of high-rises, you should be able to pick out two of the world's one-time highest buildings, the Woolworth Building and the World Trade Center, while two more, the Chrysler Building and the Empire State Building, are visible in the cluster of skyscrapers marking Midtown Manhattan.

Brooklyn Bridge Be sure not to use up all your film on the Promenade: returning to Manhattan on foot across the Brooklyn Bridge reveals the same scenes from continually shifting perspectives behind the struts of the bridge, providing endless scope for inventive photographers.

Staten Island Ferry Look across the harbor from Brooklyn Heights to see the green hills of Staten Island rising to the south. You might also spot the Staten Island Ferry as it plies between the island and the southern tip of the Financial District.

Riding the ferry is much more interesting than looking at it, however. From the vessel are dramatic views of Manhattan's skyline (best on the return leg, when the skyscrapers appear to grow bigger and bigger) and slightly less dramatic ones of Governors Island (occupied by the U.S. Coast Guard), the Statue of Liberty, and one of the world's longest suspension bridges, the Verrazano-Narrows Bridge, which links Staten Island (itself a place of attractive views) to Brooklyn.

STATUE OF LIBERTY VIEWS
At the Statue of Liberty, which sits on an island between Manhattan and New Jersey, the outlook is stirring. Across the Hudson River, Battery Park City and the World Trade Center are prominent. In the foreground, scores of yachts, tugs and pleasure boats skim by on the water, while helicopters zip past overhead.

THE TOMPKINS SQUARE PARK RIOT

In the heart of Alphabet City, Tompkins Square Park was the scene of a heavy-handed police operation on a steamy August night in 1988, when 12 mounted police, soon joined by 400 reinforcements, battled for four hours to clear the 16-acre park of the homeless people who were occupying it.

The incident was recorded on video by a local artist and the police brutality that the playback showed triggered outrage across the city, and nightly violence at the park. Mayor Dinkins closed the park for major renovations, posting police guards to keep out anyone but dog-walkers and basketball players. Reopened, the park is now fairly peaceful during the day.

Tompkins Square Park, in Alphabet City, has seen its share of problems, but it is now a fairly safe and peaceful place in daylight

► **Abigail Adams Smith Museum**　　151D3

61st Street at York Avenue (tel: 838-6878)
Open: Tue to Sun 11–4; Jun and Jul until 9 on Tue
Subway: N, R, 4, 6; 59th Street

Neither Abigail Adams, daughter of John Adams, the second president of the U.S., nor her husband, William Stephens Smith, an aide to George Washington, ever lived in what is now the Abigail Adams Smith Museum. Instead, the ashlar stone building was the carriage house of their intended 23-acre country estate on the banks of the East River.

Financial decline caused the couple to move to alternative accommodations in 1799, however. The stables were converted first to an inn and then to a private residence before being purchased in 1924 by the Colonial Dames of America, an organization pledged to preserving the history of the revolutionary period. The building was gradually equipped with Federal-period furnishings and objects which now fill nine of its rooms, making for an entertaining half-hour's viewing.

Alphabet City　　IFCC3

Subway: subway lines Second Avenue

The process of gentrification that spread through Greenwich Village in the 1970s continued into the East Village. By the mid-1980s it had reached Alphabet City (so-called for having lettered rather than numbered avenues), which lies east of First Avenue between Houston and 14th streets. With its restaurants offering cuisines from Asia to Eastern Europe, the area draws mainstream New Yorkers in search of new dining experiences. Among its resident population are those wealthy enough to inhabit a classy, if usually small, renovated apartment in one of the many former tenement blocks.

Most of Alphabet City's population, however, are Puerto Ricans who have informally dubbed the area "loisaida" (pronounced "low-ees-SIDE-ah"), a phrase reputedly first used by a local poet and playwright. The neighborhood suffered from urban blight into the early 1980s, but the efforts of the local community and a major police initiative—and the rising interest of property developers—all contributed to regeneration. Much poverty remains though, and the area east of Avenue B can seem intimidating to outsiders.

▶ American Academy and Institute of Arts & Letters   *IBCD2*

Broadway at 155th Street (tel: 368-5900)
Open: Thu to Sun 1–4
Subway: C, D, 1; 155th or 157th streets
Two august cultural bodies—the National Institute of Arts, founded in 1898, and the American Academy, founded in 1904—unified in 1977 and jointly honor American achievements in art, writing, and music.

Although much of its activity seems little more than mutual backslapping, the organization also administers grants to deserving artistic causes and stages temporary seasonal exhibitions highlighting individual members. If your favorite author, painter, or composer is being featured, it could be worth a visit.

▶ American Bible Society   *151D1*

Broadway at 61st Street (tel: 408-1236)
Open: Mon to Wed and Fri 10–6, Thu 10–7, Sat 10–5
Subway: A, B, C, D, 1, 2, 3, 9; 59th Street
A 1960s cast-in-place concrete structure a bagel's throw from busy Columbus Circle makes an unlikely home for the American Bible Society, founded in 1816 in order to circulate the Bible "without note or comment."

Over the years, historic bibles from near and far have been collected to form the society's extensive library and archive. The collection includes an illustrated Armenian account of the Four Gospels dated to the early 1400s and also a 16th-century bible translated by a New England preacher into Massachusetts (an Algonquin Native American dialect).

A few changing selections are displayed on the second-floor level, alongside a reconstruction of a Gutenberg printing press and a feature on the Dead Sea Scrolls.

AUDUBON TERRACE
The American Academy and Institute of Arts & Letters occupies one section of Audubon Terrace, a Renaissance Revival complex planned in 1908 and intended to provide a suitably imposing setting for several venerable national institutions—others among them including the American Numismatic Society (see page 65) and the Hispanic Society of America (see page 126).

Situated between Riverside Drive and Broadway and 155th and 156th streets, the scheme was never entirely successful: not only a poor architectural job, it also left its tenants in a humdrum residential area far removed from the ebb and flow of New York life.

The terrace was built on a part of the estate of John James Audubon, the eminent American naturalist of the early 1800s.

Changing exhibitions of pottery, textiles, furniture, and other artifacts can be viewed in spacious surroundings at the American Craft Museum, which show-cases the work of contemporary craftspeople

MUSEUM OF AMERICAN ILLUSTRATION
Within a few steps of the American Federation of the Arts, the Society of Illustrators (63rd Street between Lexington and Park avenues), established in 1875, holds the small but interesting Museum of American Illustration. Through lively temporary exhibitions, the museum highlights the contribution made to Americans' self-image through cartoons, advertising, book and magazine drawings, and much more.

▶▶ American Craft Museum 151C2
53rd Street between Fifth and Sixth avenues (tel: 956-3535)
Open: Tue, Wed and Fri to Sun 10–6, Thu 10–8
Subway: E, F; Fifth Avenue
From teapots and tapestries to baskets and brooches, the exhibits of the American Craft Museum are always stimulating. Chosen from the museum's own vast collection or using loaned pieces, the displays illustrate design trends and techniques and they often feature the work of the most artistic and skillful 20th-century American craftsmen and women.

The museum is run by the American Craft Council, whose purchase of a brownstone house on this site in 1959 turned out to be a wise investment. A 1980s property speculator eager to erect a high-rise here agreed to give the museum a spacious chunk of the new building's first floor, enabling the displays to be mounted around a lovely three-story atrium.

▶ American Federation of the Arts 151D2
65th Street between Park and Madison avenues (tel: 988-7700)
Call for opening times
Subway: 6; 68th Street
The American Federation of the Arts arranges traveling exhibitions for the small museums of the U.S., often finding time to display tasters of some in its own galleries. It is pot luck what might be on display but a look inside also reveals the building's lavishly decorated interior, a 1960s restoration of what was originally the home, built around 1910, of a successful stockbroker.

▶▶ American Museum of Natural History   *IFCF2*

Central Park West and 79th Street (tel: 769-5100)
Open: Sun to Thu 10–5:45, Fri to Sat 10–8:45
Subway: 1, 9, B, C; 79th Street or 81st Street

With 36 million exhibits, this is one of the world's best-stocked museums. Whether you are gazing at a saber-toothed tiger or an ancient Guatemalan inscription, there is every chance it will be among the foremost examples of its kind on show anywhere in the world.

Darwin's theory of evolution and Mendel's law of heredity were two of the natural science breakthroughs that provided the stimulus for the museum's founding in 1869. Within a decade, the collections had acquired a specially built home, a stately Romanesque structure beside Central Park.

The sheer size of the collections of the American Museum of Natural History makes it a daunting prospect even for the most enthusiastic visitor. One way to discover the best of the museum without fatiguing yourself too much is to join a free hour-long guided Highlights Tour. These depart several times daily; details from any of the museum's information desks (tel: 769-5100). Greatly improved by a $30 million restructuring, the museum's fossil collection—already among the best in the world—now forms part of a six-room, state-of-the-art complex revealing the intricacies of the evolutionary relationships as far back as the Jurassic period (180–120 million years ago). The climax of this section are the two Dinosaur Halls, which feature magnificent skeletons of Tyrannosaurus Rex and Apatosaurus.

CARL AKELEY
The Akeley Gallery at the American Museum of Natural History is named after Carl Akeley, a naturalist, explorer and inventor. Akeley twice narrowly escaped death by dangerous animal. In 1911, he was gored by an elephant but saved himself by swinging beneath the creature's body; on another occasion, he ran out of bullets while confronted by an angry leopard but saved himself by strangling it. Among his many technical innovations was a new taxidermy technique, which he employed on the seven elephants that stand in the gallery. Ironically, Akeley died in 1926 from complications arising from a gnat bite.

63

Massive exhibit in a massive museum—the Barosaurus at the Museum of Natural History

HAYDEN PLANETARIUM

Adjacent to the American Museum of Natural History is the copper-domed Hayden Planetarium, which holds astronomy exhibitions and excellent hour-long "Sky Shows," taking visitors on voyages through the cosmos using state-of-the-art technology. For details, tel: 769-5100.

The gorilla diorama at the American Museum of Natural History. Few aspects of the world's wildlife are left untouched by the museum's vast collections

Native American life and the evolution of North American animal and bird species are outlined by comprehensive but fairly dreary habitat dioramas.

More enjoyable are the excellently arranged anthropological collections on Africa, Asia, and Central and South America. This last section is particularly strong, including thousands of curious religious, ceremonial, and everyday objects. Look for the Aztec musical instruments made from human bones, the 17th-century sheet-metal ornamental llamas from the Andes, and shrunken heads from the Amazon rainforest—and be ready for intriguing insights into Mayan astronomy.

The museum unveiled a new permanent exhibition in 1993, the Hall of Human Biology and Evolution. It studies the workings of the human body, traces ancestors over the centuries, and features a computerized archeological dig and an electronic newspaper with information on human evolution.

Measuring 94 feet in length and weighing 10 tons, what is thought to be the world's largest museum exhibit replicates the world's largest mammal—the blue whale—above the Hall of Ocean Life and Biology of Fishes. The fiberglass whale steals the show, although the room's dioramas and fish skeletons do a commendable job in unraveling the mysteries of reproduction, feeding, and self-defense far beneath the ocean's waves.

Moving on, even the mindbogglingly priced gems of Midtown Manhattan's jewelry stores pale into insignificance when compared with the contents of the museum's

Hall of Minerals and Gems, a collection valued at $80 million. A great chunk of crystal-impregnated copper and scores of darkened display cases filled with sparkling, spellbinding stones are just part of a cleverly planned exhibition focusing on the natural forces that create the world's most prized pieces of rock. Some of the stones are the size of a pinhead, others are as big as your fist; the 21,000-carat Brazilian Princess Topaz weighs a quarter of a ton and is the world's largest uncut gem.

Entered directly from the museum, the **Nature Max Cinema** has screenings on natural history themes using the giant-screen IMAX system. If you have ever wanted to inspect a lion's teeth at close quarters, this is the safest way to do it. Adjacent is the museum in the Hayden Planetarium (see panel).

▶ American Numismatic Society · IBCD2

Broadway at 156th Street (tel: 234-3130)
Open: Tue to Sat 9–4:30, Sun 1–4
Subway: C, D, 1; 155th or 157th streets

A vast hoard of coins and medals that is unsurpassed anywhere in the world, the collections of the American Numismatic Society are primarily intended to aid the research of devoted coin collectors and academics. There are, however, two engaging first-floor exhibitions. The first is a spirited documentation—using maps, photographs, and remarkable specimens of very ancient money—of the origins of, and the spread of, coins throughout the world.

After viewing the coins, you may not have sufficient energy left to do justice to the extensive display of medals housed in the second exhibition. Upstairs, there is a public information desk where you can find out whether the foreign coin you have just found in your change is likely to improve your lifestyle dramatically.

▶▶ Asia Society · 151D3

Park Avenue at 70th Street (tel: 517-6397)
Open: Tue to Sat 11–6, Thu 11–8, Sun 12–5
Subway: 6; 68th Street

Founded in 1956 and pledged to improving understanding between Asia and America, the Asia Society hosts conferences, concerts, workshops, and film shows, and mounts stunning temporary exhibitions of Asian art drawn from the world's foremost collections. Displays from the society's own collections include Chinese ceramics from the 11th century BC, some very fine pre-Angkor Cambodian sculpture, and wonderful Japanese Edo-period prints, all donated by John D. Rockefeller III. The decorative lion above the entrance is based on an 18th-century bronze of a Nepalese guardian lion.

ST. JAMES CHURCH
The Sunday services at St. James Episcopal Church (861–863 Madison Avenue), a short walk from the Asia Society, draw many of New York's most wealthy believers from their Upper East Side homes. Drop in during the week to admire the church's impressive stained glass and reredos.

65

The bright interior of St. James Church on Madison Avenue—one of several notable places of worship on the Upper East Side

ST. ELIZABETH ANN SETON

The well-preserved Federal-style building at 7 State Street (tel: 269-6865)—its columns said to be cut from ship's masts—was erected in 1783 for the prominent Watson family but has found longer-lasting fame as the shrine of Elizabeth Ann Seton. She founded the Sisters of Charity, the first order of nuns in the U.S., in 1812 and in 1975 she became the first native-born American woman to be canonized by the Roman Catholic Church. This was her home from 1801 to 1803. Usually open Mon to Fri 6:30–5, on weekends and holidays; ring bell for admission.

66

Above and right: Battery Park, the gateway to the Statue of Liberty, combines history and small-time commerce

▶ Battery Park 104B1

Subway: 4; Bowling Green

A welcome open space on the edge of the Financial District, Battery Park provides 22 acres of greenery with outstanding harbor views. Historical texts are pinned to its lampposts, leaving you with no excuse for not discovering something of early New York simply by strolling the tree-lined pathways.

The park took its name from the row of cannons that the British stored during the 17th century along State Street, which now borders the park but which then marked the Manhattan shoreline.

If you are taking the ferry to the Statue of Liberty and Ellis Island, you will enter Battery Park's most interesting structure to reach the ticket booth, which is situated on the one-time parade ground of **Castle Clinton** (tel: 344-7220; *Open* daily 9–5). This circular fortification, finished in 1811, was built to repulse British attack.

Though there is little evidence of the fact today, Castle Clinton—which originally stood some 300 feet offshore and was linked to land by a causeway—has enjoyed a prominent place in New York life. As its defensive importance declined, the fort was planted with floral gardens and became the scene of well-attended concerts (some presented by 19th-century showman P. T. Barnum) and exhibitions; subsequently, it predated Ellis Island as a landing and processing point for immigrants, almost 8 million of whom came ashore here between 1855 and 1889. The castle also served a 46-year stint as aquarium for the city.

Elsewhere in Battery Park is the pint-sized Peter Minuit Plaza named after the Dutchman who bought Manhattan from its Native American inhabitants for the equivalent of $24 paid in the form of a few tools and trinkets. Occupying a granite building topped by a distinctive six-tiered roof in nearby Battery Park City (see page 18), the **Museum of Jewish Heritage** (18 First Place; tel: 968-1800; *Open* Sun to Wed 9–5, Thu 9–8, Fri 9–2) traces Jewish life through persecution in Europe to the creation of Israel and the growth of Jewish communities in the U.S.

On manic streets beneath the towering sky-scrapers, it is easy to forget that Manhattan is a small island. One of the best ways to get a grasp of its size and shape is from the water that surrounds it, on a guided boat trip.

Most boat-tour operators seem to be offering much the same thing—a sightseeing trip along the Hudson and East rivers that includes a stop at the Statue of Liberty and a view of any New York landmarks visible from the water. There are variations, however, so consider all the options to find the trip that suits you best.

In-depth sightseeing The most comprehensive sight-seeing cruise is run by **Circle Line** (tel: 563-3200). This comprises a three-hour narrated circumnavigation of Manhattan Island, passing beneath seven major bridges on the way. The same company operates a two-hour cruise after dark (Manhattan at night is not a sight to be

Even on a short stay, sightseeing by boat can make a pleasant change from hot sidewalks and traffic jams

easily forgotten) and several other options including a speedboat ride and a Latin DJ dance cruise.

Other options A touch more decadent are the eating and sightseeing trips of **Spirit Cruises** (tel: 727-2789). The company offers a two-hour Tropical Lunch Buffet cruise daily except Sunday, voyaging around Manhattan's southern tip and passing some of the city's major sights. On Sundays, the champagne-fueled Jubilee Lunch Cruise follows a similar route. Dinner and dance cruises (the food from a substantial buffet and the music from a live band, depart nightly and offer memorable views of Manhattan by moonlight.

The catamaran of **Express Navigation Tour (**tel: 800/262-8743) has the swiftest tours, zipping from the Statue of Liberty to the United Nations in 75 minutes. By contrast, **Seaport Liberty Cruises** (tel: 748-8782) uses a replica 19th-century river boat for 90-minute trips, with two-hour lunch cruises and one-hour cocktail evening spins as other options.

EAT AS YOU GO
Visitors love to sightsee but New Yorkers love to eat, and they are the people most in evidence on the lunch, brunch, and dinner cruises offered by World Yacht (tel: 630-8100). These are not calorie-counting affairs: lunch and brunch are lav-ish buffets, and dinner is a four-course treat followed by dancing.

BROADWAY'S FIRST BEND

Broadway's angular scythe through Manhattan's otherwise largely grid-style street plan gave rise to squares such as Union, Madison, and Times. Its first bend—after traveling for 3 ruler-straight miles north from Bowling Green—was due to the refusal of a Dutch landowner, Jacob Brevoort, to allow it to cross his property, a site now occupied by Greenwich Village's Grace Church.

Broadway's nerve center: the theater district near Times Square

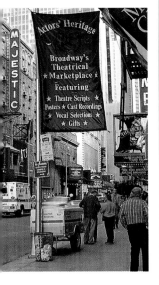

TIMES SQUARE TOURS

Call into the Times Square Visitors Center, inside the Harris Theater, 226 W 42nd Street, for the story of Times Square, told with posters and assorted memorabilia. Each Friday at noon, the center is the starting point of a free two-hour walking tour of the neighborhood, pointing out places of interest.

▶▶ Broadway   *151C2*

The story of Broadway is the story of New York. This is the city's oldest and longest thoroughfare—in one guise or another, Broadway not only runs north–south through Manhattan but continues for 140 miles to Albany. It has witnessed every good, bad, and indifferent phase in the city's growth, while its internationally famous theater district of Times Square and adjacent streets is, for many, what New York is all about.

Originally part of a Native American trail, Broadway was known to early Dutch settlers as De Heere Straat, or Main Street. It has remained New York's major (and perhaps most famous) artery ever since.

Broadway acquired the city's first numbered housing in 1793 and was also the first New York street to see its residential properties put to commercial uses. The commerce came in contrasting forms, with seedy bars, brothels, and gambling dens alongside the city's finest retail outlets. In the 1880s, a popular saying held that if you fired a shotgun in any direction at the junction of Broadway and Houston Street, you would not hit an honest man.

In the days before traffic signals and one-way streets, Broadway was bedlam. Holding the city's major businesses and being the main route north, Broadway's sidewalks were packed with pedestrians and its center a crush of handcarts and horse-drawn wagons. Police had to physically intervene to prevent the thoroughfare becoming completely blocked. Walkers took their lives in their hands when attempting to cross Broadway. The junction with Fulton Street was so infamously hazardous that, in 1867, the authorities erected a footbridge—only for it to be torn down at the insistence of store owners fearful of losing their side's share of captive pedestrians.

What evolved into New York's theater district began in Broadway's southern reaches and steadily moved north, one of the first theaters opening in 1798 at the junction with present-day Park Row. Broadway's theaters quickly forged a reputation for entertaining the city's well-to-do classes with productions of artistic merit and were considered a cut above their Bowery counterparts, popularly regarded as offering low-brow titillation for the consumption of the masses.

By the 1880s, the heyday of vaudeville and the age of stars such as Lillie Langtry, the Broadway theaters had pushed north to Union Square. Around this time, however, the Metropolitan Opera House opened on an unlikely site 26 blocks north and began drawing the city's élite to an area then dominated by livery stores and stables. Broadway crossed this area at Longacre Square.

Ten years passed before a theater opened at Longacre, but by then a section of Broadway around 34th Street had been famously labeled "the Great White Way" on account of its giant advertising billboards lit by hundreds of electric light bulbs.

Soon, **Times Square**—as Longacre Square was renamed after the publisher of *The New York Times* got permission to build an office tower above it—was similarly illuminated. Once joined to the subway system, it quickly became the heart of the city's theater district.

Broadway continued north but the theater district stayed where it was. By the 1920s many of the theaters were showing movies and, 50 years on, the oldest of them were demolished in a spate of office building.

As if to echo the sleaziness of an earlier Broadway, the area around Times Square degenerated into porno stores, prostitution, and drugdealing—though the sheer gaudiness of the place and the many genuine theaters still operating in its vicinity continued to attract a tide of tourists.

With the help of several billion dollars, a different Times Square began to appear through the 1990s: numerous new commercial developments, and considerable improvements in appearance and safety have utterly transformed the area (see pages 18 and 153).

The nighttime neon of Broadway—less stunning than in its heyday perhaps, but still dazzling visitors a century after the first electrically lit sign was switched on

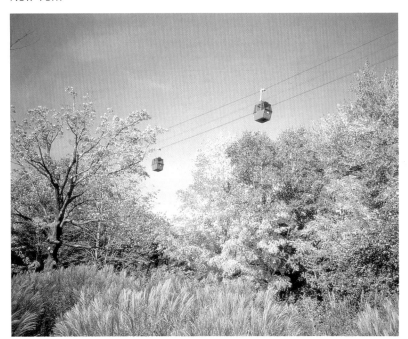

Above and opposite: riding above it on the Skyfari aerial tramway is a good way to view the re-created habitats found at the Bronx Zoo

BRONX ZOO PRACTICALITIES
The zoo's Browndale entrance is a short walk from the Pelham Parkway subway stop. An alternative route from Manhattan is with the Liberty Lines Express Bus (BxM11), which runs from Madison Avenue to the Bronxdale entrance (for details, tel: 718/652-8400).
Summer is the best time to visit (Mon to Fri 10–5, Sat and Sun 10–5:30). During the winter (November to March) many of the zoo's open-air sections are closed and the animals moved indoors (opening hours are then 10–4:30). Admission is free on Wednesday. There is a charge for using the monorails. For general information on the zoo, tel: 718/367-1010.

▶ The Bronx   49D4

That the Bronx has had a worse press than any other New York borough is largely because one section, the South Bronx, became an international symbol of the most extreme forms of urban decay. Since the 1970s, abandoned buildings stripped clean of their fittings and regularly targeted by arsonists have littered the area. A major injection of funds for the building of affordable housing for the predominately low-income population and widespread community initiatives are steadily, if slowly, having an impact, but the South Bronx's image as a place depressed is a hard one to lose.

The rest of the Bronx is quite different. Off **Grand Concourse**, a stately thoroughfare laid out in 1892 and still (though no longer deserving of its title) cutting south-north through the borough, lie safe and tidy residential areas, immense parks, and the **Bronx Zoo** (see below).

In the South Bronx, **Yankee Stadium** (161st Street and River Avenue, tour info tel: 718/293-4300 ex 552) has been the home of the New York Yankees since its completion in 1923. A $100-million renovation program carried out in the mid-1970s was intended to improve the area as much as the building. If you visit the stadium, continue to the **Bronx Museum of the Arts** (1040 Grand Concourse). Opened in 1971, the museum has exhibitions of local art and Bronx-related cultural topics.

If they are not fans of the Yankees, many New Yorkers visit the Bronx for just one thing: the **Bronx Zoo▶** (officially called the **Wildlife Conservation Park**), the largest city zoo in the nation. Spanning 265 acres, the zoo puts its emphasis on herds and flocks rather than single animals and on re-created natural habitats rather than cages. The indoor rain forest of JungleWorld, for example, finds gibbons and monkeys leering at their human visitors from across artificial rivers. You should also spot a few Indian gharials, a type of alligator whose ancestry goes back 180 million years. Rare snow leopards are the highlight of the Himalayan Highlands, while World of Darkness—where day is transformed into night—allows glimpses of foxes, aardvarks, bushbabies, and bats (including the vampire variety, which receive a daily ration of blood).

The animals of the zoo's principal open space, Wild Asia, can be viewed only on a 25-minute narrated monorail ride. The open-sided cars glide above a plain roamed by antelopes, elephants, rhinoceroses, and sika deer—a species now extinct in its native habitat.

More traditional exhibits include the ape and reptile houses, and the MouseHouse, its cages inhabited by innumerable tiny furry things. There is also a separate Children's Zoo, intended to provide young minds with an insight into animal behavior and offering plenty of cute and cuddly creatures for stroking.

Beginning across Fordham Road from the zoo, the **New York Botanical Garden▶** (tel: 718/817-8700; *Open* Wed to Fri 10–5, Sat 11–9, Sun 11–5) is a wonderful mixture of formal gardens, rock gardens, and rugged woodlands—including a 40-acre hemlock forest. In the northwest corner, the Enid A. Haupt Conservatory is filled by a glorious array of banana plants, palm trees, cacti, and other

vegetation and stages seasonal flower shows. After enjoying the vegetation, stop for refreshment at the Snuff Mill Terrace Café (*Open* summer only), invitingly shaded by trees and overlooking the Bronx River.

The **Edgar Allen Poe Cottage▶** (off Grand Concourse at East Kingsbridge Road, tel: 718/881-8900; *Open* Mon to Fri by appointment, Sat 10–4, Sun 1–5) is where the writer lived for two years during the 1840s, in the hope that the country air would improve his wife's health. In the unheated dwelling, Poe's tubercular spouse died during the first winter. Holding a few of the Poes' sparse furnishings, the cottage is an aptly bleak memorial to a man whose short life was seldom a happy one.

In the grounds of the **Bronx Community College▶** (181st Avenue and University Avenue) is the **Hall of**

71

RIVERDALE
When New Yorkers mention the Bronx, they are not usually thinking of Riverdale, part of which is the site of enviable homes and which reaches from the eastern edge of Van Cortlandt Park to the Hudson River.

One place worthy of a visit is the 1846 Fonthill Castle, a Gothic Revival structure modeled on an English folly and originally the home of actor Edwin Forrest. It now serves as the admissions office for the College of Mount St. Vincent, at Riverdale Avenue and 263rd Street. Another is Wave Hill (675 W 252nd Street; tel: 718/549-3200), 28 acres above the Hudson River holding two 19th-century mansions with gardens and greenhouses. It is the site of horticultural exhibitions and summer concerts.

The New York Botanical Garden

Fame for Great Americans. Here the bronze busts of around 100 prominent Americans are lined up along an open-air colonnade. The neoclassical style of the Hall of Fame is noteworthy and is replicated across the campus, much of which is credited to the prominent turn-of-the-century New York architect Stanford White (of the firm McKim, Mead & White).

Predating the college, and most other buildings in the Bronx, the **Van Cortlandt Mansion▶** (off Broadway between 240th and 242nd streets, tel: 718/543-3344; *Open* Tue to Fri 10–3, Sat and Sun 11–4) was built in 1748 for a family prominent in politics and farming, their land holdings consuming what are now the wild expanses of **Van Cortlandt Park**. The mansion, built in Georgian style with Dutch adornments, also provided a part-time base for George Washington, who marched from here into Manhattan to celebrate the end of the Revolutionary War. The mansion shows off its English, Dutch, and Colonial furniture, and a few other 18th-century odds and ends. Periodically, there are demonstrations of brick making and open-hearth cookery.

Strange as it may sound, a more intriguing stop than the mansion is **Woodlawn Cemetery▶** (East 223rd Street and Webster Avenue). Rather than raid the art collections of Europe or finance Manhattan skyscrapers, some ultra-rich early New Yorkers chose to spend their fortunes on extravagant mausoleums. Among those buried here are merchants Richard H. Macy, J. C. Penney, and F. W. Woolworth—whose sphinx-guarded, pseudo-Egyptian palace defies belief. Smaller tombs honor writer Herman Melville and jazz giant Duke Ellington.

New York's first black immigrants were slaves who arrived with the Dutch, by whom they were treated with comparative benevolence. However, a change for the worse occurred during the era of British dominion, when the colony's new rulers showed no respect for people whom they regarded merely as chattel. They responded to slave uprisings with public hangings and burnings. Since then, the struggle for civil rights has unfortunately been a long, uphill battle.

Early racism After the Revolutionary War, a few freed slaves attained respectable social positions, but others were illegally transported to the Deep South. All were subject to racial hostility.

By the early 1800s, New York's African-Americans encountered segregation in public places and were prevented from obtaining the necessary work skills to be employed as anything other than laborers and servants.

The rise and fall of Harlem In response, the first black churches and mutual aid societies were formed and, after years of enduring racism in the city's slums, it was amid the stylish brownstones of Harlem (originally built for wealthy whites) that New York's blacks first felt they had found a secure and self-supporting enclave.

Harlem's population doubled during the 1920s, a period when its art, music, and literature flowered into the "Harlem Renaissance." Swiftly, however, the Depression made Harlem a ghetto, and its problems, along with those of African-American communities in other boroughs, were never tackled by the authorities. The Civil Rights Movement—and the Harlem speeches of Malcolm X—brought racial issues into the public spotlight during the 1960s.

The raising of black consciousness in the 1960s was helped by public campaigners such as Malcolm X, seen here addressing a Muslim meeting in Harlem. He was assassinated in 1965

Modern times David Dinkins became New York's first black mayor in 1990, as Harlem was evolving into one of Manhattan's newest areas of tourist interest. Meanwhile, Harlem institutions such as the Schomburg Center of Research in Black Culture have earned widespread recognition.

GREEN-WOOD CEMETERY
Henry Pierrepont, the man who developed Brooklyn Heights, was not only concerned with providing homes for the living. With Green-Wood Cemetery (main entrance at Fifth Avenue and 25th Street), he created a 478-acre landscaped plot to be enjoyed by some of the most prominent New Yorkers on their earthly demise. The cemetery drew 100,000 visitors a year in its Victorian heyday to wander its 20 miles of footpaths, take in the views over New York harbor, and contemplate the many richly decorated tombs. Richard Upjohn's remarkable Gothic Revival gate and gatehouse, at the Fort Hamilton Parkway entrance, just marks the beginning. Among the 500,000 interred are Henry Ward Beecher, William Marcy "Boss" Tweed, Peter Cooper, and Samuel Morse.

Absorbed into New York City in 1898, fiercely independent Brooklyn at least has its own view of the Statue of Liberty

►►► Brooklyn 48C3

Brooklyn was once a full-fledged city in its own right, with an affluent population and revered cultural institutions. In 1898, buoyed by the opening of the Brooklyn Bridge spanning the East River, it decided (by a narrow majority) to become part of New York City.

The decision has been cursed by Brooklynites ever since. Post-independence humiliations have been many: the Depression and a huge influx of immigrants turned many of Brooklyn's stylish neighborhoods into slums and created breeding grounds for organized crime; the naval shipyards were closed down; Brooklyn's award-winning *Daily Eagle* newspaper bit the dust after a strike. Perhaps most galling of all, the Brooklyn Dodgers moved to Los Angeles in 1955.

Despite these setbacks, Brooklyn remains the most distinctive and enjoyable of the Outer Boroughs. The moderate tempo of its streets comes as a welcome relief after the bustle of Manhattan.

If it were still a city, Brooklyn would be the sixth most populous in the U.S. Within its metropolitan sprawl are four pockets of special interest. Downtown Brooklyn and the historic Brooklyn Heights lie closest to Manhattan. To the north, Fort Greene is gaining a reputation as the home of the new black artistic community. South of downtown, the elegant Eastern Parkway leads past the massive Brooklyn Museum and the Botanic Garden; farther south, on the coast, is the fabled but faded Coney Island amusement park and Russian-dominated Brighton Beach.

From the Brooklyn Bridge, any turning to the right leads into the short leafy streets of **Brooklyn Heights►►►**. The 1814 invention of the steam-powered ferry made this district, set on bluffs above the East River, a residential area coveted by the bankers and speculators active in Manhattan's Financial District, just across the water.

(Continued on page 76)

Where Brooklyn meets the Atlantic Ocean you will find not only a coastline but two contrasting images of New York life: Coney Island amusement park, world-famous but now a pale shadow of its former self, and Brighton Beach, a declining seaside resort energized and transformed since the 1970s by a massive influx of Russian émigrés.

Coney Island Up until the mid-1940s, this was many New Yorkers' idea of heaven. For a nickel subway fare they could spend a day of fun beside the ocean, munching cotton candy and making themselves dizzy on the roller coasters, or lurking around the side shows. Coney Island is undoubtedly a legend, but today it is also—in every sense—history. In the amusement park area between Surf Avenue and the Boardwalk and West 8th and West 16th streets, little more than run-of-the-mill fairground rides suggest the old days, though a 1927 roller-coaster, the fearsome Cyclone, is still in business, as is the even older wooden Wonder Wheel.

On summer days, Coney Island's beach still gets plenty of users, while remaining surprisingly clean, and the Boardwalk beside it is as atmospheric as ever—windswept, breezy, and with an exhilarating polyglot flavor.

Aquarium For Wildlife Conservation (tel: 718/265-3400; *Open* daily 10–4:45) Five species of shark, beluga whales, dolphins, and sea lions are among the inhabitants of the Coney Island Aquarium, accessed from the boardwalk. Visitors will also find the Sea Cliffs exhibition, a sophisticated re-creation of a rocky coastal habitat populated by walrus, seals, penguins, and sea otters.

Brighton Beach Continue east along the Boardwalk to reach this revitalized area where between 10,000 and 20,000 ex-Soviet immigrants form the largest Russian community in the U.S., beneficiaries of the U.S.S.R.'s relaxing of restrictions in the years before its collapse. With caviar and ice-cold vodka advertised in Cyrillic script, and the riotous restaurants along Brighton Beach Avenue known to round off the evening with frenzied dancing and the odd drunken brawl, so-called Little Odessa (many settlers arrived from the Black Sea port) is becoming one of the most celebrated areas of New York City. Bakeries and restaurants here offer Russian culinary specialties.

CONEY ISLAND'S NAME
The most plausible of many theories as to how Coney Island acquired its name is that it derives from the Dutch *Konijn Eiland*—Rabbit Island.

MAXIM GORKY ON CONEY ISLAND, 1906
"Fabulous and beyond conceiving, ineffably beautiful, is this fiery scintillation."

BROOKLYN
HEIGHTS

Stroll along the Brooklyn Heights Promenade for classic views of Manhattan. At the base of the skyscrapers is the South Street Seaport

STROLL: BROOKLYN HEIGHTS

An enjoyable way to walk off a good lunch is with a stroll along the Brooklyn Heights Promenade. Also called the Esplanade, this wide pathway overlooks the East River, and has views of Manhattan strong enough to draw Brooklyn office workers with picnic lunches and to push the prices of west-facing penthouse apartments along nearby Columbia Heights into the realms of the phantasmagoric.

(Continued from page 74)

Brooklyn Heights subsequently became covered with brownstone dwellings—Gothic, Greek, or Romanesque in style—which largely survive intact in an area that became a National Historical Landmark in 1965.

Structure your explorations sufficiently to include Orange Street and its **Plymouth Church of the Pilgrims**▶ (tel: 718/624-4743 for opening hours or appointment). It was here during the 1800s that abolutionist minister Henry Ward Beecher (see panel on page 78) delivered eloquent and impassioned sermons against slavery and made the church a platform for the leading abolitionists. He is remembered by a statue in the adjoining garden. **Brooklyn's Historical Museum**▶ (128 Pierrepont Street, tel: 718/624-0890; *Open* Tue to Sat 12–5) is another worthwhile stop with its exhibits of local memorabilia.

Below the Heights, downtown Brooklyn spills along Fulton Street, which bends around Borough Hall, an unappealing Greek Revival building erected in 1848. Of far greater interest, the **New York Transit Museum**▶▶ (tel: 718/330-3060; *Open* Tue, Thu to Fri 10–4; Wed 10–6; Sat and Sun 12–5) occupies a former subway station at the junction of Boerum Place and Schermerhorn Street. Inside, art deco air-vent coverings and mosaic-tiled station name plates recall the care that went into the early years of what became the world's second-largest mass transit system.

Between Downtown Brooklyn and the former naval dockyards, **Fort Greene**▶ is another district well endowed with leafy streets and elegant brownstones, now owned by Brooklyn's more affluent blacks among others. Many became rooming houses during the Depression, causing the area to fall into neglect.

Though signs of inner-city poverty remain apparent, Fort Greene is very much on the rise. African-Americans still make up 70 percent of the district's population, a significant number of them being successful in the arts. Artist Ernest Critchlow is a long-established local; another is film-maker Spike Lee, who resisted the lure of Hollywood and located his production company here.

Lee grew up in Fort Greene and his 1986 movie, *She's Gotta Have It*, made use of a local landmark: **Fort Greene Park**, designed in 1860 by Olmsted and Vaux (better known for Manhattan's Central Park). The Doric column was added later in memory of the 12,000 American patriots who died on British prison ships during the Revolutionary War and lie buried beneath the park.

Fort Greene sees comparatively few tourists. It is sensible to keep to the area south of the park, where you will find the most impressive of the brownstone buildings and also several churches (visit on Sunday morning for the best atmosphere).

There are many more brownstones located in the residential streets between Flatbush Avenue and Sixth Avenue, an upscale section of the Park Slope neighborhood. A much more spectacular sight in this area, however, stands at the center of Grand Army Plaza (on Flatbush Avenue by the main entrance to Prospect Park, described below): the oversized Soldiers' and Sailors'

BORN IN BROOKLYN
Woody Allen (1935), Clara Bow (1905), George Gershwin (1899), Mickey Rooney (1922), Barbra Streisand (1943), Mae West (1892), Barry Manilow (1946), Aaron Copland (1900), Mary Tyler Moore (1937), Veronica Lake (1919), Elliot Gould (1938), Neil Sedaka (1939), Phil Silvers (1912), Philip Glass (1937).

Brooklyn

THE HASIDIC JEWS
Since the 1940s, Brooklyn's Williamsburg district (north of Downtown) has been a base of the ultrastrict Hasidic community. Men wear beards, side curls, dark frock coats and hats; the heads of married women are shaven and covered by a wig. The Hasidim adhere rigidly to kosher diets, and some eschew T.V. and radio. Another large Orthodox Jewish community in Brooklyn is the Lubavitchers, adherents to a Hasidic sect that originated in 18th-century Russia.

HENRY WARD BEECHER
Clergyman at the Plymouth Church of the Pilgrims for some 40 years in the latter half of the 19th century, Henry Ward Beecher spoke out against slavery and in favor of women's suffrage. Equally controversial for the time, Beecher's writings supported Darwin's theory of evolution. His later years were dogged by allegations of adultery, charges of which he was cleared only after his death in 1887.

Memorial Arch, raised in 1892 to commemorate the Union forces who died during the Civil War.

This Brooklyn version of an imperial Roman arch was designed by John H. Duncan, who was also responsible for the similarly grandiose General Grant Memorial (see pages 110–111). The memorial's sheer size makes it much more of an architectural curiosity than a fitting shrine to the dead. The sense of pomposity is compounded by the heroic sculptures added to the memorial in 1898, though some amends are made by the finely detailed bas-reliefs that decorate the walls on the inside of the arch.

Prospect Park▶ itself is a broad and bucolic open space completed in 1874. With none of the restraints that were imposed with Central Park (such as incorporating major traffic arteries) architects Olmsted and Vaux gave their imaginations free rein here and considered Prospect Park their finest work.

The grand streets and landscaped open spaces—as well as the triumphal monuments—that Brooklyn acquired during the late 19th century were the hallmarks of a city very much on the rise. In keeping with the optimism of the times—and in an effort to create a symbol of Brooklyn's cultural superiority over Manhattan—the **Brooklyn Museum▶▶▶** (200 Eastern Parkway,

Brooklyn Heights. Not all of the city's best skyscrapers are in Manhattan

tel: 718/638-5000; *Open* Wed to Fri 10–5, Sat 11–9, Sun 11–5, 11–11 first Sat of the month) was founded in 1897 with the intention of becoming the largest museum in the world. Such great ambitions were never fulfilled, however, and this fine museum has been playing second fiddle to the better-known museums of Manhattan for decades. It is probably most renowned as the resting place for the world's third largest stock of ancient Egyptian artifacts, a remarkable collection dating from predynastic times to the Roman conquest.

The museum's fifth floor has an exceptional collection of 19th-century American portraiture, including Gilbert Stuart's iconographic image of George Washington. Elsewhere, Francis Guy's airy *Winter Scene in Brooklyn* of 1817 stands out, and a quality selection from the Hudson River School culminates in Albert Bierstadt's *Storm in the Rocky Mountains, Mt. Rosalie*, an intense landscape of rugged granite beneath brooding storm clouds.

The fourth floor of the museum has colonial-period ceramics, and interiors ranging from 17th-century farmhouses to 1920s art-deco lounges. Note the Moorish Room: a dreamy conglomeration of patterned tiles, gold-brocaded walls, oak panels, and velvet drapes which once graced John D. Rockefeller's Manhattan mansion.

Other stories are filled by comprehensive Asian art collections, while the first floor holds pottery, figurines, and votive objects from Africa, Oceania, and Central and South America. Most striking among the latter is perhaps the Paracas Textile, a 2,000-year-old Peruvian burial cloth.

The Native American collections, on the same floor, feature diverse tribes and exhibits ranging from buckskin jackets to totem poles.

After exploring the museum, head for the 52 divinely landscaped acres of the **Brooklyn Botanic Garden**▶ ▶ (tel: 718/622-4433; *Open* Tue to Fri 8–4:30, Sat and Sun 10–4:30, extended hours during summer), just to the rear.

The quiet charm still to be found in parts of Brooklyn Heights contrasts with the frenetic streets of Manhattan, just across the East River

LITERARY BROOKLYN HEIGHTS
Brooklyn Heights has strong literary associations. Poet Hart Crane and novelist John Dos Passos both lived at 110 Columbia Heights during the 1920s (Crane also resided briefly at 77 Willow Street). Henry Miller spent a short time at 91 Remsen Street during the 1920s, and Truman Capote wrote *Breakfast at Tiffany's* in the basement of 70 Willow Street. Norman Mailer wrote *The Naked and the Dead* while living with his parents at 102 Pierrepont Street (he now lives elsewhere in Brooklyn Heights). At the same address Arthur Miller wrote his play *All My Sons*, before moving to 155 Willow Street, where he is remembered by a plaque—though he wrote *Death of a Salesman* at 31 Grace Court.

BAD LUCK AND THE BROOKLYN BRIDGE

In its early years, the Brooklyn Bridge saw more than its share of tragedy. Its designer, John A. Roebling, died following an accident before his bridge was complete. His son, Washington, took over, but became paralyzed as a result of "the bends," and had to supervise the construction work from his sick bed. Twenty of the 600-strong work force died during the construction. Six days after the bridge opened, the screams of a woman who tripped on the approach caused a panic in which 12 people lost their lives, mistakenly believing the bridge was about to collapse. In 1884, however, circus-owner P. T. Barnum led 21 elephants across it; since then there have been few doubts as to the bridge's strength.

The pedestrian walkway on the Brooklyn Bridge. The towers of Manhattan's Financial District gleam behind the intricate web of suspension cables

▶▶ Brooklyn Bridge   77D1

Subway: Brooklyn Bridge

Completed in 1883, the Brooklyn Bridge was the world's first steel suspension bridge, and, for 20 years, the longest. It formed the first fixed link between Brooklyn and Manhattan Island.

Enhanced immeasurably by its two Gothic 272ft-high stone arches (when they were finished, only the spire of Trinity Church rose higher into the New York sky), the bridge is an aesthetic as well as an engineering master-piece. Many writers, including Brooklyn-based Walt Whitman, have waxed lyrical over its beauty.

Bike riders, skaters, joggers, and high winds can be a hazard to walkers on the bridge's pedestrian path, easily the best way to appreciate the structure. From Manhattan, the views used to be of Brooklyn's busy shipyards, a scene re-created by a display beside the footpath, while another recounts the bridge's origins. In the other direction is a fabulous view of Manhattan.

▶ Carnegie Hall   151C2

57th Street at Seventh Avenue (tel: 247-7800)
Guided tours: Mon, Tue, Thu, and Fri 11:30, 2 and 3
Subway: D, E, N, R; Seventh Avenue or 57th Street

Financed by a $2-million gift from steel magnate Andrew Carnegie, Carnegie Hall opened to the public in 1891 and quickly gained an international reputation for its out-standing acoustics. Its horseshoe-shaped auditorium is modeled on those of Italian opera houses. Refurbishment has restored the hall to the appearance of its younger days, best appreciated by attending a concert—a must if you have time. Tours of the building end at the **Carnegie Hall Museum** which records the hall's origins and the long list of famous names that have graced its boards. Besides Benny Goodman's clarinet and Arturo Toscanini's baton, the museum has a 1964 bookings diary with a handwrit-ten entry recording the first New York appearance of "The Beetles"(sic).

Gothic vaulting (left) and (below) a sculptural detail of what will, if and when it is completed, be the world's biggest cathedral

▶▶ Cathedral of St. John the Divine   *IBCB2*

Amsterdam Avenue at 112th Street (tel: 316-7540)
Open daily 8–6
Subway: 1; Cathedral Parkway (110th Street)

The cornerstone of the Cathedral of St. John the Divine was laid in 1892, marking the beginning of what is now an immense Episcopalian edifice spread across 11 acres—the largest church in the U.S., and the largest Gothic church in the world, yet still years short of completion.

The original plans were for a church of Byzantine/Romanesque design, but delays caused by engineering problems and lack of finance meant that only the choir and four stone arches were completed in the first 25 years. Changing tastes (and the death of the project's original architect) saw the structure remodeled in French Gothic form, and it was given a facade reminiscent of Notre-Dame in Paris.

The nave, covering a staggering 32,000 square feet, was completed in a comparatively swift 10 years, but the U.S.'s entry into World War II again halted progress, as did a decision during the 1960s to divert building money to the needs of the community. Another building program got under way in 1978, when funds were available to import a master stonemason from England to cut the Indiana limestone used in the towers and to train a small army of local apprentices.

As its towers still rise, enclosed by scaffolding, the cathedral's exterior takes on a strangely surreal appearance. Inside, the scale is breathtaking. The clash of Gothic and Romanesque/Byzantine styles is most apparent from the unfinished crossing, where the structure's anatomy is revealed and above which the red-tiled dome, installed as a "temporary" shelter during 1909, remains in place even today.

Foremost among the cathedral's decorations are two sets of religious tapestries: the Mortlake Tapestries, woven in England during 1623 from cartoons by Raphael, and the 17th-century Barberini tapestries, which were woven on papal looms.

NEW YORK PUBLIC LIBRARY: 115TH STREET BRANCH
The main branch of the New York Public Library on Fifth Avenue (see page 168) is one of the city's greatest architectural delights, and the 115th Street branch (between Seventh and Eighth avenues) is no mere pile either. Dating from 1908, the library was the work of the firm of McKim, Mead & White, and its imposing Renaissance style was intended to match the grandeur of early Harlem.

1   Charles A Dana Discovery Center
2   El Museo del Barrio
3   Museum of the City of New York
4   International Center of
     Photography
5   Jewish Museum
6   Cooper-Hewitt Museum
7   Guggenheim Museum
8   Cleopatra's Needle
9   Delacorte Theater
10 Belvedere Castle
11 Swedish Cottage
12 American Museum of Natural
     History and Hayden Planetarium
13 San Remo Apartment Building
14 Loeb Boathouse
15 Alice in Wonderland Statue
16 Hans Christian Andersen Statue
17 Frick Collection
18 Bandstand
19 Holy Trinity Lutheran Church
20 Tavern-on-the-Green
21 Heckscher Playground
22 Wollman Memorial Rink

▶▶▶ Central Park   IFCF2

From almost any high point in Manhattan, what holds the
eye longest is not the Empire State Building or the World
Trade Center but the great rectangle of greenery in the
heart of the dense urban clutter. Central Park fills 843
acres and runs for 50 city blocks between the Upper East
and Upper West sides.

The candidates in New York's mayoral campaign of
1850 were agreed on just one issue: the need for a large
public park of the kind civic leaders and journalists had
been advocating since poet and newspaper editor
William Cullen Bryant raised the idea in 1844. At that
time, property developers were breaking all records in
their northward streak across Manhattan.

In 1856, the city paid $5½ million for a tract of land—an
area well to the north of the city as then established,
dotted with pig farms and squatter camps and mostly
used as a garbage dump. Two years later work began on
the park, to the plans of Frederick Olmsted (a farmer-
turned-engineer-turned-journalist-turned-landscape
architect) and English architect Calvert Vaux.

The park's design called for a major earth-moving project as glades, copses, and rock outcrops were created,
and some 5 million trees planted. Bridges linked the
park's internal thoroughfares and cross-park traffic was
carried by sunken roads to keep the pastoral view intact.

With tree-lined driveways for the wealthy to parade in
horse-drawn carriages, and footpaths for the working
classes (who typically at the time toiled in sweatshops
and lived in filthy tenements) to experience, as Olmsted
expressed it, "a specimen of God's handiwork," the park
was an instant success.

Though now fully enclosed by buildings and with far
more monuments than Olmsted would have liked,
Central Park is still a great escape from the city streets.
The Fifth Avenue and Upper West Side apartment buildings that appear above the treetops simply add to the
park's country-in-the-city effect. Getting lost temporarily
in Central Park is surprisingly easy. Be sure to pick up a
map from one of the information kiosks before you enter.

From the south, the first place to make for is the **Dairy**. In
pursuit of a romantic rural vision, the Gothic-style Dairy
was built here in 1870 as a place where traditionally
attired milkmaids would serve fresh milk to mothers and
young children. The quaint building now holds the park's
main Visitor Center, with displays and several leaflets
describing park walks.

North of the Dairy, across the 65th Transverse, the 22-
acre **Sheep Meadow** did indeed hold sheep during the
park's earliest years, the resident flock being led across
the park's West Drive twice a day to the Sheepfold, which
occupied the site of the present Tavern on the Green.

Just east of the Sheep Meadow begins the **Mall**, one of
the first completed sections of the park and its only formal
area. Many 19th-century New Yorkers got their first taste
of European-style promenading along its tree-lined
esplanade, and some also gained their first experience of
donkey- and goat-cart riding, both of which were offered
to visitors here.

Olmsted initially resisted attempts to have statuary in
the park but eventually agreed to the memorials of

writers—Shakespeare, Robert Burns, and Sir Walter Raleigh among them—which are grouped around the Mall's southern end to form the **Literary Walk**.

Continuing north, the Mall leads into the **Concert Ground** and the **Naumberg Bandshell**, the scene of free live music on most summer weekends.

Cross the 72nd Street Transverse and you enter **Bethesda Terrace**. At its heart is the Bethesda Fountain and the elegant *Angel of the Waters* statue. One of the few pieces commissioned especially for the park, the statue, inspired by the biblical story of the Bethesda Pool in Jerusalem, was unveiled in 1873 to commemorate the opening of the aqueduct that gave New York its first regular supply of fresh water.

There is more water directly north of Bethesda Terrace, in the form of the **Lake**. A leisurely paddle along this imposingly calm body of water is a fine way to round off a park visit. Boats can be hired from the Loeb Boathouse, on the eastern banks of the lake.

If you are determined to do something more energetic, you could always cross the lake on foot by way of the Bow Bridge—one of Central Park's seven original cast-iron bridges—to **The Ramble**. Comprising 33 acres of painstakingly re-created rurality, complete with rustic

STROLL: STRAWBERRY FIELDS
From the Upper West Side, entering Central Park on 72nd Street leads into Strawberry Fields, a 3-acre section maintained by an endowment from Yoko Ono, as a memorial to her late husband John Lennon.

Overlooked by the Dakota apartment building, where the Lennons lived (see page 96), Strawberry Fields is planted with 161 species of plant, representing 161 nations of the world. The authorities were not unanimous in agreeing to the tribute: conservative elements wanted a memorial to Bing Crosby.

Central Park's Bethesda Fountain

83

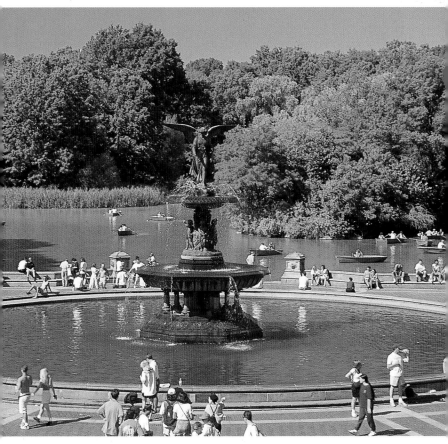

CENTRAL PARK IN STYLE
One way of seeing the park is as the city swells of the 1880s did: by horse and carriage. Buy a ticket from the stand at Grand Army Plaza (at the junction of 59th Street and Fifth Avenue) and climb aboard. Prices have risen over the last hundred years, however: expect to pay around $34 per person for a 25-minute trot.

birdhouses and beehives, The Ramble is ripe for exploration and is also an excellent location for birdwatching. It is not advisable to ramble alone, however, as this is an isolated and dangerous area.

Across the 79th Street Transverse from The Ramble, a replica Scottish castle, **Belvedere Castle** (tel: 722-0210; *Open* Tue to Sun 10–4), was erected in 1869 for no reason other than fun and holds displays on park wildlife.

To the left, a path leads to the **Shakespeare Garden**, planted with trees and plants mentioned in the bard's works, passes the **Delacorte Theater** (scene of a summer Shakespeare festival), and continues to the immaculate **Great Lawn**. Free open-air concerts are given here each year during the summer by the New York Philharmonic.

Top: a sedate tour or (above) the more energetic pastime of rollerblading

Central Park has had its share of well-publicized crimes but is generally no more dangerous than the average New York street, though there are isolated areas where lone wandering is not wise. Never visit the park after dark.

▶▶ Chelsea
East of Fifth Avenue between 14th and 34th Street
In the 1990s Chelsea evolved into one of Manhattan's most stylish neighborhoods. Former warehouses close to the Hudson River have been converted into gallery space, and Chelsea has become a thriving quarter for new art, exhibited amid truck supply stores and courier firms.

Among the galleries is the main site (there are two others in SoHo) of the **DIA Center for the Arts** (548 West 22nd Street, tel: 989-5566; *Open* Thu to Sun 12–6; *Admission charge*), with low-key exhibitions often featuring major names. Meanwhile, several river piers (west of 23rd Street) became the imaginatively designed recreational complex of **Chelsea Piers** offering skating, bowling, golf, restaurants, river cruises, and a waterside promenade.

The commercial heart of Chelsea is around the junction of 23rd Street and Eighth Avenue. The residential areas nearby are a mixture of tasteful townhouses and high-rise apartment blocks.

The Chelsea Hotel

When the Chelsea opened in 1888 at 222 West 23rd Street, it was the first apartment building in New York to have a penthouse apartment on its uppermost floor. Its facade featured wrought-iron balconies decorated with sunflower motifs. Converted to a hotel in 1905, the Chelsea became famous as a haunt of writers, painters, and composers, who gave it an unconventional ambience.

Painter John Sloan and writers Mark Twain and O. Henry (the pen name of William Sydney Porter) were among the Chelsea's early guests, but the hotel hit its artistic stride during the 1930s, after poet Edgar Lee Masters eulogized it in verse and novelist Thomas Wolfe took up residence.

Impressed by the size of his suite, Wolfe dubbed his bathroom the "Throne Room" and kept 4,000 loose pages of prose strewn across his floor. Selections from these would be assembled and supplied to his publisher as finished works.

The 1950s and 1960s Its literary links were already established by the time Dylan Thomas made the Chelsea his New York base during the early 1950s. His last conscious hours, after he had claimed to have downed 18 whiskeys in a Greenwich Village bar, were spent in room 205, and he died in hospital a few days later of suspected alcohol poisoning.

A decade later, the Irish writer Brendan Behan took shelter at the Chelsea and begged to be commemorated by a plaque—as he now is. Besides Behan, Beat writers William Burroughs and Gregory Corso, expatriate Russian novelist Vladimir Nabokov, and abstract expressionist painter Jackson Pollock were among the renegades who gathered at the Chelsea's bar (which is now a Spanish restaurant).

Its decorative design may once have been ahead of its time, but the Chelsea has long been known not as an architectural landmark but as a cultural one

Pop and punk The hotel provided a backdrop for Andy Warhol's rambling split-screen film *Chelsea Girls* (which starred Warhol acolyte Edie Sedgwick, a Chelsea resident) and through the 1960s its guests included many pop-music icons—among them Bob Dylan, who wrote his epic song "Sad Eyed Lady of the Lowlands" in one of its rooms.

The hotel's most ignominious night came in 1978, when punk rocker Sid Vicious allegedly stabbed his girlfriend to death in their suite— Ken Russell's movie *Sid and Nancy* actually featured the hotel.

Step into the Chelsea's lobby and you will find plaques commemorating its most illustrious residents and many works donated by artist guests. The Chelsea's rooms vary greatly in style, size and price, and some of them are occupied by eccentric long-term guests.

PRE-CHINATOWN REMNANTS

On St. James Place you can find the First Shearith Israel graveyard, predecessor of the cemeteries of Greenwich Village and Chelsea. The first Jewish cemetery in the United States, the site was consecrated in 1656, when it was considered to be well outside town.

On nearby James Street, St. James Church is an 1837 Greek Revival edifice. Al Smith, once an altar boy at the church, rose from this poor then-Irish neighborhood to become New York's governor and a 1928 Democratic presidential candidate.

Frenetic but fascinating, Chinatown's streetlife never takes a break

▶▶▶ Chinatown   *IFCB3*

New York streetlife enters a new dimension on the tightly clustered, densely crowded sidewalks of Chinatown, which lies between the courthouses, Little Italy, and the Lower East Side.

Stalls are laden with seafood, vegetables, or fruit; herbalist stores dispense wondrous remedies; bakeries concoct sweet cakes; and rows of gaudy neon signs advertise (in English and Chinese) the noodle stores, tea parlors, and dim sum houses that bring most non-Chinese New Yorkers to the area.

There has been a Chinese presence here since the 1850s, but only with the relaxing of immigration laws in 1965 did Chinatown really begin to expand. Spilling beyond its traditional boundaries, Chinatown now holds around half of New York's estimated 300,000 Chinese population and has been swelled by arrivals from Vietnam and other parts of Southeast Asia.

The handover of Hong Kong to Beijing has also been felt. Hong Kong banks have opened here, and brightly lit shopping malls stuffed with jewelry and electrical goods have spread along Canal Street.

Beyond business and people, there is not a lot for visitors to see in Chinatown, although a notable exception is the **Museum of the Chinese in the Americas** (second floor, 70 Mulberry Street; tel: 619-4785; *Open* Tue to Sun 10:30–5). This one-room exhibition presents a small, absorbing documentation of Chinese settlement in the U.S. The many exhibits are a hotchpotch of family photos, items from Chinese-run businesses, and objects of symbolic significance carried from the homeland. Part of the museum's aim is to help young Chinese-Americans understand their history, although the temporary exhibitions examine many aspects of the Chinese Diaspora.

Walk

the **Transfiguration**, at 25 Mott Street, predates Chinatown. Not far away, **Doyers Street** was once the

Chinatown streetlife

Effervescent streetlife is the main attraction of Chinatown, which holds few specific sights. This walk covers the main ones and captures the atmosphere of the area.

Begin at **Columbus Park**, which replaced a notorious slum and red-light area of the mid-1800s. Across Mulberry Street is the entrance to the **Museum of the Chinese in the Americas**. Walk up to **Canal Street** for Chinatown's biggest and brightest shopping emporiums before reaching Mott Street.

At 64 Mott Street, the **Eastern States Buddhist Temple** is a genuine temple but also sells souvenir Buddha figures, arranged in eye-catching rows. Built in 1801, the Georgian **Church of**

domain of opium dealers and prostitutes, and its bend was used as an ambush point during 19th- and early 20th-century Tong Wars, when rival Chinese gangs fought over who should have control of drug-trafficking, prostitution, and gambling. Nowadays perfectly safe, Doyers Street is lined by numerous restaurants.

Chinese faces were few and far between in early 19th-century New York, but nowadays the Chinese community is expanding fast in both size and importance. Whether in academia or business, Chinese-Americans are frequently among the city's most spectacular achievers.

CHINESE IN THE U.S.
Although only a few Chinese were present in New York prior to the late 1800s, they were already established in California where 25,000 had arrived in 1852. Most of them worked in the California gold mines and, subsequently, on the transcontinental railroad that linked the West Coast to the rest of the country. The Chinese gained a reputation as dependable laborers, but in the economic depression that followed the Gold Rush, they found themselves prevented from opening businesses or owning land. Banding together, the Chinese settled in what became the "Chinatown" districts of many California communities, some making the cross-country trip to the less hostile atmosphere of New York.

The 75 Chinese immigrants estimated to be living in New York in 1870 were mostly individuals who had jumped ship and assimilated themselves as best they could into established ethnic groups. By 1890, however, New York's Chinese population had rocketed to 12,000. Many of the new arrivals came here from California, where they had provided labor for the transcontinental railroad.

With their language and culture at odds with European New York, the lone Chinese males (denied the company of their relatives by an anti-immigration law of 1896) rarely strayed from Chinatown. Aided by family-based self-help organizations, they toiled in stores and laundries, sending any spare money back home.

The seamy side The popular imagination saw Chinatown as a neighborhood of incredible exotica. Gambling, prostitution (provided by white women), and opium dens did in fact exist, but usually in upstairs rooms or basements. These activities were overseen by the Tongs—an American term for a Chinese-American secret society. Many Tongs claimed long histories to impress recruits and, at a time when the Chinese were excluded from the American legal system, provided a vehicle for settling grievances.

Acceptance and expansion The Japanese invasion of China in 1937 helped unite warring factions in the Chinese community, and the subsequent U.S.–Sino military alliance reduced anti-Chinese feeling among New Yorkers. A bigger change came in 1965, when limitations on Chinese immigration were lifted and waves of new arrivals from Taiwan and Hong Kong came to Chinatown.

The new Chinese were eager to embrace American ways. They quickly made their presence felt in mainstream New York life. Their success and prosperity enabled them to become fully integrated into New York life, and to leave cramped Chinatown for more comfortable homes. Many left the inner city for suburbia as soon as they made the climb up the economic ladder.

Chinese food to go. Chinatown's eateries cover a vast range of styles and regional cuisines

*The unmistakable
Chrysler Building—New
York art deco at its finest,
and everyone's favorite
skyscraper*

THE CHEATING SPIRE
The Chrysler Building's
"world's tallest" title was
acquired through some
slightly devious behavior
by its architect, William
Van Alen. The needle-like
spire that tops its 77
stories was secretly
assembled inside the
tower and pushed through
the roof. In this way Van
Alen outwitted his former
partner, H. Craig
Severance, whose
contemporaneously com-
pleted Bank of Manhattan
Building (40 Wall Street)
would otherwise have
earned the accolade.

89

►► Chrysler Building   151B3

42nd Street at Lexington Avenue (tel: 682-3070)
Open: Mon to Fri 8:30–5:30
Subway: 4, 6, 7; 42nd Street/Grand Central
The definitive symbol of New York art deco and briefly
the world's tallest building, the 1,045-foot Chrysler
Building was completed in 1930. Its tower is still among
the city's most recognizable landmarks. More impressive
than the exterior view, however, is the lobby, retaining its
walls of red-veined African marble and a mural by
Edward Trumbull depicting the glories of world transportation. The elevators, too, still have their original decor
of laminated woods, and the entire 77-story building is
studded by automobile motifs.

► City Hall   104C2

Tel: 788-6879
Open: Mon to Fri 9–4
Subway: N, R; City Hall
A cluster of municipal buildings stands near the foot of
the Brooklyn Bridge. The oldest, the **City Hall**, a mix of
Federal and French Renaissance styles dating from 1811,
is still in use for its original purpose. The barriers that line
the front of the building are intended to prevent the frequent demonstrations in City Hall Park from blocking
councilors' access to the building. Inside, a circular staircase winds beneath the eye-catching rotunda to the
second floor, where the **Governor's Room** is lined by portraits of early New York notables and items of furniture
mostly contemporaneous with the building. To the north
stands the **Old New York County Courthouse**, intended as
a shrine to justice but a building whose financing was one
of the biggest swindles in New York history (see page 42).
It is now used as municipal offices. Across Centre Street,
the present **New York County Courthouse** has a hexagonal
shape and a magnificent Corinthian portico.

POLICE RIOTS
In 1857, City Hall Park
was the scene of violence
between New York's two
rival police forces, the dis-
credited Municipal and the
newly formed
Metropolitan. Their battles
continued into City Hall
and ended only when
National Guardsmen drew
their bayonets.
 In September 1992,
New York's finest again
disgraced themselves in
the park, when a poorly
planned demonstration
against Mayor Dinkins culminated in officers (some
of them clearly the worse
for drink) stepping over
the barricades and
blockading the entrance to
City Hall.

City dwellers love to root for the home team, and New Yorkers—with their city represented by two professional teams in football, hockey, and baseball—are no exception. Loyalties and rivalries run deep, even though the closest most people get to actual games is the couch facing the T.V. in their living rooms: tickets, especially for football games or for playoff games in other sports, tend to be hard to get hold of and very expensive.

THE NEW YORK MARATHON

What began in 1970 with 127 runners is now the world's largest urban marathon. Its 26-mile course is contested by some 22,000 runners and watched by over 2 million spectators. Usually held on the third or fourth Sunday in October, it begins on Staten Island at the Verrazano-Narrows Bridge, passing through each of the city's five boroughs to finish at Central Park's Tavern on the Green.

A great New York sporting event

Baseball Beset by off-the-field problems through the early 1990s, the New York Yankees are now putting their troubles behind them and returning to their glory days. The Yankees play at Yankee Stadium in the Bronx (tel: 718/293-6000).The season runs from April to October. Ticket prices range from around $8 (on the day) for the bleachers, where you will hear the New York crowd at its most witty but also get the worst view, to around $23 as you move up into the tiered seating.

Until recently, the more successful of the city's two teams has been the New York Mets, who play at Shea Stadium in Queens (tel: 718/507-8499) where ticket prices are similar to those for the Yankees.

Basketball From fall to spring, basketball fans can watch the New York Knicks (short for "Knickerbockers") playing at Madison Square Garden (tel: 465–JUMP). The Knicks had an all-win "dream" season in the early 1970s, but their record has been off and on since. Ticket costs vary upward of $20 and are particularly difficult to get for the end-of-season play-offs. The advent of professional women's basketball quickly found New York Liberty (tel: 564-9622) among the country's top WNBA sides. Like the Knicks, they play at Madison Square Garden, with tickets priced from $8 to $55.

Hockey The incredible lack of success of the city's New York Rangers was dramatically ended by their winning of the Stanley Cup in 1994. The Rangers face off at Madison Square Garden (ticket info, tel: 465-6741) in a season lasting from late fall to spring. New Yorkers who want to see a local hockey team with a more regular success rate are inclined to travel to Uniondale on Long Island, where the New York Islanders play at the Nassau Coliseum (tel: 516/794-9300).

Football Both of New York's two professional football teams play outside the city's boundaries, at Giants Stadium, the Meadowlands, East Rutherford, New Jersey (tel: 201/935-8222). In recent years, the Giants have been much more successful than New York's A.F.C. team, Jets. The football season runs from August through December and tickets for the Jets start at around $25. Particularly for Giant games, however, tickets are virtually impossible to obtain without marking reservations many months (if not years) in advance. Shuttle buses carry spectators from Manhattan.

Horse-racing At daily races held from May to July and from September to mid-October, thoroughbreds can be seen stampeding along the turf at Belmont Park, Elmont, Long Island (tel: 718/641-4700), and from late October to May at the Aqueduct Racetrack, Ozone Park, Queens (phone number as for Belmont Park). During August, the state's horse lovers move upstate to follow events at the Saratoga Raceway (tel: 518/584-2110) for a month-long series of meetings.

Betting on horse races If your interest in horses extends only as far as betting on them, aim for one of the many branches of New York City Off-track Betting, where bets can be placed and races watched on T.V. simulcast. Other venues for a wager are The Inside Track, Second Avenue between 53rd and 54th streets (tel: 752-1940), a sports bar in the style of an English pub with two giant screens and 15 T.V. monitors, or the elegant Select Club, 165 Water Street (tel: 785-0478).

Tennis Early in September, one of the big events in the international tennis calendar, the U.S. Open, takes place at Flushing Meadows, Queens (tel: 718/760-6200). Tickets for the later stages of the Open have traditionally been snapped up many moons in advance, though it has always been possible to see international stars play at short notice—there are often people with extra tickets trying to sell them on the boardwalk leading to the stadium area. With the completion of new, enlarged quarters, the ticket situation has loosened up considerably. The springtime Tournament of Champions draws many top players to the West Side Tennis Club in Forest Hills, Queens (tel: 718/268-2300).

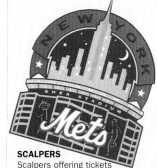

SCALPERS
Scalpers offering tickets for all major sporting events are usually found on the approach routes to the venue. Be wary of forged tickets and that prices, which can start well in excess of the ticket's face value, will drop as game time approaches.

SPORTS BARS
The city's many sports bars provide alcohol and T.V. screens tuned to every sports event anyone could possibly want. If a New York team is involved, you can also be sure of loud and frequent partisan comments and suggestions.

Informal basketball

THE GEORGE WASHINGTON BRIDGE
Look southward from any high point in or around the Cloisters and you will be able to admire the elegant form of the George Washington Bridge, spanning the Hudson River from 178th Street and once described by famed modernist architect Le Corbusier as "the most beautiful bridge in the world."

Altarpieces and chapel furnishings at the Cloisters

TWO FOR THE PRICE OF ONE
If you visit the Metropolitan Museum of Art and the Cloisters on the same day, a single ticket is valid at both. During the summer there is also a direct bus link between the two museums, which is quicker though more expensive than public transportation.

▶▶ The Cloisters   *IBCF1*

Fort Tryon Park, Washington Heights (tel: 923-3700)
Open: Tue to Sun 9:30–4:45
Subway: A; 190th Street

Manhattan and medieval European monasteries may seem an unlikely partnership, but at **Fort Tryon Park**, close to Manhattan's northern tip and perched on a spectacular site above the Hudson River, parts of five 12th- to 15th-century monastic buildings from France and Spain have been brought together to form the Cloisters, a fitting home for a large portion of the Metropolitan Museum of Art's medieval collection.

Although much of the Cloisters' architecture is new disguised as old, the genuinely historic parts—assorted columns, cloisters, chapels, apses, and much more—were gathered by sculptor George Gray Bernard as he roamed the back roads of Europe during the early 1900s. Bernard grabbed all the forgotten religious art and architecture he could lay his hands on. Some of his pieces were discovered lying in pigsties and ditches near old churches, others were being used as garden ornaments. Bernard

put the rather haphazard collection on show in Manhattan and it was brought to the Met in 1925 with funds provided by John D. Rockefeller, who subsequently commissioned the construction of the Cloisters to put it on permanent show. The exceedingly wealthy Rockefeller also owned the land that became Fort Tryon Park (see panel page 93) and donated to the Cloisters its most memorable exhibit—the Unicorn Tapestries (see below).

Each section of the Cloisters is arranged more or less chronologically, and highlights particular aspects of medieval creativity. The Romanesque Hall, for example, is entered through one of three sculptured church doorways, demonstrating the stylistic shift from 12th-century Romanesque to 13th-century Gothic. Most impressive of the three is the latest: a High Gothic masterpiece from Burgundy which shows Christ crowning the Virgin, flanked by Clovis, first Christian ruler of France, and his son, Clothaire. The two men are so realistically sculpted they seem ready to reach forward and shake your hand.

Off the Romanesque Hall you will find the apse of the 12th-century Fuentidueña Chapel, which survived as its church crumbled around it: note the frescoes and the statues of St. Martin and the Annunciation of the Virgin, both of which remain highly impressive despite the ravages of age.

Next door, stroll around the cloisters of the Benedictine Saint-Guilhem Monastery admiring the 12th-century carved capitals before passing through the Romanesque room for the Langon Chapel. During the 12th century, few places produced better wood sculpture than Autun, in Burgundy. Gaze long enough at the chapel's major piece—an Enthroned Virgin and Child—and its many subtleties of form and texture gradually become clear.

Beyond the Langon Chapel are several Gothic rooms and the Cuxa Cloister, its pink arches and columns built in 1188 for a Pyrenean monastery. Across the cloister are the amazing Unicorn Tapestries, probably 16th-century and of Flemish origin. Depicting the hunt for the mythical unicorn as an allegory for Christ's Incarnation, the Unicorn Tapestries are vivid in color and rich in detail. Pick out the images of love and fertility (within the flora and fauna), which mingle with the Christian symbols and suggest that the series may have been commissioned to celebrate a wedding.

The beauty and glowing color of the tapestries tend to outshine everything else in the Cloisters, except for the six glorious stained-glass lancet windows in the adjoining Boppard Room. Produced during the 1400s, the panels originally stood in the Carmelite Church of St. Severinus in Boppard-on-Rhine in Germany. With stunning artistry and craftsmanship, the glass shows several saints occupying canopied niches around the central figure of the Virgin.

Another important exhibit is a few steps away: Robert Campin's *Annunciation* altarpiece, an early Flemish triptych pioneering the use of oils on wood panels and also breaking new ground by using a contemporary domestic setting.

A "medieval" home for medieval treasures: the Cloisters

FORT TRYON PARK
This park, in which the Cloisters stands, was the site of the Battle of Washington Heights during the Revolutionary War. The fort that stood here then was renamed Tryon by the victorious British, after the last British governor of New York. Subsequently, its 66 acres were divided into private estates which, one by one, were later purchased by John D. Rockefeller. Rockefeller gave the land to the city in 1930, and the Olmsted Brothers (descendants of Frederick Olmsted, architect of Central Park) were commissioned to landscape the lawns, terraces, and picnic grounds that stand here now.

RIVERSIDE CHURCH

Just south of the Columbia University campus, the Cathedral of St. John the Divine rises in its monumental and still unfinished form (see page 81). Another substantial example of religious architecture sits just to the north, between 120th and 122nd streets off Riverside Drive, in the very imposing French Gothic form of Riverside Church.

The church—now interdenominational—has championed the underprivileged, and radical liberal views have often been aired from its pulpit. An elevator runs to the tower's 20th-story observation level for views of the Hudson River and over Upper Manhattan. Go after the Sunday morning service for an earful of the world's largest carillon, housed in the tower. *Open* for self-guided tours (free) Tue to Sat 11–4, Sun 12:30–4 (tel: 222-590).

Alma Mater, *Daniel Chester French's statue, outside Columbia University's Low Library*

▶ Columbia University

114th–120th streets between Amsterdam Avenue and Broadway (tel: 854-4900 for free guided tours of the campus, which run most weekdays)
Subway: 1; 116th Street

Founded in 1754 with a charter from the British king George II (it was originally named King's College) on a site in Lower Manhattan, Columbia University was intended to raise New York's cultural profile at a time when the fast-growing city was regarded as an uncouth, money-crazed upstart by the comparatively refined communities of Boston and New Haven, where the universities of Harvard and Yale were well established.

The campus occupied various locations in Manhattan. Through its steady movement northward, Columbia acquired ownership of the land that was later occupied by Rockefeller Center; it sold the prized plot during the mid-1980s for $400 million. The university arrived at its present location in 1897.

The specially designed campus (on the grounds of a former lunatic asylum) placed the academic buildings around a series of fountain-dotted plazas at the heart of which stands the majestic **Low Library**, based on Rome's Pantheon. This was the gift of Seth Low, university president and briefly, starting in 1902, mayor of New York.

An elegant three-tiered stairway leads up to the library's colonnaded entrance. Inside, you will see 16 green marble columns supporting an impressive octagonal rotunda. What you will not see is students poring over weighty tomes: the library is used only for ceremonies and exhibitions. On the second floor, the Columbiana Collection charts the history of the university with a mass of drawings, documents, paintings, and assorted paraphernalia.

On the library's steps you will pass Daniel Chester French's symbolic sculpture, *Alma Mater*, which was

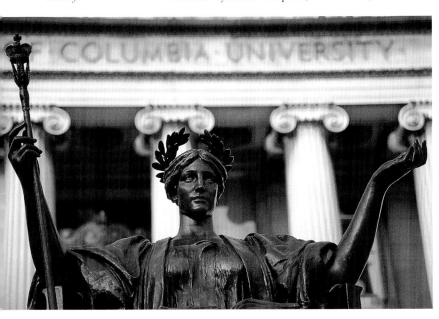

covered in gold leaf until 1962 and which formed an unlikely rallying point for the anti-Vietnam War demonstrations that spread across the campus in 1968. Just east of the library is the Italian Renaissance **St. Paul's Chapel,** which has a masterly vaulted interior.

▶▶ Cooper-Hewitt Museum 187C1

91st Street at Fifth Avenue (tel: 860-6868)
Open: Tue 10–9, Wed to Sat 10–5, Sun 12–5
Subway: 4, 6; 86th or 96th streets

Inspired by their 1897 visit to London's Victoria and Albert Museum, the three Hewitt sisters set about creating a visual library of design that would inspire new ideas. From their motley assortment of wallpaper, keys, and unusual jewelry, the Cooper-Hewitt Museum has grown into a collection of more than 250,000 items. It includes ceramics, wall coverings, textiles, decorative arts, drawings and prints, plus encyclopedic reference and picture libraries devoted to design matters.

Selections from the eclectic stocks make up the museum's thematic shows. Whether they feature 17th-century French needlework, contemporary Italian typewriters, Middle Eastern embroidery, American hatboxes, or three centuries' worth of maps (to mention a few past shows), this is where you will find some of New York's most imaginative, and sometimes most controversial, exhibitions.

The status of the museum rose greatly in 1967 when its collections, previously displayed in Lower Manhattan, were put into the care of the prestigious Smithsonian Institution and later moved to their present home, the former residence of industrialist Andrew Carnegie.

Carnegie was one of the world's richest men by the time he announced his intention to have built the "most modest, plainest, and roomiest house in New York." Not exactly plain, the 1901 Georgian mansion, in red brick and limestone, sits amid extensive gardens and has 64 rooms—intended for Carnegie, his wife and daughter, and their 19 servants.

As you wend your way around the exhibitions, notice the vaulted ceilings, the Tiffany glass windows, and the Louis XVI music room furnished with French antiques and with a set of bagpipes molded into the decorations—a reminder of Carnegie's Scottish origins.

▶ Daily News Building 151B3

220 East 42nd Street
Open: during business hours (lobby only)
Subway: 4, 6, 7; Grand Central Terminal/42nd Street

Created by Raymond Hood, who with it established his credentials as the father of New York skyscraper architecture, the 1930 Daily News Building (now called the News Building) is a landmark, a no-frills structure of thrusting verticality. Inside the largely original lobby, a frieze recounts the rise and rise (though its immediate prospects are in question) of the New York newspaper that became a legend for its punchy headlines and salacious stories. An immense revolving globe sits at the center of displays on meteorological themes. If the building seems familiar, you may be remembering the 1980s *Superman* films, in which it starred as the offices of the *Daily Planet*.

COLUMBIA UNIVERSITY RIOTS

By 1968, the student activism that had begun a few years earlier with the Free Speech Movement at the University of California at Berkeley had escalated into nationwide campus demonstrations protesting against U.S. involvement in Vietnam and inept academic administrations. In April, Columbia University saw marches, sit-ins, and the taking of five university officials hostage for 26 hours. The besieged university president eventually asked city police to clear the campus, in the course of which they arrested 698 students and injured 100—and united the student body and university staff in allegations of police brutality.

95

PETER COOPER

The fortunes of inventor and philanthropist Peter Cooper, grandfather of museum founders Sarah, Amy, and Eleanor Hewitt, were built on glue and iron. The Cooper foundry, in New Jersey, was where the tracks of the U.S.'s first great railroads were forged. Recognizing that his riches stemmed from the "cooperation of the masses," Cooper founded the first free college, the Cooper Union, which still stands in what is now the East Village (see pages 98–99).

THE DAKOTA IN MOVIES AND BOOKS

Plenty of the Dakota's residents have had leading roles in films. So, too, has the building. With its turrets, towers, and gables, the Dakota provided a suitably unsettling location for Roman Polanski's 1968 story of demonic possession, *Rosemary's Baby*. It also played a part in the 1970 time-travel novel, *Time and Again*, by Jack Finney.

The Dakota Apartments—home of the stars, and a screen star itself

▶ Dakota Apartments   151D2

1 West 72nd Street
Subway: 1, 2, 3; 72nd Street

Wealthy New York house owners of the 1880s had yet to be convinced that apartment living was the lifestyle of the future when Edward S. Clark, heir to the Singer sewing machine fortunes, commissioned a luxury apartment house in what is now the Upper West Side but was then wild, open land dotted by shanty dwellings and not even linked to the city's power supplies.

So far out was the site that critics suggested it might as well be in the Dakota territories—which is how the building got its name and the ears of corn, arrowheads, and the Native American head that decorate its entrance.

As the city spread northward and Midtown Manhattan house prices rocketed, there were suddenly lots of enthusiastic takers for the Dakota's marble floors and oak- and mahogany-paneled dwellings. The building quickly became—and continues to be—a prestigious address, with a roll call of rich and famous residents that has included Leonard Bernstein, Lauren Bacall, Judy Garland, and John Lennon—who was murdered while entering the building in 1980.

More inspired by Manhattan's celebrity-filled soirées than by its art museums, the ever-quotable Andy Warhol might be the one world-famous artist New York can call its own.

Born Andrew Warhola to Czech immigrant parents in Pittsburgh, Andy Warhol moved to New York in 1949 and within seven years was among the city's most sought-after commercial artists, much of his work appearing in high-society magazines.

Fame in a soup can Warhol loved the party-going life of New York but found his own fame—and artistic vocation—after a trip to a supermarket in 1962. As the artists of the pop art explosion created collages of consumerist images, Warhol began painting soup cans, according the gravity of serious portraiture to each one.

Be it depictions of dollar bills, electric chairs, or Brillo boxes, Warhol relished the publicity that his work aroused. A reviewer wrote that Warhol's silk-screened images of Marilyn Monroe were "as sentimental as Fords coming off the production line." In reply, Warhol declared, "I want to be a machine" and named his studio the Factory.

In the mid-1960s, Warhol's Factory became filled by every oddball character in New York, many of whom starred in the underground movies that the artist began making, including *Chelsea Girls*, described by one critic as "an image of the total degeneration of American society."

Getting rich The Factory's excesses ended in 1968, when Warhol narrowly survived an assassination attempt and found his financial affairs under scrutiny. Feeling he should be earning more money, the guru of pop art became a society portrait painter, charging $25,000 a time, while his revamped *Interview* magazine began providing lucrative advertising alongside its celebrity gossip.

Warhol's wealth and fame became greater than his creativity. Moving to an expensive Upper East Side house in 1975, he wasted a lot of time and money on several ill-fated projects and appeared happiest during his daily shopping expeditions.

Shortly before his death in 1987, Warhol opined, "Getting rich isn't as much fun as it used to be."

ANDY WARHOL SAID
"In the future, everybody will be famous for 15 minutes."
"I don't think my art has any lasting value."
"I never wanted to be a painter. I wanted to be a tap dancer."

97

LITTLE UKRAINE

In an area of the East Village around Second Avenue between 4th and 14th streets is New York's Little Ukraine. Ukrainians began settling here in the late 1800s and, though their numbers have been greatly depleted, are still much in evidence among the neighborhood's many Slavic restaurants and stores selling traditional Ukrainian crafts—such as painted Easter eggs. The tiny Ukrainian Museum, 203 Second Avenue, has changing exhibitions on past and present Ukrainian life in New York and in the homeland.

he Public Theater

- Films Du Losange

REGULAR   7.00
Little   GA 007

KESPEARE FESTIVAL PRODUCTION

▶ The East Village   IFCC3

In the 1950s, rising rents in Greenwich Village began pushing New York's more radical artists and writers across Broadway into the East Village. Here they took cheap apartments in tenement buildings otherwise inhabited by hard-up Eastern European immigrants, many of them from the Ukraine.

The heart of New York hippiedom in the 1960s and the epicenter of its 1970s punk rock scene, the East Village was regularly at the vanguard of alternative culture. Despite increasing signs of gentrification, expect to see at least one person dressed head-to-toe in leather and sporting bright green hair. Bizarre one-of-a-kind stores, ethnic eateries, and a vibrant street scene are the things the East Village does best, although a handful of historical sights are also worthy of attention.

Astor Place carries the name of John Jacob Astor, one of early 19th-century New York's wealthiest men. Like the similarly extremely affluent Cornelius Vanderbilt, Astor owned one of the series of marble-fronted houses that became known as **Colonnade Row**. Once the grandest residences in New York, those that have managed to survive, now looking rather shabby, are on Lafayette Street (numbers 428 to 434).

Across Lafayette Street, Astor financed the city's first free public library in a brownstone building which, since the 1960s, has been the **Public Theater** (originally Joseph Papp Public Theater), a venue for varied theatrical, cinematic, and other arts events.

Another 19th-century remnant is the **Cooper Union Building**, just south of Astor Place. Founded in 1859 by the millionaire railroad tycoon Peter Cooper to provide free education for all, the college was the first of its kind in the U.S. and also became an airing place for a range of political views: Abraham Lincoln was one of the famous orators who spoke here.

East of Astor Place is St. Mark's Place, where the unprepossessing building at number 77 was home to Anglo-American poet W.H. Auden from 1953. This was also where, four decades earlier in the basement, Leon Trotsky had plotted the Russian Revolution.

Nearby, the church of **St. Mark's-in-the-Bowery** (tel: 674-6377; *Open* for events only) arose on the estate of New York's Dutch governor, Peter Stuyvesant, in 1799. Its original body was later topped by a spire and fronted by a cast-iron portico. The church serves its congregation with Episcopal services, poetry readings, and performance art. On the church's eastern side, Stuyvesant and six generations of his descendants lie buried.

Walk

The East Village stores and sights

This walk touches historical sites and also highlights the contemporary flavor of the East Village.

Begin at the 1799 church of **St. Mark's-in-the-Bowery** and continue along Stuyvesant Street to the **Cooper Union Building** (1859), the U.S.'s first free college

In Astor Place is the huge Bernard Rosenthal **Alamo** cube sculpture which spins on point when pushed. Turn onto St. Mark's Place, once the center of the punk rock movement, now a touristy collection of piercing stores, cafés, and t-shirt kiosks. You can eat cheap East Village fare at **Dojo's** (24 St. Mark's Place) or French food at **Jules** (65 St. Mark's Place).

Unusual store in the East Village

Turn on Avenue A to 7th Street and walk west to 2nd Avenue for funky vintage stores, such as **Tokio 7** (64 East 7th St.). Stop for a beer at **McSorley's** (15 East 7th St.), a local landmark since 1854.

99

THE WALL OF HONOR
Running around the edge of Ellis Island close to the ferry dock, the American Immigrant Wall of Honor records 200,000 names—just a small percentage of those who became American citizens here. Ellis Island arrivals you may have heard of include Isaac Asimov, Irving Berlin, Bela Lugosi, Golda Meir, Edward G. Robinson, and Rudolph Valentino.

Ellis Island: the future of many a would-be American was determined in these buildings. Museum displays now bring to life the hopes, fears, and disappointments of those newly arrived immigrants

▶▶▶ Ellis Island   48C2

Tel: 269-5755
Ferry from Battery Park daily 9–5, longer hours during summer
Around 100 million present-day Americans have ancestors who passed through Ellis Island, a modest speck of land in the shadow of the Statue of Liberty in New York's Upper Bay. From 1892 to 1924 this was the country's busiest immigration center.

Later serving as an army hospital and as an enemy alien detention center, Ellis Island was closed in 1954 and suffered total neglect until a $160-million restoration project reopened its major building as the Ellis Island Immigration Museum in 1990.

Those who arrived at Ellis Island hoping to become Americans were drawn from Europe's underclasses (immigrants of means were processed elsewhere and allowed immediate entry into the U.S.). The elation they experienced on seeing the Statue of Liberty quickly dissipated as they reached the place nicknamed the "Island of Tears" and faced the bureaucracy that stood between them and American citizenship.

Would-be Americans were screened for contagious diseases and signs of insanity and questioned about their relatives and their work skills. Any sign of sickness, or giving the wrong answers, could mean being detained and perhaps deported.

Some also got their first taste of American corruption at Ellis Island: among the many scams were bribes for immigration officers and overpriced train tickets for onward travel in the U.S.

From statistics projecting the country's future ethnic make-up to trunks and string bags that carried treasured possessions, the museum has many eye-opening exhibits. The taped oral histories of former arrivals do most to suggest the hopes, the fears, and the sheer sense of bewilderment that most of the would-be immigrants experienced as they stepped into this building.

▶▶▶ Empire State Building   151B2

34th Street at Fifth Avenue (tel: 736-3100)
Open daily 9:30–midnight. Last elevator to the top at 11:30pm
Subway: B, D, F, N, R; 34th Street
The World Trade Center may be taller and the Statue of Liberty a more potent national symbol, but New York's most enduring emblem is the Empire State Building, rising above Midtown Manhattan with a gracious, ageless aplomb. As construction mania swept through New York

EMPIRE STATE BUILDING FACTS

Height: 1472ft.
Weight: 365,000 tons.
Number of bricks:
10 million.
Budget: $60 million.
Actual cost:
$40,948,900.
Tallest visitor: King Kong, 1933
Greatest tragedy: plane crashing into the 79th story in 1945, killing 14.

The lobby of the Empire State Building

NEW YORK SKYRIDE

If the views from the observation levels of the Empire State Building fail to satisfy, get an aerial view of the city on the New York Skyride—a flight simulator tour of the city at dizzying speed aboard a "spacecoptor." The Skyride is on the Empire State Building's second floor. *Open* daily 10–11 PM; tel: 279-9777.

during the booming 1920s, the Empire State Building was the winner in the financiers' race to create the world's tallest building, snatching the title in 1931 from the Chrysler Building and holding it until the first World Trade Center tower was finished in 1973.

Although the building rose to 1,250 feet (gaining a further 222 feet with a T.V. mast in 1951), it was constructed within only two years. The zoning laws (see page 24) of the time resulted in the tiered design that tempers the impact of the structure's bulk and contributes greatly to its elegant profile.

Conceived in an economic boom, the building was completed amid the gloom of the Depression, the Wall Street crash occurring as the 2-acre site—which held the original Waldorf-Astoria Hotel—was being cleared. Consequently, much of the office space remained unrented for years, and most of the building's early income was from tourists visiting for the views.

Admire the art deco fittings of the lobby before descending to the concourse for a ticket and the express elevator to the 86th-floor observation level (the enclosed 102nd-floor level hardly justifies the additional elevator ride to reach it). On a clear day you see for 80 miles.

▶ Federal Hall National Memorial   104B2
Wall and Nassau streets (tel: 825-6888)
Open daily 9–5, closed Sat and Sun during winter
Subway: 2, 3, 4, 5; Wall Street

Its finely proportioned steps and Doric columns impose themselves grandly in the heart of the Financial District, but a sense of history is disappointingly missing from the echoey interior of the 19th-century Federal Hall. Built as the first U.S. Custom House, it later served as a bank before being declared a national memorial in 1939.

If you are exploring the Financial District, Federal Hall ought to be on your itinerary, but do not expect anything spectacular. Inside, only a short film and a rather tame collection of exhibits record events that took place on the site: a glass-encased section of balcony railing, on which Washington leaned when addressing the crowds after his inauguration and a pair of the great man's belt-buckles form the highlights.

▶ Film Center Building   151C1
Ninth Avenue between 44th and 45th streets
Open: business hours (lobby only)
Subway: A, C, E; 42nd Street

You may not want to visit any of the many film companies that have offices here, but the Film Center Building justifies a visit to view one of the city's most stunning art-deco interiors: its lobby, vestibule, and entrance hall are all the work of Ely Jacques Kahn. Already an outstanding modernist architect, by the late 1920s Kahn also had a reputation for his distinctive interior decoration based on interlinked geometric forms—employed here to wonderful effect.

▶▶ Financial District   IFCA2

The nation's monetary institutions took root in Lower Manhattan from the early 1800s, and as the city grew, so did its Financial District, quickly becoming a global center of trade and commerce. Side by side in this compact area stand grandiose neoclassical buildings, whose form signified their status as repositories of wealth, and the high-rise glass and steel blocks that are the contemporary towers of mammon.

The exuberant 1980s saw Wall Street (just one of several thoroughfares here, but internationally synonymous with the highest of high finance) yield millions and give birth to the yuppie. But the party was over by the end of the

102

At Federal Hall National Memorial, the statue of George Washington commemorates his inauguration as president, which took place in an earlier building on the site

THE ORIGINAL FEDERAL HALL
The historic significance of the present Federal Hall is eclipsed by that of its predecessor, which housed the first U.S. government and which was where, in April 1789, George Washington was sworn in as the country's first president.

Despite its role in U.S. history, the original building reached such a dilapidated state that it was sold for scrap in 1812.

decade, when a succession of scandals put the greedy behind bars and heralded the economic uncertainties of the 1990s.

Facing Wall Street from Broadway, the striking neo-Gothic form of **Trinity Church** (tel: 602-0747) has, since the 1840s, been reminding the Financial District's power brokers of a force greater than money. Note the bronze doors and the reredos, and continue into the small church museum to look at drawings showing a Manhattan skyline dominated by church spires rather than high-rise towers. In the 17th-century graveyard (*Open* daily 8–4:30) lies Alexander Hamilton, the first U.S. treasurer.

Predating Trinity Church by almost a century is Manhattan's only surviving prerevolutionary church, **St. Paul's Chapel** (tel: 602-0874; *Open* Mon to Sat 9–3, Sun 7–3), which faces Fulton Street from Broadway. Laid out in a graceful Georgian style with a surprisingly bright interior, the chapel was regularly visited by George Washington, and dutifully maintains the Washington Pew, where the first president sat during the service marking his inauguration in 1789.

WALL STREET'S NAME
An oaken barricade erected by Dutch governor Peter Stuyvesant in 1653 to mark the northern boundary of New Amsterdam and deter British invaders was the "wall" that gave the world-famous street its name. The wall never quite fulfilled its promise, because its planks were steadily removed to build and repair the wooden homes of settlers. In 1699 its remains were finally demolished by the then well-entrenched British.

Now dwarfed by skyscrapers several times as high, Trinity Church began life as the city's tallest building, at 264 feet high

103

THE FEDERAL RESERVE
Many Financial District buildings house major financial corporations where every day millions of dollars are traded and transferred in paper and electronic transactions. One of the few that actually holds money—in the form of gold—is the Manhattan branch of the Federal Reserve (33 Liberty Street; tel: 720-6130), formally known as the Federal Reserve Bank of New York. Nationally, the Federal Reserve acts as banker to major banks and to the U.S. government, regulates monetary policy, and sets interest rates. The high security of the fortress-like building can be lawfully penetrated on guided tours, but tickets must be acquired well in advance. *Open* Mon to Fri 9–5; tours at 10:30, 11:30, 1:30, and 2:30.

Walk

Financial District architecture

Encompassing historic churches and financial and architectural landmarks, this walk is an excellent way to explore the varied facets of the Financial District.

Begin at **Trinity Church** (page 103) and continue along Wall Street,

stopping at **Federal Hall** and detouring along Broad Street for the **Stock Exchange** (page 182).

Continue along Nassau Street for **Chase Manhattan Bank**, the first international-style structure in Lower Manhattan. Across Maiden Lane, you can gaze at over 11,000 tons of gold—the wealth of many nations—stored below ground at the **Federal Reserve Bank** (advance reservations essential, tel: 720-6130). Otherwise, examine the richly decorative ironwork of the enormous building's facade.

On the corner of Broadway, the much-detested 1915 **Equitable Building** rises for 40 sheer stories; this was New York's first ever high-rise office building and the first to plunge its neighboring buildings—and much of the street below—into relative darkness. Continue along Broadway for **St. Paul's Chapel** (page 103); aim to arrive for a free lunchtime concert, and finish at the **World Trade Center** (page 193).

Tussles during the 19th century among Eastern Europe's Slavic peoples—Poles, Ukrainians, and Russians—and the totalitarian suppression of more recent times helped create two of New York's most stridently nationalistic communities: the Poles and the Ukrainians, who now coexist peaceably alongside their former foes, the Russians.

Polish-Americans Struggles against colonial oppression in their own country made New York's Poles natural allies of the Americans in the revolutionary battles with the British. Not much later, New York offered refuge to those who had led an unsuccessful Polish republican uprising in 1830. The 234 immigrants who arrived were among Poland's finest minds, and were to give New York its first Polish cultural institutions.

Later Polish arrivals found factory jobs in the Greenpoint area of Brooklyn, though some opened the stores and bookstores that would become community focal points. Soviet control of post-war Poland brought exiled intellectuals, while the collapse of Communism in the 1990s led to more arrivals.

The Ukrainians Enforced military service in the czar's army caused many Ukrainians to flee their Russian-dominated homeland during the 1800s. Arriving in New York with their families, they turned a section of what is now the East Village into the world's largest urban Ukrainian community by 1919.

Russian immigrants The bulk of Russian immigrants were Jewish refugees who had fled persecution under the czar (see page 139). More symbolic of the effect of European political upheavals, though, were the Russian aristocrats who arrived in New York as Leon Trotsky (here since the abortive 1905 revolution) left for Moscow to help the Bolsheviks seize power. Another arrival was ground-breaking ballet choreographer George Balanchine. These newly arrived Russians quickly became integrated into New York society—a far cry from the former Soviet Russians who later settled in Brighton Beach (see page 75).

THE PULASKI AND KOSCIUSZKO BRIDGES
Two of the bridges—the Pulaski and the Kosciuszko—linking Brooklyn and Queens bear the names of Poles who aided the American cause in the Revolutionary War. Cavalry expert Casimar Pulaski was noted for his bravery in battle (he died in an attack on the British); the engineering skills of Thaddeus Kosciuszko were crucial in preparing the anti-British fortifications at West Point and Saratoga.

105

The first taste of America for European immigrants: Ellis Island

*The Flatiron Building—
an unmistakable Fifth
Avenue landmark*

23 SKIDOO
A story goes that in the days when well-dressed ladies had skirts to their ankles, high winds would find voyeurs lingering outside the Flatiron Building on 23rd Street hoping to spot female legs exposed by the breeze. The shouts of the police when moving the gentlemen on are thought to be the origin of the term "23 skidoo."

DANIEL H. BURNHAM
The architect of the Flatiron Building, Daniel H. Burnham, made his name in Chicago in the 1880s, where, in partnership with John Root, he pioneered the modern skyscraper by making the first use of a steel frame to support a high-rise structure. Burnham's design ideas became a fundamental element in the highly influential "Chicago School" of architecture. Burnham's Chicago work was made possible partly because of a devastating fire that required the entire downtown area to be rebuilt. He also played an important role in the reshaping of San Francisco, wrecked by the earthquake of 1906, for which he planned a new Civic Center.

▶ **Flatiron Building**   151A2
Broadway and Fifth Avenue at 23rd Street
Subway: N, R; 23rd Street
Architect Daniel H. Burnham solved the problem of fitting a building into the triangular plot of land where Broadway crosses Fifth Avenue with the most logical solution: a triangular building. It was the world's tallest (285 feet) on its completion in 1902 and was one of the first to be erected around a steel frame—the basic support of every subsequent skyscraper.

Nowadays, it is not height or building techniques that make the Flatiron Building one of New York's most-loved structures but its pretty French Renaissance features and the fact that its limestone body tapers to an impossibly slender 6-foot-wide corner curve on 23rd Street. In recent years, the building has provided a convenient sobriquet for the immediate area, now known locally as the "Flatiron District."

▶ **The Forbes Galleries** 113C2

Fifth Avenue between 12th and 13th streets (tel: 206-5549)
Open: Tue, Wed, Fri, Sat 10–4
Subway: L, N, R 4, 6; 14th Street/Union Square

Even in New York, few magazine publishers have broken the speed record for ballooning across the country or have hurtled along Fifth Avenue on a motorcycle. Malcolm S. Forbes did both of those things, and more, in a career that began by accident and left him with wealth estimated, at his death in 1990, to be in excess of $700 million.

Born in 1919, two years after his father had founded *Forbes*, a ground-breaking magazine of investigative financial journalism, Forbes had turned the ailing title into a thriving concern by the time he took it over in 1964. One of the secrets of his success was a genius for garnering maximum publicity for himself and the magazine. Through the 1970s the media doted on Forbes and his colorful activities, which ranged from lavish parties to his offbeat collecting interests.

The Forbes Galleries bear the fruits of Forbes' quirky collecting passion. They occupy the first floor of the Forbes Magazine building. Among the displays are 500 model boats and submarines (some of them in bathtubs) viewed to the accompaniment of what purports to be the sound of the Battle of Jutland. Some 12,000 model soldiers are arranged in battle-ready poses, and there is an amazing room of trophies awarded for achievements such as having the best pure-bred bull of 1878 and the best 5 acres of turnips grown with Bradburn's manure.

The Presidential Papers room holds less eccentric material, drawn from the Forbes collection of 3,000 historical documents, while another special room displays gem-encrusted Easter eggs—and scores of other priceless objets d'art—made by master jeweler–goldsmith Peter Carl Fabergé for the last two czars of Russia.

▶▶ **Fraunces Tavern** 104A2

54 Pearl Street (tel: 425-1778)
Open: Mon to Fri 10–4
Subway: 1, 4, 9; Bowling Green, South Ferry or Broad Street

This Federal-style brick building, which looks like a dollhouse beneath the glass-and-steel high-rises of the Financial District, stands on the site of the original Fraunces Tavern, a hotbed of subversion during the 18th century, when its customers included George Washington and his fellow revolutionaries.

At the successful completion of the Revolutionary War, Washington made a famously emotional farewell to his officers here after a meal in the Long Room—a scene re-created with period furniture on the tavern's third floor, while other objects and paintings from the revolutionary period are displayed on the fourth floor.

It may seem strange today, but the tavern became the unofficial seat of several government bodies during the earliest days of nationhood and spent three years as the recognized base of the Department of Foreign Affairs, the War Department, and the Treasury, before being unceremoniously sold to a Brooklyn butcher.

Visit the tavern around lunchtime, when the atmosphere is enhanced by the smell of food wafting up from the first-floor restaurant.

THE SALMAGUNDI CLUB
At 47 Fifth Avenue, opposite the Forbes Magazine Galleries, an 1853 Italianate brownstone mansion built for a coral magnate provides a home for the Salmagundi Club. Founded in 1871 (but moving here in 1917), the Salmagundi Club is the oldest artists' club in the United States and numbered Stanford White and Louis Comfort Tiffany among its early members. Occasional exhibitions provide a chance to peek at the building's extravagantly appointed interior.

The word "salmagundi" describes a mixed salad dish popular in the 18th century, but was presumably adopted from a series of pamphlets, the *Salmagundi Papers*, written and published in the early 1800s by author Washington Irving and friends. The *Salmagundi Papers* satirized New York life and, among other things, first coined the word Gotham as an alternative name for the city.

A BOMB AT THE FRAUNCES TAVERN
George Washington was not the last revolutionary to make a point at Fraunces Tavern. In January 1975, the building was rocked by a bomb that killed four Wall Street businessmen and left 55 people injured. Responsibility was claimed by an underground group called the F.A.L.N., in revenge for the U.S. Government's resistance to Puerto Rican independence.

For those with money and a well-known face (or name) to go with it, New York can easily become the ultimate playground. What follows is a very selective Manhattan list for the well-heeled person about town. For those visitors who need to budget carefully for every cab ride, a peek inside one or two of these establishments offers a glance at the luxurious end of New York's wide spectrum of lifestyles.

108

GETTING AROUND LUXURY NEW YORK
When money is no object, travel between expensive stores in a chauffeur-driven stretch limousine. Equipped with V.C.R.s, telephones, and bars—and other features that make Manhattan's traffic-stopping gridlock almost seem attractive—stretch limos can be rented from around $50 per hour. Carey Limousines (tel: 599-1122) and Imperial Limousines (tel: 229-9292) are among the operators awaiting your call.

Daniel (East 65th Street between Madison and Park avenues, tel: 288-0033). One of the reasons Daniel Boulud decided to relocate his gastronomic temple was that he couldn't accommodate all of the power players and food lovers clamoring for reservations. Some $15 million and 40 additional seats later, you still have to book a table four weeks in advance. The new restaurant is a formal affair, an elegant combination of contemporary style and stateliness. The food is every bit as good as at the previous restaurant (now home to his more casual, more reasonably priced Café Boulud). Think ethereal soups, whole-roasted fish, succulent braised meats, and a seasonality and freshness of ingredients unsurpassed by any of the city's great restaurants.

Jean Georges (Trump International Hotel, 1 Central Park West at Columbus Circle, tel: 299-3900). Like superstar chef Jean-Georges Vongerichten himself, this four-star restaurant is sleek, elegant, and welcoming. During the day the muted tones and Asian lines are flooded with sunlight, at night the glow radiates from the beautiful crowd. In keeping with the environment, the food is conceptual and artfully presented: for example, garlic soup with frog's legs and seared sea scallops with raisin caper sauce. Equal emphasis is placed on service, and the tableside show is like a fine ballet. Don't miss the extravagant tea service and the homemade marshmallows in a variety of flavors, paraded around the room in glass apothecary jars and snipped ceremonially onto your plate.

Four Seasons (East 52nd Street between Park and Lexington avenues, tel: 754-9494). The serious trade here is power-lunching corporate executives—plus a sprinkling of lawyers, politicians, and publishers. On the ground floor of Mies van der Rohe's landmark Seagram Building, this Philip Johnson-designed restaurant features a large Picasso tapestry and other noted modern pieces. The lunch menu is designed to be good but simple, so it does not detract from the deals being struck across the tables. At dinner, the chef presents ably prepared contemporary American creations, some of which are finished at your table. A full dinner here is liable to cost $100 per person; lunch should be a comparatively modest $40.

The "21" Club (West 52nd Street between Fifth and Sixth avenues, tel: 582-7200). A row of cast-iron model jockeys stand to attention along the facade of the "21" Club, which opened on New Year's Eve 1929 and was—in those Prohibition times—just one of scores of speakeasies lining 52nd Street. The others quickly disappeared but the "21" Club endured, maturing into a favorite watering hole of the New York establishment. Despite a complete refurbishment in the 1980s, the "21" Club's dark, wood-paneled walls and deep-pile carpets offer a picture of old-style luxury New York that is rarely found today. Although appearances suggest otherwise, it is not an exclusive club, but you should not show up without a reservation. Many regulars come here to confirm their place in the New York social pecking order as much as to dine: the kitchen is experiencing a renaissance since the addition of a creative chef. You might try the famous "21 Burger," or the pre-theater prix-fixe dinner, but you probably won't have change from $30 and $50 respectively.

Le Cirque 2000 (New York Palace Hotel, 455 Madison Avenue at 50th Street, tel: 303-7788). No restaurant in New York has quite the razzle-dazzle of this celebrity shrine. Adam Tihany's futuristic circus decor for the ornate Villard mansions has been likened to a Ferrari parked in an Italian palazzo. (You either love it or you hate it.). He doesn't miss a detail of the operation. Chef Sottha Kuhn's food can be sublime, but it isn't the point. You are there to see and be seen, or to watch the people who are.

SIGHTSEEING BY HELICOPTER
One way to beat the crowds at the Statue of Liberty or the World Trade Center is to view such attractions, and the rest of Manhattan, from a helicopter. Sightseeing helicopter flights are operated day and night by Island Helicopter Sightseeing (tel: 683-4575) and Liberty Helicopter Tours (tel: 800/542-9933 or 967-6464).

109

SPECIALTY GROCERS
Manhattan's avid foodies are willing to pay high prices for superior quality and variety at fancy food emporiums such as **Balducci's** (6th Avenue. at 9th Street) in Greenwich Village, with exquisite produce, meat, fish, and pastries, and the huge SoHo trendsetter **Dean & Deluca** (560 Broadway at Prince Street) where food is displayed like art. On the Upper West Side, there's **Zabar's** (2245 Broadway at 80th Street), which sells fine foods on the street level and kitchenware upstairs. On the Upper East Side are the **Vinegar Factory** and **Eli's**, also owned by the Zabar's clan. **The Chelsea Market** (88 Tenth Avenue) is a block-long food mall with fine independent purveyors.

The luxurious Plaza Hotel: evocative of Old World elegance

Having made his fortune in Pittsburgh, industrialist Henry Clay Frick moved to New York, where he had this elaborate mansion built to house his superb collection of European art

MOVING PICTURES
Each summer, Henry Frick had his fantastic art collection packed into crates and transported in a special railroad car so he could enjoy it while staying at his estate in Massachusetts. Asked if he was worried about losing the priceless canvases through an accident in transit, Frick allegedly replied, "No, they're insured."

▶▶ **Frick Collection**   151D2

70th Street at Fifth Avenue (tel: 288-0700)
Open: Tue to Sat 10–6, Sun 1–6
Subway: 6; 68th Street

Henry Clay Frick made a fortune through coke and steel, and was little loved in his day for his mean-spirited business practices. Ironically, the Frick Collection of 14th- to 19th-century European art, housed on the first floor of the French-style mansion in which Frick spent the last five years of his life (he died in 1919), is perhaps the most loved of New York's many art collections.

The absence of ropes, descriptive texts, and other museum trappings is intended to make seeing the collection akin to visiting a private house. The collection is a triumph of quality over quantity, and there is not a single painting that does not deserve its wall space.

Highlights are many and naturally vary according to individual taste. Few could fail to be impressed, however, by Gainsborough's *The Mall in St. James's Park*, a refined vision of privileged promenaders that stands out in a dining room lined by 18th-century English portraiture.

The living hall has two particularly potent canvases: Titian's *Portrait of a Man in a Red Cap* and El Greco's *St. Jerome*. But it is on the walls of the west gallery that the cream of the collection is hung: two of Turner's studies of northern European ports resonate on facing walls, close to Rembrandt's 1658 *Portrait of a Young Artist—Self-Portrait* and the same artist's much debated (its authenticity is disputed) *Polish Rider*.

After leaving the final room, take a break in the garden court before starting through the collections once again, this time concentrating on the outstanding sculptures, tapestries, and decorative arts exhibits.

▶ **Fulton Fish Market**   104C3

South and Fulton streets (tel: 732-7678)
Subway: 2, 3, 4; Fulton Street

If you are an insomniac or a very early riser, be at the Fulton Fish Market at 6 AM prompt on the first or third Thursday of each month (Apr–Oct) for an odoriferous behind-the-scenes tour of the daily market. Here truckloads of squirming fish and creeping crustaceans are unloaded and prepared for sale to some of the city's classiest restaurants.

If you have somewhere to cook it, the market is the perfect place to pick up jumbo shrimp, swordfish steaks, Chilean seabass, squid, New England lobsters, or any of a multitude of diverse seafare.

▶ **General Grant Memorial**   IBCB2

Riverside Drive at 122nd Street (tel: 666-1640 FREE)
Open: daily 9–5
Subway: 1; 116th Street

The largest mausoleum in the U.S., its gray granite form rising 150 feet beside the Hudson and its entrance fronted by six Doric columns, the General Grant Memorial (commonly known as Grant's Tomb) holds the remains—in 9-ton marble sarcophagi—of Ulysses S. Grant and his wife Julia. As commander-in-chief of the Union forces in the Civil War, Grant achieved enormous fame: an estimated million people lined the route of his funeral procession in 1885. Inside, a chilled atmosphere prevails, and your footsteps echo as you walk around reading the brief accounts of Grant's distinguished military service and his much less successful eight-year tenure as 18th U.S. President. Outside, the mosaic-decorated benches result from a community arts project.

▶ Gracie Mansion 187C2

East End Avenue at 88th Street (tel: 570-4751)
Guided tours: Apr to Oct, Wed 10, 11, 1, and 2
Subway: 4, 6; 86th Street

The official residence of the mayor of New York since 1942, Gracie Mansion was built in 1799 as a country retreat for shipping magnate Archibald Gracie. After his business collapsed, Gracie sold the mansion, and it spent an ignominious period as a refreshment stand before being purchased by the city. Recent renovations have made the mansion a finer example of Federal architecture (the first architectural style considered distinctly American) than it ever was in its infancy. The house can be fully appreciated only on guided tours.

GRANT'S MILITARY CAREER
Following an unremarkable graduation (21st in a class of 39) from West Point Academy, Ulysses S. Grant distinguished himself in service, but resigned from the army in 1854 while stationed in California. Grant failed as a farmer (his subsequent occupation), and was working as a clerk in his father's store in Illinois at the outbreak of the Civil War. His military experience led to his appointment as brigadier of the Illinois Volunteers. A series of battle successes followed, showing a strategic brilliance that culminated in Grant's capture of the Confederate stronghold of Vickburg after a 47-day siege in 1863. The following year, Grant was made commander of all Union armies. As president, Grant faced the postwar Reconstruction period and difficulties that would have tested the skills of the most experienced politician—his battle planning skills proved no match for the chicanery of Washington DC.

HENDERSON PLACE
In a cul-de-sac on the north side of 86th Street, close to Gracie Mansion, stands the lovely row of 24 Queen Anne-style houses that constitute the Henderson Place Historic District. The houses were commissioned during the 1880s by fur-hat manufacturer John C. Henderson to provide homes for "persons of moderate means."

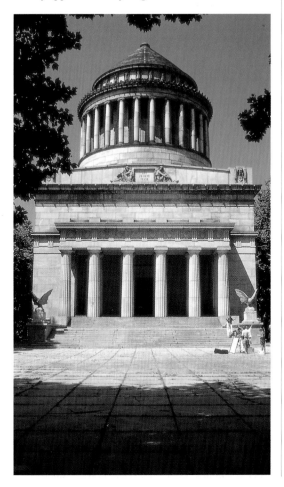

The grandiose mausoleum of Civil War general Ulysses S. Grant was inspired by Napoleon's tomb in Paris

Greenwich Village secondhand stores may not offer such good bargains as less fashionable areas of the city, but they are hard to beat for sheer variety

►►► Greenwich Village   *IFCC2*

No place in New York has a greater cultural aura than Greenwich Village. For almost 100 years this has been a breeding ground and rallying point for the nation's most inventive and imaginative minds.

From its earliest days, Greenwich Village has kept its distance from mainstream New York life. Its first homes were built to enable the wealthy to escape the outbreaks of disease that were common in the 1790s, pushing back the boundaries of the city that, until then, had been contained within present-day Lower Manhattan.

By the late 1800s, the rich were moving north again, and their Greenwich Village town houses were being converted into stores, factories, and boarding houses for immigrants. By the turn of the 20th century, Greenwich Village's diverse ethnic mix had fostered an atmosphere of tolerance that, coupled with low rents, attracted the unconventional elements that gave birth to the country's first, and eventually its most celebrated, enclave of nonconformity.

Over three decades, writers and artists from Walt Whitman to Edward Hopper were to turn American culture upside down from their Greenwich Village bases. During the 1950s, the earliest Beat writers began taking Greenwich Village still farther away from the materialist values of middle America, but rents were soon on the rise as new transit links made Greenwich Village the target of moneyed professionals in search of a well-placed neighborhood full of character.

Living in Greenwich Village today certainly requires financial security, but the lawyers and investment bankers who have flocked here have certainly not dampened the community spirit or Greenwich Village's rebellious streak. A Bohemian mood still percolates through its innumerable Italian cafés and restaurants, even though today most Greenwich Village visitors are not impoverished souls at creativity's cutting edge.

(Continued on page 116)

GRACE CHURCH
One of the few things in Greenwich Village likely to bring to mind the European Middle Ages is the 1846 Grace Church, on Broadway between 10th and 11th streets. The church's finely proportioned Gothic Revival design—among the earliest examples of the style in the U.S.—helped its architect, James Renwick, win the commission for the larger, grander St. Patrick's Cathedral in Midtown Manhattan. Set on Broadway's first curve, the church's spire could originally be seen from as far south as what is now Battery Park.

Walk

The heart of Greenwich Village

From Grace Church in the east, this walk goes through the heart of Greenwich Village, ending at the foot of Christopher Street.

Leaving Grace Church, walk along 10th Street to the 1840 **Church of the Ascension,** by English architect Richard Upjohn, also known for Trinity Church in the Financial District.

Eighth Street holds many stores and the New York Studio School of Drawing, Painting and Sculpture, first home of the Whitney Museum. This was founded in 1931 by Gertrude Vanderbilt Whitney; her own studio was a converted stable at 17½ MacDougal Alley (a private street).

In business since 1785, **Caffé Reggio** is the oldest of many cafés lining MacDougal Street; its dark interior has been seen in films such as *Godfather II* and *Serpico*.

On Sixth Avenue, Village Square is dominated by the gables, turrets, and towers of the 1877 **Jefferson Market Courthouse,** now a library. Across Sixth Avenue is **Balducci's,** a long-established purveyor of groceries and very fine foods.

Washington Square Park

Like delis and subway stations, bars are among the stock images of New York life. From rough-and-ready Bohemian hangouts to elegant hotel cocktail lounges, New York bars come in all sizes and forms. Don't miss this quintessential experience. (For guidance on New York bar-going etiquette, see pages 224–225.)

114

WINE BARS

In New York nowadays any restaurant that wants to be taken seriously offers several decent wines by the glass. But a proliferation of wine bars offering hundreds of wines has recently upped the ante. Wines are sold either as single servings or in tasting "flights" (wines grouped by region, style, vintage, or other interesting characteristics). Check out Divine Bar (244 East 51st Street and 55 Liberty St.), Le Bateau Ivre (230 East 51st St.), and Enoteca i Trulli (122 East 27th St.).

NEW YORK'S
OLDEST BAR

In business since 1854, McSorley's Old Ale House (15 East 7th Street) is justified in its claim to be New York's oldest surviving bar. For years a men-only establishment patronized by career drinkers from the Bowery's Skid Row, McSorley's began admitting women in 1970 and now attracts a young, mainly student crowd.

Writers, artists, and bars Greenwich Village is littered with bars where major names of art and literature have gathered to eat, drink, and (not infrequently) be carried home very much the worse for wear.

On his New York stays, Welsh poet Dylan Thomas held court at the **White Horse Tavern** (567 Hudson Street). One night in 1953, a drunken Thomas spluttered, "I've had my 18th whisky, and I think that's the record." Within a few days he was dead. The literary associations might seem all but buried beneath the throng of customers, but cuttings on the wall remind drinkers at **Pete's Tavern** (129 East 18th Street) that this was once a lair of O. Henry, the pen name of William Sydney Porter, short-story writer and a trenchant New York observer in the early 1900s. To sample the East Village's Bohemian ambience, slip into something black and then into **d.b.a.** (41 First Avenue), a popular local hangout with minimalist decor and a good variety of beers and single malts.

No longer in its original location, the **Cedar Tavern** (82 University Place) was a meeting place for the painters of what became the New York School of Abstract Expressionism. As Jackson Pollock and others loudly lamented the state of art, Beat writers such as the late Allen Ginsberg and William Burroughs eavesdropped from neighboring tables.

Bars for beer-drinkers Beer connoisseurs will welcome the 200 imported varieties sold at the **Peculier Pub** (145 Bleecker Street). The wooden bench tables here often overflow with New York University students. Detailed menu descriptions will help you choose from the 50 or so beers served at **The Blind Tiger** (518 Hudson Street). There's no such help at **The Ginger Man** (11 East 36th Street), but the selection of beers and single malt scotches is even larger.

Bars with a view The Manhattan skyline looks better than ever when viewed with a cocktail in your hand. At the **Greatest Bar on Earth**, on the 107th floor of the World Trade Center, the theme (and the crowd) changes every day of the week, and the views stretch for miles. In Midtown Manhattan, try the 39th-floor **Top of the Sixes** (666 Fifth Avenue), where drinks are accompanied by free snacks and a fine panorama, or the now refurbished **Top of the Tower**, at the Beckham Tower Hotel (3 Mitchell Place, off 49th Street), for a splendid view across the East River. The **Pen Top Bar** at the Peninsula Hotel (700 Fifth Avenue) offers its drinks from a roof-top terrace.

Bars for the good-looking The **Coffee Shop** (29 Union Square West) is a favorite stamping ground of the young and beautiful, with a long, snaking bar, Brazilian food, and loud music. Alternatively, try the equally hip **Fez** (downstairs from the Time Café on Lafayette at Great Jones Street), with its good jazz and basement dance floor. If you can get past the velvet ropes, the upstairs lounge at **Moomba** (133 Seventh Avenue South) is attractive and frequently star-studded with celebrities. The cavernous **10th Street Lounge** (212 East 10th Street) with low lighting and high style makes everyone look cool.

Hotel bars As well as guests, many are favored by locals for their elegant surroundings and the fact that you do not have to shout over loud music to hold a conversation. The **King Cole Bar** at the St. Regis Hotel (2 East 55th Street) serves drinks in front of an impressive Maxfield Parrish mural. For a private tryst, try the Vodka Bar of the **Royalton** (44th Street between Fifth and Sixth avenues—you can also celebrity-spot in the lobby bar), or **Fifty Seven Fifty Seven**, at the Four Seasons Hotel (57 East 57th Street), which draws publishing and media bigwigs. The scene at the lobby bar of the **Mercer Bar** (99 Prince Street) in SoHo is white hot, and the **Grand Bar** at the SoHo Grand Hotel (310 West Broadway) attracts the fashionable every night.

MARIE'S CRISIS CAFÉ
Few places symbolize changing New York better than Marie's Crisis Café (59 Grove Street). Nowadays, do not be surprised to find this lively bar packed by gay men singing hit songs from famous Broadway shows. Two centuries ago it was a home of Thomas Paine, whose publication, *Crisis*, helped fuel the American Revolution.

The photos and flags that adorn the walls of McSorley's Old Ale House suggest a time when New York bars provided informal employment centers and enabled many new immigrants to land their first jobs in the United States

115

Greenwich Village

GREENWICH VILLAGE WRITERS
James Agee, James Baldwin, Willa Cather, James Fenimore Cooper, Hart Crane, Theodore Dreiser, e. e. cummings, Henry James, Ruth McKenney, Herman Melville, Edna St. Vincent Millay, Eugene O'Neill, Anaïs Nin, John Dos Passos, Edgar Allan Poe, John Reed, William Styron, Mark Twain, Tennessee Williams, Edmund Wilson, Thomas Wolfe.

Washington Square Memorial Arch

(Continued from page 112)

There is no better place to begin exploring Greenwich Village than **Washington Square Park▶▶▶** where jugglers, thespians, unicyclists and chess-players put on a show for the families, visitors, and street-wise kids who promenade along the park's pathways.

On the park's northern side, the triumphal **Washington Memorial Arch▶▶** stands at the foot of Fifth Avenue, 77 feet high and erected by Stanford White in 1892 on a spot where he had earlier raised a wooden marker to celebrate the centenary of Washington's inauguration.

What the white marble arch does not commemorate, however, are the 22,000 people who were buried beneath the park when it served as a mass cemetery during epidemics. There is also no reminder of the fact that during the early 1800s some of the park's trees were used for public hangings.

Besides ending hangings and covering over the burial ground, the creation of the park in 1827 greatly increased the social cachet of the immediate area. Fashionable town houses rose around it, the only survivors being **The Row▶▶** on the north side: note their porticoes, shuttered windows, and elongated stoops—emphasizing the distinction between the owner's entrance and the servants' entrance at ground level.

To the park's south and east are a few of the buildings of New York University. With 14 separate schools scattered throughout Greenwich Village, the university is one of the city's major landowners.

(Continued on page 118)

INSIDE THE MEMORIAL ARCH
In 1916, maverick artist Marcel Duchamp and friends forced their way through the locked door of Washington Square Park's Memorial Arch and climbed the 110 steps to the top. Once there, they hung balloons, Chinese lanterns, and banners proclaiming Greenwich Village as the independent republic of New Bohemia. After having a picnic, Duchamp and company were forced down by militiamen.

With somewhat less spectacle, a man is thought to have lived in the arch for seven months during World War II. He was noticed only when he hung his wash out to dry.

New York City is home to one of the most vibrant gay and lesbian communities in the United States, centred around Chelsea and Greenwich Village. The contributions of its members help to make New York what it is in publishing, advertising, art and design, theater, dance, restaurants, law, business, and many other fields.

The census of 1880 found five men in prison for "unspeakable crimes against nature"—a euphemism of the time for homosexual activity. By the 1930s, a small network of gay rendezvous points had spread across Manhattan; places where discretion was uppermost and which remained invisible to the heterosexual world.

In the period following World War II, when the values of family life were extolled to the hilt, gays and lesbians increasingly felt the backlash. Sexual minorities were pilloried in the press, and the police were urged to clamp down on behavior that was feared and perceived as a menace to society.

Gay Pride In 1969, the two days of rioting that followed a police raid on Greenwich Village's Stonewall Inn became a turning point in gay history: for the first time, the community had risen up to defend itself against the authorities, and its newfound solidarity led to the founding of the Gay Pride movement.

The movement's many achievements are celebrated annually by the Gay Pride Parade along Fifth Avenue and through Greenwich Village (see page 27).

Gays have steadily become established and largely accepted throughout the city. Gay issues are now widely debated throughout mainstream media, while legal breakthroughs include the formal recognition of gay couples in 1993. In the last few year gays have also featured prominently in the rejuvenation and gentrification of the Chelsea neighborhood.

INFORMATION
For general information and the latest on gay and lesbian events, nightclubs, and more, contact the Gay and Lesbian Switchboard (tel: 777-1800). Although homophobia is much less a feature of New York than it may be in some cities, such crimes do occur and can be traumatizing, especially for visitors. An emergency telephone number is available for support and advice, tel: 807-0197.

117

Christopher Street in Greenwich Village is home to a substantial gay and lesbian community

STROLL: GREENWICH VILLAGE

The maze of side streets off Christopher Street holds some of Greenwich Village's quietest and prettiest corners. Take time to admire the lovely row of brick and brownstone Italianate houses on St. Luke's Place and venture into Bedford Street for the Isaacs-Hendricks Residence (see page 130) and the 9-foot-wide house at number 75½. Its dainty dimensions did not deter actor John Barrymore, poet Edna St. Vincent Millay or screen star Cary Grant from living in it at various times.

Its subway station has preserved its original blue tiles and the street stalls on Bleecker Street recall its place as a home for Beat writers in the 1950s and 1960s

(Continued from page 116)

Not content with his Memorial Arch, Stanford White also erected the **Judson Memorial Church▶**, on the park's south side, in largely Romanesque style. More noteworthy than the architecture are the church's stained-glass windows, the work of Hudson River artist John LaFarge.

A block away, on MacDougal Street, the unremarkable exterior of the **Provincetown Playhouse** does nothing to suggest that the group based here forged new ground in American drama in the 1910s, helped in no small measure by the talents of Eugene O'Neill.

Just south, on the corner of Minetta Lane, the **Minetta Tavern▶** displays photos and mementos from Greenwich Village's earliest days as a center for the arts.

Running across MacDougal Street, **Bleecker Street▶▶▶** holds the best of Greenwich Village's bars and clubs, though nothing these days matches the stirrings of the early 1960s when local folk clubs spawned talents such as Bob Dylan, Judy Collins, and Arlo Guthrie.

A decade earlier, the Bleecker Street cafés had reverberated to the performance poetry and drunken debates of embryonic Beat writers: Gregory Corso, Jack Kerouac, Allen Ginsberg, and William Burroughs (see page 119).

More restaurants, bakeries, and cafés line Bleecker Street as it continues westward across Sixth Avenue into the West Village, the main artery of which, Christopher Street, cuts westward from Village Square and the extraordinary **Jefferson Market Courthouse** (see page 113), toward the Hudson River; on Sixth Avenue is Balducci's (see page 113).

At 53 Christopher Street was the **Stonewall Inn**. It gave its name to the "Stonewall Riots," which united the local gay community in 1969 and led to the founding of Gay Pride (see page 117), which was to spawn similar organizations in many parts of the world.

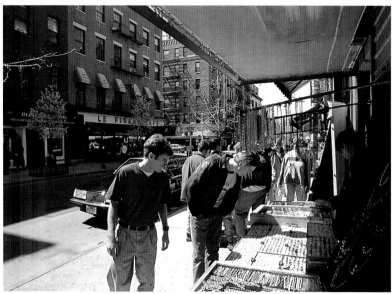

A small group of interesting characters frequenting the bars around New York's Columbia University and Greenwich Village in the 1940s evolved into what became the Beat Generation, the country's first postwar subculture and one that used drugs, jazz, and Eastern religion to inspire the new forms of writing that, for a brief time in the 1950s, seemed set to tear American society to pieces.

If the Beat Generation had a starting point, it was the West End Café (on Broadway between 113th and 114th streets) in the mid-1940s. Here teenaged student Allen Ginsberg, 30-year-old William Burroughs and 22-year-old Jack Kerouac swapped ideas, later adjourning to an apartment at 421 West 118th Street to hold lively discussions to the sound of the newly emerged bebop jazz.

Beat writing Ginsberg began writing "serious" poetry, Kerouac worked on his breathless prose style, and Burroughs steadily assembled the pieces that would evolve into his novels. By the end of the 1940s, the chief hangouts were the San Remo (189 Bleecker Street) and the Cedar Tavern (then at 24 University Place).

Success and notoriety Ginsberg was living in San Francisco in 1956 when, besides working for an advertising agency and studying Buddhism, he wrote his epic poem, _Howl_, describing characters and ideas from the past few years. The poem was published to enthusiastic reviews—and an obscenity trial that greatly increased the notoriety of "the Beats," as did _On the Road_, Kerouac's novel published the next year.

When Ginsberg and Kerouac returned to New York, the _Village Voice_ proclaimed "Witless Madcaps Come Home to Roost," and the events of a decade earlier quickly became, and continue to be, a source of legend.

WHY "BEAT GENERATION"?
Ginsberg and another writer, John Clellon Holmes, conceived the term "Beat Generation," partly from the "Lost Generation" of the 1920s and partly from a Times Square junkie who always described himself as "beat." When Holmes's novel _Go_ was published in 1952, the New York Times reviewer seized on the handy phrase, but this did not help Ginsberg, Burroughs, or Kerouac find publishers for their work.

119

The late Allen Ginsberg (left) listens to a speaker at a 1960s anti-Vietnam War rally near Tompkins Square Park

For every major religious edifice such as St. Patrick's Cathedral or the Cathedral Church of St. John the Divine, New York has dozens more places of worship that seldom receive a visit from passing travelers. Many of these are mentioned in the A to Z section of this book, but those described below are especially notable for illustrating the city's many forms of ecclesiastical architecture or for highlighting New York's endless diversity.

120

SAME CHURCH, DIFFERENT RELIGION
Indicative of the changing ethnic makeup of the Lower East Side, the 1895 Russian Orthodox Cathedral at 4th Street between Avenues C and D is now San Isidro y San Leandro Orthodox Catholic Church of the Hispanic Rite, which is serving the Lower East Side's now predominantly Puerto Rican population.

The statue of Shinran-Shonin outside the New York Buddhist Church

Greek Orthodox Just one of many churches in the Financial District that predate the high-rise glass towers and provide a striking contrast of style, the **St. Nicholas Greek Orthodox Church** (155 Cedar Street; tel: 227-0773) is New York's earliest Greek church. The interior is decorated with brass chandeliers, icons, and the model ships that are reminders of its original seafaring congregation (St. Nicholas being the patron saint of sailors). As the Greek community prospered and moved northwards, the **Greek Orthodox Cathedral of the Holy Trinity** (74th Street near First Avenue; tel: 520-3500) became its religious focal point, in 1931. The interior of the stylish Romanesque church holds more icons.

Jewish Also in what is now the Financial District, New York's first Jewish residents established the city's earliest synagogue some 300 years ago on what became William Street. A replica of the 20-seat shrine can be seen on the fifth floor of the **Wall Street Synagogue** (47 Beekman Street; tel: 227-7800). Later, the city's first Jewish architect raised the **Central Synagogue** (Lexington Avenue at 55th Street; tel: 838-1522). Its rough-hewn Moorish facade, complete with onion domes and banded arches, was intended to reflect the Jewish experience in Moorish Spain. Its interior decorated in shades of red, blue, and ocher, the synagogue was completed in 1872.

Roman Catholic In 1918, just north of the Central Synagogue, architect Bertram Goodhue produced an accomplished and imposing facade for the **Church of St. Vincent Ferrer** (Lexington Avenue at 66th Street; tel: 744-2080), but he saved his best touches for the expansive interior. Note the reredos and Charles Connick's exceptional stained-glass windows.

Russian Orthodox The seat of the Russian Orthodox Church in North America is on New York's Upper East Side, where the **St. Nicholas Orthodox Cathedral** (97th Street near Fifth Avenue; tel: 289-1915) was erected at the turn of the century, financed by donations collected across the tsarist Russian empire. The cathedral's splendidly ornate style—red brick patterned with blue and yellow tiles and five bulging onion domes—is based on the church architecture of 17th-century Moscow.

121

*From Greek Orthodox
(above left) to Buddhist
(above): New York's
places of worship mirror
its diverse ethnic makeup*

Muslim The design of St. Nicholas is strikingly different from the drab buildings around it, as is that of the **Mosque of the Islamic Culture Center** (Third Avenue at 96th Street; tel: 722-5234), which also deviates from the usual grid-style alignment of Manhattan buildings by being pointed towards Mecca. The first permanent place of worship for New York Muslims, the $12-million mosque was largely financed by the government of Kuwait.

Buddhist On the other side of Central Park, you might easily go right past the **New York Buddhist Church** (Riverside Drive between 105th and 106th streets; tel: 678-0305) without realizing the fact—were it not for the unmistakable bronze statue of Shinran-Shonin, the 13th-century founder of a Buddhist sect, that stands outside.

Abyssinian Baptist Harlem's **Abyssinian Baptist Church** (138th Street near Lenox Avenue; tel: 862-744) was founded in 1808 by, and to serve, New York's black community and quickly acquired the largest black congregation of any church in the U.S. Past ministers include Harlem's first black member of congress, Adam Clayton Powell. His struggles to end racial discrimination and raise African-American living standards made him a nationally controversial, but locally revered, figure in the 1940s. The present Gothic-style church dates from 1923 and has a display recording Powell's achievements.

▶▶▶ Guggenheim Museum   187C1

Fifth Avenue between 88th and 89th streets (tel: 423-3500)
Open: Sun to Wed 10–6, Fri and Sat 10–8
Subway: 86th Street

A member of an ultrawealthy New York family whose fortunes were founded on copper and silver mines, Solomon R. Guggenheim followed the usual track of an Upper East Side millionaire with more money than he knew what to do with by dabbling in art. Guggenheim's first purchases were unremarkable Old Masters, but his tastes were changed radically in 1927 when he met Baroness Hilla Rebay von Ehrenwiesen, an outspoken and energetic enthusiast of European abstract art.

Through the baroness, Guggenheim met artists such as Robert Delaunay, Fernand Léger, and Albert Gleizes and quickly amassed a superb stock of their work and works by other contemporary artists, particularly Wassily Kandinsky, hanging them on the walls of the rooms he occupied with his wife at New York's Plaza Hotel. At the suggestion of the baroness, Guggenheim commissioned architect Frank Lloyd Wright to design and build a museum to be called (with an ideological correctness insisted on by the baroness) the Museum of Non-Objective Painting.

Guggenheim had been dead for 10 years by the time Wright's extraordinary achievement opened in 1959, its name changed to the Solomon R. Guggenheim Museum. It proved to be the architect's only New York building, and he referred to it as his "Pantheon." By this time, Guggenheim's initial collection of abstracts had been enlarged and greatly broadened in scope by purchases and bequests, particularly the Thannhauser Collection of impressionist and post-impressionist paintings which were bequeathed by a prominent dealer and collector.

The best way to see the collection is to take the elevator to the top level and slowly work your way down the museum's remarkable spiral ramp. In this way you can study the exhibits, look over the parapet to the lobby below, and finish up where you began without ever getting lost.

Precisely what will be on show when you visit has been scheduled years in advance; the museum stages several special exhibitions each year, often focusing on the work of an individual artist. What you can be fairly certain of seeing, however, is the permanently displayed Thannhauser Collection, hung in comparatively orthodox fashion in several galleries reached off the second level of the ramp.

Highlights of the Guggenheim's permanent collections include works by Kandinsky, Modigliani, Klee, Mondrian, Braque, Chagall, Gleizes, and Malevich.

Among these, Van Gogh's painting entitled *Mountains at Saint-Rémy* is outstanding, its vibrant swirls of color painted in 1899 as the artist recovered from one of his bouts of mental illness.

Works by Cézanne include *Still Life: Flask, Glass, and Jug* and *Bibémus*, a shimmering preabstract landscape, and the slightly mystifying *Man With Crossed Arms*, described as a "proto-Cubist" piece, whose figure has been thought to embody the spirit of quiet resignation that the artist possessed during the last years of his life.

A couple of paintings by the enigmatic artist Henri Rousseau (also known as "Le Douanier"—the Customs Man) are amusing and defiantly odd. In *The Football Players*, five handlebar-moustached and ludicrously attired figures strike up absurd poses while frolicking with a ball in a forest; similarly handlebar-moustached but more correctly attired soldiers make up the core of *The Artillery Men*.

The earliest of several canvases by Picasso, *Le Moulin de Galette*, was painted in 1900 when the artist was only 19 years of age and was inspired by his first visit to Paris. The gloomy but angular figure of 1904's *Woman Ironing* is a product of the latter stages of what is known as Picasso's Blue Period; from a year or two later, *Fernand with a Black Fortilla* marks a change of style—and perhaps the first step toward Cubism.

The most striking piece in the Thannhauser Collection is also the earliest: *The Hermitage at Pontoise*, an 1867 landscape by Camille Pissarro. The artist later became a leading impressionist (Gauguin and Cézanne were among Pissarro's students and associates) but here uses a realist style that goes hard against the grain of traditional French landscape painting—and seems to make the idyllic rural scene radiate from the canvas.

RAYMOND HOOD
Architecture buffs impressed by his subsequent Daily News Building and Rockefeller Center's R.C.A. Building (or G.E. Building, as it is now more correctly known) may care to cast an eye over Raymond Hood's 1928 apartment block at 3 East 84th Street, bearing many of the features—such as pressed-metal spandrels—that later appeared in a refined form on his more well-known works.

The vertiginous interior of the Guggenheim

It has been called a doughnut, a snail, and an insult to art, but Frank Lloyd Wright's Guggenheim Museum is one of the outstanding contributions to New York architecture—even though there is plenty of truth in the accusation that it often steals the show from the art that it exhibits. Wright inserted the inscription "let every man practice the art he knows" in bronze on the entrance floor—intended perhaps as a lasting riposte to the building's critics.

124

THE GUGGENHEIM IN THE NEW MILLENNIUM

Renovation work completed in 1992 has left the Guggenheim looking almost as good as new. The following year's completion of Gwathmey/Siegel's 11-story tower, welded to the rotunda, provided much-needed extra office and exhibition space. Despite being widely criticized for its failure to blend with Wright's original building, the tower has left the museum core uncluttered by the trappings of gallery administration.

More than 40 years after it opened, the Guggenheim remains a unique feature of the New York landscape

"Organic architecture" The originator of the "Prairie style," Wright in his best architecture blended buildings into the organic, natural forms around them. The Guggenheim's predominantly curving exterior is totally out of step with the vertical lines of the neighboring Upper East Side apartment houses but has a great deal in common with the trees and shrubbery of Central Park, directly across Fifth Avenue.

With the Guggenheim Museum, his only major New York commission, Wright also made a radical departure from the traditional room-by-room gallery style. The exhibits here occupy partitioned spaces off a quarter-mile-long spiral walkway that rises six stories high, steadily growing wider as it climbs.

Controversy The architect persistently battled with the city authorities and disagreed with the museum's director over the structure's supposed failure to meet the practical needs of an art museum. All this contributed to delays, and 16 years elapsed between Wright's finished plans and the Guggenheim's opening in 1959, the year of his death. The aesthetic debate has raged ever since, though the museum is now very much part of the Upper East Side landscape.

▶ Harlem   *IBCC2*

Increasingly a part of the city's tourist circuit and long a vital and distinct component in New York's character, Harlem begins north of Central Park at 110th Street and splits into two sections.

Above the Upper West Side, West Harlem (or Harlem proper) is the longest-established home of the city's African-American population. Above the Upper East Side is East Harlem—or **El Barrio** ("the Neighborhood") —which has become New York's largest Spanish-speaking enclave, the majority of its residents having Puerto Rican origins.

During the 1890s, eager to repeat the success they had had on the Upper West Side, property speculators covered West Harlem with brownstones and apartment blocks. The anticipated buyers never materialized, however, and Harlem's homes were rented out largely to black tenants. Rents were inflated because of housing pressure—thousands of African-Americans were arriving in New York, and the competition was great. Tens of thousands of the nation's blacks fled the Deep South for Harlem, seen at the time as a promised land. By the 1920s, the Harlem Renaissance was in full swing: a flowering of African-American culture through art and literature as jazz and blues percolated through Harlem nightclubs such as the **Cotton Club** and **Smalls' Paradise**. Although Harlem has endured many inner-city problems, the past few years have seen a new spirit in the neighborhood.

FIDEL CASTRO IN HARLEM
Arriving to address the United Nations in 1960, Cuban leader Fidel Castro and his entourage spent several nights in a Midtown Manhattan hotel, reputedly running up a $10,000 bill for damage before being asked to leave. No other hotel was eager for Castro's patron-age, but Harlem's Teresa Hotel (272 West 125th Street), long known as a radicals' meeting place, filled the breach. During its week-long stay, the Cuban contingent was cheered by locals and was visited by Soviet leader Khrushchev. In 1971, the Teresa was converted into an office building.

125

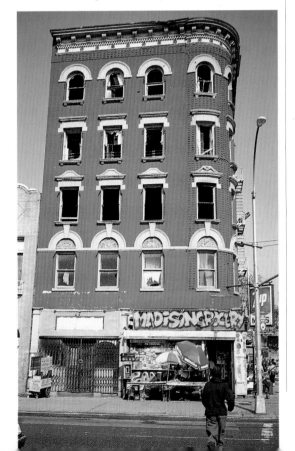

Not many people visit Harlem for its architecture, but the buildings can be just as lively as the atmosphere

MARCUS GARVEY IN HARLEM

Arriving in Harlem from Jamaica in 1914, Marcus Garvey predated the Black Panthers in the 1960s in encouraging black pride and assertiveness. Winning many followers through his brilliant powers of oration, Garvey founded the Universal Negro Improvement Foundation, published the *Negro World* newspaper and purchased two ocean liners to carry out his promised repatriation of America's blacks to Africa.

Eventually, Garvey was arrested on trumped-up charges and deported. He died in London in 1940. Garvey's doctrines became crucial elements in Rastafarianism, and in 1973 the Harlem park that straddles Fifth Avenue between 120th and 124th streets was renamed in his honor.

Unfortunately, the park, which holds a curious fire-watch tower dating from 1856, is a drug-users' hangout and is best left unvisited.

Harlem gospel choir

With leafy boulevards neighboring its low-rent housing projects, it is quite safe if you stick to daylight hours and main thoroughfares.

Along the main commercial strip, West 125th Street, you will find the **Apollo Theater** (number 253), legendary for its amateur talent nights and for showcasing every African-American jazz, blues and soul act, from Billie Holliday in the 1930s to James Brown in the 1960s. Brown's *Live at the Apollo* album was recorded here in 1962 and captures some of the venue's raw excitement. You will also find the temporary exhibitions and photographic archive of the **Studio Museum in Harlem** (144 West 125th Street; tel: 864-4500; *Open* Wed to Fri 10–5, Sat and Sun 1–6) and more soul-food restaurants than anyone could wish for.

For the best of early Harlem architecture, explore the **St. Nicholas Historic District** on 139th Street. The stylish 1890s town houses between Seventh and Eighth avenues were occupied by successful blacks from 1919 and hence earned their lasting nickname "Striver's Row."

Upbeat Sunday gospel services have become one of the major points of visitor interest in Harlem, although the tour group numbers at some churches have led to complaints that local congregations are being snubbed. One of Harlem's most celebrated churches for its outstanding choir and history of community involvement, is the **Abyssinian Baptist Church** (see page 121).

Always shabbier than its westerly counterpart, **East Harlem** was first settled by working-class Italian and Irish families but, from the 1920s on, it steadily evolved into the city's major Puerto Rican neighborhood. The **Museum of the City of New York** and **El Museo del Barrio** (see pages 156–157) stand on its fringes, but the place to make for is **La Marqueta**, found under the Park Avenue viaduct between 110th and 116th streets, where salsa music resounds among the market stalls and food stands.

▶ **Hispanic Society of America**   IFCD6

Broadway at 155th Street (tel: 690-0743)
Open: Tue to Sat 10–4:30, Sun 1–4
Subway: 1; 157th Street

Paintings by Velázquez, El Greco and Goya are among the most prized possessions of the Hispanic Society of America, founded in 1904 by Archer M. Huntington, son of magnate Collis P. Huntington. However, this collection of Spanish and Portuguese art, archaeology, tilework, and tomb decorations is overall less impressive than its setting: a sumptuous two-story Spanish Renaissance interior, decorated with ruby-red terra-cotta.

As their country is a self-governing common-wealth territory of the U.S., Puerto Ricans are automatically U.S. citizens. The right to settle freely led to Puerto Ricans forming the biggest Spanish-speaking community in New York.

Early 19th-century New York drew Puerto Ricans active in the sugar and coffee trade. Others, who were inspired by the American Revolution, came here hoping to use the city as a base to plot the overthrow of their Spanish colonial masters.

The U.S. in Puerto Rico In 1898, Puerto Rico was deeded by Spain to the United States, which established a military government on the Caribbean island and allowed American interests to rule its economy. In return, Puerto Ricans were granted United States citizenship (although not until 1917) and so were able to settle freely in the United States.

The profiteering of American companies encouraged Puerto Rican migration and, by 1930, around 45,000 Puerto Ricans had settled in New York. Many were employed in jobs formerly held by upwardly mobile Jews and Italians; others worked in their traditional trades such as cigar-making.

El Barrio Although there were Puerto Rican neighborhoods across Manhattan, the area around the low-rent apartments of East Harlem became *El Barrio*, base of Puerto Rican cultural institutions and Spanish-language cinemas and publications. Over a period of time, Fiorello La Guardia (who took office in 1933) recognized the political power of the Puerto Ricans by encouraging them to register to vote.

In the 1950s, when inexpensive flights began operating between New York and San Juan—the Puerto Rican capital—the Puerto Rican population in New York soared to 600,000, some spilling from El Barrio into the Bronx. The majority of the new arrivals had been rural-dwelling farm laborers, who subsequently found it difficult to adjust to big-city life.

Americans of Puerto Rican descent are now a major part of the city's ethnic jigsaw puzzle. While the area is celebrated among trendy New Yorkers for its spicy foods and for its salsa music, El Barrio unfortunately continues to struggle with every contemporary inner-city problem.

SAN JUAN HILL
When Yankee Stadium was completed in 1923, it was dubbed "the House that Ruth built," after baseball's most famous player. One might well call Lincoln Center "the House that Bernstein built." The great irony is that the construction of the new home of Leonard Bernstein's New York Symphony Orchestra required the utter destruction of the neighborhood that was the setting for his most famous work, *West Side Story*. More than 1,500 families in the area then known as San Juan Hill—most of them black and/or Puerto Rican—were displaced.

127

At an exhibition in Los Angeles in 1956, the phrase "the New York School" was first coined, refering to the group of artists who, in New York a decade or so earlier, had spearheaded abstract expressionism, the country's first modern art movement, thus creating a worldwide audience for American art.

THE CEDAR TAVERN
Rare is the major art movement that was not influenced to some degree by drunken debate. Abstract expressionism was no exception. The favored gathering place of many of the artists who became the New York School was the Cedar Tavern, then at 24 University Place. Here, discussions would rage into the night and sometimes culminate in an inebriated rearrangement of the furniture.

Fans of abstract expressionism who also like a drink may be pleased to know that the Cedar Tavern still exists (though it has moved to 82 University Place). These days, however, it is plain and rather uninteresting.

The Armory Show of 1913 (see page 149) not only brought modern European art to the U.S. for the first time, but also made it plain that the country had no modern style to call its own. Dadaist Marcel Duchamp summed up America's contribution to world art as "her plumbing and her bridges."

Even if they viewed it only as a stop on the way to Paris, however, New York was still a magnet for young American artists. They arrived to escape humdrum rural towns, to take classes at the city's Art Students League, and to paint in spacious light-filled loft studios available for cheap rents.

European influences As Europe moved toward war, many of the continent's most innovative and influential artistic minds fled across the Atlantic. When the Nazis marched down the Champs-Elysées, New York eclipsed Paris as the nerve center of international art.

In the late 1940s, as the conclusion of the war seemed to present a world free of the shackles of traditionalism and filled with new possibilities, the abstract expressionists emerged.

Jackson Pollock A farmer's son from Wyoming, Jackson Pollock had arrived in New York in the 1920s and was later employed for a short time at the embryonic Guggenheim Museum.

In 1947, Pollock seized one of his paintings from its easel, fixed it to the floor, and started applying paint directly from the can in great sweeping arcs across the canvas. Soon after, Pollock dispensed with easels and brushes entirely, pouring paint onto the flat canvas and manipulating it with "sticks, trowels, or knives."

As the final product depended entirely on the act of Pollock dripping and throwing paint (compared to a western cowboy's lasso skills), the technique gave rise to the term "action painting" (also called "gestural painting").

De Kooning, Gottlieb, and Rothko Another key abstract expressionist was Willem de Kooning. While de Kooning used figures much more than Pollock—often formed by white contours on black—he was every inch the action painter, attacking his canvas with an energy that sent specks of paint flying in every direction.

A major influence on the abstract expressionists was the *Pictographs*, a series of paintings by Adolph Gottlieb, each of which was divided into compartments holding a mythological figure or symbol.

128

The abstract expressionists sought to transmit primal emotional states through their work—a goal that went beyond what was possible within traditional painting and which the horrors of the war had helped awaken.

Mark Rothko, an associate of Gottlieb's, became the foremost figure of what was termed the "color field" branch of abstract expressionism. As the full terrors of the Nazi concentration camps emerged, there was a special poignancy when Rothko, the Latvian-born son of Russian Jewish émigrés, asserted that "human incommunicability" had rendered figurative painting obsolete. Rothko's work evolved into floating rectangles of color, which, he said, provided "a spiritual basis for communion."

Barnett Newman and after Barnett Newman likened the color field artists' work to that of "primitive" cultures, keen to reach a "metaphysical understanding." In the late 1940s, Newman produced the first of his "zip paintings," their flat field of color split by a narrow vertical line.

Ironically, it was a misinterpretation of Newman's work that influenced later artists such as Jasper Johns. These later artists paved the way for the break away from the mentally wrought canvases of abstract expressionism to the re-casting of familiar images practiced by the 1960s pop art movement.

Perhaps in keeping with the anguished soul-searching of their work, the lives of abstract expressionism's two major figures both ended prematurely: Jackson Pollock died after driving his car into a tree in 1956, and Mark Rothko committed suicide in 1970.

ABSTRACT EXPRESSIONISM ON DISPLAY
The Museum of Modern Art (see pages 158–160) has an excellent collection of abstract expressionist works and, besides those mentioned on these pages, also features work by other highly influential members of the movement such as Robert Motherwell, Franz Kline, and Arshile Gorky.

The Guggenheim Museum (pages 122–124) has a fair number of abstract expressionist canvases in its possession (sometimes on display in temporary exhibitions), and important works by Pollock, de Kooning, and Rothko can be seen at the Whitney Museum (page 191).

129

One, a huge canvas of 1950 by Jackson Pollock, now in MoMA

PASSENGER SHIP TERMINAL

Great ocean liners such as the *Queen Mary* and the *U.S.S. United States* would berth at the piers at the western ends of 48th, 50th, and 52nd streets (just north of the Intrepid Sea-Air-Space Museum) in the days before air travel made them uneconomic. To make the docking area as luxurious as the ships, the swanky New York Passenger Ship Terminal was completed in 1976. Unfortunately, most scheduled services had been abolished by the time, although modern luxury cruise ships can sometimes be seen docked here.

130

PHOTOGRAPHY HOUSE

One of the most handsome neo-Georgian mansions on the Upper East Side is home to the International Center of Photography. The four-story red-brick building was completed in 1914 by the firm of Delano & Aldrich for Willard Straight, a wealthy ex-diplomat who founded the influential *New Republic* magazine. The International Center of Photography also has a Midtown branch, called simply I.C.P. Midtown, at 1133 Sixth Avenue at 43rd Street.

►► International Center of Photography   187D1

Fifth Avenue at 94th Street (tel: 860-1777)
Open: Tue 11–8, Wed to Sun 11–6
Subway: 6; 96th Street

One of the world's few museums entirely devoted to photography, the International Center of Photography (ICP) has four galleries mounting changing exhibitions of both internationally established names and lesser-knowns.

One gallery is usually filled with selections from the center's permanent collection, which holds prints by almost every notable photographer you can think of: Henri Cartier-Bresson, Ernst Haas, Weegee, and Robert Capa to name a few.

► Intrepid Sea-Air-Space Museum   151C1

West end of 46th Street (tel: 245-0072)
Open: Oct to Apr, Wed to Sun 10–5; rest of year, daily 10–5
Subway: A, C, E; 42nd Street

The flight deck of the *Intrepid*, a Navy aircraft carrier, is the core of this entirely militaristic museum. Permanently moored on the Hudson River, the *Intrepid* saw action in the Pacific during World War II and served in an antisubmarine role during the Vietnam War.

The vessel is stuffed with exhibits from its own wartime adventures—its aircraft shot down 650 enemy planes and destroyed 289 ships—and from its peacetime role of retrieving Mercury and Gemini space capsules. There is a plethora of armed forces' hardware, not least the fighter and bomber planes that sit on the flight deck with their cockpits open for inspection.

Temporary exhibitions explore diverse aspects of warfare, although they tend to highlight technical achievements rather than the human experience of war. The staging of fund-raising rock concerts and dance nights at the museum in 1997, as well as alleged poor maintenance of the planes, caused a rift between the museum and the military, particularly the U.S. Navy, which owns many of the exhibits and which threatened to withdraw them.

► Isaacs-Hendricks Residence   113A2

77 Bedford Street, Greenwich Village
Subway: 1; Christopher Street

You could be forgiven for walking right past the Isaacs-Hendricks Residence without noticing it. Alterations in 1836 and 1928 have detracted from its Federal style, of which it is one of the earliest surviving examples, having been erected in 1799. The clapboard wall on the side that backs onto Commerce Street is the main clue to the house's architectural pedigree.

► Jan Hus Presbyterian Church   187B2

74th Street between First and Second avenues
Subway: 6; 77th Street

Named for the Czech martyr of the Reformation, the Jan Hus Presbyterian Church was founded in 1914 to serve Czech settlers in an area that was known as Little Bohemia into the 1930s. The church, with a bell tower modeled on the Powder Tower in Prague, is more popular for its secular activities than for its services. Musical and dramatic events are staged at the church's hall.

Only a fraction of New York's Czech-American population now lives in Little Bohemia and, besides the church, there are only a couple of notable reminders of the Czech presence, such as the run-down Bohemian National Hall, on 73rd Street between First and Second avenues, raised in 1895.

▶ Jewish Museum   187D1

Fifth Avenue at 92nd Street (tel: 423-3200)
Open: Sun, Mon, Wed, Thu 11–5:45, Tue 11–8
Subway: 6; 96th Street

An imitation French Gothic château might seem a strange home for the largest stock of Judaic ceremonial art and historical objects in the U.S., but the fine collections of New York's Jewish Museum have been housed in just such a place since 1944. It was then that the premises were bequeathed to the museum by the widow of their original owner, banker Felix M. Warburg.

Some of the tremendous stash of coins, household objects, and religious pieces dates back to Roman times; much more is representative of Jewish life from medieval times into the present century. One exemplary feature is the re-created turn-of-the-century café in which visitors can select oral histories of Jewish lives in various European cities of the time, and of early Jewish arrivals to the United States.

The Jewish Museum also stages lively and sometimes provocative temporary exhibitions that are designed to explore the Jewish experience from new and challenging perspectives. There is also a Childrens' Activity Center which offers arts and crafts projects related to Jewish culture and traditions.

The Intrepid-Sea-Air-Space Museum

From the major T.V. networks to the loony public-access channels and from the venerable New York Times *to free magazines packed with ads for tarot readers, media is a big part of New York life; information pours from all sides.*

Television All New York's daily newspapers carry full listings of T.V. programs. A full week's listings is also included as a separate magazine with the many sections of the Sunday *New York Times*. The latest local news and weather can be found on NY1, a 24-hour channel devoted to the city. While all hotel rooms will have T.V.s, budget-priced rooms rarely come equipped with cable channels, and even medium-priced options tend to be skimpy on the cable selections available. One perk of more costly hotels is a fuller range of viewing options, sometimes including Manhattan's public-access channels on which people—crazed astrologers and self-styled sex therapists alike—pay to make a half-hour show.

Radio New York has many radio stations: your best bet is to turn the dial until you find what you like. FM frequencies offer a wide choice of stations, each with its own specialty, from round-the-clock hip-hop, soul, funk, jazz, country, heavy rock, or classical sounds. Stations on the AM wavebands are primarily spoken word, and include phone-ins of the kind that launched pioneering shock-jock Howard Stern. At the very least, such shows soon acquaint visitors with the New York accent.

The cast of international comedy hit "Friends," which is set in New York

Newspapers Of New York City's daily newspapers, *The New York Times* is unmatched for in-depth coverage of international and national affairs, while its Metro section delivers the New York news that matters. The special features of the *Times* provide intriguing insights into city life, and the Friday edition is invaluable for its listings of weekend events and activities. The Sunday edition, particularly as the Christmas-shopping season advances, becomes, literally, a heavyweight as its pages fill with ever more tempting advertisements. While the city once had several flourishing dailies, the general falling off in newspaper readership has left the *New York Times* as a virtual monopoly when it comes to the serious reader—except for the businessman and, increasingly, the general investor, who turn to the *Wall Street Journal* for their daily news-fix.

While the *Times* is regarded as politically liberal, the tabloid *New York Post* is the home of conservative reaction, despite having some sharp columnists. The Page Six gossip column (which may not be on page 6) is avidly read. New Yorkers who hate the *Post*'s politics but love tabloid headlines turn instead to the *Daily News*. The *Daily News* has built its reputation on well-written racy stories which match its famously racy headlines. It can be relied upon to reveal the most heinous of crimes and the juiciest of scandals.

The weekly *Village Voice* began in the mid-1950s as an alternative paper (author Norman Mailer was one of its cofounders) and is now as much a part of the city as the Empire State Building. It explores city politics and fringe issues with relish and carries comprehensive arts and entertainment listings. However, the *Voice* faces competition from other weeklies such as the entertaining, easier-to-read, and better presented *New York Press*, and the *New York Observer* with its engaging news, features, and arts reviews.

Magazines Appearing in weekly editions, the *New York* magazine is a glossy celebration of the New York lifestyle and has an extensive events-listing section. The *New Yorker*, also published weekly, is noted for long, detailed articles written by literary heavyweights. The *New Yorker* is hardly light reading, although there are many who buy it solely for its thoughtful film reviews, its cartoons, and its humor columns.

Free publications Many free publications are found in New York's stores, restaurants, bars, and hotel lobbies, and in special bins around the city. Some specialize in particular areas, such as pet care, advancing your career, or the beliefs of the New Age; others are neighborhood publications such as *The Villager, Resident,* and *Tribeca Trib* and well worth reading for gossip and local news. *Blade* is a free weekly with news and features of interest to the gay community.

A sense of occasion is never lacking at the Metropolitan Opera House: the crystal chandeliers above the auditorium are sucked into the gold-leafed ceiling before a performance

GUIDED TOURS OF LINCOLN CENTER
Hour-long guided tours depart from the concourse level fairly frequently on most weekdays. The anecdote-packed tours weave through the major buildings (except the Metropolitan Opera House; see below), visiting backstage areas and often catching rehearsals in progress (tel: 875-5350). Tours of the Metropolitan Opera House leave from the entrance foyer of the Met, Mon to Fri at 3:45 PM and on Sat at 10 AM (tel: 769-7020).

▶ Lincoln Center for the Performing Arts   151D1

62nd to 66th streets between Columbus and Amsterdam avenues
Subway: 1, 66th Street/Lincoln Center

The buildings and plaza of the Lincoln Center for the Performing Arts are looking somewhat dated, but what takes place inside is impressive.

The complex arose in the 1960s as part of a Utopian plan to give New York a single cultural rendezvous point. One element in Lincoln Center's genesis was the decision of the New York Philharmonic, faced with what seemed likely to be the imminent destruction of Carnegie Hall, to seek a home of its own. Philharmonic Hall was completed here in 1962, changing its name in 1973 to Avery Fisher Hall in honor of the man who parted with $10 million to improve its atrocious acoustics (not completely brought up to snuff until the 1980s).

The Philharmonic's search for new premises coincided with that of the Metropolitan Opera; the 10-story **Metropolitan Opera House** (tel: 769-7000) now rises boldly above the plaza, two enormous Marc Chagall murals visible through its windows.

The **New York State Theater**, designed by architect Philip Johnson, is the permanent home of the New York City Opera and New York City Ballet.

Eero Saarinen's **Vivian Beaumont Theater** (tel: 362-7600) ironically has until recently endured poor reviews for its cultural offerings. Next door, the **New York Public Library for the Performing Arts** (tel: 876-1600) holds 50,000 tomes and finds room for three separate galleries hosting temporary exhibitions.

On the north side of the complex is the world-famous Juilliard School, which numbers violinist Itzhak Perlman and actor William Hurt among its alumni. Beside the school, **Alice Tully Hall** (tel: 875-5000) provides a refreshingly intimate and acoustically brilliant home for the Lincoln Center Chamber Music Society—and for free concerts given by students, which usually take place on Wednesday lunchtimes.

►► Little Italy   87B2

Both Italian and not very large, Little Italy has had its boundaries steadily eroded by the expansion of Chinatown and by the drift of its original inhabitants to Italian enclaves in the Outer Boroughs. Between 1890 and 1924, however, 145,000 migrants from Sicily and southern mainland Italy settled here, in an area between Houston and Canal streets.

After years of decline the area is showing signs of gentrification with stores and restaurants spreading from SoHo and the East Village into its northern edge, now dubbed **NoLita** (north Little Italy). Many of the few thousand Italians remaining in the neighborhood are employed in the restaurants, cafés, and bakeries along Grand and Mulberry streets. The food is good but far from cheap, and the cost-wise way to take in Little Italy's atmosphere is with a cappuccino at an outdoor table.

The closest the district comes to a genuine Italian landmark is **Umberto's Clam House** (129 Mulberry Street), which acquired fame for all the wrong reasons in 1972, when, in settlement of a gangland feud, "Crazy" Joe Gallo was shot while dining on a seafood supper.

The local Irish, who predated the Italians, had their spiritual needs fulfilled by what is now **"Old" St. Patrick's Cathedral** (264 Mulberry Street; tel: 226-8075; *Open* daily 7–8:45). The city's earliest Gothic-style building, it lost its original facade in an 1866 fire and was demoted to a parish church when a new St. Patrick's Cathedral was consecrated in Midtown Manhattan in 1879.

Take a look at the **Old Police Headquarters** at 240 Centre Street. This Renaissance palace, topped by a green dome, was an immeasurably imposing symbol of law and order when it arose in the midst of one of the city's most crime-ridden districts in 1909.

Walk on to the **Puck Building** at 295–307 Lafayette Street. This was completed in 1886 to house the *Puck* satirical magazine and, with its deliriously complex red brickwork, was instantly revered as a prime example of New York commercial design.

FESTIVAL OF ST. GENNARO
Each September, Little Italy's Mulberry Street is lined by makeshift stalls selling homemade sausage, calzone and other Italian specialties (plus an increasing number of Chinese ones) and jumps to the sound of marching bands in a two-week celebration of the Feast of St. Gennaro. The religious aspect of the festival, honoring the patron saint of Naples, is evident as a likeness of the saint is carried along the streets and showered with dollar bills. In 1995, the festival was almost canceled following allegations that most of the estimated $10 million raised by the event went to one of New York's Italian crime families. Mayor Giuliani refused to licence stallholders until guarantees were made that the proceeds would reach charities.

The tenements of Little Italy. Many of them have a restaurant or a café at street level—worth a stop at any time for a cappuccino, ice cream, or a pizza

As an ethnic group, the Italians arrived in large numbers during the 1880s. Through a combination of hard work, traditional values, and business acumen, the Italian community had become sufficiently prosperous to take the helm of the city by the 1940s.

A refuge for Italian liberals and revolutionaries through the 19th century, New York's first Italian neighborhood was on Bleecker Street during the 1860s. Its population was chiefly made up of sophisticated northerners. By contrast, the grinding poverty of rural southern Italy triggered the massive influx of the late 1800s, and 145,000 people were soon packed into the tenements of what became, and still is, Little Italy.

Many Italians work in the restaurant industry, providing New Yorkers and visitors alike with pasta, pizza, and other universally popular specialties

Exploitation of immigrants

Speaking little or no English, these new arrivals were exploited, not least by their fellow countrymen who had been in the U.S. long enough to learn the language yet who still knew enough about traditional Italian values to overwork and underpay the immigrants.

Little Italy's men built New York's sewers and subways and its women worked in garment industry sweatshops. Any spare money was sent home to their villages. Many Italians had escaped Little Italy for East Harlem by the 1910s, and by the 1940s had become wealthy enough to move to suburban areas in the Outer Boroughs.

Rising fortunes It was from East Harlem that Fiorello La Guardia emerged. This Protestant Italian son of a Jewish mother was destined to be remembered as the best mayor the city of New York ever had. La Guardia's rise was a symbol of the assimilation of Italian-Americans into city politics, a sphere where they replaced the Irish as the dominant ethnic group.

With descendants of the first Italian-Americans excelling in every walk of New York life, a new wave of immigrants appeared almost unnoticed during the prosperous 1980s. In contrast to the Italian arrivals of a century or more earlier, these Italians were affluent and stylish. They moved into the Upper East Side and opened the upscale boutiques and wonderful Italian restaurants that won the hearts and wallets of New Yorkers who could afford to eat there.

►►► Lower East Side   *IFCB3*

Don't come to the Lower East Side expecting epoch-making architecture, fashionable faces, glamorous boutiques, or expense-account restaurants. While new bars and boutiques are making in-roads, this is still downbeat New York with few pretensions. It is traditionally the first stop for newly arrived immigrants from around the world whose priority is to work hard and earn enough money to move on.

The first to arrive in the Lower East Side were the Irish, fleeing their homeland's famine in the mid-1800s. They were followed by successive waves of German and Eastern European immigrants, including the 2 million Jews who turned the Lower East Side into the world's largest Jewish community.

Living in windowless rooms in overcrowded tenements and often working in sweatshops for breadline wages, the immigrants nonetheless founded cultural institutions and places of worship and established the educational organizations that were to make their children's lives easier than their own.

The 1924 tightening of immigration laws slowed the European influx into the Lower East Side, although by then its more successful inhabitants had moved on and established ethnic pockets elsewhere, and it was to these districts that new arrivals headed.

With land here yet to become valuable, many Lower East Side tenements remain, as do the delis, garment and jewelry stores on which the first locals made their money. Nowadays, the owners are likely to be Indian or Korean, representing the latest waves of immigration.

Less immediately obvious to outsiders are the Lower East Side's Caribbean immigrants, including the many Puerto Ricans who dominate a broad area east of Essex Street and spill north across Houston Street into Alphabet City (see page 60).

It is the stores and their heavily discounted prices that bring most visitors to the Lower East Side. The area is at its busiest on Sundays when bargain-hunting New Yorkers descend on the narrow streets off Delancey Street

TENEMENT LIFE: THE ANNUAL MOVE
Few Lower East Siders ever stayed in a particular tenement for longer than they had to, and the offer of a free month's rent in return for a year's tenancy was usually sufficient inducement for tenement dwellers to up stakes and move every 12 months. It also became common for entire families to move back and forth across the same street, often moving in and out of the same tenements many times over at yearly intervals.

137

For vast stocks of cut-price clothing, the stores and stalls of Orchard Street, at the heart of Jewish New York on the Lower East Side, are hard to beat

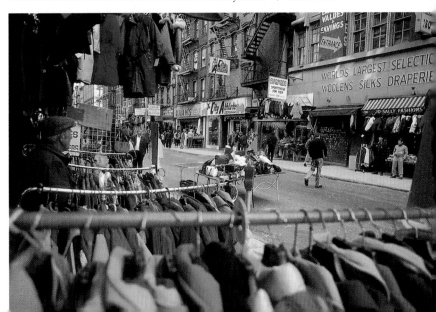

HOW THE OTHER HALF LIVED

Photographs and text by Jacob Riis, published as *How the Other Half Lives* in 1894, focused attention on the grim realities of everyday life in the Lower East Side and were instrumental in bringing about laws improving housing and working conditions. Nonetheless, for most Lower East Side residents, the only real escape was to save enough money for a move to Brooklyn, the Bronx, or Queens.

WALKING TOURS

The Lower East Side Tenement Museum organizes various walking tours, each concentrating on a specific facet of Lower East Side life—such as ethnic heritage, the lives of women, tenement architecture, and the exploits of New York's earliest street gangs. The walks are not cheap but they are enjoyable and informative. For details and reservations, tel: 431-0233.

Typical Lower East Side tenements on Delancey Street. Buildings like these sprang up in the 19th century to house newly arrived immigrants—often in very overcrowded and unhealthy conditions

for some of the biggest clothing discounts to be found in the city. The crush is fiercest outside the garment stores lining **Orchard Street▶**. When the crowds become overwhelming, explore the marginally less busy neighboring streets such as Allen, Grand, and Essex.

The tumult of Sundays is not repeated during the week, when the streets are much quieter—and actually rather dull. An exception to this is the **Essex Street Market▶**, where Lower East Siders buy their fresh meat, vegetables, and fruit.

The current ethnic mix of the area is evident in the conversations carried out here in Yiddish, Spanish, and Chinese—and in the plantains and bean sprouts sitting alongside the Jewish staples. The market is closed on Sundays. If you plan a weekend visit, it is useful to bear in mind also that many stores are closed on Saturdays in observance of the Jewish Sabbath.

After shopping, taking in the atmosphere, and sampling fresh-made knishes (doughy pastries filled with meat or potatoes) from one of several dozen Jewish bakeries, be sure to visit the **Lower East Side Tenement Museum▶▶▶** (97 Orchard Street; tel: 431-0233; *Open* Tue to Fri 12–5, Sat and Sun 11–5. Guided tours are available Apr to Dec) is situated in a six-story tenement that was built in 1863 and housed 11,000 people over a 70-year period.

The museum provides a fascinating background to Lower East Side life and reveals countless illuminating facts about the deprivations of tenement living, at least for those tenement dwellers of an earlier age. The upper floors have been re-created to show the conditions that the house's tenants endured.

Since 1654, when 23 Sephardic Jews deported from Brazil landed in New York and resisted the Dutch governor's attempts to remove them, the Jewish community has shaped the character of New York life. The city's Jewish population has given the world everything from bagels to Irving Berlin.

Established and respected in the commercial life of colonial America, the Sephardic community—which traces its origins back to Moorish Spain—continued to flourish after the American Revolution.

In the 1830s, arrivals from Germany, the Ashkenazy—who had a different set of Jewish traditions—began looking for new opportunities in the city.

Germans and Russians Assisted by mutual aid societies, the Germans settled in the Lower East Side and were soon establishing the area's jewelry and garment industries. Such businesses employed other Ashkenazy: Russian Jews who arrived during the late 1800s, fleeing the pogroms of Tsar Alexander III. For the most part, these Russians shunned the charity offered by the German Jewish aid societies and formed their own self-help organizations. In the garment industry sweatshops, the Russians formed powerful labor unions.

The Ashkenazy immigrants also brought a rich cultural life to the Lower East Side, particularly with the Yiddish theaters in an area which became known as the "Yiddish Rialto." Although the Yiddish theater began with vaudeville and farce, the arrival of Jacob Gordin, a leading Russian playwright, helped it develop serious drama and stage works by the likes of Norwegian playwright Henrik Ibsen and Russian playwright Maxim Gorky. Future stars such as Walter Matthau and Edward G. Robinson cut their teeth before the lively Yiddish theater audiences. At the same time, the smoke-filled Lower East Side cafés became centers of political and literary debate, as well as the venues for closely fought chess matches.

Some anti-Semitism was encountered, but New York immigrants never suffered the hostilities that had been their fate in Europe, and Jewish culture soon became deeply embedded in New York life.

Later arrivals The Lower East Side was still the first area of settlement for poor Sephardic arrivals from Turkey, Greece, and Syria during the Balkan Wars of the 1910s. By the 1930s, however, Europeans fleeing the rise of Nazism were able to move directly into comfortable Jewish enclaves established in the Upper West Side and the Outer Boroughs.

In the 1970s, a few Soviet Jews began settling in Brooklyn's Brighton Beach. Today, the most conspicuous aspects of New York's Jewish community are seen in areas dominated by ultra-orthodox sects, such as the Satmarers and Lubavitchers.

Black hats (fur trimming denotes a rabbi) and matching long coats make men belonging to the rigidly orthodox Satmar sect instantly recognizable

Many visitors come to New York for no reason other than to shop. Once the designer outlets and the big-name department stores have been exhausted, however, the attention of the serious shopper turns to the city's flea markets and secondhand stores—where the quest for that elusive item at a giveaway price can bring hours of sheer pleasure to many.

THRIFT STORES
The intrepid bargain-hunter might not want to leave New York without delving into at least a few of its thrift stores. Often linked to a church and run by volunteer labor with the proceeds going to charity, thrift stores are filled with cast-off clothing, house-hold objects, books, and other items. For a full list, consult the Yellow Pages.

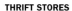

Flea markets Wherever the New York sidewalk is wide enough you are likely to find an impromptu flea market. The merchandise will probably range from out-and-out junk to stolen goods (often with fake designer labels). Resist temptation and instead visit one of the city's four main official flea markets, where better fare turns up.

Every weekend between March and December, the **Annex Antiques Fair and Flea Market** (Sixth Avenue between 24th and 26th streets) features a varied stash of bric-a-brac, clothing and jewelry. The quality is highly variable, but a browse can be worthwhile. Nearby is the **Chelsea Antiques** building (110 West 25th Street), where vendors sell everything from exquisite jewels to novelty items. Next door is the **Chelsea Antiques Garage** (112 West 25th Street), a weekend emporium of fine and mediocre used goods.

Prices are higher at the Saturday **Greenwich Village Flea Market** (Greenwich Street at Charles Street), although this small market merits a visit if you are explor-ing the neighborhood.

On Sunday, the **Green Flea Indoor/Outdoor Market** (Columbus Avenue between 76th and 77th streets) is a larger and somewhat more commercial affair, with clothing, jewelry, ornaments, and furniture. On Saturday, the same market can be found at 67th Street, between First and York avenues.

Books Not only do they love bargains, New Yorkers also love to read. Spend a whole day browsing in the **Strand Book Store** (Broadway at 12th Street) and you will barely make an impression on its 8 miles of shelves; the stocks range from dog-eared paperback best-sellers to discarded review copies of pristine hardbacks—all sold for a fraction of their original price.

Much smaller but equally interesting, the intimate **Bleecker Street Books** (350 Bleecker Street) carries general-interest subjects. By contrast, a massive, unclassified clutter of paperbacks fills **Ruby's Book Sale** (119 Chambers Street), where you might also be tempted by piles of vintage magazines.

Clothing The city's more affluent elements may shop for clothes among the designer-name stores that proliferate in Midtown Manhattan, but the sartorially adventurous—and those in search of a bargain—target the array of vintage clothing stores downtown in Greenwich Village and SoHo.

ANNUAL FAIRS

There are several annual neighborhood fairs that allow residents and retail establishments the opportunity to peddle their wares or get rid of old junk, as the case may be. The Atlantic Antic, on Atlantic Avenue in Brooklyn each September, is one the best. Also noteworthy is the Stuyvesant Town Fair each May.

Left: you will find plenty of junk (and, just possibly, a bargain or two) on sale in Canal Street

The enormous stocks of **Antique Boutique** (712–714 Broadway) have plenty to keep the vintage-clothes fanatic engaged, although dedicated bargain-hunters might be better served by a search through the racks at **Stella Dallas** (218 Thompson Street) or **Cheap Jack's** (Broadway between 13th and 14th streets).

Clothes of the 1950s are the specialties—though far from the total extent—of the reasonably priced stock at **Love Saves the Day** (119 Second Avenue at East 7th Street), while **The Family Jewels** (832 Sixth Avenue at 29th Street) carries everything from 1920s evening gowns to 1960s miniskirts, along with an eclectic mix of hats, purses, and shoes. **Church Street Surplus** (727 Church Street at Canal Street) also stocks a broad range of vintage clothing, as well as used army–navy gear. **The Quilted Corner** (Fourth Avenue at Twelfth Street), stocks vintage clothes alongside curtains and fabrics. Another happy hunting-ground is **Alice Underground** (Broadway between Broome and Grand streets). Here there are great collections of very classy,but attractively priced,clothes.

It is hard not to be overwhelmed by the sheer volume of print at the Strand Book Store, which claims to be the world's largest second-hand bookstore

C.D.s and Records New York has a massive audience for all kinds of music, but predominant on the secondhand racks are indie rock and classical rarities. Underground rock music and hot dance cuts are found at **St. Mark's Sounds** (20 St. Mark's Place). **Stoor Records** (122 East 7th Street) has a stellar supply of new and used records and c.d.s ranging from jazz to hip-hop. **Footlight Records** (113 East Twelfth Street) is the city's prime source of show music, big band records, and movie soundtracks, and also has a strong jazz selection. Classical music fans should explore the used records section of **Academy Records** (12 West 18th Street) and seek out the costly rarities at **Gryphon Records** (33 West 72nd Street).

The Met's imposing neoclassical entrance

THE ORIGINAL BUILDING

Few New York facades are as overwhelming in their grandeur as that of the Metropolitan Museum of Art, even though the exuberant neoclassical features that greet visitors to the Met's Fifth Avenue entrance are but one of many additions made to the museum's original body. In 1880, in an effort to blend the planned museum into its setting on the edge of Central Park, its original architects Jacob Wrey Mould and Calvert Vaux (one of the park's co-designers) devised a High Gothic form for the main facade, which then faced the park.

As its collections grew, so too did the museum building. In 1902 it gained the Fifth Avenue entrance that remains in place today. Only a segment of Mould and Vaux's work can still be seen, inside the much more recent Robert Lehman Wing.

▶▶▶ **Metropolitan Museum of Art**   *187C1*

Fifth Avenue and 82nd Street (tel: 535-7710)
Open: Sun, Tue to Thu 9:30–5:15, Fri and Sat 9:30–9
Subway: 4, 6; 86th Street

Founded in 1870, the Metropolitan Museum of Art is now among the world's most important art museums. Over the years, the collection has been greatly swelled by donations from some of America's richest people. The Met will exhaust you long before you exhaust it. The best way is to think of it as a dozen or so separate museums.

Plan your visit bearing in mind that some galleries close in rotation. Schedules are available from the desk. If you cannot decide where to begin, aim first for the European paintings on the second floor.

The Dutch galleries include almost a whole room of Rembrandts and five of Vermeer's 40 extant paintings.

Among the Spanish contributions, focus on El Greco's *View of Toledo*, a striking depiction of the 16th-century religious center below menacing clouds and Velázquez's *Juan de Pareja*, a portrait of his assistant, painted in the 1640s during his second trip to Italy.

Moving on, the French rooms reveal choice works spanning three centuries. Among many striking pieces, George de la Tour's *The Penitent Magdalen* has a rare ability to draw the viewer into its dark corners, and Rousseau's *The Forest in Winter at Sunset* seems to resonate with the primeval forces of nature.

After the changing displays of drawing and photography you reach the 19th-century European painting and sculpture. The galleries of French impressionists and post-impressionists include contributions from Manet, Monet, Cézanne, Gauguin, and Renoir, but winning the day are the canvases of Van Gogh, among them *Self-Portrait with a Straw Hat* and the stunning *Cypresses*.

(Continued on page 144)

Detailed explanatory labels are an essential aid to comprehending the Met's Egyptian collections, an otherwise overwhelming stash of 40,000 objects that stretch from predynastic times to the arrival of the Romans.

You don't need to be a scholar to enjoy the collections or the lasting impression they provide of one of the world's greatest civilizations. Some of this colossal stock of treasures were donated by individuals but many come from the Met's own 30-year excavation program. The single biggest exhibit, the Temple of Dendur (see panel), was a gift from the government of Egypt to the United States in the 1960s.

Although the walk-through Tomb of Perneb—a structure that draws attention as soon as you enter the Egyptian galleries—is a reconstruction, most of the objects on display are originals in such excellent states of preservation that they seem far younger than they really are; their imagery, and their often extravagant use of color are surprisingly forceful.

The trappings of death The most powerful examples are the numerous brightly decorated coffins, that of the 12th-dynasty (1897–1843 BC) Khnumnakht being particularly notable for its painted eyes—intended to allow the dead to look intensely into the land of the living.

The smaller items, too, can be striking. From the Ptolemaic period (332–30 BC) are a sculptured Anubis, the jackal-headed god of embalming who watched over the dead, and the erect and disconcertingly alert bronze likeness of a cat, used as a coffin for the animal regarded by some ancient Egyptians as sacred. Look also for the detailed 11th-century (2009–1998 BC) house and garden models from the tomb of Mekutra, used to show the layout of the deceased's property.

THE TEMPLE OF DENDUR
Destined to be submerged following the construction of the Aswan Dam, this 2,000-year-old temple was packed up and transported to the museum from its original site on the banks of the Nile. The sandstone temple, a monument to Isis and two Egyptian brothers who drowned in the Nile, was constructed around 15 BC in an effort by the Roman emperor Augustus to win the hearts of the conquered locals. It manages to be both spectacular and disappointing, overwhelmed by the modern gallery that was built to contain it and overlooked, through a vast glass wall, by the trees of Central Park and the penthouses of Fifth Avenue.

The Temple of Dendur stands in its own huge gallery

(Continued from page 142)

The American Wing holds an outstanding collection, defining the development of art and design in the U.S. as European traditions were by stages mimicked, absorbed and finally submerged, as American styles developed.

Foremost among the paintings are the finely detailed landscapes of the Hudson River artists, many of which captured the continent's natural breadth and diversity as white settlers steadily forged westward. A series of period rooms shows the progress of the decorative arts, from Queen Anne armchairs and Philadelphia Chippendale chests of drawers to the unique art nouveau glasswork of Louis Comfort Tiffany, who worked in Long Island, and a large living room that brilliantly expresses the vision of Frank Lloyd Wright's Prairie-style architecture, intended to replicate the wide open spaces of the American heartland in a domestic setting.

Compared with their American counterparts, the European period rooms seem vulgarly stuffed with finery—they include Venetian bedrooms, English interiors by Robert Adam, and a Louis XIV state bedchamber. The phenomenal collection of clocks, mirrors, and objets d'art lining the adjacent passageways is enough to bring tears to the eyes of any passing antique dealer.

Just a few steps away, a flamboyantly decorated 16th-century Spanish patio leads to the stairwell and the main entrance to the museum's cache of medieval art. Should medieval art be your abiding interest, make this your first call. Only with a clear head are the 4,000-odd exhibits—from the fall of Rome to the dawn of the Renaissance and from a tiny 3rd-century Alexandrian medallion to a three-story-high wrought-iron choir screen from 17th-century Spain—likely to fall into a comprehensible pattern.

(Continued on page 146)

MORE MEDIEVAL ART
After a thorough rummage through the Met's main collections, true medievalists might consider forsaking the remainder of the museum for New York's second batch of medieval treasures, displayed at the Met's Cloisters wing (see pages 92–93). Admission tickets are valid at both locations on their day of issue.

144

One of the less well-known and more restful corners of the labyrinthine Met: the Petrie Sculpture Court

Documenting the origins and spread of Islam through the highly skilled and often beautiful art and craft works that it inspired, the Met's Islamic art collections fill 10 galleries on the third floor. Though these are among the Met's 'lesser-known exhibits, they make up one of the finest such displays in the world.

After a bright introductory room describing the founding of Islam by Muhammad in 622 and the religion's steady outward spread from Mecca, the sides of the initial galleries are lined with dozens of well-stocked display cases, each holding a wonderful assortment of gold and silver pieces such as beads, pendants, and plaques from the craftsmen of Egypt, Iran, and Syria during the 9th, 10th, and 11th centuries.

A side room is even more copiously stocked, holding the enormous collection of ceramics unearthed during the Met's own excavations in Nishapur during the 1930s and 1940s. The Iranian town was a 10th-century center of Islamic creativity.

Calligraphy and ceramics Flanked by exquisite mosque lamps and perfume sprinklers, another gallery holds a series of leaves from the Koran, demonstrating the development of calligraphy from angular kufic scripts on parchment from 9th-century Egypt to the final refinement of cursive scripts achieved by the oblique cutting of the pen nib in 13th-century Iraq. In the same room stands a 14th-century prayer niche (Mihrab), each of its tiny ceramic tiles individually fired to maximize the glaze and heighten the floral decoration. Since it showed the direction of Mecca, the Mihrab was (and still is) the most important item in a Muslim place of worship.

Small is beautiful Many exquisite examples of 14th-century miniature painting, used in text illustration and characterized by pure and harmonious colors and a strong sense of patterning, are displayed in rotation. The influence of miniature artwork was carried over into Islamic carpet design in later years, and carpets and prayer rugs are the prize exhibits of subsequent galleries. Look especially for the lavish textiles—some decorated with gold leaf—with which Mogul emperors lined their tents. Finally, peer into the Nur ad-Din Room, a reassembled winter reception room typical of a wealthy Syrian home of the early 1700s: heavily decorated wood-paneled walls rise from a patterned marble floor and reach up to stained-glass windows and a sumptuous beamed ceiling.

A 14th-century gilded and enameled glass mosque lamp

145

New York

PRINTS AND PHOTOGRAPHS

As comprehensive and as engrossing as any other section of the museum, the Met's collections of prints and photography include everything from Rembrandt etchings to Russian constructivist photography. Every print-maker and shutter-clicker that you have ever heard of—and many less famil-iar—are represented.

(Continued from page 144)

Unlike the tightly packed rooms of the main museum, the newer Lila Acheson Wallace Wing holds spacious, light-soaked galleries and makes an excellent setting for the museum's 20th-century art.

Picasso's portrait of Gertrude Stein is a piece that stands out, though the bulk of the collection is provided by Americans—de Kooning, Lichtenstein, Pollock, and O'Keeffe among them. This is not the greatest collection of modern art in New York (for that, see the Museum of Modern Art, pages 158–160), but the side room holding selections from the Berggruen collection of Paul Klee drawings is a definite plus. So, too, is the rooftop sculpture garden, reached by elevator. Its views across Central Park tend to draw your attention away from the

Changing exhibitions of sculpture and sweeping views over Central Park are two good reasons to visit the Met's rooftop

sculpture, which is taken from the permanent stock in the museum and exhibited on a rotating basis.

The Michael C. Rockefeller Wing, named after the col-lector who disappeared (presumed drowned) on a trip to Papua New Guinea in 1961, houses the art of Africa, Oceania, and the Americas. Of a large, wide-ranging, and constantly intriguing assemblage, items from the Asmat tribe of Irian Jaya (the region of Indonesia adjoining Papua New Guinea) are perhaps the most absorbing.

The **Greek and Roman art** collections include Cypriot, Greek, and Roman sculpture, painted Greek vases, Roman portrait busts, one of the few surviving Etruscan chariots, and some remarkable wall paintings from a villa at Boscoreale, buried by the AD 79 eruption of Mt. Vesuvius. Another engaging piece is the diminutive *Seated Harp Player*, a marble Cycladic sculpture.

Since the early 1970s, the museum has developed its **Asian Art** holdings into one of the world's best. The collection of early Chinese art includes major Buddhist sculptures, ceramics and jade.

(Continued on page 148)

> *Bequeathed by a millionaire banker who allegedly spent his youth roaming Europe tracking down masterpieces and telegramming his father for the money to buy his discoveries, the Robert Lehman Collection provides a relaxing interlude from the museum's more popular galleries.*

The Lehman Collection's more important paintings, chiefly 14th- and 15th-century Italian works, are all on display on the second floor in reassembled period rooms from the Lehman house at West 54th Street. The various other paintings vie for attention with the temporary exhibitions of drawings at first-floor level, including work by Dürer and Rembrandt.

Botticelli Modest in size but immense in its importance, the highlight of the collection is perhaps Botticelli's *Annunciation*, revealing the achievements of late 15th-century Florentine art in the use of perspective. The painting sets a row of classical pillars between a resonant Virgin and the Archangel Gabriel. God's message arrives as light through a doorway, the rays cutting a diagonal path, splitting the painting's horizontal and vertical lines and linking the two figures.

Venetian painters The Bellini family is represented with a Madonna and Child by Jacopo Bellini and an early work by his more famous son, Giovanni, placed at around 1460 and depicting the Madonna and Child in intense poses before an eerily still landscape. From a few years later, another Venetian, Jacometto Veneziano, contributes two portraits: *Alvise Contarini* and *Nun of San Secondo*, intriguing works prefiguring the Venetian portrait style that came to prominence during the 1500s.

Giovanni da Paolo Among a strong complement of Sienese works, da Paolo's *Expulsion from Paradise* stands out, not least for its lively use of color. The painting shows God soaring above an intensely vibrant constellation, pointing a finger at a barren Earth—the destination for a spindly Adam and Eve who are being shooed out of Eden by a nervous angel.

Another interesting Sienese contribution in the Lehman pavilion is the painting, *Temptation of Saint Anthony Abbot*, credited to the Osservanza Master.

FRENCH WORKS
The collection's 19th-century French paintings are less inspired despite bearing famous names: Monet's unusually airy *Landscape near Zaandam* is worth a look, as are *Promenade among the Olive Trees* (above) by Matisse, and Cézanne's *House behind the Trees on the Road to Tholonet* and *Girl Bathing*.

147

Jacopo Bellini's Madonna and Child

EATING AND DRINKING AT THE MET

A thorough exploration of the Met calls for great stamina, and even if you have consumed a hearty breakfast before arriving, you will be in need of farther nourishment well before it is time to leave.

On the museum's first floor, near the entrance to the Michael C. Rockefeller Wing, a spacious atrium holds a self-service cafeteria, with a choice of hot and cold dishes at reasonable prices, and a slightly more expensive waiter-service restaurant.

If you are only pretending to visit the museum—or its size simply becomes too much to bear—you could while away the day over a glass or two of something deliciously tempting at the atrium's bar.

Figures and figurative art: visitors and exhibits at the Metropolitan Museum of Art

(Continued from page 146)

Astor Court, a re-creation of a Ming-era scholar's garden in Soochow, is a centre for traditional garden architecture, built by craftsmen from that city.

The Japanese collections span thousands of years but their heaviest holdings are undoubtedly the wonderful screen paintings of the Edo period, when years of peace and stability enabled great blossoming of artistic talent: Ogata Korin's *Waves* is just one eye-catching example.

The Met has a couple of offbeat departments that—though not designed for the purpose—might well come as a godsend if you have young minds to keep occupied.

The Musical Instruments galleries house 4,000 weird, wonderful, and sometimes priceless tune-making devices. Among the displays, look for the remarkably unattractive legs of the world's oldest existing piano—dated 1720 and a product of the workshops of Bartolommeo Cristofori—and a Stradivari violin made in 1691 which has been restored to its original appearance.

Strange instruments are plentiful, such as the 19th-century Indian mayuri, a kind of bowed sitar in the shape of a peacock, and a Native American shaman rattle, its carved animal emblem intended to symbolize the transfer of magical power from the spirits to the shaman.

Though it gets comparatively scant attention from the public, the Met's Arms and Armor collection is among the best of its kind to be found. Close study of the massed rows of suits of armor, from the 15th century onwards, reveals the high level of artistic flair and craftsmanship that went into the creation of battle apparel.

In temporary exhibitions, the **Costume Institute** displays selected parts of its enormous wardrobe of 60,000 items—from every corner of the world—of clothing and accessories, spanning everything from 19th-century Parisian ballgowns and Mary Quant mini-skirts to Korean bridal gowns and African tribal wear, not forgetting items from the United States itself.

▶ ▶ ▶ Midtown Manhattan *IFCD2*

Midtown Manhattan is the New York of popular imagination: a place where battalions of power-dressed office-workers march along packed sidewalks to the sounds of wailing police sirens and bumper-to-bumper traffic, as street vendors dispense hot dogs and pretzels in the shadows of the striking high-rise architecture.

In reality, such scenes unfold only between 42nd and 59th streets, an area with many highlights, most of which are detailed elsewhere in this book and explored by the walks on page 150. To New Yorkers, Midtown is usually the section bounded on the north by 59th Street and on the south by 34th Street. The Midtown map on page 151, however, extends the area south to 14th Street.

Where Broadway crosses 14th Street, busy **Union Square▶** was ringed by elegant homes and became the center of the city's theater district in the late 1800s. By the early decades of the 20th century, the social life had moved north, and Union Square had become a left-wing rallying point. In 1927, police hoisted machine guns onto nearby rooftops during a demonstration. Three years later, a 35,000-strong protest against unemployment ended in fierce pitched battles between police and protesters.

Now, Union Square is home to two new art deco subway entrances and the **Farmers' Market**, where fruit, cheeses, vegetables, and homemade bread are sold from stalls on Wednesdays, Fridays, and Saturdays.

Just east along 14th Street, the offices of Consolidated Edison—the firm responsible for providing New York's power supply—fill a building notable at night for its illuminated facade and clock tower and by day for its **Energy Museum▶** (tel: 460-6244; *Open* Tue to Sat 9–5. *Admission free*), which records the triumph of Thomas Edison in electrifying the city. Audiovisual displays explain the vine-like entwinements of pipes and cables beneath a typical New York street.

(*Continued on page 152*)

The Venetian-style Metropolitan Life Insurance tower, once the world's tallest building, dominates the Midtown skyline near Madison Square Park

149

THE ARMORY SHOW
The 69th Regiment Armory, on Lexington Avenue between 25th and 26th streets, is not the only National Guard barracks to be modeled on a medieval fortress, but it is the only one to have staged the legendary Armory Show of 1913, the first exhibition of modern European art in a country then still obsessed with traditional landscapes and portraiture. The work of Marcel Duchamp and others shocked critics and public alike and the Armory Show's effect on American art was profound. A small plaque on the Armory's facade notes the historic event.

Midtown Manhattan landmarks

Beginning at the Empire State Building and finishing at the United Nations complex, this walk passes seven decades' worth of landmark New York architecture.

After visiting the **Empire State Building** (pages 100–102), continue north along Fifth Avenue to the **New York Public Library** (page 168), its entrance set back from the street and guarded by sculptured lions. Behind the library is the restored **Bryant Park**, landscaped in 1934. Walk east along 42nd Street to Grand Central Terminal (pages 166–167) and the **Philip Morris Headquarters**, on Park Avenue, a modern building with a gallery holding exhibits from the Whitney Museum of American Art.

Farther east on 42nd Street, pass through the cast bronze doors of the 1923 **Bowery Savings Bank** (now the Home Savings Bank of America) to see the lavish Romanesque interior. Close by, note the stunning art deco bas-reliefs by Edward Trumbull on the exterior of the **Chanin Building**. Ahead are the unmistakable **Chrysler Building** (page 89) and **Daily News Building** (page 95), while turning north on First Avenue reveals the **United Nations** complex (page 184).

Midtown churches and museums

Beginning and ending at Rockefeller Center, this walk includes several Midtown churches, the **Museum of Modern Art** (pages 158–160), and the **American Craft Museum** (page 62).

Facing **Rockefeller Center** (pages 173–174) across Fifth Avenue, the twin-spired **St. Patrick's Cathedral** was completed in 1878 in rich, carved Gothic form. Inside, the chapels and shrines glow with candlelight.

On East 50th Street, the art deco **Waldorf-Astoria Hotel** has accommodated royalty and every U.S. president since its opening in 1931. Inside, admire the art deco interior and the lobby stores that cater to every whim of the well-heeled traveler. Nearby, the slim octagonal brick tower of the **General Electric Building** is another art deco landmark. Byzantine-style **St. Bartholomew's Church** boasts a splendid triple-arched entrance portal and a mighty dome which adds to the interior's sense of airyness. Back on Fifth Avenue, a single corner tower gives **St. Thomas' Episcopal Church** a disjointed look, but don't miss the striking reredos inside. The architect, Bertram Goodhue, also designed St Bartholomew's and had a hand in several other noted Manhattan churches.

View of St. Patrick's Cathedral and the Olympic Tower

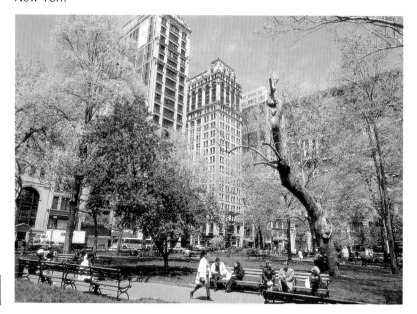

Madison Square Park: the square holds several tributes to notable figures in U.S. history

BASEBALL'S BIRTHPLACE
Baseball was introduced to the U.S. in 1842, but not until 1845 did a group of enthusiasts—who had been playing the game regularly at what later became Madison Square Park—band together to create a fixed set of rules and the first baseball club, the Knickerbocker Club. As baseball spread in popularity across the country, it was known at first as the "New York Game."

(Continued from page 149)

During the mid-1800s, the city's elite relocated from Greenwich Village into the new areas of **Gramercy Park▶** and **Murray Hill▶**. Favored by more prominent citizens were the brownstone town houses around **Gramercy Park▶▶**, between 20th and 21st streets, part of a residential area laid out in imitation of the grand squares of London. An aura of wealth and understated elegance still lures well-heeled but publicity-shy New Yorkers to Gramercy, where Gramercy Park is the city's only private park. Look through the park's high railings and you will see statues that include a likeness of actor Edwin Booth in the role of Hamlet. In 1888, Booth founded the influential **Players Club▶** in an 1845 building at 16 Gramercy Park South. Ornamental theatrical masks decorate its entrance, designed by Stanford White.

The codesigner of Central Park, Calvert Vaux, added the Ruskin-influenced Gothic features to the building next door, now the **National Arts Club** but earlier occupied by Samuel Tilden, governor of New York from 1874. Tilden's stand against corruption in New York public life did not alleviate his fears of public insurrection: he had a secret passageway set under the house to hasten his escape if angry mobs barricaded the entrance.

A few blocks east, at 235 East 20th Street, the **Police Academy Museum▶▶** (tel: 477-9753; *Open*: Mon to Fri 9–3, *Admission free*) has many intriguing exhibits, among them Al Capone's machine-gun and a stash of terrifying weaponry collected during amnesties.

Heading west, 20th Street holds the **Theodore Roosevelt Birthplace** (see page 182), while 23rd Street leads into **Madison Square Park**. On the south side of the park is the **Flatiron Building** (see page 106) and on the east side is the 1893 **Metropolitan Life Building**, which gained its tower in 1909.

When asked to provide a funeral for an actor in 1870, one Murray Hill church representative said "we don't accept actors but there's a little church around the corner that does." From then on, the 1849 Church of the Transfiguration, on 29th Street just off Fifth Avenue, became better known as the **Little Church Around the Corner**▶▶, serving New York thespians in spiritual need. A picturesque garden fronts the church, and the intimate interior holds several memorials to actors.

Moving north, McKim, Mead & White's monumental 1913 **Post Office**▶, on Eighth Avenue at 33rd Street, fills an entire block and is accessed by an impossibly long flight of steps. Directly across Eighth Avenue is the mighty complex of **Madison Square Garden**▶, one of the city's major venues for sports, concerts, and large-scale shows and exhibitions.

Follow 34th Street into the **Garment District**, the powerhouse of the city's fashion industry. Ten blocks farther (north and east), Broadway crosses Seventh Avenue at **Times Square**▶▶, an area benefiting enormously from 1990s neighborhood improvement initiatives. The **Times Square Visitors Center** (1560 Broadway, between 46th and 47th Streets; tel: 768-1560; *Open* daily 8–8), is the departure point for Friday's **free walking tour** of the area.

Cheek-by-jowl Midtown skyscrapers—with a view!

153

It was an Irishman, Thomas Dongan, who gave his name to the charter of 1686 that created New York's modern system of administration. As governor of a British colony, however, Dongan probably never expected that in years to come his countrymen would flock to New York to free themselves of British oppression and take a controlling grip on New York life.

THE UNWELCOME IRISH
Most of the large numbers of penniless Irish that arrived in the city during the 1800s were forced to occupy the worst areas, and some turned to petty crime in order to make a living. In so doing, they incurred the wrath of many long-established New Yorkers. Some turned against Irish immigrants as a whole. The auctioneer and one-time city mayor Philip Hone wrote of New York's Irish population: "they increase our taxes, eat our bread and encumber our streets, and not one in twenty is competent to keep himself."

St. Patrick's Day (March 17) sees the city's biggest street parade, along Fifth Avenue

Under British rule, Protestant and Catholic Irish were established in professional life in New York, but—mindful of British treatment of the Irish at home—both groups embraced the American Revolution and saw their chance to build a truly democratic, self-governing society.

Fall and rise The potato famines brought tens of thousands of Irish into New York during the 1800s. They arrived on the "Irish berths": cramped, airless sections of ships where disease was rife, and once ashore, the penniless Irish—faced with growing anti-Catholic feeling—were forced to occupy crowded rooms, often in atrocious conditions.

By 1860, Irish Catholics made up a quarter of the city's population and were the backbone of the police force, fire-fighting teams, and building trades. Irish organizational skills created powerful unions and paved the way for Irish domination of New York's entire administrative machine from the 1870s to the 1940s.

Church and tavern One symbol of the Irish Catholic ascendancy in New York was the building of St. Patrick's Cathedral in 1878. But while the church was important in Irish immigrant life, so too was the tavern. A first stop for new arrivals, taverns were informal clearinghouses for jobs. Some served free lunches to Irish workmen.

Irish-Americans are still strongly represented in New York public office. New York's last outpost of authentic Irish culture is Bainbridge, in the Bronx. First settled in the 1840s by Irishmen who saw its enticing greenery while working on the Harlem Railroad, Bainbridge's bars are the genuine article, without an ornamental leprechaun or bottle of green beer in sight.

▶ **Museum for African Art** 113A3

Broadway between Houston and Prince streets (tel: 966-1313)
Open: Tue to Fri 10:30–5:30, Sat and Sun 12–6
Subway: N, R; 6 Prince Street or Spring Street

Arts and crafts from sub-Saharan Africa form the core of the temporary exhibitions staged in this highly respected museum, one of the U.S.'s major spaces for African art, along with the Smithsonian Institution. Far from being static displays, the shows frequently take provocative directions.

▶ **Museum of American Financial History** 104B2

Broadway at Bowling Green (tel: 908-4519)
Open: Mon to Fri 11:30–2:30
Subway: 4; Bowling Green

This one-room collection need not detain you long, but it is an appropriate stop when touring the Financial

*Woven hangings at the
Museum of American
Folk Art—a showcase for
the talents of craftspeople
from all over the Americas*

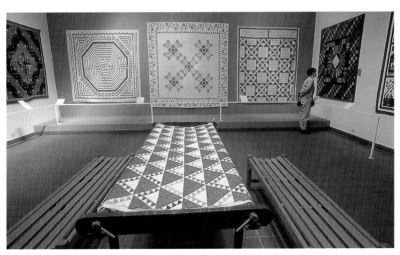

District. Inside the former Standard Oil Building, once presided over by multimillionaire John D. Rockefeller, the changing exhibitions explore diverse historical avenues in the U.S. economy.

▶▶ **Museum of American Folk Art** 151D1

Lincoln Square (tel: 595-9533)
Open: Tue to Sun 11:30–7:30. Admission free
Subway: 1; 66th Street

From toys and weather vanes to carved walking sticks and gravestone rubbings, the collections of the Museum of American Folk Art are drawn from the output of artists and craftspeople—many of them revered figures within their own communities—from all over the Americas. Be it Mexican wooden animal figures or Navajo blankets, the work on display is frequently of an exceptionally high standard and decorated with symbolic detail that only becomes apparent with close inspection.

In a city that falls over itself to honor the art of Europe, these exhibitions of indigenous American culture—a mix of permanently shown items and various temporary shows—are very welcome.

THE NEWSEUM
This museum fills 72,000 square feet of space with temporary inter-active exhibits on news-gathering, reporting, and photo-journalism. Accompanying the exhibits (as diverse as documentary studies of Tibetan culture to the role of the media in U.S. politics), are regular talks and lively discussions on media-related issues. (580 Madison Avenue, junction with 57th Street; tel: 317-7503; *Open* Mon to Sat 10–5:30; for recorded events info, tel: 317-7596).

The Museum of the City of New York, whose dignified grand entrance on Fifth Avenue is the gateway to a mixed collection charting aspects of the Big Apple through the ages

THE NEW YORK ACADEMY OF MEDICINE
A short walk from the Museum of the City of New York is the New York Academy of Medicine (2 East 103rd Street; tel: 822-7200), which occupies a 1926 building raised with Byzantine, Italian, and Romanesque features. Inside, the academy's library is open to the public. One reason to drop in might be to view the collection of 4,000 cookbooks (many of them rare), donated by a physician who believed that the key to good health was a nutritious diet. *Open* Mon to Fri 9–5.

SPECIAL EVENTS
The Museum of the City of New York organizes numerous special events, including puppet shows for children and classical concerts and lectures for adults. During the spring and fall, the museum also runs four-hour guided walking tours through different sections of the city. For details on any or all of these events, tel: 534-1672.

► **Museum of the City of New York**　　　*IBCA3*
Fifth Avenue at 103rd Street (tel: 534-1672)
Open: Wed to Sat 10–5, Sun 1–5
Subway: 6; 96th Street

Chronicling the rise and rise of one of the world's most diverse and colorful cities is no easy task, and while the Museum of the City of New York has its share of interesting bits and pieces from the early years of the great metropolis, it struggles to bring them together with any cohesion. Many of the museum's exhibits seem lost in the spacious innards of this neo-Georgian building.

The devoted history buff will find plenty here to mull over, however. Chronologically, things begin on the third floor with staid dioramas of Native American life in the years leading up to European discovery. Far more intriguing are the earliest maps of the New York area and drawings and paintings from the mid-1600s, thought to be the earliest depictions of what was then the Dutch trading post of Nieuw Amsterdam.

Six undistinguished period interiors give a very general impression of the furnishings—from simple Dutch tables to ornate English colonial cabinets—that stood in New York drawing rooms from the 17th to the early 20th century. Close by, several cases hold a glittering array of New York-made silver tea caddies, tankards, and cutlery that graced the kitchens of the city's most illustrious residents from the late 1700s.

A few figureheads and many model ships and boats are the principal pieces in a forgettable room intended to document the city's growth into a major seaport. Take care, though, to look at the paintings—such as Alonzo Chappel's simple but expressive *Bowery on a Rainy Day*, painted in 1849, and another that shows ice-skaters in Central Park during 1865—that hang on nearby walls and do more to evoke the New York of their period than many of the more valuable exhibits around them.

The museum enjoys its finest moment on the fourth floor, where a glorious collection of toys (some dating to the mid-1700s) includes a room filled by elaborate three- and four-story dollhouses. The dolls, too, are as impressive as the houses and include a specimen of almost every type produced in the U.S. from the late 18th to the mid-19th centuries. The oldest doll is a French-made import dating from 1724.

The Rockefeller Rooms on the museum's sixth floor comprise the master bedroom and dressing room from the mansion purchased in 1884 by John D. Rockefeller at West 54th Street—a site which is now consumed by the garden of the Museum of Modern Art. A wealth of intricately carved woodwork with mother-of-pearl inlays inspired by English designer Charles Eastlake, the rooms were the height of fashion in Victorian New York. What is not on view here is the mansion's wonderful Moorish room, which is now to be found in the Brooklyn Museum (see page 79).

Temporary exhibitions fill the first-floor rooms, while the museum's basement is occupied by poorly arranged memorabilia from New York's earliest fire-fighters. The centerpiece is a well-maintained hose-carriage of 1865, but smaller and more revealing pieces fill the surrounding display cases. Among the helmets, lamps, model fire-appliances, and press clippings detailing New York's most famous fires and the men who put them out, look for the fire-fighters' ear trumpet—a device intended to improve communication in blazing buildings. When plugged at one end, it also served as a beer-drinking vessel and a handy weapon for when the "fire laddies" (as they were known) gathered for an evening in a tavern.

EL MUSEO DEL BARRIO
A few strides across 104th Street from the Museum of the City of New York, El Museo del Barrio (tel: 831-7272; *Open* Wed to Sun 11–5) is very much a product of its East Harlem environment, evolving from a local school classroom into a museum devoted to the cultures of Latin America, particularly that of Puerto Rico. The small permanent collection of pre-Columbian objects is regularly eclipsed by temporary exhibitions that span paintings, sculpture, video, and more, reflecting diverse aspects of Latin American life, past and present.

157

Times change: one of the museum's dioramas shows what New York's East River waterfront looked like in the 1850s

THE MOMA BUILDING
In 1939, MoMA acquired not only its current home but also what would, on completion, be one of the first international-style buildings in the U.S. Architects Philip Goodwin and Edward Durrell Stone interrupted West 53rd Street's row of brownstones with a facade of marble, tile, and glass. The very term "international style" had been coined at a MoMA exhibition in 1932 by Philip Johnson, who was later to oversee several additions to the building, most notably the Sculpture Garden.

Van Gogh's Starry Night

▶▶▶ Museum of Modern Art   151C2

53rd Street between Fifth and Sixth avenues (tel: 708-9480)
Open: Sat to Tue, Thu 10:30–6, Fri 10:30–8:30
Subway: E, F; Fifth Avenue

Nowhere in the world will you find a museum so well stocked, so aptly designed to illustrate the principal movements and trends, and showing so many of the major works of the past 150 years of artistic achievement.

Paintings and sculpture form the core of the museum's permanent stock, but there are also excellent collections of photography, drawings, prints, and illustrated books, a section on architecture and design and an encyclopedic film and video archive.

It may seem hard to imagine today, but when MoMA (as it is known) staged its first exhibition in 1929, the artists it featured—Cézanne, Gauguin, Seurat, and van Gogh— were not represented in any other New York museum. The otherwise all-encompassing Metropolitan Museum of Art was just one that considered such names to be too much of a risk. Nonetheless, 47,000 people visited the MoMA exhibition in a single month.

A decade later, MoMA acquired its present site (a gift of the Rockefeller family) and through the energy of its young director, Alfred H. Barr, Jr., and the benevolence of a host of millionaire benefactors, it steadily became the world's primary repository for modern art's most influential works, acquiring a prestige all of its own.

The museum itself is a stimulating place, with escalators linking the multilevel galleries and natural light in abundance, enabling visitors to enjoy its contents without suffering exhaustion or eye strain. The painting and sculpture galleries are arranged broadly in chronological sequence across the second and third floors, starting with a room of post-impressionists richly hung with canvases by Cézanne,

Toulouse-Lautrec, Seurat, and notable others. It is van Gogh's mighty *Starry Night*, however, that stands out, arguably the museum's most celebrated possession.

Given a corner of its own outside the post-impressionist galleries, Monet's *Water Lilies*, painted in 1920, is a remarkable study of the subtleties of light and shadow on water and on land, the ripples of color appearing to undulate before your eyes.

The next sequence of galleries picks out some of the seminal works of cubism—pioneering pieces like Picasso's *Three Women* and Braque's *Man With a Guitar*, which can be contrasted with offerings from the genre's other leading proponents, such as Gris and Léger.

Moving on, you will pass prime examples of expressionism and futurism, before entering a room dominated by Mondrian's colorful geometric grids—the New York-influenced *Broadway Boogie-Woogie* being prominent.

In a later gallery, you will find the pick of MoMA's extensive Matisse holdings (where *Dance* holds center stage). Beyond it, a single room is devoted to Klee paintings and drawings. Finally, you will reach an entire wall

THE SCULPTURE GARDEN
Directly opposite the lobby, and a great place to pass an hour on a sunny afternoon after viewing the interior exhibits, is MoMA's Abby Aldrich Rockefeller Sculpture Garden, filled with an excellent and diverse collection of sculpture. Highlights include Henry Moore's *Family Group*, Picasso's *She Goat*—and Rodin's striking *Memorial to Balzac*, a towering bronze that was rejected by its Parisian commissioning committee in the 1890s.

159

covered by works by Picasso. Dating from the 1930s, some of these arresting images show the impact on Picasso of Europe's slide into war. They include the hauntingly grim *Charnel House*.

A wealth of works by Miró—who had tremendous influence on New York artists in the 1940s—dominates the surrealist rooms, though it is the arguably less accomplished pieces by Dali (*The Persistence of Memory*) and Magritte (*The False Mirror*) that provide instantly familiar, if no less surreal, images.

Also on the second floor are temporary photographic exhibitions, drawn from a permanent stock that ranges from Cartier-Bresson to Diane Arbus.

The third floor is detailed on page 160. Taking the escalator to the fourth floor, you will pass beneath an aluminum-bodied Pinin Farina sports car and a 1945 Bell helicopter as you enter the architecture and design exhibitions. These feature architectural models and drawings from Frank Lloyd Wright, Le Corbusier and others. The permanent collection covers everything from Tiffany lamps to state-of-the-art Italian saucepans.

Inside the MoMA building—New York's earliest piece of architecture in the international style and a fitting home for some of the most famous paintings and sculptures of the 20th century. Clever design, using plenty of natural light and with space to stand back and relax, allows unhurried appreciation of the exhibits

The Museum of Modern Art's third floor holds some of the most influential works in modern American art: from seminal abstract expressionist canvases to mixed-media experiments.

TEMPORARY EXHIBITIONS AT MOMA
It hardly need be said that a museum of MoMA's standing has no trouble in attracting temporary exhibitions of international repute. This is great news for art-loving New Yorkers, but not so good for visitors who may have traveled to New York only to find that their favorite artworks have been stored away to make room for a blockbusting temporary show. To avoid this, contact the museum (tel: 708–9480) or the New York Convention & Visitors' Bureau (tel: 800/NYC–VISIT or 484-1222) before making travel plans.

European influences Many items here reveal the influence of Europeans such as Matisse and Miró, both of whom have later works displayed here. An entire room, in fact, is devoted to Matisse's wonderful *The Swimming Pool*, a large-scale paper mural that originally decorated a wall of his home.

The New York School The most important galleries chart the development of abstract expressionism and the New York School (see pages 128–129). The influence of the surrealists' concern with the subconscious and universal myths is seen in early works by Jackson Pollock (*The She-Wolf* and *Gothic*) and Willem de Kooning.

Similar themes are explored by the so-called gesture artists, among them Franz Kline and Robert Motherwell, who used large blocks of black and white. By contrast, the color field artists such as Barnett Newman and Mark Rothko used shimmering bands of luminous color to evoke emotional states.

Move through the chronologically arranged galleries and the abstract expressionist canvases grow steadily bigger and bolder, reaching their apotheosis in Pollock's monumental *One*.

Recent works After the draining and intense works of the abstract expressionists, it comes almost as light relief to enter the galleries of contemporary art, including Jasper Johns' *Target with Four Faces*; Robert Rauschenberg's study in mutating forms, *Bed*; the comic-strip paintings of Lichtenstein; and Claes Oldenburg's enjoyable oversized papier-mâché models of America's favorite foods.

Painting from one of the Museum of Modern Art's excellent third-floor galleries

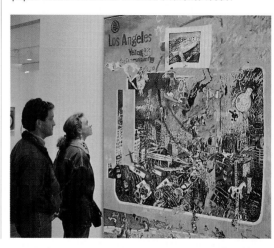

▶▶ **Museum of Television and Radio**   *151C2*

25 West 52nd Street (tel: 621-6800 for daily events, 621-6600 for general information)
Open: Tue to Sun 12–6, theaters until 8 on Thu and 9 on Fri
Subway: E, F; Fifth Avenue

For serious media students and couch-potatoes alike, the Museum of Television and Radio is the stuff that dreams are made of. For almost anyone else, a visit will be a highly entertaining experience—and a perfect antidote to the more run-of-the-mill forms of sightseeing. More than 40,000 American television and radio broadcasts from the 1920s to the present are stored here, all of them available to the public at little more than a flick of a switch. Several thousand new programs are added every year.

A number of small screening rooms show selections from the museum's televisual archive (schedules are available from the lobby, or tel: 621–6800), while the headphones in the cozy radio listening room can be switched to one of five separate channels, each exploring a different area of broadcasting history—from a landmark Metropolitan Opera broadcast to a wartime comedy

A T.V. addict's dream come true—the Museum of Television and Radio offers your own choice of viewing at one of around 100 individual video consoles

show. More demanding visitors can riffle through the library's computerized cataloguing system and make their own selections from the entire collection. Not only listing television program titles, the database also carries details of the personnel involved in each production—a handy resource if you have forgotten who played Thing in *The Addams Family* or want to discover the real-life identity of your favorite *Batman* villain.

Once you have made your choice (restricted to two hours of viewing time), leave the library for the viewing room, where your selection will be made ready almost immediately (though there may be a three-day wait for particularly obscure items) for private watching at a video console.

Commercials—of which the museum has 10,000 in stock— feature among the daily screenings, Also on view are television shows from other countries, from heavy-weight documentaries to vintage episodes of *Monty Python's Flying Circus.*

THE MUSEUM BUILDING
You may be too eager to renew your acquaintance-ship with Perry Mason or Lou Grant to notice, but the building that houses the Museum of Television and Radio is a curious blend of classical and modern styles from architects Philip Johnson and John Burgee. With its 16-story limestone-clad tower, the structure has been described as the world's first vertical museum.

The advent of art deco coincided with the skyscraper boom that gripped New York during the 1920s, and the new decorative style was seen as the natural accompaniment to the world's most adventurous architecture. Walk around the city and you will find the art deco influence everywhere, from world-famous buildings to fine details of decoration.

ZONING LAWS
In 1915, when the Financial District's Equitable Building rose straight up in the air, robbing adjacent streets and buildings of their sunlight and breezes, the city authorities responded with the U.S.'s first set of building regulations—or zoning laws. The Zoning Law of 1916 divided New York into commercial and residential plots; high-rise buildings had to recede as they rose above the street. This greatly affected the architecture of the city for the next 50 years.

Art deco sculpture in Rockefeller Center

Art deco first emerged in 1925 at the Paris Exposition Internationale des Arts Décoratifs, a show intended to highlight the fine skills of French craftsmen at a time when the German Bauhaus was revolutionizing the world of the decorative arts.

New York was already aware of the art deco style, however, as the Metropolitan Museum of Art had amassed a collection of the finest European work and inadvertently aided the creation of an American art deco style dubbed "moderne." With the emphasis on overall effect rather than individual craftsmanship, art moderne was tailor-made to the needs of the American market. Mass-produced terra-cotta and bronze friezes covered with geometric designs and floral patterns, available by mail order, soon began appearing on buildings all over the country.

This new style began to affect interiors, too. Some of New York's finest art deco entranceways and lobbies, such as the Film Center Building (see page 102), are the work of the talented architect Ely Jacques Kahn.

One of the city's earliest art deco buildings was the **New York Telephone Company** (also called the Barclay-

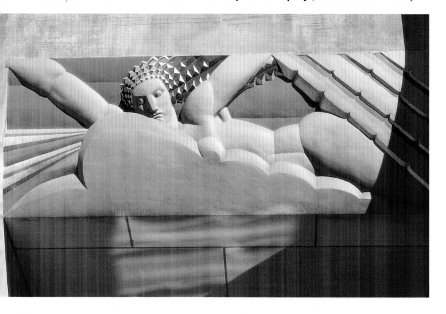

Vesey Building, 140 West Street), described by one critic as "Mayan art deco." To get around the constraints imposed by the narrow street, designer Ralph Walker gave the building a series of pedestrian arcades decorated by a cast-concrete frieze cluttered with depictions of bunches of grapes, rabbits, elephant heads, bells, and much more.

Chrysler Building The single most spectacular and lastingly impressive art deco building in New York, the Chrysler Building (see page 89) was one of the first buildings to use exposed metal. It rises in a series of cutbacks with each new level marked by a different type of decoration—a brickwork frieze of car wheels or immense winged radiator caps. Its most distinctive feature, however, is the seven-story dome, which takes the form of a tiered arch with triangular dormer windows encased in chrome steel.

Empire State Building The Chrysler Building's status as the world's tallest building was soon eclipsed by the Empire State Building. Built purely for commercial renting, every inch of the Empire State Building was critical, and consequently the decoration was kept to an absolute minimum—allowing the structure to emerge as a fine specimen of skyscraper art deco at its most restrained and dignified.

Chanin Building Sculptor René Chambellan's facade for the Chanin Building (122 East 42nd Street), which draws the eye away from the nearby Chrysler Building, depicts swooping birds on a bronze band that winds around the building below a terra-cotta frieze of geometric animal forms. Inside the bronze- and marble-dominated lobby, farther bas-reliefs depict the "City of Opportunity"—or New York as it was for the building's owner, Irwin Chanin, a property developer who struck it lucky.

Raymond Hood Destined to become one of the leading architects of Rockefeller Center, Hood used black brick and gold terra-cotta to emphasize the upright form of the **American Radiator Building** (40th Street between Fifth and Sixth avenues). He later developed this idea with vertical columns of windows and spandrels for the **Daily News Building** (see page 95).

In the former **McGraw-Hill Building** (42nd Street between Eighth and Ninth avenues), with its green and gold terra-cotta, Hood continued his move towards the international style, but the building's lobby retains its impressive art deco interior.

With **Rockefeller Center** (pages 173–174), New York art deco had its greatest day. Raymond Hood had a large hand in the center's showpiece R.C.A. (now G.E.) Building. At the foot of the building, Paul Manship's golden *Prometheus* sculpture is the first of scores of art-deco items decorating the entire complex. Meanwhile, Rockefeller Center's **Radio City Music Hall** takes art-deco into another dimension. Its vast and extraordinarily theatrical interior is intended to be just as much a part of the evening's entertainment as the performers appearing on the stage.

The Chrysler Building, resplendent with eagle gargoyles

164

OUR LADY OF LOURDES CHURCH
Sections from the Gothic-influenced 1865 home of the National Academy of Design (which stood at 23rd Street and Park Avenue South), together with pieces of other buildings, were incorporated into the very bizarre facade of Harlem's Our Lady of Lourdes Church, on 142nd Street between Amsterdam and Convent avenues.

▶ National Academy of Design ⠀⠀⠀⠀187C1
Fifth Avenue at 89th Street (tel: 369-4880)
Open: Wed and Thu 12–5, Fri 12–6, Sat and Sun 12–5
Subway: 4, 6, 86th Street
Founded in 1825 by a group of accomplished artists, architects, sculptors, and engravers—including the artist/inventor Samuel Morse and the creator of Washington Square's handsome town houses, Ithiel Town—the National Academy of Design was established with the intention of becoming an artist-run school and museum. Selections from the permanent collections are shown in the upstairs galleries, but one piece you can be certain of seeing is the sculptured figure of Diana by Anna Hyatt Huntington, which pivots at the foot of an elegant staircase leading up to the Academy's galleries.

▶▶ National Museum of the ⠀⠀⠀⠀104A2
⠀⠀⠀⠀⠀⠀⠀American Indian
U.S. Custom House, Bowling Green (tel: 668-6624)
Open: daily 10–5. Admission free
Subway: 4; Bowling Green
For many years, the U.S.'s major collection of Native American artifacts was housed in the Audubon Terrace complex in Harlem, where its geographical distance from most of the city's major museums caused it to be neglected by the majority of New York visitors.

In the early 1990s, the majority of the collection was moved to the Smithsonian Institution in Washington, D.C., but the city retained enough to fill several floors of the architecturally distinguished U.S. Custom House (see page 190).

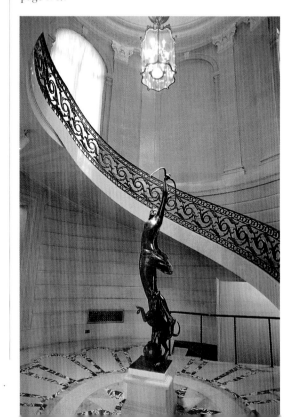

A focal point at the National Academy of Design: Anna Hyatt Huntington's statue of Diana

As the rights of indigenous peoples are slowly being recognized by the powers that be, some items formerly in the museum's possession have been returned to the Native American tribes that produced or owned them. Nonetheless, the museum retains a colossal collection. Baskets, quilts, and pottery drawn from the many and extremely diverse cultures of North, South, and Central America are among some of the objects displayed. Other fascinating exhibits include some of the infamous treaties that paved the way for European colonization of Native American lands.

Early equipment on display at the Fire Museum

▶ New York City Fire Museum   IFCB2
278 Spring Street, SoHo (tel: 691-1303)
Open: Tue to Sun 10–4, Thu 10–9
Subway: 6; Spring Street
It may not be at the top of every New York visitor's itinerary, but the New York City Fire Museum fills three floors with the buckets, hand-pumps, and horse-drawn fire-appliances that saved the city from near-total destruction on more than one occasion. The antiquated carriages are exhibited alongside an impressive collection of hose-pipe nozzles, ladders, axes, tools, fire alarms, extinguishers, uniforms, and helmets.

▶▶ New-York Historical Society   IFCF2
Central Park West at 77th Street (tel: 873-3400)
Open: Wed to Sun 12–5
Subway: 1; 79th Street
Predating all the city's other museums, the New-York Historical Society was founded in 1804 (its hyphen dates from then) and was uniquely placed to receive the bequests of wealthy New Yorkers. The society has a substantial collection of works, from early portraits of significant New Yorkers to important canvases from the country's first home-grown art movement, the Hudson River School. The society also holds a sizeable Louis Comfort Tiffany collection and all extant watercolors in Audubon's *Birds of America* series.

THE GREAT FIRE OF 1835
The temperature in New York City on December 16 and 17, 1835, was well below freezing, but that did not stop one of the most destructive fires in the city's history from razing 674 buildings on a 13-acre site in and around the Financial District.
    Crowds arriving from the notorious Five Points slums looted the burned-out buildings and helped the flames engulf many more. With insurance companies enduring the same losses as many of their clients, many of the city's banks and financial institutions were unable to reopen and as a result New York endured galloping inflation for the next two years.

In the 1930s, passengers boarding the New York–Chicago early evening service from Grand Central Terminal were, quite literally, given the red carpet treatment. Few who trod the venerated carpet, however, would have thought that just a few decades later the terminal—an architectural tour de force that was dubbed "the gateway to the nation"—would be threatened by cheap air travel and by the rising value of the land on which it stands.

GRAND CENTRAL STATION?

Many people, including lifelong New Yorkers, often erroneously refer to Grand Central Terminal as "Grand Central Station." In fact, as trains can only begin or end their journeys there, "terminal" is the correct word to use. The confusion was not helped by an enormously popular radio drama series which began in 1937, set in New York and titled *Grand Central Station*.

In the 1960s, the Penn Central Railroad (the company in charge of Grand Central Terminal and previously responsible for the demolition of the original and much-loved Pennsylvania Station) proposed to raise a 55-story office tower above the terminal, but these shortsighted plans were luckily thwarted by public pressure, and the building eventually became an official New York City landmark (in 1978), gaining lasting protection.

Grand Central Terminal was completed in 1913 on a plot of land that then marked New York's northern edge. The land had been purchased by transportation magnate Cornelius Vanderbilt (see page 37), who had gained control of all rail routes into New York. After a 10-year period of construction, the station was unveiled to wide public acclaim both as an engineering marvel and as a delight to the eye. It remains one of the world's great railroad stations: an enduring symbol of the city.

Architectural elegance The terminal's construction was a joint effort. The engineer William Wilgus and the architects Reed & Stem devised the innovative split-level design that allowed for a smooth flow of traffic—either train, subway, or pedestrian—into and through the station; Whitney Warren focused on creating the terminal's graceful Beaux-Arts style. Since it was the arrival and departure point for millions of travelers (by 1939, as many people were passing through Grand Central Terminal each year as lived in the entire U.S.), stores, hotels, restaurants, and offices opened up in close proximity to the terminal, making the site a prime Midtown Manhattan plot. Many side entrances and maze-like tunnels link the terminal with its surrounding streets and adjacent office towers such as the former Pan Am Building (now the Metropolitan Life Building, see panel on page 183), just to the north. On the terminal's southern facade you will first see Jules-Félix Coutan's 48-foot-high figures of Mercury, Hercules, and Minerva, draping themselves around an American eagle. There is also a bronze likeness of Cornelius Vanderbilt—seemingly counting potential railway passengers as they pass.

The interior Once inside, head for the terminal's second story and look upward. On the 150-foot-high vaulted ceiling, French artist Paul Helleu used 2,500 electric lights to replicate the zodiacal constellations. The design is based on a medieval manuscript illustration, and the debate continues as to whether or not Helleu was aware that medieval illustrators commonly depicted the heavens reversed—giving God's view.

Look toward the northwest corner to spot the dark rectangle that provides an intentional reminder of the grime that had darkened the ceiling over 50 years and was removed (using a specially prepared organic soap) during the late 1990s. Another ceiling oddity is the segment that was cut out to accommodate the tip of a nuclear missile, part of a military display staged here in the 1960s.

The grandeur of the **Main Concourse** is often obliterated by the half a million commuters each day. Nonetheless, try to find a slow moment to descend the marble flight of steps onto its floor and seek out a quiet corner to contemplate its 75-foot windows, its claim to be the world's largest room (it is 375 feet long and 120 feet wide), and the once serious suggestion to develop the concourse into three separate bowling alleys.

A pearl of a restaurant The terminal's balconies and lower levels hold a number of stores and restaurants, and a branch of the **New York Transit Museum** (tel: 878-0106; *Open* Mon to Fri 8–8, Sat 10–4. *Admission free*; see page 76). The restaurants include that of basketball superstar Michael Jordan and the **Oyster Bar**. The latter is known not only for its diverse selection of oysters and other seafood, but also for its low ceiling, covered by tan-colored Guastavino tiles. In a vaulted area just outside the restaurant, a whisper into one corner can be distinctly heard in the other corner. However, the restaurant proper has no such magical acoustics, being one of the noisiest in the city. Still, there are few better places in the city for listening in on the lunchtime gossip of New York executives, although the suggestions that fortunes have been made on the Stock Exchange by inspired eavesdropping are apocryphal at best.

The huge scale and grand style of the Main Concourse (said to be the largest room in the world) affirm Grand Central Terminal as a monument to the halcyon days of train travel

GUIDED TOURS
For a more detailed exploration of Grand Central Terminal, join the guided tour run by the Municipal Art Society (tel: 935-3960), which begins at 12:30 PM each Wednesday from the Information desk on the Main Concourse.

The imposing main entrance to the New York Public Library on Fifth Avenue

►►► New York Public Library   151B2

Fifth Avenue and 42nd Street (tel: 869-8089)
Open: Mon 10–6, Tue and Wed 11–7:30, Thu to Sat 10–6
Hours for special exhibitions vary
Guided tours: Mon to Sat 11 and 2
Subway: B, D, F; 42nd Street

You cannot borrow a book at this branch, the Central Branch of the New York Public Library (the 3 million or so tomes are for reference only), but you can explore one of the city's finest expressions of architecture, a Beaux-Arts temple created by the legendary firm of Carrère & Hastings and opened in 1911. Its terrace and elegant steps are decorated by twin sculptured lions, fountains fronting statues symbolizing Truth and Beauty, and bronze flag-pole bases cast at Long Island. The triple-arched portico entrance leads into the exquisitely proportioned Astor Hall—named after John Jacob Astor, founder of the nation's first library (one of the three that combined to create the present library's original holdings). The information desk here dispenses floor plans and marks the starting point for the free tours.

Immediately ahead, Gottesman Hall stages some of the library's temporary exhibitions. Turn left for the De Witt Wallace Periodical Room at the end of the corridor. Publisher De Witt Wallace spent many hours in this room scanning periodicals and abridging their contents for his fledgling venture, the *Reader's Digest*. His profits financed the room's 1983 restoration: its brass lamps and walnut chairs were joined by Richard Haas' murals of *New York* magazine and newspaper offices. Climb the marble stairs to the fourth floor, noting the original lamps and the lions'-head drinking fountains on the way to the vaulted McGraw Rotunda, decorated in 1940 by Edward Laning's murals. This marks the entrance to the public catalog room, complete with computer databases. Beyond the catalog room lie the main reading rooms—the most beautiful part of the library. Across the corridor is the Edna Barnes Salomon Room, which displays the library's paintings and selections from its printed treasures.

THE LIBRARY'S TREASURES

The New York Public Library has an extraordinary stock of rare and valuable books and prints, some of which may be on display. These include a Gutenberg bible; a 1493 folio edition of a Christopher Columbus letter describing his American discoveries; the first full folio edition of Shakespeare, from 1623; the 1640 Bay Psalm Book (the first English book published in America); a handwritten copy of George Washington's farewell address; and an early draft of Jefferson's Declaration of Independence.

▶▶▶ Pierpont Morgan Library   151B2

36th Street at Madison Avenue (tel: 685-0610)
Open: Tue to Fri 10–5, Sat 10:30–6
Subway: 6, 33rd Street

Born into wealth and educated in Europe, J. Pierpont Morgan had become one of New York's leading financiers by the closing decades of the 19th century. But, unlike his nouveau riche contemporaries, he trusted his own taste and judgment as he lavished a fortune on European cultural treasures, acquiring rare books, manuscripts, and drawings that by 1890 had become one of the finest private collections in the country.

In 1902, Morgan commissioned the leading architect of the day, Charles F. McKim, to create the Renaissance-style Pierpont Morgan Library. The Palladian porch that marks the library's original entrance on 36th Street merits a special look, though the present entrance is on the Madison Avenue side and enters a 1928 annex on the site of Morgan's son's brownstone residence.

The temporary exhibitions could hold your attention for hours, but look first around the library itself, starting at the West Room, where Morgan's study is preserved as it was on the financier's death in 1913. Once described as "the most beautiful room in America," the study is lined by Italian Renaissance paintings and dominated by Morgan's immense wooden desk.

From the study, free-standing columns of green-veined marble mark the way to the imposing rotunda and the East Room. In a nutshell, the East Room is one of the plushest reading rooms you are ever likely to see. Three tiers of bookcases, fashioned from bronze and inlaid walnut, rise to a ceiling covered by colorful murals of artists and scholars (and signs of the zodiac), while above the fireplace hangs a 16th-century Flemish tapestry.

Sumptuous though it certainly is, the East Room is never overbearing, and you could spend a long time here, poring over priceless letters and manuscripts.

THE PIERPONT MORGAN COLLECTIONS
The following are just a few items from the vast collections of the Pierpont Morgan Library: three Gutenberg bibles; a Shakespeare first folio; an autographed manuscript of Milton's *Paradise Lost;* manuscripts and early editions of Rudyard Kipling, Oscar Wilde, and Gertrude Stein bearing the authors' doodles and changes; musical scores from the hands of Bach, Brahms, and Beethoven; etchings and prints by Rembrandt, Rubens, and Degas; and a huge selection of pre-19th century paintings and *objets d'art.*

169

Space for the studious: the reading room of New York Public Library. Choose your tome from the library's many miles of shelving and consult it here

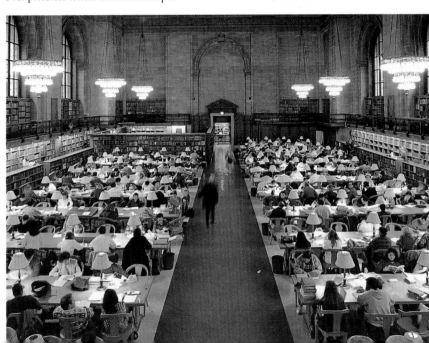

STREET NUMBERING IN QUEENS

Anyone who has spent several days mastering the Manhattan street-numbering system will find the streets of Queens even more of a challenge. Part of the price for Queens affiliating itself to New York City in 1898 was the loss of its named streets for a numbering system imposed by the civic powers in Manhattan.

The system, it seems, is still having teething troubles. Usually streets and avenues run at right angles to each other, and an address such as 10–35 14th Street will be located on 14th Street near the junction with 10th Avenue. This is not always the case, however, and most problems occur when neighborhoods run into each other at something other than a perfect right angle. If you get lost, the solution might be to ask a local. But then again it might not: Queens residents are often as baffled by the system as everyone else.

The interior of Bowne House, the oldest building in Queens

▶ Queens

48C3

An almighty slab of land holding 2 million people and spreading across 119 square miles of western Long Island, Queens is completely incomprehensible unless you think of it as its residents do: a network of separate and self-contained communities, many of which are ethnically distinct and have nothing except geography in common with the neighborhood that happens to be found right next door.

While much of Queens fits the sprawling-house-and-two-car-garage image of the typical American big-city bedroom community, many portions reflect New York's immigration patterns. Large communities of Koreans, Indians, and Japanese nestle beside other areas long dominated by Greeks or Puerto Ricans.

Even though you probably failed to realize it at the time, if your arrival point in New York was **La Guardia** or **JFK** airport, you have already had a brief taste of Queens. Both airports are sited in the borough. Planes into JFK swoop above the 20 square miles of marshlands comprising the **Jamaica Bay Wildlife Refuge** (tel: 718/318-4340), a place much more interesting to migrating birdlife than to all but the most ornithologically obsessed humans.

You will need a car and a very detailed map to explore all of Queens but the main points of interest—which will also give a broad flavor of the borough's ethnic mix—are slotted into a handful of key areas, easily reached by public transportation from Manhattan.

Take the subway from Manhattan to **Flushing**, for example, and you will soon see why the route is unofficially dubbed the "Orient Express." What Flushing's Japanese supermarkets, Korean restaurants, and Chinese dim sum houses do not suggest, however, are the town's 17th-century links with Quakers.

At 137–16 Main Street, a Friends' Meeting House has stood since 1694 and, on a nearby corner, the 1661 **Bowne House▶▶** (tel: 718/359-0528; *Open* Tue, Sat and Sun 2:30–4:30), one of the city's oldest houses has further connections with the Society of Friends. The house's owner, John Bowne, was exiled for defying a ban on Quaker meetings. However, he persuaded the Dutch West India Company —who did not want to risk losing any would-be settlers—to insist that all religious groups would be tolerated in the new colony: a step toward the religious freedoms later enshrined in the Constitution.

The house holds some of Bowne's colonial furnishings, plus those of his descendants, who lived here until the 1940s. Tours of the small modest dwelling wend their way into the kitchen, where the clandestine Quaker meetings took place. A short walk from the Bowne House, the 1774 **Kingsland Homestead** (tel: 718/939-0647; *Open* Tue, Sat, and Sun 2:30–4:30) is an example of the Dutch and English architectural mix typical of Long Island farmhouses of the period.

A mile east of Flushing, **Flushing Meadows-Corona Park▶▶** (tel: 718/699-8283) began life as a swamp and garbage dump, but by 1939 it was drawing millions to the World's Fair, which symbolized New York's emergence from the Depression. A few relics from the 1939–1940 fair remain, as do many more from a second World's Fair held here in 1964–1965. Among these are Philip Johnson's **New**

The Unisphere in Flushing Meadows-Corona Park—a relic of the 1964–1965 World's Fair

York State Pavilion Building—the architectural highlight of the 1960s show, but these days in a much crumbled condition that reflects poorly on the construction ideas of the time—and the 140-foot high Unisphere, intended to represent the Earth and its satellites.

Another 1960s survivor, the New York Hall of Science▶ (tel: 718/699-0005; *Open* Jul and Aug, Mon 9:30–2; Tue and Sun 9:30–5; rest of the year Mon to Wed 9:30–2, Thu to Sun 9:30–5. *Admission free* Thu and Fri, Sep to Jun), is these days crammed with hands-on computer exhibits illustrating the rudiments of science to children.

More modest-sized memorabilia from both world fairs is displayed inside the Queens Museum of Art▶ (tel: 718/592-9700; *Open* Wed to Fri 10–5; Sat and Sun 12–5) housed in a structure that dates from the 1939–1940 fair. What fascinates most here is the Panorama: a scale model of New York City that covers 18,000 square feet and includes every building in the city.

The park is also home to the Queens Wildlife Center (tel: 718/271-1500; *Open* winter Mon to Fri 10–5, rest of year daily 10–4:30) a small zoo of North American animals, as well as the National Tennis Center—where the annual U.S. Open is held.

THE UNITED NATIONS IN QUEENS
The City Building, which houses the Queens Museum in Flushing Meadows-Corona Park, was used by the United Nations as the organization awaited the completion of its site in Manhattan. Among the motions carried here was the one in 1947 that paved the way for the creation of the state of Israel.

A busy street in Queens

Roosevelt Avenue, in the Jackson Heights neighborhood of Queens, is known for its bakeries and restaurants

Baseball fans and devotees of the Fab Four might care to note that **Shea Stadium**, home of the New York Mets and the venue of a now legendary concert by the Beatles in 1965, stands in the northerly section of the park.

On the borough's northern side, facing the Bronx across the East River, **Astoria▶** is one of the world's largest Greek communities. Lining 31st Street and Ditmars Boulevard are countless Greek bakeries, cafés, and restaurants, and even the graffiti on the walls is in Greek.

Not remotely Greek, though, is Astoria's **American Museum of the Moving Image▶** (36–11 35th Avenue; tel: 718/784-0077; *Open* Tue to Fri 12–5, Sat and Sun 11–6), which occupies part of a working studio complex. During the 1920s, Paramount shot silent movies here with legendary figures such as Rudolph Valentino, Clara Bow, Gloria Swanson, and the Marx Brothers, before they relocated to Hollywood.

The museum shows cinematic classics and carries temporary exhibitions on various aspects of movie history. On permanent display is a large but only mildly interesting collection of props, costumes, filmmaking equipment, fan magazines, and vintage movie posters.

Heading back toward Manhattan is heavily industrialized **Long Island City**, which is forging a reputation as an artists' enclave. In its early days, the area of Long Island City known as Hunters Point was linked by ferry to Manhattan, encouraging business development here. Some of the old warehouses and factories have been turned into artists' studios.

In Long Island City is the riverfront **Isamu Noguchi Garden Museum▶▶** (32–37 Vernon Boulevard; tel: 718/204-7088; *Open* Wed to Fri 10–5, Sat and Sun 11–6) devoted to the acclaimed sculptor. The son of a Japanese poet who emigrated to California, Noguchi's unconventional ideas were at first derided, but his extraordinary imagination and tremendous creativity is clear enough throughout the 12 galleries that chart his long career (Noguchi died in 1988, aged 84), and in the gardens that hold still more of his enigmatic creations.

STEINWAY
Just east of Astoria is the town of Steinway, created by William Steinway when he moved his piano factory here—partly to escape the power of unions—from Manhattan in 1872. The factory still stands at 19th Avenue and 39th Street. Steinway himself, meanwhile, moved into a stonework Italianate villa overlooking the East River at 18–33 East 41st Street. The slightly spooky villa has certainly seen better days, as has the now entirely unsalubrious neighborhood that surrounds it.

▶▶ Rockefeller Center *151C2*

47th–52nd streets between Fifth and Sixth avenues
Subway: B, D, F, 1; 47th Street—Rockefeller Center

This is the world's largest commercial and entertainment complex, through which a quarter of a million people pass each day. The project changed the face of American urban planning from the 1940s on.

The center is named after multimillionaire John D. Rockefeller, Jr., who was approached in 1928 by the Metropolitan Opera with a view to his developing a down-at-the-heel Midtown site, on land rented from Columbia University, as a new Opera House. Rockefeller agreed, but the Wall Street crash led to the shelving of the plans and left him with 11 acres of land and a very large debt. In the country's first major pooled architectural project, Rockefeller commissioned several firms to erect 14 buildings on the site with the proviso that the structures form an aesthetically unified entity and that the complex should be a pleasing environment for working, eating, shopping, and relaxing.

As a result, the art deco buildings themselves take a secondary role to the numerous cafés, restaurants, underground walkways, and shopping plazas secreted in and around them, allowing a flow of light and easy movement of people. This became the blueprint for city-center renewal initiatives throughout the country.

To reach the heart of the complex, enter from Fifth Avenue along the short Channel Gardens to the sunken **Plaza▶**, which holds an open-air restaurant and a wintertime ice rink and is presided over by Paul Manship's 1934 figure of *Prometheus*.

Rising above Prometheus' head, the 70-story **G.E. Building** (better known by its original title, the R.C.A.

173

Summertime brings bright umbrellas and a holiday atmosphere to the sunken plaza amid the office buildings of Rockefeller Center

Building) is the heart of Rockefeller Center. Enter the lobby and note the murals by José Maria Sert—replacements for those of Diego Rivera, who refused to appease the anticommunist Rockefellers by removing a handsome likeness of Lenin.

Take the elevator to the **Rainbow Room** restaurant complex, in whose **Rainbow Promenade Bar**, for the price of a drink, you can gaze out over Manhattan. Return to the lobby to collect a free map from the information desk, essential as you begin weaving deeper into Rockefeller Center's impressive labyrinth.

Simple wanderings will reveal much of interest, but one place not to be missed is **Radio City Music Hall**. The hall's 1932 gala opening was attended by the likes of Charlie Chaplin and Clark Gable, and it instantly became one of the great American entertainment palaces. More recently a favored location for live concerts and the occasional film premiere, the 6,000-seat hall is still an art deco delight and can be seen on guided tours (tel: 632-4041; *Open* Mon to Fri 10–5, Sun 11–5). Less glamorous but still in the realms of the showbiz world, the offices and studios of **N.B.C. Television** (tel: 623-4041; can be viewed on hour-long guided tours, daily 9–5).

174

GETTING TO ROOSEVELT ISLAND
A road bridge crosses from Queens to Roosevelt Island, but to reach the island from Manhattan, use either the subway (lines B or Q) or (much the best choice) the cable car, which makes a 3-minute jaunt over the East River from a terminal at Second Avenue and 60th Street.

The Roosevelt Island cable car

▶ Roosevelt Island   187A2

Once given over to 27 hospitals that kept the incurably sick and insane (and the simply scandalous, such as Mae West) segregated from the rest of New York society, Roosevelt Island is today regarded as one of the most successful attempts at integrated mixed-income housing. Would-be residents now have to wait several years to get an apartment in the area. Besides near-total absence of crime, Roosevelt Island dwellers also enjoy automobile-free streets and a sight of the Midtown Manhattan skyline unsurpassed in few other locations in the city. For visitors, the peacefulness and the views (and the cable car that crosses to the island) are the only attractions, though the ruins of the old hospitals add a distinctly eerie note.

▶▶▶ SoHo   113A2

Named for being SOuth of HOuston Street (and bordered also by Canal, Lafayette, and Sullivan streets), SoHo is dominated by large cast-iron factory buildings put up in the mid-19th century.

The determined efforts of conservationists saved the area and its unique buildings from demolition following a decade of neglect and after 10 years of colonization by up-and-coming artists who were attracted by spacious rooms lit by immense windows, SoHo entered a period of swift gentrification. Its loft-style apartments found favor with the city's rich and trendy—and with the art dealers who made the area internationally synonymous with contemporary art. With chic clothing stores and fashionable restaurants alongside scores of art galleries, SoHo is now transformed—but it is the dozens of remaining cast-iron buildings that shape its character.

Among the earliest examples of the cast-iron form, the **Haughwout Building** (488–492 Broadway) dates from 1857, rising in four tiers of arched windows and Corinthian columns. On Greene Street, numbers 28–30 and 72–76 show the artistry that later ironwork facades acquired, while the **Little Singer Building** (561–563 Broadway) suggests the next great architectural step: replacing cast-iron floor supports with steel—the basis of the modern skyscraper.

Art lovers not exhausted by SoHo's many galleries can also visit the **New Museum of Contemporary Art** (Broadway between Houston and Prince streets; tel: 219-1355; *Open* Wed to Fri, Sun 12–6, Sat 12–8;) often showcasing newer artists who are making an impact; the **Alternative Museum** (Broadway between Houston and Prince streets; tel: 966-4444; *Open* Tue to Sat 11–6) has exhibits of art often inspired by social and political issues; and the **SoHo Guggenheim** (Broadway at Prince Street; tel: 423-3500; *Open* Wed to Fri, Sun 11–6, Sat 11–8), uses a warehouse remodeled by top architect Arata Isozaki for changing displays drawn from the main Guggenheim Museum (see pages 122–124) and from quality traveling exhibitions.

Creativity is all around you in Soho

175

RICHARD HAAS' SOHO MURAL
Since 1973, at the junction of SoHo's Prince and Greene streets, the neighborhood's bringing together of contemporary art and historic cast-iron buildings has been celebrated in a witty trompe l'oeil by Richard Haas, which cleverly confuses the actual features of the buildings with painted representations.

You do not have to be an art dealer or critic to find New York's thousand or more art galleries fascinating. Many galleries are clustered close together in Chelsea and SoHo—very much the international nerve center of contemporary art—though others are well established on the Upper East Side and around 57th Street. Take the time to see the nonprofit galleries, too, showcasing the work considered too risky by the commercial galleries.

THE GALLERY GUIDE

The *New York Times*, the *Village Voice*, and many special art publications carry art gallery listings, but the most comprehensive details are provided by *Gallery Guide*. A publication listing over 700 galleries and providing maps to help locate them, the *Gallery Guide* is published monthly and distributed free in galleries and a few selected bookstores. The thinner *New York Art World* has similar information. Many Chelsea galleries stock the free bimonthly gallery listing, *Chelsea Art*.

Upper East Side galleries The epitome of Upper East Side elegance and sophistication, the Paris-founded **Wildenstein & Co.** (19 East 64th Street; tel: 879-0500) specializes in French impressionist works, but its holdings extend from contemporary paintings to antique objets d'art.

The diverse stocks of **Hirschl & Adler** are displayed in three separate galleries at the same address (21 East 70th Street; tel: 535-8810). The main gallery carries a broad selection of 18th- and 19th-century European pieces; Hirschl & Adler Folk gallery holds American folk art, from paintings to crafts, while **Hirschl & Adler Modern** gallery specializes in American and European names from the mid-1950s.

Focusing on modern American painters, the **Gagosian Gallery** (Madison Avenue between 76th and 77th streets; tel: 744-2313) provides a museum-like exhibition space for lesser-known works of art by well-known names, such as Jackson Pollock, Willem de Kooning, Andy Warhol, and Cy Twombly.

The pocket-sized **Kahan Gallery** (922 Madison Avenue; tel: 861-3682) has a well-justified reputation for 19th- and 20th-century European works, Picasso among them. New York's oldest gallery, **Knoedler & Company,** helped develop many major private collections from the 1920s and continues to display works of note. **Margo Feiden** (699 Madison Avenue; tel: 677-5330) is lined by Al Hirschfeld's theatrical caricatures.

57th Street area galleries If you only have the opportunity to visit one 57th Street gallery, make it **Pace** (32 East 57th Street; tel: 431-3292). This deserves its place among the world's leading galleries for a stock that includes virtually every European and American name of major significance from the last 30 years.

Extremely influential in the emergence of pop art and noted for the high quality of its purchases, the **Janis Gallery** (110 West 57th Street; tel: 586-0110) has been a fixture on the New York art scene for four decades and continues to present established and new names in stimulating exhibitions.

Abstract expressionists turn up in many New York galleries but one of the better places to find works by the color field artists is the **André Emmerich Gallery** (41 East 57th Street; tel: 752-0124).

Some intriguing historical documents from the turbulent 1930s can be seen alongside fine examples of German expressionism at **Galerie St. Etienne** (24 West 57th Street; tel: 245-6734).

First established in SoHo, the **Mary Boone Gallery** (745 Fifth Avenue; tel: 752-2929) is what serious art watchers ignore at their peril. Through the 1980s Mary Boone helped launch some of the brightest new names in American art, such as David Salle and Julian Schnabel.

Around the corner on Fifth Avenue is the **Edwynn Houk Gallery** (745 Fifth Avenue; tel: 750-7070), exhibiting works by some of the world's best photographers; and the **Tibor De Nagy Gallery** (724 Fifth Avenue; tel: 262-5050) is a champion of emerging contemporary artists since the 1950s.

NONPROFIT GALLERIES
SoHo has several non-profit galleries. **Artists' Space** (38 Greene Street, tel: 226-3970) is a launch pad for artists working with installations and video; a SoHo branch of DIA (141 Wooster Street; (tel: 473-8072; see page 84) holds Walter de Maria's **New York Earth Room** with its 14 tons of soil; and the **Visual Arts Gallery** (137 Wooster Street; tel: 598-8221) exhibits student works.

SoHo galleries In the early 1960s, the **Leo Castelli Gallery** (2nd floor, 420 West Broadway; tel: 431-5160) brought artists such as Andy Warhol, Roy Lichtenstein, Jasper Johns, and Frank Stella to wide attention. The gallery has a graphic arts annex, which can be found at 578 Broadway. Another SoHo pacesetter is the **Molly Solomon Gallery** (172 Mercer Street; tel: 941-5777).

Minimalist and conceptual art is the stock-in-trade of the highly regarded **John Weber Gallery** (142 Greene Street; tel: 629-5711), closely linked with figures such as Sol Lewitt and regularly showcasing new artists.

Chelsea galleries Many galleries occupy former ware-houses on the western edge of Chelsea. They include **Cheim & Read** (521 West 23rd Street; tel: 242-7727), **Feigen** (535 West 20th Street; tel: 929-0500), and **Metro Pictures** (519 West 24th Street; tel: 206-7100).

Over the past 20 years, numerous small galleries have opened in Chelsea, providing launch pads for many new names in the art world

South Street Seaport and the cargo ship Peking

▶ South Street Seaport   104B3

Eastern foot of Fulton Street (tel: 748-8600)
Open: Mon to Wed, Fri and Sun 10–6, Thu 10–8
Subway: 2, 3, 4; Fulton Street

A large collection of stores, seafood restaurants, bars, craft centers, and galleries make up the South Street Seaport district, which transformed an abandoned area beside the East River—the place where New York's 19th-century maritime trade flourished—into a history-themed pedestrian mall.

By day, however, most visitors come to Seaport itself to explore the vintage ships of the **South Street Seaport Museum** complex—which jump-started the area's gentrification some two decades ago—moored beside the South Street piers. The most interesting exhibit is the 1911 *Peking*, a four-masted cargo vessel that spent its glory days shifting nitrate from South America to the U.S. and made several roundings of Cape Horn.

Climb aboard and descend to a lower deck where a pictorial display recounts the ship's working life. Back on dry land is the **Museum Gallery**, which has a minor exhibition of maritime photos and ships-in-bottles and certificates and documents attesting to New York's historical place as one of the world's great seaports.

▶▶ Staten Island   48B1

A ride on the Staten Island Ferry (see the panel opposite) is reason enough to make the crossing from the Financial District to the hilly chunk of land wedged between New Jersey and Brooklyn, but Staten Island has much more than a ferry to call its own. Settled by Dutch and French farmers in 1661 and an important British base during the Revolutionary War, the island has evolved into leafy suburbia with a tranquil mood that makes it seem a million miles from the hurly-burly of the rest of New York City. It also has some surprising collections among its museums.

The ferry docks at St. George, the island's least enthralling community. Two miles west (take bus S40 from the ferry terminal), Sailors' Snug Harbor is a better

SOUTH STREET SEAPORT MUSEUM

SEPTEMBER 11,
MUSEUM ADMISSION

TICKET VALUE: $8.00

YSTEM IS MADE POSSIBLE BY A GENEROUS G

STROLL: WATER STREET
Water Street, between Wall Street and South Street Seaport, was New York's main riverside thoroughfare in the 19th century, lined by sailors' boarding houses, bars, and brothels.

first stop. Founded in the 1800s as an institution for "decrepit and worn-out sailors," it is now better known as **Snug Harbor Cultural Center**▶ (tel: 718/448-2500; *Open* daily dawn to dusk. *Admission free*). Restoration has kept a number of its imposing 19th-century buildings intact.

It is farther south that Staten Island's real treasures are to be found (take bus S74). Visiting in 1991, the Dalai Lama himself described as "accurate" the stone cottage on Lighthouse Hill intended to replicate a Tibetan mountain temple and provide an apt home for the **Jacques Marchais Center of Tibetan Art**▶▶▶ (tel: 718/987-3500; *Open* Apr to Nov, Wed to Sun 1–5), a wondrous stock of sculptured deities, ritual objects, incense burners, and many other items from the world's Buddhist cultures.

Now the largest private gathering of such material in the western world, the collection was inspired by the discovery in 1880 by the young Jacqueline Norman Klauber (who later renamed herself Jacques Marchais) of 12 Tibetan figurines that her great-grandfather had brought back from a voyage to India and stored in the family attic. This experience stimulated a lifelong fascination with

THE CONFERENCE HOUSE
Students of international summitry might consider making a trip to the Conference House (tel: 718/984-6046; *Open* mid-April to Nov, Fri and Sun 1–4). In September 1776, the stone-built house became the venue of the only peace talks attempted between the British forces and the American revolutionaries. The house served as a rat-poison factory before becoming a museum in 1926. The interior has period furniture and numerous items recording the revolutionary conflict, and the failed attempt to broker peace.

179

Buddhism and its sacraments, and no opportunity was missed to expand the collection.

Whether you are looking at the Buddhist Wheel of Life or musing over a yak butter burner, informative explanatory texts make sense of the exhibits, and illuminate their complex symbolism.

A mile south is the 100-acre **Richmondtown Historic Restoration**▶▶ (tel: 718/351-1611; *Open* Jul and Aug, Wed to Fri 10–5, Sat and Sun 1–5; rest of the year Wed to Sun 1–5), which shows the fruits of half a century of gathering and restoring buildings dating from the 17th to the 19th centuries and equipping them with (usually) the original occupants' possessions. Local history buffs, dressed in period costume and keen to pass on their knowledge, lead tours around the old homes. These buildings range from a sparsely furnished Dutch building which doubled as local church and schoolhouse to a general store packed with 1840s consumer goods—all providing insights into earlier ways of life.

Also within the complex, the Island Historical Museum presents a chronological record of Staten Island's growth, with many enjoyable exhibits from some of its early industries, which over the years have ranged from brewing to oyster harvesting.

The Staten Island Ferry terminal

THE STATEN ISLAND FERRY
The actual vessel is entirely ordinary, but the views from the Staten Island Ferry can be wonderful. The Statue of Liberty, Governor's Island, and the Verrazano-Narrows Bridge all appear as the skyscrapers of Lower Manhattan shrink into the distance and the green hills of Staten Island draw nearer. The ferry (pedestrians only) takes half an hour to make the 5-mile crossing, and the journey is free.

WILD STATEN ISLAND
The hilly, bucolic interior of Staten Island holds many acres of unspoiled land, parts of which can be explored on marked walking trails. The Greenbelt (tel: 718/667-2165) spans wetlands, woodlands, streams, rivers, and parks; organized weekend activities include horse-back-riding and guided nature hikes. The one-time mining of clay on Staten Island's southwest shore has helped create the 250-acre Clay Pit Ponds Preserve (tel: 718/967-1976), with pine woods and many man-made ponds that now provide wildlife habitats.

STATUE OF LIBERTY FACTS
Height: 151ft. 1in.
Weight: 450,000lbs.
Length of hand: 16ft. 5in.
Length of index finger: 8ft.
Length of nose: 4ft. 6in.
Thickness of waist: 35ft.
Best movie role: in Alfred Hitchcock's *Saboteur*.
Biggest fictional blunder: Liberty's torch is described as a sword in Franz Kafka's *America*.

If you have time to spare, visit the **Alice Austen House**▶ (tel: 718/816-4506; *Open* Thu to Sun 12–5), a bayside home on Staten Island's eastern edge, dating from 1710 and filled by some of the 8,000 photographs taken by the untrained Alice over a 50-year period to 1934. In 1951, *Life* magazine discovered and published some of her work. Her talents were soon recognized far afield, yet she spent her poverty-stricken old age in a public workhouse.

Another small and equally unexpected collection is the **Garibaldi Meucci Museum**▶ (tel: 718/442-1608 FREE; call for hours), where Giuseppe Garibaldi—one of the founders of unified Italy—spent two years in the 1850s in the home of American-Italian Antonio Meucci. Garibaldi's place in history is assured, but fate was unkinder to Meucci, an inventor who developed a proto-type telephone but failed to patent the idea. To reach both this and the Alice Austen House, take bus S51 from the ferry terminal.

▶▶ Statue of Liberty   48C2

There is no greater symbol of the nation and its promise of freedom and opportunity for all than the Statue of Liberty, which has held the flame of liberty above New York harbor since 1886. From Manhattan, a visit to the statue begins with a ferry ride from Battery Park Pier. Boats to the statue also stop at the excellent Ellis Island (see page 100).

At the statue, there are two options. If you have the time and energy, begin an assault on the 354 steps that lead up to the crown—but be warned that the staircase is narrow and that you can only climb as fast as the person in front (the ascent can take three hours). Alternatively, take the elevator to the pedestal level, from which the views are only marginally less impressive than those from the crown. On the way down, visit the museum recording the creation of the statue and the effect it had on newly arrived immigrants when seeing it for the first time. The Statue of Liberty Ferry (tel: 269-5755) from Battery Park runs daily 9–5, longer in summer.

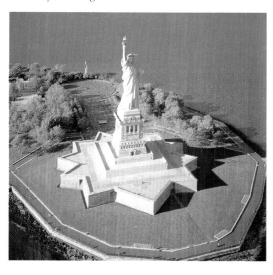

Liberty Island is in fact closer to New Jersey than to New York, but its statue is universally regarded as a funda-mental part of the city

Originally intended to stand in Egypt, partly funded by a French lottery, and at first regarded in the U.S. as a waste of money, the Statue of Liberty may be America's most famous landmark, but the story of its construction is much less straightforward than most people may realize.

Liberty in Egypt? A sculptor with a taste for monuments on the grand scale, Frenchman Frédéric Auguste Bartholdi visited Egypt and presented to the Egyptian sultan his plans for a gigantic figure of a robed female peasant holding a torch, to be sited at the entrance to the Suez canal.

The sultan rejected the scheme, but Bartholdi, on a trip to the U.S. in 1871, found the perfect spot for his torch-carrying lady at the entrance to New York's harbor, 4,000 miles from her original intended location.

French friendship The idea of a gift from France to the U.S. to mark the nations' shared belief in democracy had been around for some time, and Bartholdi's statue idea was taken on board by France's new Third Republic, busy modeling its constitution along U.S. lines.

As a sign of friendship, both governments agreed that the work would be shared, Bartholdi producing the statue while its pedestal was made in New York. In France, a popular lottery raised 250,000 francs toward the project, but in the U.S., the idea was greeted with apathy.

As *Liberty Enlightening the World* (as the statue is officially titled) took shape outside Bartholdi's Paris studio—being too large to fit inside—the pedestal had barely left the drawing board, and the American press was full of satirical cartoons and articles condemning its expense.

Raising the money After Congress rejected a bill allocating $100,000 to the work, and the mayor of New York vetoed a plan for the city to donate $50,000, newspaper publisher Joseph Pulitzer attacked the miserliness of the nation's rich, and appealed for contributions—no matter how small—from ordinary Americans.

Packed into 214 crates, the finished statue arrived in New York in June 1885. Two months later, Pulitzer announced that the goal of raising the necessary sum of $100,000 had been reached.

The statue was hoisted onto its pedestal in May, 1886 and unveiled in October. The response of the public, as Pulitzer's newspaper recorded, was "one long cheer."

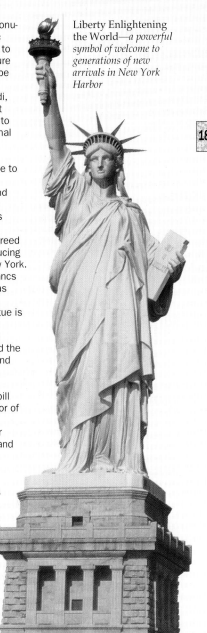

Liberty Enlightening the World—*a powerful symbol of welcome to generations of new arrivals in New York Harbor*

181

Stock Exchange 104B2

Broad Street near Wall Street (tel: 656-5168)
Open: Mon to Fri 9:15–4. Admission free
Subway: 4; Wall Street

Housed in a 1903 neoclassical building, the New York Stock Exchange might be expected to form the highlight of a tour around the Financial District. Unless you have a vested interest in the ups and downs of the Dow Jones average, however, the exchange's 37,000-square-foot dealing floor—populated by color-jacketed brokers, reporters, and pages—looks as uninteresting from behind the glass of the public viewing gallery than it does on T.V.

The exhibits on the exchange's history, and on share dealing in general, do nothing to lessen the sense of anticlimax. Nonetheless, if you want to view the spot where the crash of 1929 plunged the nation into the Great Depression, it is best to pick up your ticket, free and time-stamped for the half-hourly tours, from the entrance soon after 9 AM.

▶ **Theodore Roosevelt Birthplace** 151A2

20th Street between Broadway and Park Ave (tel: 260-1616)
Open: Wed to Sun 9–5
Subway: 6; 23rd Street

The nation's future 26th president, Theodore Roosevelt, entered the world in 1858 in a Midtown Manhattan brownstone, a building subsequently demolished but precisely reconstructed on its original site in 1923 to house a museum honoring the only president to have been a New York native.

The lower floor carries an absorbing exhibition on Roosevelt's life, from his childhood struggles with asthma and the tragedy of the deaths of his mother and his wife on the same day, to his entry into politics on a ticket of ending the corruption endemic in New York affairs and his rise to become the nation's youngest ever president in 1901, aged 42.

Upstairs, more than half the furnishings in the period rooms come from the original Roosevelt house. Best capturing the personality of Roosevelt himself is the room stuffed with hunting trophies and outdoor memorabilia.

▶ **TriBeCa** IFCB2

Subway: 1; Franklin Street

TriBeCa—the TRIangle BElow CAnal Street (bordered on the east by Broadway and continuing west to the Hudson River)—became the stamping ground of the artists who were priced out of their SoHo lofts (see page 175) as that district's property values soared throughout the 1970s.

Like SoHo, TriBeCa's old warehouses—formerly at the center of New York's dairy and poultry trade—offer apartments with ample space and natural light, making perfect studios. Also like SoHo, however, TriBeCa is increasingly taking the fancy of upscale residents in search of stylish Lower Manhattan living and sound property investment, so prices have risen here too.

Besides providing as good a picture of New York-style urban regeneration as you are likely to find, a walk through TriBeCa uncovers something of note at almost every turn. Art galleries, much less slick than their SoHo counterparts, occupy many of the former industrial

182

The Stock Exchange

A RADICAL EXORCISM AT THE STOCK EXCHANGE
The bulletproof glass screen that shields the trading floor of the Stock Exchange from the public gallery has been in place since 1967, the year when yippie (a twist on the term "hippie") Abbie Hoffman and friends tossed 300 one-dollar bills on to the trading floor. Traders went scurrying for the cash and one of Hoffman's co-activists described the incident as "exorcising the evil spirits of the Stock Exchange."

buildings. A notable example is the **Clocktower** at 108 Leonard Street. Dozens of pricey restaurants nourish fashionable faces while, at 37–41 Harrison Street, a primly restored row of early-1800s Federal-style town houses makes a wholly incongruous appearance.

Trump Tower   151C2

Fifth Avenue at 56th Street
Subway: E, F; Fifth Avenue

High-profile property tycoon Donald Trump was brave enough to put his name to this horrid glass tower—a monument to the booming economy of the early 1980s and the frenzied building that it financed. He also became one of the people actually to live in one of the 263 plush apartments that fill the tower's upper levels.

Although the facade is among the city's least inviting, it is worth stepping inside Trump Tower for some serious window-shopping. Serenaded by the tinkling of a five-story waterfall, you can explore a host of designer-name boutiques here—though the pink marble surfaces and the obsessively manicured shrubbery might have you running for the exit surprisingly quickly. Just next door at 727 Fifth Avenue are the classy baubles of **Tiffany & Co**, the renowned jewelry store.

THE FORMER PAN AM BUILDING

Bauhaus architect Walter Gropius was among the team that designed the Pan Am Building on Park Avenue, adjoining Grand Central Terminal. The largest commercial office building ever constructed, it is also possibly the only one so closely resembling an aircraft wing. Following the demise of Pan Am, the Metropolitan Life Insurance company purchased the building in 1992 and set about removing its much-photographed Pan Am logo. The building itself remains as familiar a sight as ever, though still blocking the view along Park Avenue.

183

STROLL: DUANE PARK

By day, the streets around TriBeCa's Duane Park provide fruitful territory for a stroll. Head northward along Hudson Street, and turn off to explore Harrison and Leonard Streets.

Inside or out, nothing is understated at Trump Tower

UN GROUNDS AND GARDENS

Besides its three main buildings, the 18-acre United Nations site also holds several sculptures, a small park and a rose garden. Two of the sculptures, Barbara Hepworth's bronze *Single Form* and Henry Moore's *Reclining Figure* commemorate Dag Hammerskjöld, Swedish UN General Secretary killed in a plane crash in 1961. More sculpture, each piece donated by a member state, lines the walk to and through the relaxing rose garden, where views reach across the East River to Queens and the southern tip of Roosevelt Island.

The General Assembly in session. The immense hall can accommodate delegations from up to 179 countries, and proceedings are conducted in six official languages

▶ United Nations 151C3

First Avenue between 42nd and 46th streets (tel: 963-7713)
Tours daily, every half hour 9:15–4:45
Subway: 4, 6, 7; 42nd Street—Grand Central

Given the problems blamed on its huge and infamously cumbersome bureaucracy, it might seem apt that the main building of the United Nations—the organization of world states formed in San Francisco in 1945 and operating on this plot since 1947—should be the entirely uninspiring Secretariat Building. This structure houses the U.N.'s 16,000 pen-pushers and rises for 39 marble-and-glass stories above the East River.

The U.N.'s public entrance is through the General Assembly Building. The lobby carries temporary exhibitions on international themes, and from here a stairway leads down to the souvenir store, post office (selling United Nations postage stamps, valid only on mail that is posted here), and also to a rather gloomy cafeteria.

To see any more of the U.N., other than the Delegates Dining Room (reservations essential, see Restaurants) and the grounds and gardens, you need to buy a ticket for a guided tour. Departing every 15 minutes or so from the lobby, the tours last around an hour and sweep through the various U.N. buildings, pausing on the way at displays on the work of the U.N. and at artworks donated by member states. None of these matches the emotional impact of the half-melted items culled from the ruins of Hiroshima and Nagasaki, which are also on display. Assuming no meetings are in session, the tour stops by the Security Council chamber—where the calmness imposed by the empty chairs and desks belies the fact that this is the only U.N. body with any teeth, able to impose economic sanctions and instigate military actions—and the General Assembly room, the very size of which suggests it can never be anything more than a debating chamber.

The gridlock that ensues whenever heads of state arrive to take their places at the United Nations now seems such an established part of New York life that it is easy to forget that the organization came within a whisker of opting for Philadelphia as its permanent home. What is more, present-day budget problems are causing the U.N. to reassess not only its expenditure but also its continued presence in the Big Apple.

The United Nations Charter was signed by represent-atives of 50 countries in San Francisco in April 1945, but the General Assembly held its first meeting in London in 1946, a year during which the scramble among several cities to become the organization's permanent base grew intense. San Francisco, Boston, and Philadelphia were in the running before New York's application to become the U.N.'s home was instigated by the city's most famous (some would say most infamous) planning department chief, Robert Moses, who promised that a successful bid "would make New York the center of the world."

185

Philadelphia or New York? Among those on the city's campaign committee was Nelson Rockefeller, of the Rockefeller banking dynasty, who was carving a political career for himself with the ambition of becoming presi-dent. Rockefeller persuaded U.N. officials to use New York as their base when sizing up the rival bids during 1946, but by December it seemed that Philadelphia would be chosen, and that city's authorities began preparing the future U.N. site. Meanwhile, property devel-oper William Zeckendorf had been buying land alongside New York's East River for residential use. Rockefeller made Zeckendorf an offer he could not refuse for the land, presented the site to the U.N. officials and won the bid—the land being paid for with an $8½ million grant from Rockefeller's father. The complex of buildings was completed in 1963, designed by an international team of architects led by William K. Harrison.

Considered by many to be New York's most boring building, the U.N. Secretariat towers above the East River and is home to the organization's huge administrative machine

Mixed feelings Although not all New Yorkers could see the wisdom of diverting their taxes into easing the U.N.'s arrival and providing incentives for its diplomats, the organization's presence took the city's prestige through the roof and injected millions into its economy.

Overstaffing and well-publicized expenses abuses caused streamlining to be ordered in 1992, and the U.N. Children's Fund and U.N. Development Program consid-ered leaving bases for rent-free accommodations elsewhere. Meanwhile, in a move certain to gain the favor of New Yorkers (and encourage their support in a forth-coming election), mayor Giuliani announced in 1997 that U.N. officials would no longer be able to claim diplomatic immunity when issued with parking tickets.

Gracie Mansion, official residence of the mayor of New York, echoes the opulent feel of the Upper East Side

MUSEUM MILE
The Upper East Side holds almost all of New York's finest museums on a stretch of Fifth Avenue that has become known as Museum Mile. From 79th Street going north, you will find the Metropolitan Museum of Art, the Guggenheim Museum, the Cooper-Hewitt Museum, the Jewish Museum, and the Museum of the City of New York. Just outside the officially defined mile are the Frick Collection on 70th Street, the Whitney Museum of American Art on Madison Avenue, and Museo del Barrio on 104th Street.

▶▶▶ Upper East Side   151D3

Manhattan is money-mad, but nowhere is the sheer pleasure of being incalculably wealthy so clearly evident as amid the mansions, high-rent apartment houses, and ultra-chic stores of the Upper East Side, synonymous for a century with the kind of lifestyle only a bottomless bank account can buy.

A vacant space until the creation of Central Park and Manhattan's steady northward population shift made it ripe for development, the Upper East Side's first homes were modest affairs alongside new elevated train lines that ran above Park Avenue, and the streets to its east, from the 1870s.

By the 1890s, the city's wealthiest people began eyeing the two-block corridor formed by Fifth and Madison avenues. The richest of the rich erected grand mansions in styles ranging from mock-Gothic to imitation Italian Renaissance along the former, while the merely very rich moved into the fine brownstone town houses constructed along the latter.

With a few exceptions, such as the 64-room former home of Andrew Carnegie (now the Cooper-Hewitt Museum) and that of Henry Clay Frick (site of the Frick Collection), the Fifth Avenue mansions were demolished during the 1920s to make way for the luxury apartment houses that stand here now, their windows giving priceless views over Central Park and their entrances guarded by white-gloved doormen.

Through the 1950s, the Madison Avenue brownstone buildings were steadily converted to stores and offices,

Art and elegance

Giving a taste of the Upper East Side's elegance and taking in several interesting but often overlooked buildings, this walk also includes a couple of important art collections.

Begin on 65th Street at **Temple Emanu-El**, a 1929 synagogue with space for 2,500 people. Its design incorporates Romanesque and

Temple Emanu-El

Byzantine features, a mixing of East and West.

Two blocks east and to the north is the **Seventh Regiment Armory** with a drill hall for shows and sales.

Ahead, on Park Avenue, is the **Asia Society** building (page 65), west of which stands **St. James' Episcopal Church** (1884), with its two tiers of stained-glass windows and impressive reredos.

Facing Fifth Avenue, the former mansion home of Henry Clay Frick holds the **Frick Collection**, mostly of European Old Masters (page 110). By contrast, four blocks north and to the east, the very best of modern American art is the specialty of the **Whitney Museum** (page 191).

and now fashionably groomed locals patronize the art galleries, antique stores, and designer clothing outlets of one of the nation's most exclusive—and expensive—commercial strips.

Strolling Madison Avenue dreamily window-shopping and eavesdropping on neighborhood banter is the perfect way to acclimatize yourself to Upper East Side life.

Additional reasons to come to this area are the so-called Museum Mile (see the panel), and Gracie Mansion—the official residence of New York City's mayors since 1942 (see page 111).

"He adored New York City. He idolized it out of all proportion." These lines from the opening of Woody Allen's **Manhattan** *could easily be applied to the director himself, whose films have regularly celebrated New York and its inhabitants—and done so more convincingly than perhaps any other film-maker.*

WOODY ALLEN VERSUS MIA FARROW
In the summer of 1992, New York was gripped by the acrimony between Allen and his long-time companion Mia Farrow, following her allegations of child abuse and the revelation that Allen had had an affair with Soon-Yi, Farrow's 21-year-old adopted daughter. In June 1993, Allen was found not guilty of abusing Dylan, the couple's 7-year-old adopted daughter. He subsequently married Soon-Yi.

In 1942, the six-year-old Allen Konigsberg rode the subway from Brooklyn with his father and emerged onto 42nd Street. He would later recall that he was "in love with Manhattan from the earliest memory."

Home to New York By the mid-1950s, Konigsberg had become Woody Allen and was working as a TV gag-writer in Los Angeles when (legend has it) he proposed by phone to his Brooklyn sweetheart because he needed someone to go with to see *Casablanca* on the weekend.

Meanwhile, Lenny Bruce and Mort Sahl had reshaped stand-up comedy and paved the way for the stage-shy Allen to progress swiftly from playing tiny Greenwich Village nightspots to becoming a major figure on the national comedy circuit.

A television appearance by Allen led to his (by then ex-) wife mounting an unsuccessful $1 million lawsuit for defamation of character, but Allen's anti-wife jokes did not prevent him from remarrying, this time to an Upper East Sider through whom he claimed to have assumed "citizenship of Manhattan."

WOODY ALLEN'S
MANHATTAN

The films Allen's first film to give New York a starring role was *Annie Hall* (1977). In it Allen cast himself as a stand-up comic and writer devoted to New York but hopelessly ill at ease in Los Angeles.

Two years later, from its George Gershwin soundtrack to its monochrome photography, *Manhattan* was as much an ode to New York as it was a tale of the "emotional alienation of the Manhattan intelligentsia." Key scenes unfolded in Central Park, the Whitney Museum of American Art, and the New York Aquarium.

Perhaps Allen's best 1980s New York film, however, was *Hannah and Her Sisters* (1986), with its complex relationships and dilemmas of upper-middle-class Manhattan intellectuals. *Annie Hall* star Diane Keaton returned for the genial *Manhattan Murder Mystery* (1993) and Allen's prodigious output continued with New York-set films such as *Bullets Over Broadway* (1994), the musical *Everyone Says I Love You* (1997), and found a return to monochrome in *Celebrity* (1998).

▶▶ The Upper West Side 151D1

Between the modernism of Lincoln Center and the turn-of-the-century mood of the Columbia University campus, the largely residential Upper West Side has remained solidly bourgeois over the past hundred years.

Still standing in a neat cluster around 72nd Street are some of the city's first luxury apartment houses. The Dakota, the earliest of them all, is described on page 96. Another one which is well worth a second glance is the Kenilworth Apartments, at the corner of Central Park West and 75th Street. The limestone twirls decorating its facade bring fresh meaning to the term "wedding-cake architecture." Elsewhere, gracefully aging town houses cover large sections of the area and, close to the Hudson River, several streets contain picturesque Queen Anne-style homes.

While its buildings remain, recent decades have seen marked changes in the Upper West Side's social make-up. The park-facing apartments along Central Park West have always been occupied by the well-to-do, but much of what became Lincoln Center was a slum during the 1950s, and not by accident was it chosen as the site of the 1960 film *West Side Story*.

THE NICOLAS ROERICH MUSEUM
Born in Russia in 1874, Nicolas Roerich's life was devoted to art, archeology, and philosophy. In 1929, his "Peace through Culture" banner, intended to indicate and safeguard cultural monuments and institutions during times of war, earned him a Nobel Peace Prize nomination. The Nicolas Roerich Museum (319 West 107th Street; tel: 864-7752; *Open* Tue to Sun 2–5. *Admission free*) remembers this remarkable character with a few of his books and possessions and many of his enigmatic paintings, often depicting a lone figure striving to find enlightenment amid Himalayan landscapes.

189

Lincoln Center's arrival was followed by an influx of academics and media folk—many of them fleeing the rising rents of Greenwich Village. They have made the Upper West Side a liberal and cultured enclave boasting bookstores, cafés, and some fashionable bars. Other new arrivals are high-earning professionals with young children, taking advantage of the neighborhood's proximity to the green vistas and playgrounds of nearby Central Park and Riverside Park.

The American Museum of Natural History is one of the Upper West Side's main draws for visitors. From it you are well placed for further exploration on foot. Aim also to investigate the curious Nicolas Roerich Museum, on the northern edge of the Upper West Side (see panel).

Central Park West from the bridge on the Lake. The Dakota and other prestigious apartment houses arrayed along here have much-prized views over the park

A 1939 OPINION
Appreciation of the Custom House's Beaux-Arts style seems to be a recent phenomenon. In the 1939 W.P.A. (Works Progress Administration) *Guide to New York* the building is described as "somewhat ponderous in its neo-classical treatment."

▶ **U.S. Custom House**   *104A2*

Broadway at Bowling Green (tel: 668-6624)
Open: daily 10–5
Subway: 4; Bowling Green

On the site of Fort Amsterdam, Manhattan's first permanent European settlement, the 1907 former U.S. Custom House is an eloquent Beaux-Arts statement designed by the previously unknown Cass Gilbert.

The Custom House cost a staggering $7 million, but at the time of its construction, customs revenue was the biggest contributor to the Treasury's coffers. New York's customs—with the city established as a major seaport—were the most lucrative of all.

Heavily endowed inside and out with symbols of maritime trade, the building has at its entrance several Corinthian columns topped by the head of the Roman god of commerce and holds a frieze etched with dolphins, anchors, masts, and other nautical emblems.

Raised on pedestals on the Custom House's steps, four limestone sculptures by Daniel Chester French (best known for his statue of Abraham Lincoln in Washington, D.C.) represent the four great trading continents: Asia contemplating her navel, Europe looking to the past, Africa an unknown quantity—and America, lively enough to leap from her seat and sprint across Bowling Green. Inside, the building is capped by an impressive rotunda and decorated by a series of 16 frescoes by Reginald Marsh, commissioned by the Works Progress Administration, a government office that created work for American artists and writers during the Depression. It shows the travels of American explorers and—much more interestingly—an ocean liner docking in New York, with Greta Garbo among the disembarking passengers.

The U.S. Custom Service moved in 1973, and the building was closed. One section, ironically in a building packed with markers to the glories of commerce, reopened as the city's bankruptcy court. Since 1994, the U.S. Custom House has held the National Museum of the American Indian (see pages 164–165).

Though no longer used by U.S. Customs, the lavishly built Custom House at Bowling Green stands as testimony to the prosperity that maritime trade once brought to New York

▶▶ Whitney Museum of American Art   187B1

Madison Avenue at 75th Street (tel: 570-3676)
Open: Wed 11–6, Thu 1–8, Fri to Sun 11–6
Subway: G; 77th Street

Most of the big names of 20th-century American art are represented at the Whitney Museum

In one form or another, the Whitney Museum has ignored fashion, upset critics, baffled the general public, and been single-minded in its devotion to supporting emerging American artists for eight decades. It now finds itself in possession of some of the most important names—and works—of 20th-century art.

Wealthy would-be sculptor Gertrude Vanderbilt Whitney began supporting young artists in the 1910s, purchasing and displaying their output at her Greenwich Village studio. During the 1920s, she presided over the Whitney Studio Club, a celebrated art forum that displayed works by Edward Hopper, Stuart Davis, and John Sloan. These and other Whitney-backed artists emerged as major creative forces in contemporary American art, though they did not do much to impress the Metropolitan Museum of Art, who rejected Whitney's offer of her personal collection in 1929. The snub encouraged Whitney to found her own museum, which moved to its present home—a severe rectangular block of granite-clad reinforced concrete designed by Marcel Breuer—in 1966.

First held in 1932 (and continuing in odd-numbered years), the Whitney Biennial continues to be a controversial, invitational exhibition of the country's latest trends—often meeting the mixed response that greeted Gertrude Whitney's earliest buys. Despite the museum's attention to emerging artists and its strong temporary exhibitions, it is the long-established names that provide the main appeal for first-time visitors. The Permanent Collection galleries are a roll-call of American greats and include such influential figures as Claes Oldenburg, Mark Rothko, Jasper Johns, Roy Lichtenstein, Andy Warhol, Willem de Kooning, and Jackson Pollock. Within this area, three galleries are devoted to equally important artists with close links to the Whitney: Alexander Calder, Georgia O'Keeffe and Edward Hopper.

THE WHITNEY BRANCH MUSEUMS
In 1973, the Whitney opened its first branch museum—staging free exhibitions on special themes—in the Financial District. By the late 1980s it had four such branches elsewhere in Manhattan (and another one in Connecticut).

Sadly, the effects of the recession have left just one branch museum remaining in the city: at the Philip Morris Building, 120 Park Avenue.

▶▶▶ Woolworth Building 104C2

Broadway between Barclay Street and Park Place
Subway: 2, 3; Park Place

Nowadays dwarfed—but certainly not outshone—by the nearby twin-towers of the World Trade Center, the Woolworth Building became the world's tallest building on its completion in 1913, when its 800-foot-high tower, with Gothic pinnacles, canopies, and gargoyles, became an instant city landmark. The Woolworth Building retained its title of "world's tallest" until it was overtaken by the Chrysler Building in 1929.

Commissioned by Frank W. Woolworth as a headquarters for his ultra-lucrative chain of 2,000 five-and-dime stores, the building was designed by Cass Gilbert (also responsible for the U.S. Custom House, see page 190) and officially opened in April 1913 by President Woodrow Wilson. He flicked a switch in the White House to bathe the building—nick-named "the Cathedral of Commerce" by a commentator of the time—in the glow of 80,000 light bulbs.

The exterior of the Woolworth building may be impressive, but the lobby—one of the richest in New York—with entrances on Broadway, Barclay Street and Park Place, is the real treat. Step inside to admire the blue, green, and gold mosaics on the vaulted ceiling, wonder at the grand marble staircase, and look for the sculptured caricatures of Woolworth (depicted in the process of counting his nickels and dimes) and Gilbert (holding a model of the building), alongside other worthies.

F. W. WOOLWORTH
Rags-to-riches stories are seldom more spectacular than that of Frank Winfield Woolworth. He began his retail career as a humble clerk during the mid-1800s—an era when customers had to approach staff to ask about merchandise and, as likely as not, haggle over a price. In 1879, the first Woolworth five-and-dime store broke new ground by allowing customers to pick up and examine the stock, which was priced at either 5¢ or 10¢. By the time the Woolworth Building was commissioned, Woolworth presided over 2,000 stores and was able to uphold their no-credit credo by paying for the building in cash—a total of $13½ million.

STROLL: BATTERY PARK AREA
After visiting the World Trade Center, take a stroll towards the Hudson River, stopping by the palm-tree-decorated atrium of the World Financial Center and then continuing to the riverside Esplanade of Battery Park City.

Symbol of a world-famous empire: the Woolworth Building

▶ World Trade Center   *104C1*

Church Street between Liberty and Vesey streets (tel: 323-2340)
Open: Jun to Sep daily 9:30–11:30; rest of the year 9:30–9:30
(observation deck)
Subway: E; World Trade Center

Reaching more than a quarter-mile above Lower Manhattan, the twin towers of architect Minoru Yamasaki's World Trade Center became the world's tallest building in 1973. The W.T.C.'s height was topped by Chicago's Sears Tower in 1974 and it has the least aesthetic appeal of New York's better-known skyscrapers, the towers' unadorned, stainless-steel bodies expressing monotony on a massive scale and serving to

The roof of the World— 1,350ft. up, on the 110th floor

A CURIOUS FACT
From the southern tower's rooftop observation level, the northerly tower of the World Trade Center is farther away than it is at ground level—an effect caused by the curvature of the earth.

193

make the bland T.V. mast, atop the southernmost tower, look positively thrilling.

Yet more than a million visitors come here each year—not for the architecture but for the views from the observation deck. Tickets are available from the concourse level of the southernmost tower. An unexpected bonus is the elevator that speeds to the 107th floor in 58 seconds flat: you may not feel the elevator move, but you will feel the air pressure change.

The south, west, and east sides of the enclosed observation deck give a panoramic view far beyond Manhattan; only looking north does the view encompass what you can see from the Empire State Building—Midtown skyscrapers are toy-like, not seemingly near enough to touch (as they are uptown), and Central Park is just a big patch of green. An escalator winds up farther still to the vertiginous open rooftop level (closed in bad weather).

The towers are but two of the seven buildings that make up the World Trade Center, set around a 5-acre plaza that is the site of free open-air concerts in summer and holds sculptures—by Fritz Koenig, James Rosati, and Masayuki Nagare—unsuccessfully intended to humanize the scale of the complex.

To escape the feelings of architecture-gone-out-of-control go to the subterranean level, where an assortment of stores and restaurants serves the needs of the 50,000 people who work in the World Trade Center towers—employees of the many companies who rent the center's 10 million square feet of office space. Six people died and more than 1,000 were injured when a bomb exploded in an underground parking lot in February 1993.

Excursions

WHEN TO GO
Wherever you go within easy reach of New York City, it's best to visit between April and September. Not only will this avoid potentially chilly temperatures, it will also enable you to enjoy the dozens of local festivals that take place throughout the summer and to visit the local museums, many of which are closed throughout the winter.

194

Riverside living in the tranquil surroundings of the Hudson Valley. It is hard to believe the frenetic streets of New York City are barely 30 miles away

Excursions

Their affluent forebears may have had summer residences the length and breadth of the state, but many New Yorkers today go weak at the knees at the thought of leaving the familiar confines of the great metropolis.

Those who take the plunge, however, are rarely less than pleasantly surprised. Within an hour's drive of Manhattan lies a countryside thick with placid villages and abundant in blissfully rural vistas.

The Hudson Valley North of the city, the Hudson River flows through the 140-mile-long Hudson Valley (see pages 200–205). Once the major transit route into New York from New England, the river was of great strategic importance during the Revolutionary War, and several forts were founded along its course, one of which evolved into the famous Military Academy at West Point.

Though the battle sites remain, the valley no longer echoes to the sound of musket fire: its verdant hillsides and farmlands, studded with vineyards and orchards, are the embodiment of pastoral tranquility. These are the scenes that inspired the nation's first homegrown art movement, the Hudson River School; many examples of the artists' work can be seen in the region's museums.

Within the valley's nooks and crannies are many surprises: stately American Gothic homes, millionaires' mansions, and the homes of Washington Irving (author of *Rip Van Winkle*), and Samuel F.B. Morse, the inventor of Morse code. The valley stops at the urban jungle (relatively speaking) of Albany, capital of New York State.

The Catskill Mountains Halfway up the Hudson Valley, the Catskill Mountains loom to the west (see pages 196–199). The highest peak in the Catskills, Slide Mountain, reaches only slightly above 4,000 feet, and rather than providing scope for rock-climbers, the so-called mountains—their sides coated by pine forests and cut by tumbling streams—provide a postcard-perfect natural setting for the dozens of tiny communities enclosed in their folds. The rounded tops of the mountains are a legacy of the last ice-age, as are the deep gorges that sometimes hold spectacular waterfalls.

Photogenic views are abundant on the lanes that wind around the hills, and the Catskills' largest village, Woodstock, has a reputation for arts, crafts, and culture stretching back to the early part of the century. With streets lined by clapboard homes and dozens of galleries and craft stores displaying and selling locally produced works, Woodstock is a lovely place to succumb to the Catskills' rural pace, and its sidewalk cafés are prime vantage points for people-watching.

Long Island With its south coast bordered by the Atlantic Ocean and its north coast by the Long Island Sound, the appropriately named Long Island (see pages 206–211) runs for 125 miles east from New York City, becoming progressively less populated as it does so.

Farming and seafaring were the traditional staples of Long Island life, but New Yorkers began frequenting the south shore's fine beaches a century ago: a group of pretty seaside villages called the Hamptons became a summer retreat for the wealthy, and to this day they remain a vacation destination for affluent beach lovers.

There are more excellent beaches along the protected dune-covered sand spit of Fire Island (a popular gay getaway), though many of Long Island's more intriguing stops are on the north shore, where old whaling centers and immaculately preserved farming villages nestle among mansion homes built for families such as the Roosevelts and the Vanderbilts.

Clear skies, cool temperatures, and fall colors make autumn a good time for touring the Catskills

CAR RENTAL AND PUBLIC TRANSPORTATION
In the following pages, the excursions are described on the assumption that you are traveling by car. Note, though, that you will save money by renting a car outside New York City. All the main towns of the Hudson Valley and Long Island are well served by public transportation and have offices of the major car-rental companies, so it makes sense to rent once you have arrived. A healthy alternative is to combine public transportation with exploration by bicycle. Bike-rental outlets are plentiful in most towns during the summer. To discover the best of the Catskill Mountains, however, you will certainly need a car.

Drive

196

Catskill Mountains

This drive goes from Kingston to Saugerties, twice crossing the ear-popping Catskill highlands and also passing some of the region's most interesting villages along the way.

The drive takes you through the popular village of Woodstock and continues through several smaller towns, skirting forested hillsides beneath high peaks.

The breathtaking scenery is found on the drive's eastward leg, on Route 23A, as it climbs from Prattsville to Hunter—famous for its winter skiing and summer festivals. An alternative route from Prattsville would take you to East Durham, worth a detour for its two museums.

The final stretch of the drive descends sharply into the Hudson Valley towards the serene village of Saugerties. A lovely, seldom crowded place, with quaint antique stores and preserved homes, Saugerties is also within easy reach of Slabsides, the log cabin of venerated local naturalist John Burroughs.

All the important points of interest that you will pass as you travel along the route are covered in detail on pages 197–199.

▶▶ Catskill Mountains 196

Kingston and Hurley While forest-covered hills and tiny villages secreted along winding lanes are what the Catskills are really all about, the region's largest town, **Kingston▶▶**, should not be overlooked. Kingston began as a Dutch trading post in 1616. By the mid-1700s it had evolved into a significant commercial base and during the Revolutionary War it became the first capital of New York state.

At 312 Fair Street is the **Senate House State Historic Site▶** (tel: 914/338-2786; *Open* mid-Apr to Oct, Wed to Sat 10–5, Sun 1–5, also open Memorial Day, Independence Day, and Labor Day), which has been restored to its 1777 style to mark Kingston's two months as the seat of statehood; the senate swiftly moved south as the British approached from the north. An adjoining building displays a selection of paintings by locally born Hudson River artist John Vanderlyn and a few by his peers.

The Senate House is one of several 17th- and 18th-century Dutch-built stone houses that occupy the Stockade District, within fortifications erected in 1658 to protect the town from Native American attack. The same area holds the **Urban Culture Park Visitor Center▶▶** (tel: 914/331-7517; *Open* daily 11–5), outlining Kingston's history, and stands within easy reach of the **Old Dutch Church▶** (tel: 914/338-6759; *Open* Mon to Fri 10–4). Though built in 1852, the church was founded in 1659, and its cemetery bears Dutch tombs from that time.

Kingston's second historical area is the riverfront **Rondout** district, where the indoor and outdoor exhibits of the **Hudson River Maritime Museum** (tel: 914/ 338-00 71; *Open* May to Oct, daily 11–5) chronicle the town's heyday as a boat-building and river trade center.

A few miles west, Hurley▶ had a brief spell as the state capital during 1777 and retains its share of Dutch-built stone houses. Ten of these, on Main Street, open their doors to the public every year on the second Saturday in July.

NEW PALTZ
New Paltz, south of Kingston on Route 32, was settled in 1677 by a refugee community of French Huguenots. They were no slouches at home building, and six of their houses remain in excellent condition along the appropriately named Huguenot Street. From the 1692 Deyo House (tel: 914/255-1660; *Open* Wed to Sun 9:30–4), the local historical society leads tours of the homes, furnished in period style and illustrating the trials and tribulations of local 17th-century life.

On Route 42 near Shandaken

Woodstock The best-known and busiest of the Catskill villages, **Woodstock▶▶▶** (8 miles west of Kingston on Highway 212) gave its name to the legendary rock festival of 1969, even though the actual gathering took place 60 miles away. Nonetheless, if the festival had taken place here, it would have been well in keeping with the village's long-established Bohemian character.

HUNTER AND ITS FESTIVALS
New Yorkers know Hunter (north of Woodstock on Route 214) best as a ski resort, but when the snow leaves the slopes of Hunter Mountain the area kicks into its summer season with a series of festivals remarkable for their diversity. Early July finds an Italian festival, closely followed by a German Alps festival, and the first part of a country music festival. August sees the National Polka Festival, a Celtic festival, the second part of the country music festival, and a Golden Oldies festival. Rounding out the season is the Mountain Eagle Native American Indian Festival, in early September.

In the early 1900s, an Englishman inspired by the Utopian ideals of John Ruskin and William Morris founded the **Byrdcliffe Arts Colony** (tel: 914/679-2079 or 914/339-9935) on a 30-acre site in the hills around Woodstock (look for the signposted road off Highway 212). Artists and artisans arriving to live and work in the studios helped create a rich program of cultural events in the village, a tradition which still continues into the present day.

West from Woodstock Continuing deeper into the Catskill hills, the roads weave and pass tiny villages such as **Phoenicia** and **Shandaken**, where white-water rafting and a rich sprinkling of gourmet-class French restaurants are the main sources of local income. Both appeal to well-heeled weekending New Yorkers, who regard this area as their own piece of heaven.

On the western side of the Catskills, **Arkville** offers a touch more diversity with the **Delaware & Ulster Rail Ride▶** (tel: 914/586-3877; *Open* late-May to Oct, Wed to Sun 10–5), which operates over a 12-mile segment of a historic railroad that makes a jaunt to Halcottsville and back, several times a day.

Roxbury and Prattsville North of Arkville, **Roxbury** acquired the **Jay Gould Memorial Reform Church** in 1892. This imposing structure of limestone and oak was erected by the children of the unloved robber baron Gould, who was born here in 1836.

A more worthwhile call is to the **John Burroughs Memorial State Park▶** (tel: 315/492-1756; grounds: *Open* daily dawn to dusk), 2 miles west. Here the Catskills' foremost naturalist was born in 1837 and was buried in 1921. Burroughs accompanied the likes of Theodore Roosevelt, Thomas Edison, and Henry Ford on camping trips into the Catskills and introduced the wonders of its nature to many more in his informative writings.

Named after local tannery-owner Zadock Pratt, **Prattsville▶ ▶** claims to be the first planned community in the country and backs up this assertion with some excellently maintained 1830s houses.

One of them, the home of Pratt himself, now stores the local history collections of the commendable **Zadock Pratt Museum▶** (tel: 518/299-3369; *Open* May to Oct, Wed to Sun 1–5).

In **East Durham** on the Catskills' northern edge, you will come across an entertaining collection with something to catch the interest of almost everyone. There are a variety of farm tools, fossils, Native American artifacts, military paraphernalia, and miscellaneous household furnishings displayed in the **Durham Center Museum▶** (tel: 518/239-4313; *Open* Apr to Oct; Wed, Thu, Sat, and Sun 1–4). The building itself is a former schoolhouse which was built in 1825.

In complete contrast, the watery rides of the **Zoom Flume Water Park▶** (tel: 518/239-4559; *Open* June to Labor Day, Mon to Fri 10–6, Sat and Sun 10–7) close by on Shady Glen Road are the perfect way to keep cool on a hot day. Take a picnic lunch and some children with you and make the most of it.

PRATT ROCKS
Just outside Prattsville, on Route 23, are the Pratt Rocks, which carry engravings depicting Pratt and his horse. They were commissioned by Zadock Pratt during the 1860s, to enable an itinerant stone-cutter to earn the money to pay for lodgings.

Left, below and bottom: aspects of Woodstock, the classic Catskills village

199

Drive

Hudson Valley

Ever-changing views of the Hudson River and its beautiful tree-studded valley will guarantee lasting memories of this drive.

See map opposite.

Take two or even three days to make the most of the route, visiting some of the valley's many unique communities and historic homes—some of which have been a feature of the Hudson Valley region since its earliest European settlement.

The drive ends at Albany, New York's capital and one of the few Hudson Valley towns where modern buildings are as much in evidence as those from times long past.

The points of interest you will pass along the route are covered in detail on pages 200–205.

The Philipsburg Manor, north of Tarrytown: scenes of rural New York life during the 17th century

►► Hudson Valley

Yonkers to Tarrytown Although it is unrepresentative of the pastoral scenes farther to the north, industrial **Yonkers** should be your first stop out of New York City on the Sawmill River Parkway or via Metro North (taxis at every train stop will transport you locally for a few dollars).

The evocative Hudson River School landscapes gracing Yonkers' **Hudson River Museum▶** (tel: 914/963-4550; *Open* May to Sep, Wed to Sun 12–5, Fri 12–9; rest of the year Wed to Sun 12–5) will whet your appetite for what lies ahead.

Nearby, a taste of Hudson Valley history is provided by the stone-built **Philipse Manor▶** (tel: 914/965-4027; *Open* Apr to Oct, Wed and Thu 11–2, Sat 12–5), where Frederick Philipse III—grandson of a Dutch settler who made a fortune through shipping and slavery—led a life of ease until he was imprisoned during the Revolutionary War for supporting the British.

Farther north on Route 9, just south of Tarrytown, a neo-Gothic castle, complete with towers, spires, and battlements, stands beside the river, screened by woodlands. Known as **Lyndhurst▶▶▶** (tel: 914/631-4481; *Open* May to mid-Oct, Tue to Sun 10–5; rest of year Sat and Sun 10–5), the exuberant structure is among the finest examples of American Gothic architecture and is the work of the genre's leading practitioner, Alexander Jackson Davis.

Built in 1838, Lyndhurst was purchased by the despised robber baron Jay Gould in 1880. To his credit, Gould maintained the structure well, and his descendants lived here until 1961. The building sits in 64 acres of sumptuously landscaped grounds, and its interior is filled by a grand collection of Victoriana.

As Lyndhurst was nearing completion, author Washington Irving moved into a far less ostentatious dwelling a mile away at **Sunnyside▶▶** (tel: 914/631-8200; *Open* Mar, Sat and Sun 10–4; Apr to Dec, Wed to Mon 10–4), where he added Dutch gables and a Romanesque tower to what was originally a 17th-century farmers' cottage. Guided tours explore the 17 rooms where the creator of *Rip Van Winkle* and *The Legend of Sleepy Hollow* spent the later years of his life.

Off Route 9 north of Tarrytown is the **Philipsburg Manor▶▶** (tel: 914/631-8200; *Open* Mar, Sat and Sun 10–4; Apr to Dec, Wed to Mon 10–4). This building is a reconstruction of the 17th-century mill at the heart of the Philipse family's empire. With livestock in the yard and the gristmill and granary in operation, the tours led by guides in 1750s attire are informative and fun.

Sunnyside, home of author Washington Irving, is one of several preserved buildings near Tarrytown

201

Little more than a pitchfork's throw from the manor, the **Old Dutch Church▶** (for information call Tarrytown Historical Society tel: 914/681-8374) was built at the direction of Frederick Philipse I in 1697. Alongside those of numerous Dutch settlers the cemetery holds the tombs of Andrew Carnegie and Washington Irving. The headless hero of Irving's *Legend of Sleepy Hollow* arose from his eternal slumbers here.

Tarrytown to West Point On the Hudson's west bank, accessible via the Tappan Zee Bridge (1-287 west) Route 9W passes close to the village of **Nyack▶**, birthplace of the great American realist artist Edward Hopper in 1882. The artist spent much of his life here, at what is now the **Hopper House Arts Center** (82 North Broadway; tel: 914/358-0774; *Open* Thu to Sun 12–5). His finest canvases are hung in prestigious museums elsewhere, but devotees will find a few of his local landscapes here, plus a large number of souvenir prints and books.

Farther north off Route 9W is the **Stony Point Battlefield State Historic Site▶** (tel: 914/786-2521; *Open* mid-Apr to Oct, Wed to Sat 10–5, Sun 1–5, also Memorial Day, Independence Day and Labor Day), the remains of a British fort attacked and captured in a daredevil midnight raid by General "Mad" Anthony Wayne in 1779. A small visitors' center describes the battle and its significance.

Beyond Stony Point, Route 9W climbs into the **Hudson Highlands**: an area of rare beauty, where the river narrows and the increasingly sheer tree-clad valley walls are studded with exposed rock.

Route 218 wends a scenic route above the river, passing through the **United States Military Academy at West Point▶** (tel: 914/938-2368; museum: *Open* daily

THE NAMING OF TARRYTOWN
According to author Washington Irving, local Dutch wives were responsible for the naming of Tarrytown. It was "due to the inveterate propensity of their husbands to linger about the village tavern on market day." Less romantically inclined sources suggest the name was a corruption of the Dutch word for wheat, *Tarwe*.

202

The campus of the Military Academy at West Point. Visitors here can stroll in the footsteps of many famous Americans

10:30–4:15). Since 1802, West Point has sought to instill discipline, moral fiber, and leadership qualities into its cadets. Numerous presidents, generals, and astronauts have graduated from here; even among the drop-outs there have been some famous names, such as 19th-century author Edgar Allan Poe and the late Timothy Leary, the LSD guru of the 1960s.

Ports of call here include the **West Point Museum**, room after room of mementos—guns, flags, uniforms, medals, and more—from every conflict that has ever involved the U.S.; the remains of the Revolutionary-era **Fort Putnam**, perched 450 feet above the Hudson; and the **Drill Ground** (known as the "**Plain**"), where some of West Point's 4,000

203

cadets may sometimes be seen marching along with their geometric precision.

West Point to Poughkeepsie At **Newburgh**, the next major settlement, George Washington occupied a stone dwelling, built by Dutch settler Jonathan Hasbrouck, at 84 Liberty Street during the 16 months between the British surrender and the signing of the peace accord in Paris. Preserved as **Washington's Headquarters/Jonathan Hasbrouck House▶** (tel: 914/562-1195; *Open* mid-Apr to Oct, Wed to Sat 10–5, Sun 1–5, also Presidents' Day, Memorial Day, Independence Day, Labor Day and Columbus Day), the house is one of several 18th- and 19th-century homes that make a short stroll around the town worthwhile.

A better picture of the stresses of the Revolutionary period is provided by the **New Windsor Cantonment State Historic Site▶▶** (tel: 914/561-1765; *Open* mid-Apr to Oct, Wed to Sat 10–5, Sun 1–5, also Memorial Day, Independence Day and Labor Day), southwest of Newburgh near Vails Gate. Here, 10,000 of Washington's troops were accommodated in log cabins at the end of the war; only a speech by Washington himself quelled a mutiny in their ranks. During the summer months, local history buffs re-create bygone scenes here, some of them firing replica Revolutionary-era weaponry.

North of Newburgh lie the foothill villages of the Catskill Mountains. In contrast, on the east bank of the Hudson is **Poughkeepsie**. A venerable institution from Poughkeepsie's past is **Vassar College▶** (for information tel: 914/437-7300), an all-female college founded in 1881.

Nothing out of place: the Plain, West Point's parade ground

VASSAR COLLEGE
Strange as it may seen, profits from the production of beer helped fund Vassar College—founded in 1861 by local brewer Matthew Vassar. The intention of the rich and philanthropic Vassar was to offer women the liberal arts education that was available to men. The college did begin to admit men in 1969, although its student body remains overwhelmingly female. Besides male students, another comparatively recent addition is the Frances Lehman Loeb Art Center, built by architect Cesar Pelli to house the college's artworks. Pelli is better known for the far grander World Financial Center in Manhattan.

Excursions

THE SHAKERS

Founded in 1747, the Shakers—so named for the ecstatic trembling that followed their ritualistic dances—became one of the largest and most respected of the religious sects of the post-Revolutionary era. By the 1840s, more than 4,000 Shakers were living in twenty Shaker villages spread from Maine to Kentucky. Shaker skills and craftsmanship (their furniture is still highly coveted) had enormous impact on rural America, and the sect's many inventions included the flat-headed broom, the wooden clothespin, and the circular saw. Increasing wealth led to conflict within Shaker communities, which steadily declined from 1875. Many Shakers, however, retained their beliefs until death.

204

ALBANY'S EGGSHELL

What looks like a gigantic upturned eggshell in the center of Albany is in fact the home of E.S.I.P.A., or Empire State Institute for the Performing Arts (tel: 516/473-1061; *Open* daily 8:30–5). Inside, the eggshell has seating for 900 and a regular program of varied musical and theatrical events.

A 2-mile detour south from Poughkeepsie on Route 9 leads to **Locusts Grove**▶▶ (tel: 914/454-4500; *Open* Memorial Day to late Sep, 10–4). The house was bought in 1847 by inventor Samuel Morse, who enlisted the aid of Alexander Jackson Davis to transform it into a Tuscan-style villa. A pile of Morse's telegraph equipment shares the interior of the building with a diverting cache of Victorian furnishings.

Poughkeepsie to Albany Morse may be remembered by the code that bears his name, but he could not match the achievements of a latter-day local, Franklin D. Roosevelt. Destined to become the nation's longest-serving president, Roosevelt was born in a clapboard house beside the Hudson in 1882, near the hamlet of Hyde Park, on Route 9 north of Poughkeepsie.

Roosevelt converted the house into a 35-room Georgian-style mansion in 1916 and used it to treat royalty and heads of state to Hudson Valley views. It is now preserved as the **Franklin D. Roosevelt National Historic Site**▶▶ (tel: 914/229-9115; *Open* daily 9–5), and everyone is welcome to step inside and admire the Roosevelt taste in interior design.

On the grounds is the **Franklin D. Roosevelt Library and Museum**▶ (tel: 914/229-8114; library: *Open* Mon to Fri 9–4:45; museum: *Open* daily 9–5), which stores the presidential archive and has an exhibition on Roosevelt's life and achievements. A shuttle bus continues to the **Eleanor Roosevelt National Historic Site**▶ (tel: 914/229-9115; *Open* May to Oct, daily 9–5). This building was used by Roosevelt's wife Eleanor as a summer resort and as a permanent home during her widowhood.

The **Vanderbilt Mansion National Historic Site**▶▶ (tel: 914/229-9115; *Open* May to Oct, daily 9–5, rest of the year Wed to Sun 9–5) stands 2 miles farther north. Frederick W. Vanderbilt, grandson of millionaire Cornelius Vanderbilt, lavished $2 million of the family fortune on this three-story Beaux-Arts mansion. Inside, the Persian rugs, Flemish tapestries, and other expensive features are on display. When Vanderbilt's niece could not find a buyer for the house in 1940, she donated it to the nation.

The most imaginative home in the Hudson Valley is not a multimillion-dollar mansion but **Olana**▶▶ (tel: 518/828-0135; *Open* Apr to Oct, Wed to Sat 10–4, Sun 12–4), on Route 9G southwest of Hudson. An inspired mix of Moorish and Middle Eastern building styles, Olana arose in the 1870s as the home of a leading Hudson River School artist, Frederick Church. Decorated with Islamic and Byzantine motifs, Olana's arched doors and windows frame gorgeous views. The interior is crammed full of rugs, ornaments, and treasures from all points east.

On the final stretch toward Albany, make an eastward detour to Old Chatham, a base of the religious community of the Shakers from 1787. The **Shaker Museum**▶▶ (tel: 518/794-9100; *Open* Wed to Mon 10–5, in Nov and Dec Thu to Sun 10–5. *Closed* Jan to Mar) at Old Chatham has the most comprehensive collection of their simple and superbly crafted furnishings. There are eight buildings displaying numerous examples of Shaker achievements in carpentry, metalwork, and weaving. Other exhibits detail the history of the community and its beliefs.

Marking the northern end of the Hudson Valley is **Albany**▶▶, which boomed during the 18th century as a trade and transportation center, becoming New York's state capital in 1797. A thorough restoration program has kept many of Albany's 19th-century buildings in good order, but what dominates the town center is the 1960s white marble modernism of **Empire State Plaza**, whose quarter-mile-long walkway is decorated by free-form sculpture. Take the elevator to the observation gallery on the 42nd floor of the plaza's tallest building, the **Corning Tower**▶ (tel: 518/474-2418; Observation deck: *Open* Mon to Fri 9–3:45, Sat and Sun 10–3:45; New York State Capitol tours Mon to Fri hourly 9–4, Sat and Sun 10, 11, 2, 3; *Admission free*), for views across the valley.

At ground level, the plaza runs out beneath the pink granite exterior of the 1898 **New York State Capitol**▶▶▶ built at a cost of $24 million and gaining French, Italian, and Romanesque features as tastes—and architects—changed during its 30 years of construction. Guided tours wind up an elegant marble staircase to the restored legislative chambers.

Across the plaza is the **New York State Museum**▶▶▶ (tel: 518/474-5877; *Open* daily 10–5), which uses exhibits and walk-through dioramas to describe the region's history, shedding light on subjects as diverse as the geology of the Adirondacks and Manhattan's architecture.

There is more on show at the **Albany Institute of History and Art**▶▶ (125 Washington Avenue, tel: 516/463-4478; *Open* Wed to Sun 12–5), with Dutch settlement furniture, crockery, and aristocratic portraiture, alongside a selection of Hudson River School paintings.

The state government of New York has its offices in Albany's Empire State Plaza

THE SCHUYLER MANSION
If traveling through the valley has not exhausted your appetite for period homes, the pick of Albany's stately residences is the 1762 Schuyler Mansion (32 Catherine Street; tel: 518/434-0834; *Open* mid-Apr to Oct, Wed to Sat 10–5, Sun 1–5). It was built for the well-connected Philip Schuyler, a successful businessman who served with distinction as an officer during the Revolutionary War.

Excursions

Drive

Long Island

This drive takes in some of Long Island's beaches, historic homes, and atmospheric fishing ports.

From the beautifully landscaped Old Westbury Gardens, the drive continues to popular Jones Beach before passing the south-shore communities of Sayville and Patchogue. The route then passes tiny farming hamlets before reaching the picturesque villages of Setauket and Stony Brook on the north shore.

The Vanderbilt mansion can be reached down a side road off the main route, or you can continue direct to Walt Whitman's birthplace and the one-time whaling settlement of Cold Spring Harbor. The final stop is at Sagamore Hill, the stately home of Theodore Roosevelt.

The points of interest you will pass along the route, as well as other highlights of a more extended visit to Long Island, are covered in detail on pages 207–211.

The beaches on Long Island's south shore are extensive enough to absorb any number of vacationing New Yorkers

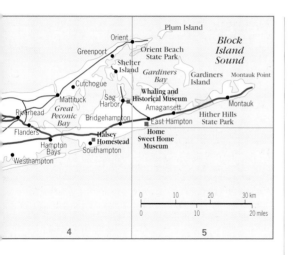

| 0 | 10 | 20 | 30 km |
| 0 | | 10 | 20 miles |

4   5

►Long Island

Old Westbury and Old Bethpage Much of western Long Island is now seamless suburbia criss-crossed by freeways, but a century ago it was rural. John S. Phipps, the son of Andrew Carnegie's business partner, chose a plot near Old Westbury as the site for a rambling country estate. Phipps' red-brick Westbury House was completed in 1903. Today, the 100-acre grounds, known as **Old Westbury Gardens▶▶** (tel: 516/333-0048; *Open* May to mid-Dec, Wed to Mon 10–5), are the main attraction for visitors who beat a path to the wrought-iron gates. Landscaped and planted to perfection, the gardens have thousands of mature trees and an aromatic rose garden in their midst.

Long Island provides not only an escape from New York City but also, in **Old Bethpage Village▶▶** (tel: 516/572-0526; *Open* Mar to Oct, Mon to Fri 10–5; rest of the year reduced hours), an escape from the 20th century. Crushed-oystershell lanes lead into this re-creation of an

AMITYVILLE
A house on a hill in Amityville, in deepest Long Island suburbia, caused its occupants to flee in terror during the early 1970s. After the subsequent book and film, both called *The Amityville Horror*, describing (and apparently greatly exaggerating) the events, were released, locals found themselves spending a lot of their time directing sightseers to the scene of the grisly goings-on. Not surprisingly, the house has proved difficult to sell over the years and still casts a strange spell over this otherwise rather ordinary community.

207

THE WILLIAM FLOYD ESTATE

Close to Mastic Beach, where the road to eastern Fire Island meets the mainland, the William Floyd Estate (tel: 516/399-2030; *Open* daily 10–4) is what is left of the plantation owned by General William Floyd, one of the signers of the Declaration of Independence. The simple house Floyd built in 1724 remains at the center of the 600-acre estate, greatly added to by successive generations of his descendants. The last of them lived here until 1975, while many of the others lie buried within the grounds in the family cemetery. The house's 25 rooms unfurl a fascinating tale of changing family fortunes.

The north shore of Long Island has great appeal for New Yorkers seeking a place in the country

1800s farming village, typical of those that dotted Long Island long before the days of freeways and suburbia. As the village's tailor, blacksmith, quilters, and storeowners go about their daily tasks, explaining them to visitors, it is hard not to be impressed by the thoroughness of it all.

Jones Beach and Fire Island Most New Yorkers hitting Long Island, however, are thinking not of old farming ways but about bronzing themselves on the south shore. On any summer weekend, **Jones Beach** is a picture of New York at play. For space and solitude make the short trip east to **Fire Island National Seashore►**, which has the added appeal of a 19th-century lighthouse now employed as a visitors' center.

The 1,000-acre state park consumes the western extremity of **Fire Island►►** (tel: 516/289-4810), longest of the sand spits that flank the southern shore of Long Island. Enormously popular as a gay vacation area, Fire Island runs for 32 miles and, other than the road links near both ends, can be reached only by ferries from various points on the mainland.

All of Fire Island is public land, although several sections are dominated by private resort communities, each with its distinctive social makeup. Day-trippers are not always welcomed with open arms at the more exclusive places. One welcoming day-trip spot, which can be reached by ferry from Sayville, is **Sailor's Haven►►** (tel: 516/597-6183). The fine beach, the nature trails weaving around the dunes, and the hardy vegetation forming the **Sunken Forest►** should not be missed. A visitors' center provides absorbing background material on Fire Island's subtle ecology.

The Hamptons East of Fire Island, the settlements collectively known as the Hamptons sat placidly at the center of windmill-studded farmland until the late 19th century, when wealthy New Yorkers began discovering their vacation potential and transformed them into highly desirable seaside resorts. The Hamptons are still a getaway for the rich whose huge mansions stand close to fine beaches, chic boutiques and pricey restaurants.

Southampton► is one of Long Island's oldest towns, and the 1648 **Halsey Homestead►** (tel: 516/283-3527; *Open* mid-June to mid-Sep, Tue to Sun 11–5) claims to be the oldest timber-framed house in the entire state. The best-looking of the Hamptons is **East Hampton►►**, with its narrow streets bordered by neatly trimmed hedges and picket-fenced cottages. The locally born actor and dramatist John Howard Payne liked the place so much that he composed the most sentimental of songs, "Home Sweet Home," here; a fact duly acknowledged by the preservation of his house as the **Home Sweet Home Museum▶** (tel: 516/324-0713; *Open* Mon to Sat 10–4, Sun 2–4. *Closed* holidays), which is mostly filled with a collection of 18th-century ceramics.

On Main Street, the 1784 **Clinton Academy▶** (tel: 516/324-6850; *Open* Jul and Aug, daily 10–5; Jun and Sep, Sat and Sun 10–5), once a revered seat of learning, now carries exhibitions on varied facets of local life.

Cross the Robert Moses Causeway to reach the south shore

209

Sag Harbor Unless you want to make the 20-mile drive to the eastern end of Long Island (see panel), head northwest from East Hampton to **Sag Harbor▶▶**. Though few people would believe it on first sight, this sleepy waterside community was once a busy port, second only to New York City in its importance. Until 1871 it boasted the world's fourth largest whaling fleet.

Perhaps even less believably, you need to pass through a whale's jawbone framing the doorway of a former Masonic Temple to enter the town's **Whaling and Historical Museum▶▶** (tel: 516/725-0770; *Open* mid-May to Sep, Mon to Sat 10–5, Sun 1–5), where piles of scrimshaw and nautical objects are stacked to the ceiling.

The 1789 **Custom House▶** (tel: 516/725-0250; *Open* Jul and Aug, daily 10–5) is another survivor of Sag Harbor's seafaring heyday, as is the **Whaler's Church▶**, built in 1841 in a curious Greek-Egyptian style. As if to mark the decline of Sag Harbor's sea trade, the church's steeple—long a navigational aid to shipping—was blown down by a fierce hurricane in 1938.

Shelter Island A quick ferry ride (pedestrians and vehicles) north from Sag Harbor brings you to **Shelter Island** which is not only a shortcut to Long Island's north fork (a second ferry crosses to Greenport) but also an ideal spot to relax among narrow, weaving lanes that are flanked by attractive Victorian cottages. It was previously a haunt of 18th-century pirates and Prohibition-era bootleggers.

LONG ISLAND'S EASTERN TIP
If you drive east from East Hampton to Montauk, you will kick yourself for not continuing a further 5 miles to Montauk Point, the last stop before the Irish coast. A lighthouse, built on the instruction of George Washington in 1797, sits at the easternmost point. The rewards for braving vertigo and dizziness to climb its 138 steps are views of Rhode Island and the Connecticut coast.

Sagamore Hill was completed in 1885 for the only U.S. president to have been born in New York City, Theodore Roosevelt; cost of the 22-room house was $16,975

RIVERHEAD
One reason to visit Riverhead, a town off the main routes between the Hamptons and the north shore, might be the Suffolk County Museum (tel: 516/727-2881; *Open* Tue to Sat 12:30–4:30), whose exhibits range from local Native American cultures to whaling. Another reason could be the produce of the Palmer Vineyards (tel: 516/722–WINE; *Open* daily 11–5). If you are visiting in mid-August, Riverhead's Polish Street Fair and Festival should not be missed.

The north shore An exploration of Long Island's north shore is best begun at **Sagamore Hill▶▶▶** (tel: 516/922-4447; *Open* daily 9:30–4:30), a three-story house set in 80 green acres just east of Oyster Bay and completed in 1884 as the summer home of Theodore Roosevelt.

Two floors of the main house hold roomfuls of Victorian furnishings and an extraordinary number of Roosevelt's hunting trophies, not least the array of moose- and deer-heads. The spacious wood-paneled rooms provided the setting for Roosevelt's peace-brokering between warring Russia and Japan in 1905, for which he was awarded the Nobel Peace Prize. Further exhibits, and a short film detailing Roosevelt's life, can be viewed in the adjoining Old Orchard Home Museum, added by his son in 1938.

Continuing east on Route 25A is the **Whaling Museum** at **Cold Spring Harbor▶** (tel: 518/367-3418; *Open* Tue to Sun 11–5), which remembers the nine-ship whaling fleet based here during the mid-1880s. The exhibits include one of the few existing complete whaling vessels, and numerous smaller pieces—examples of scrimshaw, harpoons, and the tools used to separate blubber from bone.

When the Cold Spring Harbor whaling fleet was still sailing the high seas, Walt Whitman—born in 1819, 2 miles away in Huntington—was busy overturning the rules of traditional verse to create *Leaves of Grass*, the work that sealed his place among America's literary greats. The two-story shingled dwelling built in 1816 by Whitman's father is now the **Walt Whitman Birthplace State Historic Site▶▶** (tel: 516/427-5240; *Open* Memorial Day to Labor Day, daily 11–4; Sep to May, Wed to Fri 1–4, Sat and Sun 11–4), with exhibits recounting his adventure-filled life.

North of Centerport is the Spanish-style **Vanderbilt Mansion▶** (tel: 516/726-4625; *Open* Tue to Sat 10–4, Sun 12–5), which belonged to William K. Vanderbilt II, great-grandson of Cornelius Vanderbilt. He combined his taste for opulent living with an interest in natural history, acquiring the 17,000 specimens of stuffed and mounted creatures that make a strange addition to the antiques and original furnishings on display in this shrine to luxury living. The adjacent Vanderbilt Planetarium has views of the heavens, which fail to match up to those across Long Island Sound.

Stony Brook and Setauket An almost too perfectly preserved village, **Stony Brook►►** was saved from neglect by wealthy philanthropist Ward Melville during the 1930s. Melville also financed the **Museums at Stony Brook►►►** (tel: 518/751-0066; *Open* Jul and Aug, daily 10–5; rest of the year, Wed, Sat, and Sun 10–5), a complex that focuses on 19th-century Long Island life. Pride of place goes to the vintage carriages, and the paintings by William Sidney Mount, a Stony Brook resident who emerged as one of the country's most original and daring artists during the mid-1800s.

First known as a portraitist, particularly noted for his painting of prominent statesmen, Mount acquired more lasting fame by capturing rural scenes on canvas, and was the first major painter to produce sympathetic images of African-Americans.

Close to Stony Brook is the similarly pretty village of **Setauket►**, which was a hotbed of espionage during the revolutionary years of the late 1700s, and the birthplace of what is believed to have been the nation's first spy cell. One technique employed to outwit the occupying British troops was the conveying of messages using a local housewife's clothesline. The combination of clothing on the line corresponded to a prearranged code and did most damage—as far as the British were concerned—when used to alert George Washington to the approach of the French Expeditionary Force in 1780.

A TRIP TO CONNECTICUT?
Should the combination of Long Island's sea air and nautical museums give you the urge to take to the waves, you can seize the opportunity at Port Jefferson, 3 miles east of Setauket. From here, a ferry (taking both cars and pedestrians) makes the 20-mile crossing of Long Island Sound to Bridgeport in Connecticut, several times daily.

211

Framed by formal gardens, the 24-room Vanderbilt Mansion near Centerport sits at the heart of a 43-acre estate and provides a taste of high-class living, although most visitors come for the excellent planetarium and natural history exhibits

HOTELS: THE FACTS
The New York Convention and Visitors' Bureau (2 Columbus Circle, New York, NY 10019; tel: 800/NYC–VISIT or 397-8222) publishes a free guide to hotels listing their addresses, phone numbers, and prices, and indicating their location on a map. More opinionated descriptions of New York hotels can be found on pages 262–268.

Accommodations

From side-street fleabags with naked lightbulbs to world-class lodgings with en suite Jacuzzi and antique furnishings, the one thing all New York hotels share is inflated prices. True bargains are extremely difficult to find; and when you do, you sometimes wish you hadn't.

Budget hotels Any hotel room priced under about $100 is unlikely to offer anything more than the basic necessities: a roof over your head and a mattress under your back, with the bathroom likely to be a shared one at the end of a corridor and equipped with erratic plumbing.

Shabby though they may be, hotels at the rock-bottom end of the market are usually safe, though some near Times Square are an exception and should be approached with caution.

Basic comforts For $100–$200, you can expect a comfortable, if basic, room with color T.V. (television addicts should ensure their hotel has cable channels) and a bathroom and telephone.

As you dig deeper into your budget and spend $150–$200, rooms become slightly larger and more elegantly furnished. The T.V. carries more channels, a good range of complimentary soaps and shampoos should be found in the bathroom, and sometimes a complimentary newspaper will be delivered to your door each morning.

Spoiling yourself To taste the New York good life means kissing goodbye to at least $200 a night. Do this, and you will be able to stretch out on a giant-sized bed in a large-sized room, with a fully equipped bathroom. Further spending will be encouraged by 24-hour room service. There should be a knowledgeable concierge available to recommend sightseeing trips, shows, galleries, restaurants, and to assist with reservations and tickets.

212

You will need to have a taste for opulent living, and ample funds, to enjoy a stay at the large and very plush Helmsley Palace on Madison Avenue

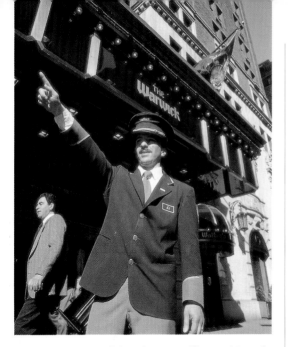

The Warwick is just one of many comfortable hotels conveniently located in northern Midtown, where some of the city's top luxury establishments are also to be found

Hidden extras For all but the most affluent visitor, the basic rates quoted by hotels (and given above) are frightening enough. There is also a string of taxes to be added: sales tax (8.25 percent), New York City hotel tax (5 percent), and a $2 occupancy tax, per room, per night.

Therefore, what might seem an $80 bargain will actually cost $92.60, and stretching your budget to its limits for a $250 treat will land you with a bill close to $285.

Quoted rates do not include tax, and do not usually include breakfast either. Some hotels have restaurants, but going for breakfast at a nearby coffee shop or diner is always cheaper and a quintessentially New York way to start the day.

Special deals Slightly better news on the financial front is that hotel prices are often lower on weekends, when many establishments seek to tempt suburb dwellers to spend some time and money in the city by offering special cut-rate weekend deals.

Such packages can bring savings of up to 40 percent on regular prices and are chiefly advertised in New York area newspapers. It is always worth inquiring whether a package is available. Longer-term visits will often also attract reduced rates: a few hotels give discounts for stays of two weeks or more.

Seasonal factors New York never runs short of visitors, but the peak tourist seasons match the clemency of the weather. The prime months are April, May, and June. In the fall, many hotels are filled by delegates who attend the numerous business conventions held in the city, and the months up to Christmas are spectacularly busy.

So, make it a point never to turn up in New York without prearranging accommodations, at least for your first night, and do so well in advance of the date you expect to arrive.

DISCOUNTED ROOMS
In the hospitality industry, hotel rooms (like airplane seats) are considered extremely "perishable" because as soon as the night is over, the potential revenue for the room is lost. Quikbooks operates like an airline broker for hotel rooms, making last-minute reservations for people in the city's best properties, often at seriously discounted rates (tel: 800/789-9887).

The Upper East Side is a fittingly exclusive setting for the art deco Carlyle, a truly grand hotel

CREDIT CARDS

Most hotels accept credit cards as payment and, in fact, require an imprint upon check-in to cover incidentals. All major cards are widely accepted.

THE RAINES HOTEL LAW

In an effort to cut down the level of alcohol consumption among the city's down-and-outs, the Raines Hotel Law of 1896 made it illegal to sell liquor in New York on a Sunday, except in hotels to accompany meals. To circumvent this law, every seedy bar with a few spare rooms declared itself a hotel and offered inedible sandwiches to its oblivion-seeking customers. The law was soon repealed.

Reservations and payment To secure a room in advance, you will be asked to place a deposit. The simplest way of doing this is by quoting your credit card number by phone (or by fax). If you reserve a room without a deposit during a busy period and arrive after 6 PM you may find the room has been re-allocated. Always reconfirm your reservation as close to your arrival date as possible.

Payment for your full stay (or at least a large part of it) is sometimes expected on arrival by credit card, traveler's check, or cash (though carrying large amounts of money is not advisable in New York—see pages 54–55).

Areas of the city Manhattan is quick and simple to travel around, so you can be selective about where you stay. By far the densest concentration of hotels is in the section of Midtown Manhattan bordered by 44th and 57th streets, where some of the grandest and priciest accommodations can be found, in a knot around Grand Central Terminal and at the southern end of Central Park. The cheaper Midtown hotels (mostly around Times Square) can be unappealing, and you will get better value elsewhere.

In the southern reaches of Midtown Manhattan, where noise and traffic levels are more bearable, residential areas such as Chelsea and the Gramercy Park district hold several hotels full of character with attractive rates.

A handful of classy hotels with sky-high rates sit in the moneyed environs of the Upper East Side. On the other side of Central Park, the limited number of hotels on the Upper West Side are better value, especially if you like a large room, but are usually considerably less elegant.

In Lower Manhattan, many high-rises in the Financial District are aimed at the expense-account traveler. In SoHo are hip hotels that cater to affluent hipsters who desire a downtown aesthetic. More affordable and interesting lodgings are hotels dotted (albeit very thinly) through Chinatown, SoHo, and Greenwich Village.

Bed and breakfast Bed-and-breakfast accommodations are an increasingly popular alternative to staying in a hotel, but prices are not significantly lower: such is the demand for accommodations of every kind in the city that real bargains are hard to come by.

New York B.&B.s fall into two categories. "Hosted" means that guests occupy a spare room or two in the apartment of a New Yorker who will provide at least a modest breakfast. Hosted B.&B.s can be a source of useful insider information on the city, but there is always the risk that you might find yourself at odds with the host. With "unhosted" accommodations, guests get the run of a New York apartment whose owner is out of town.

B.&B. prices vary according to the facilities and neighborhood. Many B.&B.s are in outlying locations, so bear this in mind when booking. A hosted bed and breakfast is generally a cheaper option ($60–$150) than its unhosted equivalent ($80–$200). Rooms should be booked well in advance for the widest choice, although you can book the day before, if necessary. Among a growing number of bed and breakfast agencies are City Lights (P.O. Box 20355, Cherokee Station, New York, NY 10028; tel: 737-7049) and Urban Ventures (P.O. Box 426, New York, NY 10024; tel: 594-5650).

STUDENT DORMS
Further inexpensive accommodations are available (during short vacation times) in the student dorms of New York University. There is a minimum stay of three weeks, and the cost per week is around $70. These accommodations are extremely limited and are quickly snapped up. If you are interested, consult the New York telephone book and contact the housing office listed under the university entry.

215

Cheap and cheerful If hotels and B.&B.s are beyond your budget but you still wish to see the Big Apple, the city has three Y.M.C.A.s that, for slightly less than the cost of the cheapest hotel room, offer single, double, and family rooms plus a range of facilities to men, women, and family groups. The West Side Y.M.C.A. occupies an elegant historic building at 5 West 63rd Street (tel: 787-4400).

You do not have to be a youth to stay at Hostelling International—New York's stylish and well-equipped New York hostel (891 Amsterdam Avenue; tel: 932-2300), although you do have to be a member of the International Youth Hostel Federation. Prices depend on whether you opt for a dormitory bed or a private room, but either way are substantially lower than hotels or B.&B.s. It is wise to make reservations in advance.

Home comforts, attractive bedrooms, and excellent value for money make the Wyndham popular with New York regulars, so book well in advance

Food and drink

City that never sleeps it may be, but New York is also a city that never seems to stop eating. This gastronomic obsession is easily explained: no city on earth has such an abundance or such a variety of food available—from burgers, blintzes, and catfish to dim sum and goulash—around the clock and at prices most people can afford.

Meals on the move The busier the street, the more vendors it will have! Most street vendors serve hot dogs—even the humble frankfurter in a bun has a place in New York culinary legend, and is regarded as a must-eat snack when visiting Coney Island (see page 75)—and also knishes (a doughy pastry filled with potatoes), bags of roasted chestnuts, and huge soft pretzels, crusted with salt—each for around a dollar ($1.50 in the pricey heart of Midtown Manhattan).

You are never far from the next snack in Manhattan

216

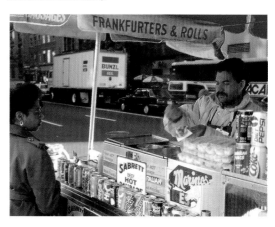

Another common sight are falafel carts and, occasionally, soup vendors. In the morning, you'll often see stands stuffed with breakfast pastries, oversized bagels, and the like—breakfast-on-the-run.

In the Financial District, traders and other money people are to be seen not at chic restaurant tables, but eating their midday meal from rows of ethnic vendors lining the main thoroughfares. These pushcarts are the most convenient and quickest places to grab a bite. Here steaming piles of meat or seafood and noodles are sold for only a few dollars.

The deli: a New York institution Street vendors apart, what New York has more of than any other American city is delis. The old-timers of the breed, known for their mile-high sandwiches stuffed with Eastern European meats such as pastrami, are nowadays few and far between. However, they have given their name to a variety of food sources all over the city where overstuffed sandwiches are served to eat in or take out.

More recently, Korean immigrants have given the word a whole new meaning, installing salad bars holding trays of cooked meats, seafood dishes, stir-fries, hot and cold vegetables, casseroles, salads, fruit, even sushi.

TIPPING
In any eating place that has waiter or waitress service, you are expected to leave a tip. Restaurant and coffee-shop staff depend on tips for a large part of their income, which is why the majority will eagerly attend to your needs. The precise amount that you leave should be judged according to the standard of service, but a tip of around 15 percent of the bill is considered average. One way to estimate a tip is to double the amount of sales tax (which is 8¼ percent) shown on your bill.

Just fill a plastic container and pay by the weight. Depending on the price per pound and how much you eat, you can have your fill for between $4 and $10. Many establishments have tables, but you may prefer to eat outside on the nearest bench while people-watching.

Most New York delis also serve a mind-boggling variety of sandwiches. Along with the traditional corned beef and pastrami on rye, you can also get heros (a.k.a. submarine sandwiches), as well as sandwiches based on food specialties of the individual deli owner's native land. In delis owned by Greeks and Middle Easterners, for instance, you may find gyros—spit-roasted beef or pork stuffed inside a pita bread envelope. Even ordinary sandwiches, such as turkey or tuna fish, are often unbelievably thick—at least an inch of meat as filling.

Bagels are served everywhere with many weird and wonderful toppings, but it is hard to beat the traditional New York way of eating them: hot out of the oven and smothered in (or with just "a schmear" of) cream cheese.

Every New Yorker has a favorite deli. Once you have found yours, start exploring the other traditional deli specialties such as thick soups, chicken soup with the dumplings known as matzoh balls, sponge cakes and mile-high meringue pies, and blintzes—similar to crêpes wrapped around cream cheese or fruit fillings. And don't forget to try the famous New York cheese cake.

Coffee-shop breakfasts If you are not in a rush linger over breakfast in a coffee shop or diner. Such establishments are as prevalent as delis and street vendors and draw an equally devoted clientele. Sit at a table or at the counter and choose from a menu which is likely to include sausages, bacon, lox (smoked salmon), pancakes, waffles, French toast, scrambled eggs, omelets with a host of mix-and-match fillings, and fried eggs. Coffee-shop breakfasts are usually served with hash browns (a.k.a. home fries), and toast. Often your cup of coffee will be refilled for free, for as long as you like to linger there.

EATING WITH CHILDREN
New York can be a wonderful and exciting place for children to eat. There are scores of diners, theme restaurants, pizzerias, and casual ethnic eateries from which to choose. Even the city's best restaurants have a reputation for being accommodating, provided junior is well heeled and well behaved. If a children's menu is not offered, don't be afraid to ask for something simple; New Yorkers are not shy when it comes to ordering in restaurants.

217

A New York legend—the original Jewish deli

A coffee-shop breakfast, consisting of eggs, toast, home fries, and coffee, will cost around $5. There are also many cafés that serve less greasy alternatives like homemade muffins, oatmeal, granola with fresh fruit and fresh squeezed juices.

Lunchtime fare Lunchtime in New York usually begins at 11 and ends around 2, though it isn't hard to find something to eat the rest of the afternoon. Sandwiches and salads are popular choices for lunch, and several establishments, such as the **Cosi Sandwich Bar** and **Mangia** food stores, have turned sandwich and salad making into an art. Here you can find savory items such as fresh mozzarella and sun-dried tomatoes on a whole wheat baguette, and smoked turkey and avocado on Russian black bread; sometimes these sandwiches are so large you can barely fit them into your mouth. The **Daily Soup** and **Souperman** chains serve a wide variety of homemade soups as an alternative to the sandwich.

Among New York's sandwich specialties are the "Reuben" (corned beef with Swiss cheese and sauerkraut on rye bread) and the "Club" (turkey with bacon, lettuce, and tomato on toasted white bread). Coffee shops also serve salad plates that could feed an army and offer variations on the plain and simple hamburger such as bacon-and-cheese burgers, chili-cheese burgers, and pizzaburgers as well as one made from ground chicken.

An even cheaper lunch may be found at a neighborhood pizza joint, where slices are sold with your choice of toppings. Several pizza parlors also offer Italian hero sandwiches filled with meatballs, chicken cutlets, or eggplant and overstuffed calzones with cheese, broccoli, spinach, or sausage fillings.

Many New York restaurants, whatever their culinary leaning, offer specially priced lunch menus or lunch buffets for under $8, which not only means good eating at a great price but also makes lunchtime a golden opportunity to begin your investigation of the city's innumerable ethnic cuisines. Seldom will you have the chance to sample so wide a choice of restaurant fare at such affordable prices. Some of the city's finest restaurants also offer very reasonable prix fix deals at lunch. During Restaurant Week the top eateries 3-course menus are priced to correspond to the year ($19.99, $20.00 etc), and many extend the promotion through the summer.

Italian restaurants Throughout the city, Italian restaurants can be relied upon for excellent food at very fair prices. If you are interested in good food, avoid Little Italy, where the atmosphere and the prices are designed exclusively for tourists. In its highest form, Italy's *alta cucina* carries a heavy price tag, but outside of its homeland, you won't find such impressive renderings.

Chinese specialties

Little Italy's prices are also higher than they deserve to be. If money is no object and you are neatly dressed, head instead for the gourmet Italian restaurants recently opened on the Upper East Side.

Chinese food Within a toothpick's throw of Little Italy are the restaurants of Chinatown,

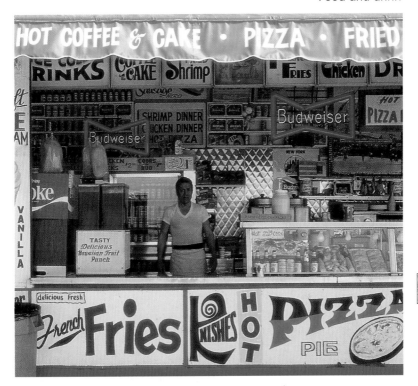

which are unmatched for value. Because their trade is largely drawn from New York's Chinese community, Chinatown's eateries can stay in profit without compromising their quality to suit western tastes.

Nobody should leave New York without dropping into a Chinatown restaurant during its hours of dim sum service. Usually served until mid-afternoon on the weekends, dim sum comprises steamed dumplings and baked buns filled with meat, seafood, and/or rice and noodles. Diners choose from trolleys pushed between the dining tables. Just point at what looks good—even though it might be chicken feet. When you cannot eat another thing, let the waiter or waitress know and the bill will be assessed by the number of empty plates on your table.

Return to Chinatown at night, when the dinner options span Cantonese, Hunan, and Szechuan specialties as well as some obscure regional cuisines.

Japanese food New Yorkers first got excited by Japanese sushi and sashimi during the late 1970s when a rash of new restaurants appeared. These were intended to serve the city's fast-growing Japanese population but found themselves besieged by locals entranced by the exotic combination of raw fish and tatami mats.

The city is still an excellent place for sushi and sashimi (ask any New Yorker for their suggestions), although the latest craze among devotees of Japanese food are the *okonomiyaki* restaurants, where large crêpes containing your choice of meat, seafood, vegetables, or noodles are prepared on a hot slab in full view.

Affordable food to suit most tastes

MEALTIMES
To avoid crowds, or to avoid having a restaurant to yourself, be aware of the city's popular dining times. Most coffee shops open for breakfast around 6 AM and are at their busiest around 8 AM. By 10 AM, the pace has slowed as most New Yorkers are already planning their lunch. Some people eat their midday meal as early as 11:30 AM but around 1 PM is more common. By 2:30 or 3 PM coffee shops start preparing for the dinner rush, from around 5 PM to 7 PM. In restaurants, lunch hours tend to be similar to those of coffee shops but the peak restaurant dinner period is between 7 and 10:30 PM. Some of the noted after-theater dining spots do most of their business between 11 PM and midnight.

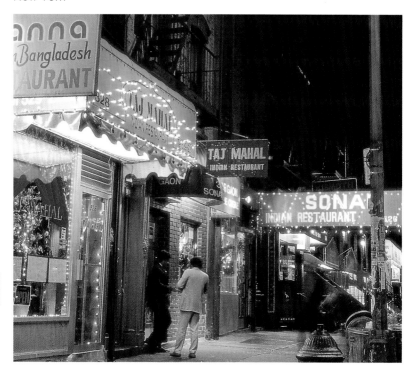

Head for 6th Street in the East Village for a dazzling array of Indian restaurants

CROSSBRED CUISINES
New York's ethnic cuisines are quick to mix with one another. To become a gastronomic explorer at the frontiers of culinary adventure (which is sometimes a long way from culinary excellence), seek out the city's Chinese pizzerias, Kosher-Italian delis and Indian-Mexican fast-food outlets, among dozens of bizarre crossbreeds.

Korean and Indian Korean is the other Asian cuisine firmly established in New York, even though few out-of-towners ever stumble on the Korean business district. Here, within a few blocks of the Empire State Building, off Fifth Avenue in the West 30s, a number of Korean restaurants maintain around-the-clock service.

With its emphasis on barbecued beef and pork, Korean eating might be less gastronomically adventurous than Chinese or Japanese, but anyone with a liking for spicy meat should enjoy Korean *jeyuk gui*, strips of barbecued pork smothered with a very hot sauce and the huge variety of *kimchee* (pickled condiments).

Indian food has been popular in New York for decades. The section of 6th Street between First and Second avenues in the East Village is packed with mediocre Indian restaurants, and another more authentic and higher quality group is to be found in Midtown Manhattan, around Lexington Avenue between 27th and 30th streets.

Spanish and Greek New Yorkers often combine dining out with a trip to the theater, but not if they are planning to tackle one of the gargantuan helpings of paella (which might well take most of the evening to devour) served at the convivial Spanish restaurants dotted throughout the city, with several notable examples in Greenwich Village and Chelsea.

Outside the strongly Greek-populated Astoria area of Queens, Greek food is getting easier to find. Simple Greek dishes such as spinach pie and moussaka often appear in coffee shops, many of which are managed by Greeks.

South American and Caribbean food You're assured of a lively evening in any of the city's increasingly well-regarded Brazilian restaurants. Churrascarias, where waiters circle the room with mammoth skewers of meat, are usually all you can eat. They offer great value and a guaranteed good time. Several Puerto Rican restaurants are along 116th Street in East Harlem, and they will be more than happy to serve you barbecued pig (the island's national dish).

Less daunting Puerto Rican specialties are also served, but East Harlem can be intimidating after dark and it is definitely sensible to restrict your food forays into the area to lunchtime.

Eastern Europe In the Yorkville district, in the 70s and 80s streets of the Upper East Side, several Hungarian, German, and Czech-Slovak restaurants are reminders of the Eastern European communities that settled here before departing for the suburbs. Look no farther for rich, heavy soups, stuffed cabbage, and extremely large portions of goulash.

Similarly solid but tasty fare turns up in the Ukrainian eateries of the East Village and in the Polish cafés that survive on the Lower East Side. In Brighton Beach's Russian restaurants, meanwhile, be ready for a Cyrillic menu—or choose from a buffet table and be prepared to dodge the vodka-sozzled dancers as you are doing so.

New York may be hard to beat for ethnic cooking but the great all-American snack still has plenty of devoted fans

221

Recipes from the regions With the foods of the world providing such competition, the regional cuisines of the nation battle hard to be noticed. Nonetheless Cajun, Tex-Mex, and southwestern cooking all have their devotees. Fried catfish, grilled swordfish, jambalaya, gumbo soup, and even stuffed armadillo are among their offerings.

Being hungry in Harlem is a perfect excuse to discover soul food. Order a plateful of fried chicken or beef ribs coated in gravy, and don't skimp on the side dishes, such as black-eyed peas, corn bread, and grits.

Vegetarian food Although New Yorkers are known to love steak, they are also known to start (and follow) trends. In some circles vegetarianism has become chic and the food offerings available to its practitioners have become vast and varied. Ethnic restaurants, particularly Southern Indian and Chinese, have much to offer. Most American restaurants offer at least one or two vegetarian entrees, and many of the fancier restaurants actually have vegetarian tasting menus available.

Steak houses One kind of establishment into which vegetarians *will* fear to tread is the New York steak house. Carnivores, however, will soon be salivating in these citadels of meat-eating, where large, thick, and juicy hunks of charcoaled prime beef are served. A la carte side dishes, like hash browns or creamed spinach, are the popular accompaniments.

The crème de la crème At the top end of the dining spectrum, New York's finest restaurants not only employ some of the world's best chefs, they also engage the top waiters (some of whom are famously surly) and leading interior designers and have a maître d' who is liable to put the fear of God into staff and diners alike.

To experience New York eating at this rarefied level requires much more than mere appetite and a big bank balance. You will also need to make a reservation (for some a few weeks in advance). Unless you are an extremely famous face (and sometimes even then), you will be shown the door (or, at best, a table completely out of view of the other diners) if you are not dressed in your best for the occasion.

Expensive restaurants sometimes allow you to sample their premier offerings with fixed-price *menus dégustation,* or "tasting menus." These menus enable you to try several dishes, usually between 5 and 10, at a price below what it would cost to order them à la carte.

SMOKING IN RESTAURANTS
Any smoker who can survive without a puff for the duration of a restaurant visit would be well advised to do so. Most New Yorkers are very aware of health issues and their fear of passive smoking has helped make tobacco addicts the scourge of the city. In January 1995, smoking was made illegal in restaurants seating 35 or more people, except at separate bar areas or rooms with independent ventilation.

222

A revered New York institution: the steak house

Coffee and tea Coffee is always freshly brewed and available in regular and decaf (decaffeinated) forms. Cappuccino, caffe latte and espresso coffee, costing around $2–$3 per cup, are also extremely popular, especially on the sidewalk tables of Italian cafés. All types of coffee may be ordered "to go" from delis and street vendors, at prices graded according to the size of the cup or container. Always ask for "regular" coffee if you want milk but no sugar—to get sweetened brew, ask for "regular with sugar."

Another Manhattan phenomenon is the coffee bars, which specialize in serving several different fine coffee blends (and usually a variety of teas and soft drinks). In addition to a variety of strengths, coffee may be obtained with the addition of specialty syrups such as hazelnut or caramel. Customers order their drinks at a counter rather than being served. Although convenient, these places are more suitable for brief stops, or for "coffee to go" rather than for lingering.

Some bookstores (such as the Barnes & Noble chain, for example) now have in-store cafés: a perfect opportunity to sit and browse through a book or magazine while you sip your coffee.

Some New Yorkers have developed a taste for iced coffee, although far more have a liking for iced tea. Both are great drinks for cooling you down after a hot day on the city streets.

Most coffee shops and delis in New York will serve hot tea if requested, but it is generally best avoided (unless you happen to like it weak and made with lukewarm water) if it is not featured on a menu. Where it is a house specialty, tea will usually be offered in a variety of Chinese, Indian, and herbal blends. The better restaurants have now begun to offer impressive selections of teas, sometimes presented for you to sniff before you make up your mind.

For something different, try the **Wild Lily Tea Room** in Chelsea or the fairy-tale like tea at **Mackenzie-Childs** on Madison Ave.

Sample the wide variety of worldwide fare available in New York

223

TEAROOMS
There are few more welcoming sanctuaries from the mayhem of Manhattan's streets than the city's elegant tearooms (often in deluxe hotels) between 2 and 5 PM on a weekday afternoon. At this time, for a price ranging from $15 to $20, you can partake of tea—the list of blends usually spans Chinese, Indian, and Russian—and nibble selectively from a silver tray laden with chicken, ham, and smoked salmon sandwiches, chocolate cakes, delicate pastries, and scones topped with Devonshire thick cream.

New York

Relaxing outside the Victory Café on the Upper East Side

NEW YORK'S NEW BEERS
Partly as a reaction against mass-produced beers and partly because New York loves a new trend, microbrewed beers (produced in small batches, often by the bar that serves them) have become increasingly common through the late 1990s. Hop enthusiasts can sample the likes of Brooklyn Brewery Black Chocolate Stout, Weinhard's Red, Rockefeller Red, Hudson River Porter, Gotham City Gold, Empire State Bitter, and Lady Liberty Light. At the Fraunces Tavern (see page 107) they can imbibe the creamy Swig Tavern Keeper, supposedly similar to that brewed when George Washington propped up the bar.

Juice bars Sodas are fast declining in popularity among some of the more health-conscious New Yorkers, who, after a workout at the gym or a jog, refresh themselves instead with the nutritious fruit juices sold in the city's specialized juice bars. As well as fresh orange, grapefruit, and carrot juice, some juice bars offer power-packed juices blended from parsley, ginger, spinach, and root vegetables; expect to spend $1–$4 for a glassful.

Bars and beers Bars, which stay open from around midday to the early hours (legally they must stop serving at 4 AM), range from the chummy neighborhood variety to those patronized almost exclusively by a particular social set—be it stockbrokers, art dealers, or punk rockers. For more insights into the diversity of New York bars, see pages 114–115.

Most bars, especially larger ones and those with outdoor tables, have waiter or waitress service, though usually you can go to the bar and order drinks directly from the bartender—as you can if you sit at the bar. In all bars, the bartender will expect you to leave a tip when buying a round of drinks or when leaving.

Mass-market beers such as Budweiser, Miller, and Rolling Rock are served in virtually every bar. Many establishments also carry a commendable selection of bottled European beers (occasionally found on tap) and Mexican beers.

Adventurous beer-drinkers should also investigate the output of the nation's many microbreweries: Anchor Steam Beer, brewed in California, is not the best of the bunch but is the most commonly found.

Sports bars New Yorkers can watch the playoffs in sports bars with multiple extra-large television screens. Some favorite ones in the city include **Entourage Sports** (1571 Second Avenue between 81st and 82nd Street), **Polo Grounds** (1472 Third Avenue between 83rd and 84th streets), **Sporting Club** (99 Hudson Street at Franklin Street), **Sports Page** (90 Second Avenue at 5th Street), baseball-mad **Mickey Mantle's** (42 Central Park South), **Runyons** (932 Second Avenue between 49th and 50th streets), and **Rusty's** (1271 3rd Avenue at 73rd Street), owned by former Met Rusty Staub.

Wines and liquor Alongside the beer, New York bars also stock a selection of wines from Europe and the United States—many of which are available by the glass. The more elegant the bar, the more extensive (and expensive) its wine stocks will be. Some good restaurants produce wine lists on regularly updated computer print-outs. Behind every bar will be a very well-stocked rack of liquor, including malt whiskies, Russian vodka, and various bourbons.

Cocktails Any bar describing itself as a cocktail lounge— particularly in parts of Midtown Manhattan and in the Upper East Side—is likely to be either a watering hole for the wealthy or a meeting place for the tragically hip. For eavesdropping on high-society gossip and poodle-grooming tips, cocktail lounges are unrivaled, but to spend an evening inside one you will need to be very well dressed (in black if you're downtown) and not afraid to spend $10 or more on a single drink—and on no account should you topple drunkenly from your stool.

Theme bars There are many interesting spots that are off the beaten path, and offer quirky themes along with strong cocktails. Idelwild (145 East Houston St), named for New York's old airport, is set up like the interior of an airplane, complete with reclining seats and servers in groundcrew uniforms.

VINTAGE CLASSICS
Hotel bars provide exhausted sightseers with some of the best places in Manhattan. The **Plaza Hotel's Oak Bar** (Fifth Avenue and 59th Street) continues to age well with its plummy, dark-wood furnishings; it draws sophisticates, shoppers, and celebrities. The **Carlyle** (35 East 76th Street) contains the charming **Bemelman's Bar** with whimsical animal murals, painted by Ludwig Bemelman, and live jazz piano music at night. At the art deco-style **Essex House** (160 Central Park South), **Journeys** bar has pure English country-style decor with rich carved wood, sporting scenes on the walls and a large fireplace. One of the most elegant, venerable spots in New York to have a glass of wine (or a cup of tea) remains the **Algonquin Hotel Lounge** (59 West 44th Street), with its many literary associations.

225

Views across to South Street Seaport and Lower Manhattan complement the food and wine at Brooklyn's River Café

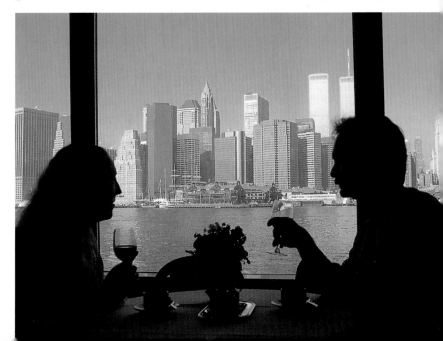

THE WINTER ANTIQUES FAIR
One way to keep warm in New York during January is to pay a visit to the Winter Antiques Fair, held at the Seventh Regiment Armory (see page 187). With all of New York's antiques dealers and antiques lovers gathered under one roof, you might not be able to afford anything, but eavesdropping on the chit-chat can be fascinating. There are plenty of fine antiques to admire, too.

Union Square now teems with shoppers choosing fresh produce at the popular Farmers' Market, which is held several times a week

Shopping

From the ultra-exclusive antiques stores of the Upper East Side to the discount clothing stores that proliferate in Lower Manhattan, New York is not only the most exciting place in the world to buy things, but also the easiest and sometimes even the cheapest. Not surprisingly, New Yorkers often like to "shop till they drop."

Antiques The New York millionaires who plundered the treasures of Europe and the Far East to furnish their mansions contributed to the city's emergence as the center of the international antiques trade. For serious buyers, there is no better place to locate that elusive Japanese watercolor or Swiss music box. There is plenty to drool over in the upscale antiques stores of the Upper East Side. The more affordable stuff, meanwhile, can be found elsewhere.

Among the city's top-range antiques stores, **A La Vieille Russie** (Fifth Avenue at 59th Street) highlights the achievements of czarist Russian craftsmen with Fabergé enamelware, jewel-encrusted icons, snuff boxes, clocks, and assorted silverware—none of which would disgrace the finest palace.

Japanese prints, books and ornaments (18th and 19th century) are among the Far Eastern treasures that can be found at **Things Japanese** (60th Street between Park and Lexington avenues). Connoisseurs of art deco will find plenty to please amid the pricey rarities at **Delorenzo** (Madison Avenue between 75th and 76th streets).

Several hours might be needed for a thorough exploration of **Asia House** (56th Street between Sixth and

Seventh avenues), packed with porcelain, lamps, vases and much more from points East. Meanwhile, **America Hurrah Antiques** (Madison Avenue at 66th Street) elevates the untutored skills of early U.S. settlers—displayed in everything from weather vanes to decoy ducks—to the status of fine art and prices it accordingly.

Antiquated melodies accompany browsing at **Rita Ford Music Boxes** (65th Street between Madison and Fifth avenues), a colossal collection of music boxes and miniature handmade carousels, which the staff are easily persuaded to demonstrate.

A change of identity? Anything is possible in the stores of Greenwich Village

If you lack the nerve to pose as a genuine customer in the more exclusive antique stores, you might aim instead for the friendlier environs of the **Manhattan Art & Antiques Center** (Second Avenue between 55th and 56th streets). At the **Laura Fisher Gallery**, one of the center's 104 separate stores, you will learn more about American quilts than you thought you could know.

Another low-key spot high on potential is the **Chelsea Antiques Building** (110 West 25th Street), where 150 dealers are spread across twelve floors, and sell items ranging from 18th and 19th-century furnishings to toys, books, and comics.

The mood in SoHo antiques outlets, typically set in warehouse-like stores, is much less stuffy than that of the Upper East Side stores and the prices are lower (but by no means a bargain). Among the inventory of **Back Pages** (Green Street between Prince and West Houston streets) you will find Wurlitzer jukeboxes, vintage pool tables, and vending machines.

Big Apple detritus forms the eclectic stock of **Urban Archeology** (285 Lafayette Street). This is just the place to pick up a bizarre bathroom fitting or a vintage barbershop chair. Similar ephemera fills **Secondhand Rose** (275 Lafayette Street), among it neon-lit Coke signs and dilapidated peep-show machines. There are also some bizarre specialist stores: see panel.

Books New Yorkers love to read. A proliferation of **Barnes & Noble** and **Borders'** superstores cover all bases and offer pleasant environments (many with cafés) in which to browse and read. Independent booksellers tailor their collections with more personality. Try **Shakespeare & Co.** (716 Broadway), **St. Marks Bookshop** (31 Third Avenue), or **Coliseum Books** (1775 Broadway). With used, review copies, and remaindered books, **The Strand** (828 Broadway) is a New York institution.

Specialty book stores also abound. If your interest lies in people's lives, check out the **Biography Book Shop** (400 Bleecker Street). For mysteries and crime try **Murder Ink** (2486 Broadway) or **Partners & Crime** (44 Greenwich Avenue). If you prefer looking at pictures, venture into **A Photographer's Place** (133 Mercer Street) or flip through the pages at **Printed Matter** (77 Wooster Street). The shelves are filled with children's books at **Books of Wonder** (16 West 18th Street). The country's largest selection of gay and lesbian books is stocked at **A Different Light Bookstore** (151 West 19th Street) and the oldest at the **Oscar Wilde Memorial Bookstore** (15 Christopher

UNUSUAL STORES
New York has an unusual store at every turn. Among the curiosities you might stumble across are: New York Firefighter's Friend (Lafayette Street between Prince and Spring streets), selling firefighting paraphernalia from model fire engines to helmets and hose nozzles; Maxilla and Mandible (82nd Street at Columbus Avenue), packed with skeletons and individual bones from humans, animals, and birds; Little Rickie (First Avenue at 3rd Street), where an extra-ordinary assortment of tasteless merchandise includes Elvis Presley clocks and lamps; and Tender Buttons (62nd Street between Third and Lexington avenues), with nothing but buttons—new and antique—tens of thousands of them.

227

Shopping

BUYING RECORDS AND C.D.S

With 75,000 square feet of floor space, the Virgin Megastore (Broadway between 45th and 46th streets) claims to be the world's largest music and entertainment store. As you pore through rack after rack of records, c.d.s, laser disks, and cassettes, and pass through a classical section that includes space for a concert pianist, the claim is easy to believe. A second outlet recently opened on Union Square. Other only slightly smaller stores are the several branches of Tower (692 Broadway; Trump Tower, 725 Fifth Avenue; and Broadway at 66th Street); and the four branches of HMV (in Midtown Manhattan at Fifth Avenue and 46th Street).

A window-display at Armani

MUSEUM SHOPS

Many museums have excellent shops. The Museum of Modern Art (pages 158–160) and the Guggenheim Museum (pages 122–124), in particular, are excellent places to find art books, unusual badges, T-shirts, and other souvenirs marking their major exhibitions. A branch of the Guggenheim Museum in SoHo (575 Broadway) also has a good range of art-related merchandise, and the Cooper-Hewitt Museum (page 95) has tomes covering all aspects of the decorative arts.

Street). Serious cooks pilgrimage to **Kitchen Arts & Letters** (1435 Lexington Avenue). Comic book lovers can lose themselves at **St. Marks Comics** (11 St. Marks Place, 598-9439). For other special interests, foreign language books, religious, scholarly, or used texts, consult the Manhattan *Yellow Pages*.

C.D.s and records C.D.s and tapes can be found to fit all tastes amid the eclectic and vast stocks of **Tower Records** (Broadway at 4th Street), **J.&R. Music World** (23 Park Row, in the Financial District) and those listed in the panel on this page.

Clothing The latest in leather, rubber, and plastic street fashions can be seen being worn around the East Village, and, in general, New York is a fashion capital. Every major designer has an outlet there. Dozens of discount stores sell American casual clothing, as well as discounted designer merchandise, for a song.

Those clothes-conscious people who do not need to worry about their credit limits—or about being patronized by snooty staff—always do much of their shopping amid the designer-name stores of Midtown Manhattan and the Upper East Side. These areas are positively cluttered with the stores of world-famous names such as **Giorgio Armani** (Madison Avenue at 65th Street), **Gucci** (there are two stores on Fifth Avenue at 54th Street—numbers 685 and 689), **Hermès** (57th Street, between Madison and Fifth avenues) and **Yves St. Laurent** (Madison Avenue at 71st Street).

One pedigree designer you should visit for the setting alone, however, is **Polo/Ralph Lauren** (Madison Avenue at 72nd Street). The company occupies a French Renaissance-style Upper East Side mansion that is a show in itself. Another is **Comme des Garçons**, whose trend-setting futuristic store in Chelsea is like an attraction at an amusement park.

Giorgio Armani also has a downtown store, **Armani A/X** (Broadway at Prince Street). This is pitched at the younger designer-dresser, though you will probably need more than your weekly allowance to afford anything inside.

The person of average income in search of quality clothing should aim instead for the scores of discount outlets, where designer clothing is unceremoniously discounted and sold for as little as half their regular prices. Although their prices may be comparatively inexpensive, the stores themselves can be as classy as any. Among them are **Century 21** (22 Cortlandt Street), which sells an amazing array of discounted merchandise for men and women; **Michaels'—The Consignment Shop For Women** (1041 Madison Avenue), a favorite of well-heeled Upper East Side ladies; and **Pretty Plus Plus** (1309 Madison Avenue), which stocks bargain designer wear for the larger woman.

There are some lower-priced (but not inexpensive) designer stores which specialize in chic clothes and accessories for the style-conscious traveler. One such place is **Betsey Johnson** (138 Wooster Street), which adapts New York street fashion into loud and colorful garments.

Also in SoHo is **Catherine** (468 Broome Street), a funky clothing store known for cowboy hats in every color of the rainbow, and **Kate Spade** (454 Broome Street) a wildly popular designer of bags and other accessories, available in a wide range of colors and styles. Style conscious men will love **Sean** (132 Thompson Street), where proper cotton shirts come in an interesting array of colors, and **Beau Brummel** (421 West Broadway), which carries what is arguably the best selection of men's ties in the city, as well as a host of stylish suits.

Just East of SoHo is the fashionable neighborhood of NoLiTa where independent designers peddle their wearable wares in tiny storefronts. Check out **Lucien Pellat-finet** (226 Elizabeth Street) for chic (and expensive) designs, all made from the most luxurious cashmere available, and **Wang** (219 Mott Street) for colorful women's clothes in wearable, downtown styles.

For true bargain hunters there's Orchard Street on the Lower East Side, where stores sell leather accessories, shoes, and some designer duds at discount prices. (But most of Orchard Street shuts down on Saturday.)

Lower Manhattan is a good area for bargain clothing stores and stalls such as this one on West Broadway

A NOTE FOR BARGAIN-HUNTERS
Photographic and electrical goods can bring real bargains in New York. It is vital, however, to know exactly what you want before entering a store and to resist the seductive patter of the salesperson. This is especially true of electrical goods, even if the sales pitch suggests otherwise.

The largest photographic discount store is 47th Street Photo (main branch on 47th Street between Fifth and Sixth avenues; others listed in the *Yellow Pages*). It also carries a large range of videos, computers, and all kinds of electrical gadgets.

Mainstream American-made clothing, particularly Levi jeans, represents exceptionally good value (especially for the European visitor); prices are lowest in the scores of discount stores on and around the SoHo section of Broadway: the biggest is **Canal Jean** (between Broome and Spring streets), with a massive stock of jeans, T-shirts, jackets, sunglasses, beachwear, loud ties, all kinds of practical traveling accessories, and secondhand clothing at extremely tempting prices.

Army/Navy (328 Bleecker Street, one of three Manhattan branches) is another dependable provider of items such as jeans, plaid shirts, T-shirts, and reasonably priced leather jackets.

Department stores Immortalized in film, fiction, and folklore, Manhattan's department stores are the stuff of legend. Generations of New Yorkers have grown up unable to imagine life without these totems to 20th-century consumerism, and while they are superficially similar, each one has a character and cachet very much its own and its own band of loyal supporters.

Among them is **Macy's** (34th Street and Sixth Avenue), famously described as the world's largest department store. The claim seems justified as you wind up its 10 floors and find half a million items for sale. There is even a section for buying pets and a branch of the Museum of Modern Art's gift store. Large this store certainly is but, despite revamping its image during the 1970s, Macy's is far from being the world's most exciting department store, having built its reputation by supplying middle-income family purchasers with the most middle-of-the-road tastes.

By contrast, **Bloomingdale's** (Third Avenue at 59th Street) is a wonderful store in which to buy cosmetics, accessories, men's and women's fashions, and much more. Although it is not cutting edge, Bloomies does feature a wide range of designers, in a wide range of prices.

Bloomingdale's was the first New York department store to feature now-established designers such as Yves St. Laurent, Calvin Klein, and Ralph Lauren, and it supports many newer ones as well. Elsewhere, there are souvenirs, the latest in electrical gadgetry, a furniture department, a well-stocked bookstore, and even a fine-food level that devotes a whole section to caviar.

More opulent still is **Bergdorf Goodman** (Fifth Avenue between 57th and 58th streets). This is where the ladies of the Upper East Side shop beneath crystal chandeliers for clothes, jewelry, perfumes, and other luxury items. Their latest husbands, meanwhile, sift through the $100-a piece tie racks in the most elegant men's store, **Bergdorf Goodman Men**, directly across Fifth Avenue.

Spread over nine artfully designed floors, **Barneys** (660 Madison Avenue) offers all the stylish and successful

Manhattanite could wish for: cutting edge designer names by the score, and beautiful jewelry and accessories, and some classic New York attitude. Barneys also prides itself on its window displays—especially at Christmas.

The antidote to glitz and ostentatious wealth is **Saks Fifth Avenue** (Fifth Avenue between 49th and 50th streets), which simply offers tasteful, stylish and high-quality merchandise—clothing, linens, cosmetics—in an orderly setting with efficient service.

Jewelry Dozens of jewelers occupy Manhattan's "diamond district," which fills a block of 47th Street immediately west of Fifth Avenue. This wholesale jewelry trading district is where diamonds are cut and polished, jewelry is repaired, gems are set, and deals are done above the ground level shops. More famous stores include **Tiffany & Co** (Fifth Avenue between 56th and 57th streets), with three floors of highly desirable pieces, not all of which cost the earth, and the more conservative **Cartier** (Fifth Avenue at 52nd Street), worth a call not least for the landmark building which it occupies. Another, less classy, stalwart is the **World's Largest Jewelry Exchange** (55 West 47th Street), more than a hundred retailers and repairers under a single roof providing ample opportunity for browsing and comparing prices.

Shoes Shoe stores abound in New York, and if you cannot find what you want (whether it's handmade Italian loafers, kitten heels, or streetwise sneakers), you are simply not trying. Aside from numerous upscale outlets on the Upper East Side, and the extensive stocks of most department stores, many Lower Manhattan discount stores offer good deals in footwear. Manhattan also has two "shoe districts," where you will see rows of shoe stores—on West 8th Street and on 34th Street between Fifth and Sixth avenues.

At **Susan Bennis/Warren Edwards** (Park Avenue and 56th Street), the handmade, limited-edition footwear for men and women comes in all manner of styles.

Everything under one (huge) roof: Macy's

PERSONAL SHOPPING
If the prospect of many hours of roaming the city's department stores fills you with dread, each store has a team of personal shoppers who will make your purchases for you. All you have to do is pay for the goods—and for the personal shopper. Telephone for details: Bergdorf Goodman (tel: 753-5300); Bloomingdale's (tel: 800/777-0000); Macy's (tel: 560-4181); Saks Fifth Avenue (tel: 753-4000).

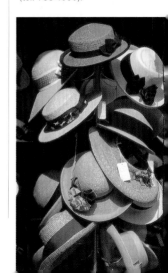

Nightlife

New York nightlife is never boring, and it's more plentiful and more diverse (and often of a higher standard) than almost anywhere else in the world. To enjoy it, all you need is energy and, in most cases, plenty of money.

Most New York-based publications carry extensive nightlife listings. The most thorough are *Time Out New York,* the *Village Voice,* and the Friday and Sunday editions of *The New York Times.* For new movies and plays, the *New Yorker* is also an excellent source of opinionated reviews and information.

Theater From the *Ziegfeld Follies* to *The Phantom of the Opera*, the theater has been an integral part of New York nightlife for years. The section of Broadway nearest Times Square has long been established as the flag-carrier of commercial American theater.

Big-time New York theater has hit a rough patch, however. Incredibly high production costs have resulted in high seat prices (as much as $100) and only financially

low-risk plays seem to be contemplated. The result is an endless stream of lavish musicals, comedies, and unadventurous drama, usually with a big name or two to spark interest. The hit shows continue to be packed, but, overall, Broadway theaters have been hit by declining attendances and have had more flops than ever before.

Nonetheless, even if the show could be a little better, a good reason for splurging on a night inside one of the 34 official Broadway theaters is to enjoy the sumptuous auditorium and get a taste of a little of the history and folklore that every Broadway theater has in abundance.

Regularly hosting the city's major shows are the **Eugene O'Neill Theater** (230 West 49th Street), probably the biggest and best of the neighborhood playhouses; the **Broadway Theater** (1681 Broadway); the **Neil Simon Theater** (250 52nd Street); the **Palace Theater** (1564 Broadway); the **Richard Rogers Theater** (226 West 46th Street); and the **Roundabout Theater** (1530 Broadway). Another worth trying is the **Walter Kerr** (219 West 48th Street), as much for a renovation job that has brought back something of the 1920s' grandeur of the place as for the shows themselves.

Another venerable New York dramatic institution is the **Public Theater** (425 Lafayette Street; tel: 260-2400—formerly the Joseph Papp Public Theater). Here you will discover provocative new plays and controversial adaptations of the classics in six separate theaters. Originally named for Joseph Papp, the director and producer whose credits included *A Chorus Line* and *Hair*, and who saved the building from demolition, the Public Theater hosts the New York Shakespeare Festival in Central Park for over six weeks each summer.

Smaller than their Broadway counterparts, Off-Broadway theaters (seating 100–499) are a little more adventurous and among them they offer an excellent choice of musicals, comedies, revivals, classics, and new works that few cities can equal. Top playwrights and leading professional actors are no strangers to Off-Broadway productions, and many of the more successful make the transition to Broadway.

Most of the leading Off-Broadway theaters can be found in and around Greenwich Village, and they include the **Circle Repertory Theater** (159 Bleecker Street; tel: 254-6330), **Orpheum** (Second Avenue at 8th Street; tel: 477-2477), and **Actor's Playhouse** (100 Seventh Avenue South; tel: 239-6200).

You can go even further afield and and try your luck at an Off-Off-Broadway venue. The dozens of tiny Off-Off-Broadway theaters (seating under 100) are often housed in places like converted churches or vacant schoolrooms. It is here that daring and experimental plays are performed by unknown but often very talented actors. It is seldom necessary for you to pay more than $15 for a seat, and ticket availability is likely to be less of a problem than trying to get last-minute seats for a Broadway hit.

These also stage performance art and alternative cabaret. Among the longer-lasting are **The Kitchen** (19th Street between Tenth and Eleventh avenues; tel: 255-5793), **The Ohio Theater** (66 Wooster Street; tel: 226-9044), and **P.S.122** (First Avenue at 9th Street; tel: 477-5829).

THEATER INFORMATION
Besides the listings in the *New Yorker, New York Times* and *Village Voice*, 24-hour recorded information on what is playing where, and on ticket availability, can be found by calling the NYC/ON STAGE hotline (tel: 768–1818).

SHAKESPEARE IN THE PARK
The Public Theater's former director, Joseph Papp, instigated the popular "Shakespeare in the Park" series: the bard's plays in Central Park's open-air Delacorte Theater (near the 81st Street entrance on the Upper West Side) between June and August. Tickets are free but limited to two per person. A very long line begins forming around noon—entertainers stroll and everyone chats and picnics: the tickets are distributed at 6 PM.

233

Bright lights in the theater district

The golden age of neon may be long since gone, but the gaudy excitement of Times Square remains legendary

Films New York has always had a special relationship with the cinema, playing a part in countless films over a period of more than 60 years (see pages 14–15 and 188). The city is also a great place to watch movies. Not only do most high-budget Hollywood features get their first screenings here in state-of-the-art cinema complexes, but dozens of smaller film houses specialize in new independent films and rarely seen foreign movies. Nostalgia buffs are in for a treat, too, with oldies—from world cinema classics to kitsch 1940s musicals—regularly showing.

Multiscreen complexes show the latest releases all over the city; most art house and revival cinemas are downtown in the Village, Soho, and TriBeCa. They include the six-screen **Angelika Film Center** (Houston Street at Mercer Street; tel: 995-2000); the **Anthology Film Archives** (Second Avenue at 2nd Street; tel: 505-5181); **Cinema Village** (12th Street between Fifth and Sixth avenues; tel: 924-3363); **Cineplex Odeon Art Greenwich** (971 Greenwich Avenue, tel: 505-CINE); **Film Forum** (Houston Street at Varick Street; tel: 727-8110); **The Screening Room** (Varick Street; tel: 334-2100); and the **Walter Reade Theater** (70 Lincoln Center Plaza; tel: 875-5600).

Many city museums have projection facilities and mount film series linked to a particular exhibition. The **Museum of Modern Art** and the **Metropolitan Museum of Art** also have extensive film archives of their own, and the **Museum of Television and Radio** (see page 161) is another potential source of delight for movie-lovers. During the summer Bryant Park (42nd Street and Sixth Avenue) has free outdoor movie screenings on Monday nights.

Classical music From free open-air recitals to concerts featuring the biggest in big names, the serious music lover will find plenty to cheer about.

Lincoln Center's Avery Fisher Hall is the home of the **New York Philharmonic**, whose season runs from mid-September to June (for information, tel: 875-5656). During July, the orchestra undertakes a free concert series in the parks of each of the city's five boroughs.

THE NEW YORK FILM FESTIVAL
Each September, specially selected new American and foreign-made films are screened at the New York Film Festival, held at Alice Tully Hall at Lincoln Center. The festival is organized by the Film Society of Lincoln Center, and tickets tend to be in short supply (tel: 875-5610).

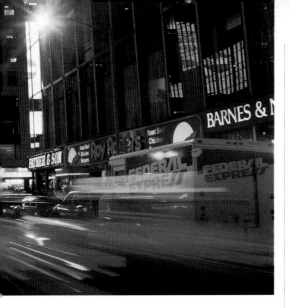

THE MOSTLY MOZART FESTIVAL

For six weeks each July and August, New Yorkers shake off their summer slumbers with the enormously popular Mostly Mozart Festival, held at Lincoln Center's Avery Fisher Hall. Featuring many star performers and conductors, the festival is also the only chance many people get to afford front row seats: for the festival, all seats are charged at a single (low) price.

The **New York Chamber Symphony** (tel: 996-1100) is based at the 92nd Y (92nd Street at Lexington Avenue). The oak-walled **Kaufmann Theater** (also 92nd Street Y) is strong on both acoustics and atmosphere and is a popular venue with visiting soloists and other chamber groups.

At Lincoln Center, **Alice Tully Hall** (tel: 875-5050) is another good place for chamber music, and all around the city numerous other venues regularly give all forms of classical music an airing. Historic **Carnegie Hall** (Seventh Avenue and 57th Street; tel: 247-7800) offers chamber music and solo recitals; the compact **Merkin Concert Hall** (67th Street between Broadway and Amsterdam Avenue; tel: 362-8719) showcases more unusual fare, such as ethnic music and choral groups; a broad-ranging program is offered at the **Town Hall** (43rd Street between Sixth Avenue and Broadway; tel: 997-1003).

Music fans of meager means should scan the newspapers' listing section for free and moderately priced concerts, held at the Financial District's **St. Paul's Chapel**, the Upper West Side's **Riverside Church**, and at the city's schools of music—the major one being the **Juilliard School of Music** at Lincoln Center.

Ballet and dance Based at Lincoln Center's **Metropolitan Opera House**, the **American Ballet Theater** (tel: 362-6000) gets rave reviews for its interpretations of classical and contemporary pieces. The season runs from April to June. **New York City Ballet** is based at Lincoln Center's **New York State Theater** (tel: 870-5570). Their performances run from November to February and from April to June, with the *Nutcracker* on during the Christmas season. Tickets vary widely in price and sell out in advance. Sometimes you can pick up tickets at the box office on the day of the performance, or (sold at face value or less) outside the theater just before curtain time.

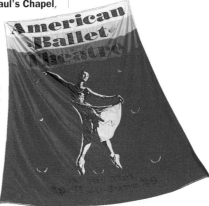

Many of the world's finest dancers perform at the Met

New York

THE FIRST MET
Generation after gener-
ation of New York's
longstanding wealthy
would demonstrate their
social aloofness by occu-
pying all of the few boxes
available during the opera
season at the Academy of
Music (on Irving Place),
leaving the *nouveau riche*
of the mid- to late-19th
century to face the social
indignity of sitting below
them. In retaliation, millionaires William Henry
Vanderbilt and Jay Astor
financed the first
Metropolitan Opera
House. The huge building
that arose, opening in
1883, was criticized for
its ugliness, but did provide the grand boxes from
which the city's self-made
millionaires could
symbolically flaunt their
affluence.

In summer, top international guest companies, such as
the Bolshoi or the Paris Opera, often come for a two-week
run. Bear in mind that the cheaper seats are very high and
far from the stage, not really a great bargain in the theater.

Another important but much more intimate dance
venue, **City Center** (55th Street between Sixth and
Seventh avenues; tel: 581-1212), hosts a trio of innovative
companies: the **Alvin Ailey American Dance Theater**; the
Dance Theater of Harlem; and the **Merce Cunningham
Dance Company**. A further small but interesting venue is
the **Bessie Schonberg Theater** (219 W 19th Street between
Seventh and Eighth avenues; tel: 924-0077), where the
Dance Theater Workshop pioneers experimental dance.
Bigger and more mainstream than the DTW, but smaller
than the City Center, the **Joyce Theater** (175 Eighth
Avenue; tel: 691-9740) has the Feld Ballet in residence
amongst others. The promising talent of many future
dance stars can be seen in the workshop performances of
the prestigious **American School of Ballet** (tel: 877-0600)
at Lincoln Center's **Juilliard School of Music**.

Such is the excellent quality of its productions that
dance-loving Manhattanites regularly cross the East River
to attend shows at the **Brooklyn Academy of Music** (tel:
718/636-4100). The U.S.'s first center for the performing
arts, the Academy was founded in 1861 and moved to its
current site in 1908. Artists from Enrico Caruso to Laurie
Anderson have graced its boards. Established as a major
center of modern dance, the academy hosts the spectacular Next Wave festival each fall.

Opera During its late September to mid-April season at
Lincoln Center's vast **Metropolitan Opera House**,
the **Metropolitan Opera** company's performances

*The Metropolitan
Opera House*

(tel: 362-6000) are as much social as musical occasions, especially Monday evenings. The company is criticized as unimaginative but seldom turns in anything other than exceptionally polished performances. Tickets are highly priced and can be hard to get without booking a long time in advance. Standing room tickets are available.

Also based at Lincoln Center is the increasingly innovative **New York City Opera** (tel: 870-5600), usually performing at the **New York State Theater**.

Among a sprinkling of smaller opera companies, with lower prices and cozier settings, is the **Amato Opera Company** (319 Bowery; tel: 228-8200). From June to August, **New York Grand Opera** (tel: 245-8837) mounts free shows at Central Park's Summer Stage.

Comedy clubs New York's comedy clubs have given a break to the careers of Eddie Murphy, David Letterman, Robin Williams, and innumerable others over the years. Don't expect Las Vegas-style gags and routines—New York comedy clubs can be boisterous places and the crowds may be cruel if they dislike a particular comic.

Most clubs have two shows nightly. It is wise to make a reservation for performances on Fridays and Saturdays.

Expect to pay more (if you can get tickets) for a "name"; "open mike" nights (when amateurs take a turn, usually on Mondays) are almost always free, but you will still be expected to buy a drink

The most extensive comedy club listings are carried by the *Village Voice*. With a range of well-chosen up-and-coming talent, and the occasional big name, the most reliable clubs are **Caroline's Comedy Club** (Broadway between 49th and 50th streets; tel: 757-4100); the **Comic Strip Inc** (Second Avenue between 81st and 82nd streets; tel: 861-9386); **Dangerfield's** (First Avenue between 61st and 62nd streets; tel: 593-1650); and **Stand Up N.Y.** (78th Street and Broadway; tel: 595-0850).

Nightclubs New York nightclubs are always in a state of flux. The last 15 years have seen the rise and fall of the jet-set Studio 54; the arty Mudd Club, which helped rejuvenate SoHo; and a batch of punky East Village clubs that reshaped many New Yorkers' notions of what a night out could be.

THE POETS' SLAM
Listening to unknown poets reciting their latest verse may sound like an unexciting way to pass an evening, but at the Nuyorican Poets' Café (234 E 3rd Street between avenues B and C; tel: 505-8183), the Friday night "Poets' Slam" finds a bunch of rowdy poets locked in combat, each one hoping to impress the audience—and a panel of invited judges—with their work. A winner is chosen at the end of this lively and bizarre—but very New York—event. Nuyorican also hosts some other interesting events like wild Latin jazz nights and experimental film screenings.

237

Music is a way of life for many New Yorkers. The city offers plenty of scope for talented performers

238

Bright lights on the club scene

The city's nightclub scene in general is thriving. One recent development is that the action has tended to move further downtown, away from the traditional midtown area, but there are still scores of places of different kinds where you can dress up (or dress down), pose, preen, or just dance—well into the small hours.

For nonregulars, the biggest potential hazard at any club is the doorman, who will decide whether you are a suitable person (judged by your clothes and general manner) to be admitted. The arrogance of doormen is legendary, but being turned away is no problem—simply try somewhere else.

No nightclub worth its salt gets into gear before 1 or 2 AM in the morning (most are open until 4 AM and some until noon the next day). Arrive before midnight and you will probably have the place to yourself. One advantage of arriving early, however, may be a reduced admission charge. Drinks in nightclubs are more expensive than in bars, and sometimes extortionately so.

Many clubs have different entertainment, and therefore an entirely different crowd, on particular nights of the week: always phone ahead to check. The best places for information on the club scene are *Time Out New York* and *Paper Magazine*.

New York nightclubs open, close, and change address with incredible rapidity; the following suggestions are intended as a representative cross-section.

One of the longer-established upscale clubs, the polo-stick-and-croquet-mallet-decorated **Au Bar** (58th Street between Madison Avenue and Park Avenue; tel: 308-9455) attracts a designer-dressed and rather staid crowd, dancing primly to fairly bland disco music.

Occasionally visited by rock-and-roll celebrities, the **China Club** (Broadway at 75th Street; tel: 877-1156) is an enjoyable mainstream rock-and-roll disco. Likewise, **Webster Hall** (11th Street between Third and Fourth avenues; tel: 353-1600) is unadventurous, but appreciated by its regular crowd of suburbanites.

Lively and youthful, and packed to the gills on busy nights, **Tunnel** (220 Twelfth Avenue; tel: 695-4682) is an entertainingly varied club with different rooms featuring different sounds, from hip-hop to acid jazz; the audience can be similarly eclectic. **Tuilo**, across the street, boasts the strongest sound system in town. Also boasting diverse music is **Coney Island High** (15 St. Mark's Place), a spacious dance spot for specialist sounds ranging from 1950s rockabilly to 1970s funk and soul. There are more Latin American rhythms—and mambo lessons—at **S.O.B.s** (Varick Street at Houston Street; tel: 243-4940).

Opening in the mid-1980s, the subdued ambience of **Nell's** (14th Street between Seventh and Eighth avenues; tel: 675-1567) was intended as an antidote to flashing lights and pulsating music; this Victorian-style living room has faded from fashion but is still worth a visit.

239

Radio City Music Hall is a popular rock venue

However, a new trend is rapidly evolving: the"lounge", a quiet place where the more sedate nocturnal New Yorker can just lounge and chat.

Rock music Rock music's big names always include New York on their international touring schedules. If they are not popular enough to fill the 55,000-capacity Shea Stadium in Queens, they are most likely to be found in venues such as the **Beacon Theater** (Broadway at 75th Street; for ticket info tel: 307-7171), **Madison Square Garden** (Seventh Avenue between 31st and 33rd streets; tel: 465-6741), or **Radio City Music Hall** (Sixth Avenue at 50th Street; tel: 247-4777) which stages musicals, dance and rock music shows.

Up-and-coming bands from the U.S. and Europe who have outgrown the small club scene but are not yet ready for the large concert halls turn up most nights of the week in mid-sized venues such as **Irving Plaza** (17 Irving Place; tel: 777-6800), the **Roxy** (515 W 18th Street; tel: 714-8001), and **Roseland** (52nd Street between Eighth Avenue and Broadway; tel: 249–8870), the legendary ballroom of the Big Band era.

ROCK MUSIC TICKETS
Tickets for major rock shows (usually $15–$30) and for most shows at medium-sized venues ($10–$20) can be booked by phone and paid for by credit card through Ticketmaster (tel: 307-7171).

Other venues worth checking out are **The Bottom Line** (4th Street near Fifth Avenue; tel: 228-7800), showcasing new signings to major labels and also booking some aging 1960s cult names, and **Wetlands** (Hudson Street, three blocks south of Canal Street; tel: 966-4225), with 1960s psychedelic décor, organic food, and books and pamphlets on ecological issues—as well as a full roster of rock, reggae, and funk bands.

Another dependable spot for local talent and sometimes more, is **Brownies** (169 Avenue A, between Tenth and Eleventh Streets; tel: 420-8392).

New York's own rock music scene is highly incestuous—some bands might be huge in a particular neighborhood but unknown outside it. Plenty of exotically named hopefuls can be heard every night for free, or a few dollars, in dozens of tiny clubs secreted throughout the East Village and SoHo. For details, read the ads in the *Village Voice* or look for the handwritten notices pinned up in local cafés and bars.

Talking Heads and Blondie were just two of the big names that emerged from the New York punk scene of the mid-1970s, which centered on the still-surviving **C.B.G.B.** (Bowery at Bleecker Street; tel: 982-4052). Unknown bands play here every night of the week, while performance art and readings are also billed at the **C.B.'s 313 Gallery** next door (tel: 388-2529).

Experimentally minded musicians explore rock's avant-garde fringe at the **Knitting Factory** (Houston Street near Mulberry Street; tel: 219-3055).

A popular jazz venue, Birdland is named after a club that was a 1940s legend

Jazz and blues Since the 1940s, New York has been well endowed with smoky jazz clubs, usually occupying basements in Greenwich Village. Their floorboards will have been trodden by many of jazz's most illustrious figures.

Most jazz clubs have two or three nightly shows. Cover charges range from around $8 to $20 or more and, depending on the venue and, sometimes, the band playing, you may have to pay per set, rather than for the whole evening. Sometimes there will also be a two-drink minimum charge (around $6).

The long-established and excellent **Village Vanguard** (Seventh Avenue at 11th Street; tel: 255-4037) epitomizes the dark-and-smoky Greenwich Village basement jazz club. Several top names play here regularly. Major jazz stars are also frequent visitors to the atmospheric **Blue Note** (3rd Street at MacDougal Street; tel: 475-8592), where cover charges can sometimes be very steep.

Among the city's newer jazz venues is **Iridium Room** (48 W 63rd Street; tel: 582-2121), highly rated for its excellent roster of live acts and its quirky architecture, which was designed to resemble frozen music. An older venue in a fresh setting is **Birdland** (315 W 44th Street; tel: 581-3080) which aims to re-create the style of a 1940s supper club. It offers three nightly jazz sets as well as a Sunday jazz brunch session.

A couple of lower-key Greenwich Village venues are **Sweet Basil** (Seventh Avenue at Bleecker Street; tel: 242-1785) and **55 Bar** (55 Christopher Street; tel: 929-9803), where quality piano and bass duos and more thrive in an intimate atmosphere.

Elsewhere around town, the pricey **Michael's Pub** (118 West 57th Street; tel: 758-2272) specializes in New Orleans-style jazz. On Monday nights, Woody Allen usually adds his clarinet to the exuberant musical melee. An appreciative audience helps make **Smalls** (183 West Tenth Street; tel: 929-7565) a likely place to catch emerging talents, and the **Knickerbocker Bar and Grill** (9th Street and University Place; tel: 228-8490) offers some line-ups that include established jazz stars.

Headliners play **The Jazz Standard** (116 East 27th St; tel: 576-2232), where the sets at 8 PM and 10 PM are designed to be more accommodating to people who want to eat in the excellent restaurant upstairs.

Blues and R.&B., meanwhile, seldom come rawer or raunchier than the nightly acts at **Manny's Car Wash** (1558 Third Avenue at 87th Street; tel: 369-BLUES) or **Terra Blues** (149 Bleecker Street; tel: 777-7776).

Folk Greenwich Village was the epicenter of the early 1960s folk revival. Judy Collins, Bob Dylan, and other legends started here. The days of hootenannys are long gone, but legendary folk venues such as the **Bitter End** (147 Bleecker Street; tel: 673-7030) remain, alongside newer ones such as the small and welcoming **Centerfold Coffeehouse** (Church of Sts Paul and Andrew, 263 West 86th Street; tel: 866-4454).

Greenwich Village jazz: a costlier night out than 50 years ago, but the atmosphere remains the same

COUNTRY MUSIC
Listening to country music seems somewhat incongruous in ultra-urban New York, but the large and brassy Full Moon Saloon (Eighth Avenue at 46th Street) features a mixture of new wave and traditional country sounds. Some smaller country venues are O'Lunney's (44th Street near Fifth Avenue; tel: 840-6688) and the Rodeo Bar (Third Avenue at 27th Street; tel: 683-6500).

FOR CHILDREN IN THE OUTER BOROUGHS

Brooklyn's Children's Museum (145 Brooklyn Avenue) is an architecturally innovative affair, with exhibits to encourage understanding of the basics of science and nature. Older children might prefer a romp through the vintage subway cars displayed at the New York Transit Museum (see page 76).

A ride on the Staten Island Ferry is enjoyable in its own right. Once ashore, the Richmondtown Historic Restoration (see page 179) has traditionally attired guides bringing local history to life in a colorful and informative way. Elsewhere, the Bronx Zoo (see pages 70–71) has a children's section; in Queen's, the New York Hall of Science (page 171) has a mass of entertaining hands-on exhibits.

Alice and friends in Central Park

New York for children

A number of Manhattan museums have sections intended for children but only the **Children's Museum of Manhattan** (in the Tisch Building, 83rd Street between Broadway and Amsterdam Avenue) is purpose-designed: a wonderful play-as-you-learn facility using computerized interactive exhibits and displays. The Children's Museum's four floors of informative fun include the Brainatarium, exploring the functions of the human brain, and the Time-Warner Center for Media, where children can film, edit, and star in their own videos. The Urban Tree House explores the environmental conflicts between city life and the natural world.

Still with an educational role, the **American Museum of Natural History** (see pages 63–64), with its dinosaur skeletons, giant model whale, and scores of stuffed creatures, is usually popular. At the **Sony Wonder Technology Lab** (550 Madison Avenue), there are regular programs for children which explore animation and other media-related subjects with interactive computers and special workshops.

For city views, the **World Trade Center**, with its elevator ride, wins out over the **Empire State Building**, although the latter's **New York Skyride** provides thrills. A boat trip (page 67) can be combined with a clamber around the historic ships of the **South Street Seaport** (page 178).

In Central Park, the main **Central Park Wildlife Center** is behind the Arsenal at 64th Street and Fifth Avenue (tel: 408-0271). Sea lion feeding times are at 11:30 AM, 2 PM, and 4 PM. Storytelling takes place Saturdays at the Hans Christian Andersen statue by Conservatory Water (tel: 794-6564 for details). On the northern edge of Central

Park are the exhibits of the **Charles A. Dana Discovery Center** (110th Street and Fifth Avenue), which explore environmental themes. Special events include beginners' birdwatching and walks.

For a treat, go to the delightful **Enchanted Forest** (85 Mercer Street), where expensive stuffed animals inhabit a make-believe medieval forest, or **F.A.O. Schwarz** (Fifth Avenue between 58th and 59th streets), packed with the kind of toys children dream about—including top-of-the-line items.

Above: Getting to grips with the game in Central Park

Above left: The Bronx Zoo, described on pages 70–71

Left: Rollerblading in Central Park

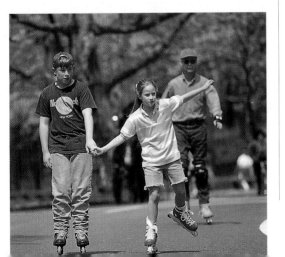

FREE IN THE OUTER BOROUGHS

The Brooklyn Historical Museum is free every day. Throughout the summer, the Brooklyn Arts Council (for details, tel: 718/625-0080) hosts free musical events at several locations, including Brighton Beach. The Bronx's Hall of Fame for Great Americans (page 72) is always free, as is the Bronx Zoo (pages 70–71) from Tuesday to Thursday, although a voluntary donation is expected. In Queens, the New York Hall of Science (page 171) does not have an admission charge but suggests a donation. Staten Island's Garibaldi Meucci Museum (page 180) has free admission, and there is no charge for the July concert series at Snug Harbor (tel: 718/448-2500).

New York for free

Even paupers can have fun in the Big Apple. Many of New York's finest things—architecture, pulsating streetlife, distinctive neighborhoods, fantastic department stores—can be seen without spending a cent. Study the suggestions below for even more ways to enjoy New York for free.

Free in Manhattan Several of the city's major museums described in the A to Z section of this book offer free admission on selected weekday evenings: the **Cooper-Hewitt Museum** (*Open* Tue 5–9 PM); the **Guggenheim Museum** (*Open* Fri 5–8 PM. *Admission charge* donation); the **Museum of Modern Art** (*Open* Thu 5–8:30 PM. *Admission charge* donation); and the **Whitney Museum of American Art** (*Open* Thu 6–8 PM). Among the smaller institutions with temporary shows, the **National Academy of Design** allows free entry to its exhibitions on Tuesday evenings (5–8 PM), as does the **International Center of Photography** (*Admission charge* donation).

Museums and galleries to which admission is free are the **American Numismatic Society** (page 65); the **American Bible Society** (page 61); the **Forbes Magazine Galleries** (pages 107); the **Hispanic Society of America** (page 126); the **Museum of American Folk Art** (page 155; there is a suggested donation of $2); the **Museum of American Illustration** (see page 62); the **Nicolas Roerich Museum** (page 189); and the **Police Academy Museum** (page 152).

Visiting **Federal Hall** (page 102) and the **General Grant Memorial** (page 110) costs nothing, and both **Lincoln Center** (page 134) and the **Stock Exchange** (page 182) offer free guided tours. When tickets are available, you can listen for free to delegates' speeches at the **U.N. General Assembly** (page 184).

Free musical and theatrical entertainment can be found in the summer in **Central Park** (tel: 794-6564), at **Rockefeller Center** (tel: 632-4000), on the plazas of **Lincoln Center** (tel: 875–5350) and the **World Trade Center** (tel: 435-4170), and at **South Street Seaport** (tel: SEA PORT).

Window-shopping, Manhattan-style: a live window display at Macy's department store

Travel Facts

Arriving and departing

By air Flights into New York land
at John F. Kennedy Airport
(tel: 718/244-4444; in Queens, about
15 miles east of Manhattan), at La
Guardia (tel: 718/533-3400; also in
Queens, 8 miles east of Manhattan),
and at Newark (tel: 973/961-6000; in
New Jersey, about 15 miles west of
Manhattan). La Guardia Airport is
almost exclusively for internal flights.

Many international airlines will
offer connecting flights (with their
own domestic service or with that of
their U.S. partners) at little, if any,
extra cost above the transatlantic fare.
It is usually a simple matter to arrive
and depart from different airports
within the U.S., provided travel is
with the same airline. Remember that
domestic flights over holiday periods
are always heavily booked.

Wherever you land, travel into
Manhattan is fairly straightforward if
somewhat time-consuming.
Depending on traffic, travel from the
airport to the city can take from 30
minutes to an hour and a half. Each
airport has a Ground Transportation
Desk where you can check routes,
times and fares into the city.

Besides the public transportation
services detailed below, taxis operate
from each of the three airports and
should be taken from the clearly signposted official taxi dispatch lines,
outside the terminals. Any taxi driver
who approaches you in person is

Use only licensed yellow cabs

likely to be unlicensed. Never ride in
independent cabs; stick with yellow
cabs, and look for the medallion—the
official flat bronze-colored disk
affixed to the vehicle's hood.

Taxi fares from the airports into
Manhattan are high: expect to spend
around $40–$50 (road and bridge tolls
are extra) from Newark, $17–$29 from
La Guardia. From JFK there is a flat
fare of $30 plus tips and tolls. "Share
and Save" group rates are available
8 AM to midnight at Newark and La
Guardia; make arrangements with the
airport's taxi dispatcher. Bear in
mind, too, that traffic can be dense
around each airport and can add
further to taxi charges.

From J.F.K. Free shuttle buses run
to the nearest subway station, at
Howard Beach, which leaves a 60-
minute ride into Manhattan. Other
buses link the airport to other subway
lines, intended for New Yorkers who
want to get home without changing
lines. (See **Public transportation** on
pages 252–253.)

Many tourists and locals carrying
luggage use the van service provided
by Gray Line Air Shuttle (tel:
800/451-0455). Purchase a one-way
($14) or round-trip ($28) ticket from
an agent at the "Ground
Transportation" desk near the bag-
gage claim. The vans run from 7 AM to
11:30 PM and stop at Manhattan hotels
between 23rd and 63rd streets. Note
that the fare *to* the airport is $19.

From Newark Olympia Trails
Airport Express (tel: 212/964-6233)
has separate buses traveling from
Newark to Grand Central Station,
Penn Station, Port Authority, and 1
World Trade Center. The $10 ticket is
sold at the "Ground Transportation"
desk, and by the driver. Buses depart
between 6:15 AM and midnight,
roughly every 20 minutes. Service to
Port Authority runs 24 hours.

As from J.F.K., Gray Line Air
Shuttle (tel: 800/451-0455) operates
shared vans from Newark airport to
hotels in Manhattan.

From La Guardia Local buses run to
the rest of Queens, but the best way to
reach Manhattan is with a Gray Line
Air Shuttle van (tel: 800/451-0455).
The vans have the same schedule and
stops as those serving JFK.

Helicopters provide a speedy but costly way to sightsee or reach the airport. Most travelers prefer to use the bus

By boat New York's great days as a seaport may be long gone, but the Q.E.2 keeps the tradition and the sheer luxury of transatlantic ocean-liner travel very much alive. After the ocean crossing, you will glide into New York beneath the Statue of Liberty, travel a short distance up the Hudson and put ashore at Midtown Manhattan's gleaming Passenger Ship Terminal, which is situated on Twelfth Avenue between 50th and 52nd streets.

By bus Long-distance buses into New York complete their journeys at the country's largest and busiest bus station: Port Authority Bus Terminal (tel: 564-8484), which stretches between 40th and 42nd Street on Eighth Avenue.

By train Most local commuter trains pull into Grand Central Terminal, at 42nd Street between Lexington and Park Avenue, while Amtrak's long-distance train service arrives at New York's other station, Penn Station, at 31st Street and Eighth Avenue. For Amtrak information, tel: 800/872-7245.

Car breakdown

In the unlikely event of your rental car breaking down, simply phone the car rental firm you rented from. With luck, the rental company represent-ative will shortly arrive with a replacement car in which you can continue your journey.

Should you break down far from a phone, stay with your vehicle and wait for a police officer to come by.

A piece of fabric hung from a side window is a common distress alert. If a passing motorist stops to offer help, there is every chance that the approach will be genuine—but treat the offer with caution. Usually, the best help such a person can provide is to make a telephone call on your behalf, probably from their mobile.

Car rental

With traffic lights on almost every block and a lack of affordable parking, as well as the constant threat of gridlock, Manhattan—and New York City generally—is a difficult place in which to drive. For excursions outside the city, however, a rental car is almost essential. A few taxi rides cost less than a space in an overnight parking lot, so no Manhattanite drives his own car in the city unless he has to. If you're planning an excursion, rent a car just before departure.

You will save time and money if you travel out of the city by public transportation and then rent a car in a smaller town. All the major international car-rental companies have desks at New York's airports (and offices in the city), where you can collect a prebooked car or rent one on the spot. Renting a car at an airport branch is usually less expensive than at the same agency's Manhattan branch.

The address of the nearest major car-rental outlet can be found by calling the following toll-free numbers: Avis (tel: 800/331-1212); Budget (tel: 800/527-0700); Hertz (tel: 800/654-3131); National (tel: 800/227-7368). Many more rental firms are listed in the *Yellow Pages*, though the big international companies are often safest.

New York has outlawed the sale of the Collision Damage Waiver (C.D.W.), an optional form of insurance that can add considerably to costs. In New York you pay only for the first $100 of damage to a rental car. Check also whether or not the vehicle has to be returned with a full tank of gas.

Anyone under the age of 25 and/or without a credit card may have problems renting a car in New York.

Climate

Although there's an occasional bone-chilling winter day, with winds blasting in off the Hudson, snow is hardly ever a problem in the city (the skyscrapers trap enough heat to melt most snowfalls). Summer is the only unpleasant time of year, especially the humid, hot days of July and August, when many New Yorkers vacate the island for summer homes. Most hotels are air-conditioned, but if you're traveling in summer and

The view that confirms you have really arrived in the Big Apple

choosing budget accommodations, it is a good idea to check beforehand whether your room has an air conditioner. Air-conditioned stores, restaurants, theaters, and museums provide respite from the heat; so do the many green expanses of parks. Subways and buses are usually air-conditioned, but subway stations in summer can be as hot as saunas (and considerably dirtier).

For advice on when to travel outside New York City, where summer activities can be much more pleasant, see the panel on page 194.

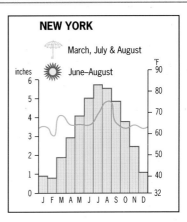

NEW YORK

March, July & August

June–August

Crime
New York has become a much safer city in recent years. Stay alert and read the Survival Guide on pages 54–55 of this book, and you will reduce what is already a statistically very slender chance of your being robbed or attacked.

Don't leave money and valuables in your hotel room: inquire whether the hotel has a safe. Don't carry easily snatched handbags and be careful not to leave your wallet sticking out of your back pocket.

Lost or stolen traveler's checks are relatively easy to replace (read the instructions when you buy the checks and make a note of all the relevant details).

Driving tips
It is never a good idea to bring a car into Manhattan—not least because New Yorkers drive like maniacs, and parking can be very expensive. Where less-expensive parking lots do exist, they are rarely the most central. Free parking on the street is almost impossible to find in Midtown, except on Sunday mornings. If you *do* bring a car into Manhattan, note that parking infringements attract stiff fines or worse (your car could be towed), so always read the signs carefully. Never park within 10 feet of a fire hydrant. If possible, avoid leaving any valuables in the car: if you can't take them with you, make sure that they are out of sight.

Venture beyond the city to the Catskill Mountains, the remoter parts of the Hudson Valley, Long Island, or New Jersey—or farther afield—and

wheels of your own become essential (see pages 194–211).

There is a speed limit of 55 m.p.h. or 65 m.p.h. in force on interstates (in some places there may also be a minimum limit). In built-up areas, lower speed limits are indicated. An extremely dim view is taken of drinking and driving—it is not unusual for hefty fines and prison sentences to be imposed for such an offence. New York City now has a policy of confiscating drunk drivers' cars—permanently.

Tolls are charged for some Manhattan bridges and tunnels, and for some stretches of road in the Outer Boroughs.

If you are a member of an automobile club, such as the A.A.A., be sure to have its emergency road service phone number handy in case of a breakdown.

Emergency telephone numbers
For **ambulance**, **police** or **fire**, dial 911 (no money required) and ask for the relevant service.

Other emergency numbers include **Victim's Services** (tel: 577-7777), **New York Gay and Lesbian Anti-violence Unit** (tel: 714-1141), **Sex Crimes Report Line** (tel: 267-7273).

Lost property
Lost at J.F.K. Airport, La Guardia Airport, or Newark, contact relevant airline.

Lost in a taxi, tel: 692-8294, 9 AM to 5 PM. Lost on a bus or the subway, tel: 718/330-3000, 8 AM to 6 PM.

Media

New York has hundreds of T.V. and radio channels and newspapers and magazines. Free publications aimed at visitors litter every hotel lobby. The best sources of what's-on information are the weekly *Time Out, Village Voice,* and *New York* magazine. For a full run-down on the city's media, see pages 132–133.

Money matters

Automated-teller machines (ATMs) are abundant; many are tied to international networks such as **Cirrus** and **Plus**. You can use your bank card at ATMs away from home to withdraw money from your checking account and get cash advances on a credit-card account (providing your card has been programmed with a personal identification number, or PIN). Check in advance on limits on withdrawals and cash advances within specified periods. Remember that finance charges apply on credit-card cash advances from ATMs as well as on those from tellers. And note that transaction fees for ATM withdrawals outside your home turf will probably be higher than for withdrawals at home. For specific Cirrus locations in the U.S. and Canada, call 800/424-7787 (for U.S. Plus locations, 800/843-7587), and press the area code and first three digits of the number you're calling from (or the calling area where you want an ATM).

Elevated subway in Williamsburg

American Express Company's **Express Cash** system lets you withdraw cash and/or traveler's checks from a worldwide network of 57,000 American Express dispensers and participating bank ATMs. You must enroll first (call 800-CASH-NOW for a form and allow two weeks for processing). Withdrawals are charged not to your card but to a designated bank account. You can withdraw up to $1,000 per seven-day period on the basic card, more if your card is gold or platinum. There is a 2% fee (minimum $2.50, maximum $20) for each cash transaction made, and 1% fee for traveler's checks (except for the platinum card), which are available from American Express dispensers.

At AmEx offices, cardholders can also cash personal checks for up to $1,000 in any seven-day period; of this $200 can be in cash, more if available, with the balance paid in traveler's checks, for which all but platinum cardholders pay a 1% fee. Higher limits apply to the gold and platinum cards.

Older travelers

The American Association of Retired Persons (A.A.R.P., 601 East St, N.W., Washington, D.C. 20049, tel: 202/434-2277) provides independent travelers with A.A.R.P. membership, the Purchase Privilege Program which offers discounts on hotels, car rentals, and sightseeing, and the A.A.R.P. Motoring Plan, provided by Amoco, which furnishes domestic trip-routing information and emergency road-service aid for an annual fee of $39.95 per person or $47.95 per couple ($54.95 for a premium version). A.A.R.P. membership is open to those aged 50 and over; annual dues are currently $8 per person or couple.

Two other membership organizations offer discounts on lodgings, car rentals, and other travel products, along with magazines and newsletters. The National Council of Senior Citizens (8403 Colesville, Suite 1200, 1 Silver Springs, MD, 20910, tel: 301/578-8800) is a nonprofit advocacy group with some 5,000 local clubs across the United States; membership costs $13 per person or couple annually. Mature Outlook Plus

(6001 North Clark Steet, Chicago, IL 60660, tel: 800/336-6330), a Sears Roebuck & Co. subsidiary with 800,000 members, charges $39.95 for an annual membership.

Note: When using any senior-citizen identification card for reduced hotel rates, mention it when you are booking, not when checking out. At restaurants, show your card before you're seated; though few city restaurants offer discounts and you may find that any are limited to certain menus, days, or hours. If you are renting a car, ask about promotional rates that might improve on your senior-citizen discount.

Opening hours

New York store opening hours vary greatly. Many big stores will open on weekdays and Saturdays from 9 AM to 8 PM, but smaller or more specialty stores may open as late as 11 AM or noon and close at 9 PM or 10 PM. On Sundays, opening times are from 11 or 12 till 6 or 7.

Museum opening times also vary. Many are open from 10 or 11 AM to 6 PM on weekdays and Saturdays (though several are closed on Monday). Some also open on Sundays, and several keep late hours on Tuesdays or Thursdays.

Bank opening hours are Monday to Friday from 9 AM to 3 or 3:30 PM (6 PM on Thursday at some branches).

Places of worship

New York's places of worship are many and varied. Some of the main ones are described in the A to Z section of this book and on pages 120–121. Your hotel will be able to advise of those in your neighborhood, and the telephone book carries a comprehensive list. **Penny Sightseeing Harlem Tours** (tel: 410-0080) offers Sunday gospel trips to Harlem.

Police

"New York's Finest," the city's police, are helpful and efficient in almost every situation. Besides patroling in cars, officers are regularly seen on the street, and the police are well represented in crowd situations.
If you are unfortunate enough to be the victim of theft, you will need to

CONVERSION CHARTS

FROM	TO	MULTIPLY BY
Inches	Centimeters	2.54
Centimeters	Inches	0.3937
Feet	Meters	0.3048
Meters	Feet	3.2810
Yards	Metres	0.9144
Metres	Yards	1.0940
Miles	Kilometers	1.6090
Kilometers	Miles	0.6214
Acres	Hectares	0.4047
Hectares	Acres	2.4710
U.s. Gallons	Liters	3.7854
Liters	Gallons	0.2642
Ounces	Grams	28.35
Grams	Ounces	0.0353
Pounds	Grams	453.6
Grams	Pounds	0.0022
Pounds	Kilograms	0.4536
Kilograms	Pounds	2.205
U.S. Tons	Tonnes	0.9072
Tonnes	U.S. Tons	1.1023

MEN'S SUITS

U.S.	36	38	40	42	44	46	48
U.K.	36	38	40	42	44	46	48
Rest of Europe	46	48	50	52	54	56	58

DRESS SIZES

U.S.	6	8	10	12	14	16
U.K.	8	10	12	14	16	18
France	36	38	40	42	44	46
Italy	38	40	42	44	46	48
Rest of Europe	34	36	38	40	42	44

MEN'S SHIRTS

U.S.	14	14.5	15	15.5	16	16.5	17
U.K.	14	14.5	15	15.5	16	16.5	17
Rest of Europe	36	37	38	39/40	41	42	43

MEN'S SHOES

U.S.	8	8.5	9.5	10.5	11.5	12
U.K.	7	7.5	8.5	9.5	10.5	11
Rest of Europe	41	42	43	44	45	46

WOMEN'S SHOES

U.S.	6	6.5	7	7.5	8	8.5
U.K.	4.5	5	5.5	6	6.5	7
Rest of Europe	38	38	39	39	40	41

visit a police station to have your insurance claim authorized. Every New York neighborhood has a police station. To find the one nearest you, dial 374-5000. If you need the police in an emergency, dial 911.

Post offices

New York's main post office, at Eighth Avenue between 31st and 33rd streets, stays open around the clock, every day of the week. Elsewhere in the city, larger post offices are open Monday to Friday from 8 AM to 6 PM and Saturday from 8 AM to 1 PM. Smaller post offices keep shorter hours.

Stamps can also be bought, sometimes at inflated prices, through vending machines found in some stores and in many hotel lobbies.

Public transportation

Spending most of your time in Manhattan will leave you much less reliant on public transportation than you might expect. Not only are distances small, but much of Manhattan is best seen on foot.

If you are in a rush, planning to visit the Outer Boroughs or simply commuting between uptown and downtown, you will need to make use of the city's buses, subway, or taxis.

City buses Substantially slower than subway trains, New York buses at least allow passengers to view the city as they travel through it. Many people find them less intimidating than the subway system. The bus network is comprehensive (free maps are available from the tourist information offices listed on page 256), and the majority of routes run north–south and east–west (crosstown), with free transfers provided between the two.

Bus stops are close to street corners—marked by a blue sign and a yellow painted section of curb—and most have a route map and frequency schedule for the buses that use that stop. The route is displayed on the front of each bus.

Most buses stop every two or three blocks; those marked "limited" (which only run at rush hour) make fewer stops, usually only at major

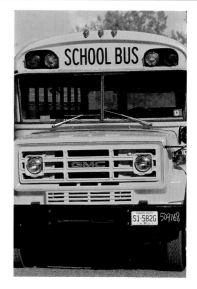

It is illegal to pass a stationary school bus

junctions. As with the subway, there is a flat fare (currently $1.50) for all journeys. This can be paid in coins (exact change only; no dollar bills) or with a subway token (see below), either of which should be dropped into the box beside the driver, or with a swipe of a MetroCard.

If you need a transfer, ask the driver as you pay and he or she will hand you a transfer slip. Transfers can be used only for continuing travel, not as round-trip tickets. They are valid for a few hours from the time punched on them and can be used only on the bus routes printed on their reverse side.

Especially during rush hours, New York buses can become packed; crosstown buses make only slightly better headway than pedestrians. If you are wedged in a crowded bus and think your stop may be coming up soon, start making your way towards the exit doors (which are in the middle of the bus—though you can also get off at the front door where you entered) in plenty of time; otherwise there is every chance you will not reach the doors before they shut and the bus moves on. A bell signal strip runs along both sides of the bus, but it is rare for the bus not to make each stop anyway.

The subway The much-maligned New York subway system is a swift, inexpensive, and largely efficient way to get about the city.

A tangle of lines denoted by numbers and letters, the subway system map (available free from subway station token booths and from provided the tourist information offices listed on page 256) initially seems hopelessly confusing. In fact, the system is relatively easy to use provided you remember that "Uptown" trains go north (toward the Upper West and East sides and Harlem) and "Downtown" trains travel south (toward Lower Manhattan). Any train labeled "Brooklyn Bound" is indeed bound for Brooklyn but will make stops in Lower Manhattan on the way.

What can be more confusing is the choice between "Express" and "Local" trains. While local trains stop at all stations on a particular line, express trains stop only at selected stations. Board an express train by mistake and you can sometimes find yourself some distance from where you want to be, and possibly in a dangerous neighborhood. If this happens,

City streetlife takes many forms in the Big Apple

cross over to the other platform and take the next train back.

Provided you know which line and which direction you want before entering the station, follow the relevant signs to the platform. If you do not know, inquire at the ticket booth or ask someone. New Yorkers are usually sympathetic and pleased to help visitors find their way. Even New Yorkers become baffled when trains are re-routed or stop running due to frequent construction projects (especially on weekends). The fuzzy public address system is rarely intelligible. Each train has the relevant letter or number and its destination shown along its side, in a color that corresponds to the colors on the subway map.

During the day, trains arrive every 10–15 minutes (more often in rush hours). Between midnight and 5 AM (the service operates around the clock), the usual wait is around 20–30 minutes.

To enter the subway system, you will need to drop a subway token (which currently costs $1.50) into a slot, or swipe your MetroCard through an electronic reader, and pass through a turnstile. Tokens and MetroCards can be bought from the booths found at every station

253

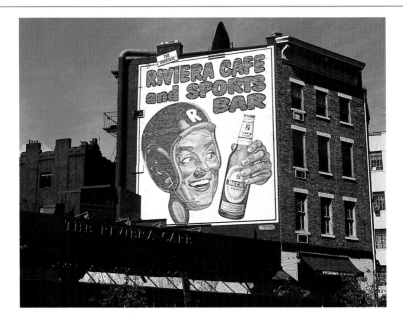

(almost all booths are open 24 hours) and also from a few major museums. Electronic MetroCards are generally a more cost-effective way to pay for multiple trips.

The MTA sells three kinds of gold plastic MetroCards: unlimited rides, pay-per-ride, and the Fun Pass. For $17, you can buy a card that lets you take an unlimited number of trips in a 7-day period (a saving if you plan to take at least 13 trips). Turnstiles will allow one person at a time to swipe in on the unlimited ride card, so each person in your party must have one if you are riding together. With a pay-per-ride card, which can hold from $3 to $80 dollars, you can swipe in as many people as you like on one card, as long as it has enough credit to cover each $1.50 fare. The $4 Fun Pass allows one day of unlimited travel for one person (from first use to 3 AM the following day). With the MetroCard, you can transfer free from bus to subway or subway to bus within two hours.

The subway, like other locations in New York and other large cities, does have its share of pickpockets—but providing you remain with the crowds and stay alert, you should have no problems with serious crime (see pages 54–55).

Street advertising is an art form New York could call its own

Taxis

New York taxis are expensive and liable to be stuck in traffic for long periods of time. Sometimes cabs are the most time-efficient way to get where you are going, however, especially at night. When you want one, raise your hand to hail the next empty one to pass by. You know a cab is empty if the sign on its roof is lighted.

Always wear the seat-belts provided—the security barriers can be lethal to teeth in sudden stops—and get a receipt from the driver before leaving. If you leave something in the cab, the receipt could help in getting it back.

Use only the official "medallion" cabs. These are yellow with "N.Y.C. Taxi" stenciled on the side, a light on the roof, and a medallion on the hood. Any other vehicle looking for passengers will be unlicensed (known colloquially as a "gypsy cab") and should be ignored.

Official taxi charges currently begin at $2 and gain 30¢ for each ⅕ mile traveled and 20¢ for each minute stopped in traffic; a 15 percent tip is the norm. After 8 PM, there is a 50¢ surcharge.

Rest rooms
Public rest rooms in New York run the gamut when it comes to cleanliness. Facilities in Penn Station, Grand Central Terminal, and the Port Authority bus terminal are cleaned regularly but are still slightly unpleasant. Do not use rest rooms in subway stations. Instead, try Midtown department stores such as Macy's, Lord & Taylor, and Bloomingdale's, museums, and large hotels. Public atriums, such as the Citicorp Center and Trump Tower, also provide reasonable public facilities. Restaurant rest rooms are usually for patrons only. If you're dressed well and look as if you belong, you can just sail right on in. Cinemas, Broadway theaters, and concert halls have limited amenities, and there are often long lines before performances, as well as during intermissions.

Student and youth travel
Students in full-time education and anyone under 26 may qualify for discounted flights offered by travel agents that specialize in youth and student travel. Students carrying International Student Identity Cards (I.S.I.C.s) will be entitled to reduced admission to many New York museums and other attractions.

While not exclusively for young and student travelers, the city's Y.M.C.A.s and youth hostels (see page 215) offer budget-priced accommodations and a chance to socialize with other young New York visitors from around the world.

Telephones
You'll find payphones in the street, in hotel lobbies, in train and bus stations, in bars and restaurants, and in most public buildings.

Almost without exception, hotel room telephones have charges much higher than those of public telephones. Sometimes hotels even charge for dialing toll-free numbers!

Emergency calls (dial 911); calls to the operator (dial 0); or the international operator (dial 1-800/874-4000) or calls for directory assistance (411) are free.

St. Paul's Chapel on Fulton Street was built in 1766

Throughout this book, toll-free numbers are given where available. The area code for Manhattan, (212), is omitted on the assumption that you are calling from another Manhattan number. Brooklyn and Queens share the (718) code.

Time
New York uses Eastern Standard Time, three hours ahead of the West Coast, 5 hours behind England.

Tipping
How much you tip is entirely up to you, but the usual rule in a restaurant or coffee shop is to leave the person who served you 15–20 percent of the total bill. (An easy way to calculate the approximate amount is to double the sales tax figure—which is 8.25 percent—shown at the bottom of the bill.) Do not leave a tip at any food outlet where you serve yourself or where the food is sold to be taken out.

After a taxi ride, it is customary to tip the driver around 15 percent of the

255

(www.newyork.citysearch.com) and the New York City government (www.ci.nyc.ny.us). Many of these are extremely useful and may allow you to make reservations using a credit card.

Tours on foot
There are many guided tours on offer in New York. The **Museum of the City of New York** (tel: 534-1672) and **New York City Cultural Walking Tours** (tel: 979-2388) visit the city's architecture, landmarks, and historic sites. Other guided tour companies include **Adventures on a Shoestring** (tel: 265-2663), **Citywalks** (tel: 989-2456), as well as **Urban Explorations** (tel: 718/721-5254), and **River to River Downtown Walking Tours** (tel: 321-2823).

The **Big Apple Greeters** (tel: 669-8159), will match your particular interest in the city with a local who can tell you all about it on a 2 to 4-hour jaunt. The service is free and tips are not accepted. More walking tours are suggested in the panel on page 56.

Gray Line New York (tel: 397-2620) tours the city in buses. You can hop on and off the authentic London double-deck buses run by **New York Doubledecker Tours** (tel: 967-6008).

Travelers with disabilities
In New York, facilities for travelers with disabilities are not only impressive, but are also improving all the time. By law, public buildings have to be at least partially wheelchair-accessible, and all must provide accessible toilet facilities. Almost all New York buses have rear-door "elevators" for wheelchair-users, and most also have a "kneel" step to make it easier to get onto the bus from the curb. The subway, however, is nearly impossible to use for those in wheelchairs.

Trains and airlines are obliged to provide services for travelers with disabilities if requested, and Amtrak has earned a reputation for doing this well. Though less comfortable than the trains, Greyhound buses are more frequent and will allow a companion to travel free provided that you have a doctor's certificate stating that this is necessary.

fare. The amount need not be exact, however, and most people (if the amount works out within reason) allow the driver to keep the change from whatever bills they've handed over in payment.

Tipping hotel porters is also expected. Again, the amount you tip is entirely discretionary, but plan on $1 per bag. If a porter simply helps move your luggage from the lobby into a taxi outside the hotel, a total of $1–$2 should usually be sufficient. Leave the chambermaid $1 per day if you wish.

Tourist information
The multilingual staff of the New York Convention and Visitors Bureau (NYCVB), 810 Seventh Avenue between 52nd and 53rd streets (tel: 800 NYC VISIT for ordering printed materals or 484-1222 to speak to a counselor; Mon–Fri 8.30–6, Sat and Sun 9–5) can answer queries, provide free bus and subway maps, and has racks of leaflets detailing restaurants, hotels, and tourist attractions.

Web sites
Many New York museums, tourist attractions, newspapers, hotels and restaurants, have their own world wide web sites. Details of them and much more information can be found from general sites such as that of the NYCVB (www.nycvisit.com), or those of Citysearch

Some major car-rental companies can arrange vehicles with hand controls provided they receive advance notice.

For brochures and further information, contact the **Mayor's Office for People with Disabilities** (52 Chambers St., Office 206, New York, NY 10007, tel: 788-2830). Blind or visually impaired visitors may appreciate a visit to the **Andrew Heiskell Library for the Blind and Physically Handicapped** (40 West. 20th Street (tel: 206-5400), a public library branch with a large collection of Braille, large-print, and recorded books, housed in a layout specially designed for easy access by the visually impaired.

The Society for the Advancement of Travel for the Handicapped (S.A.T.H., 347 5th Ave., Suite 610, New York, NY 10016, tel: 212/447-7284, fax: 212/725-8253) provides lists of tour operators specializing in travel for people with disabilities, an information sheet on traveling with specific disabilities and to specific countries, and a quarterly newsletter. Annual membership is $45, $30 for students and senior citizens. Non-members may send $5 and an S.A.S.E. for information on specific destinations. S.A.T.H. members receive a color magazine, *Open World*, which provides a wide range of travel information for travelers with all kinds of disabilities.

The **Big Apple Greeters**, volunteers who show visitors around (see **Tours on foot** page 256), extend their service to those with disabilities.

Traveling with cameras, camcorders, and laptops

About film and cameras
If your camera is new or if you haven't used it for a while, shoot and develop a few rolls of film before leaving home. Pack some lens tissue and an extra battery for your built-in light meter, and invest in an inexpensive skylight filter, to both protect your lens and provide some definition in hazy shots. Store film in a cool, dry place—never in the car's glove compartment or on the shelf under the rear window.

Films above I.S.O. 400 are much more sensitive to damage from airport security X-rays than other films; very high speed films, I.S.O. 1,000 and above, are exceedingly vulnerable.

To protect your film, don't put it in checked luggage; carry it on your person in a plastic bag and ask for a hand inspection. Such requests are usual and should be honored at American airports.

Don't depend on a lead-lined bag to protect film that you have packed in with checked luggage—the airline's security may very well turn up the dosage of radiation to see what you've got in there. Actually, airport metal detectors do not damage your film, although the alarm will go off if you happen to walk through one with a roll of film in your pocket. For information and advice call the Kodak information Center (tel: 800/242-2424) for details.

257

Subways are the fastest way to get around New York

About camcorders
Before your trip, put new or long-unused camcorders through their paces, and practice panning and zooming. Invest in a skylight filter to protect the lens, and check the lithium battery that lights up the L.C.D. (liquid crystal display) modes. As for the rechargeable nickel-cadmium batteries that are the camera's power source, take along an extra pair, so while you're using your camcorder you'll have one battery ready and another recharging.

About videotape
Unlike still-camera film, videotape is not damaged by X-rays. However, it may well be harmed by the magnetic field of a walk-through metal detector. Airport security personnel may want you to turn the camcorder on to prove that that's what it is, so make sure the battery is charged when you get to the airport.

About laptops
Security X-rays do not harm hard-disk or floppy-disk storage. Most airlines allow you to use your laptop aloft but request that you turn it off during takeoff and landing so as not to interfere with navigation equipment.

Make sure the battery is charged when you arrive at the airport, because you may be asked to turn on the computer at security checkpoints to prove that it is what it appears to be. If you're a heavy computer user, consider traveling with a backup battery.

Further reading
Many a famous writer has set down his or her impressions of this fascinating city. Some of the best full-length accounts are Christopher Morley's *New York*, a mid-1920s essay; *Walker in the City*, by Alfred Kazin; and *Apple of My Eye*, a 1978 account of writing a New York guidebook, by Helene Hanff. *New York Style*, by Suzanne Slesin, Stafford Cliff, and Daniel Rozensztroch, has several sections on the city. Dan Wakefield recalls his early literary days in *New York in the 50s*. Perhaps the best is E.B. White's 1949 essay "Here is New York."

The early history of New York is wittily told in the classic *Knickerbocker's History of New York*, by Washington Irving. For a fine historical introduction to the city, find the heavily illustrated *Columbia Historical Portrait of New York*, by John Kouwenhoven. *New York, New York*, by Oliver E. Allen, is a well-rounded, up-to-date history of the city. *You Must Remember This*, by Jeff Kisseloff, is an oral history of ordinary New Yorkers early in this century. *The Park and its People*, by Roy Rosenzweig and Elizabeth Blackmar, tells how Central Park evolved.

Fiorello H. La Guardia and the Making of Modern New York, by Thomas Kessner, is a biography of the charismatic Depression-era mayor. *The Power Broker* by Robert Caro is a fascinating biography of Robert Moses, one of the city's most influential parks commissioners. Robert Daley's *Prince of the City* is a true-life drama of New York police corruption.

Highly critical accounts of the city's recent politics can be found in *The Streets Were Paved with Gold*, by Ken Auletta; *The Rise and Fall of New York City*, by Roger Starr; *Imperial City*, by Geoffrey Moorhouse; and *City for Sale*, by Jack Newfield and Wayne Barrett. *A License to Steal*, by Benjamin J. Stein, concerns Wall Street's notorious Michael Milken, as does *Den of Thieves*, by James B. Stewart.

Theater lovers may want to read *Act One*, the autobiography of playwright Moss Hart, or *Bring on the Girls* and *Performing Flea*, P.G. Wodehouse and Guy Bolton's entertaining account of their years spent writing for musical comedy; for more up-to-date essays on the city's theater scene, try David Mamet's *The Cabin* or William Goldman's *Broadway*.

The Kingdom and the Power, by Gay Talese, offers a behind-the-scenes look at the *New York Times*; life at one of the city's most venerable magazines is recounted in *Here at the New Yorker*, by Brendan Gill. Speaking of that august publication, *Up in the Old Hotel* brings together Joseph Mitchell's *New Yorker* stories which deal with colorful New York characters.

From Manet to Manhattan, by Peter Watson, explores the city's art world. *Literary New York*, by Susan Edmiston and Linda D. Cirino, traces the haunts of famous writers, neighborhood by neighborhood. *The Heart of the World*, by Nik Cohn, is a block-by-block history of Manhattan's most famous street, Broadway.

A.I.A. Guide to New York City, by Elliot Willensky and Norval White, is the definitive guide to the city's many building styles; Paul Goldberger's *The City Observed* describes Manhattan building by building.

John Kieran's *A Natural History of New York* explores the wildlife of the city's parks, while Eugene Kinkead concentrates on the most famous city landmark in *Central Park: The Birth, Decline, and Renewal of a National Treasure*.

Perhaps because so many writers have lived in New York City, there is a wealth of fiction set here. Jack Finney's *Time and Again* is a delightful time-travel story illustrated with 19th-century photos; *Winter's Tale*, by Mark Helprin, uses surreal fantasy to create a portrait of New York's past. Novels set in 19th-century New York include Henry James's *Washington Square*, Edith Wharton's *The Age of Innocence*, and Stephen Crane's *Maggie, A Girl of the Streets*.

259

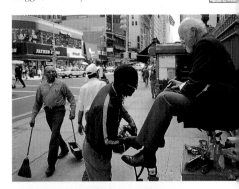

From a restaurant meal to a shoe-shine ... don't forget that tipping is expected

O. Henry's short stories depict the early years of this century, while Damon Runyon's are set in the raffish underworld of the 1930s and 1940s. F. Scott Fitzgerald (*The Beautiful and Damned*, 1922), John Dos Passos (*Manhattan Transfer*, 1925), John O'Hara (*Butterfield 8*, 1935), and Mary McCarthy (*The Group*, 1938) also wrote about this city. J. D. Salinger's *Catcher in the Rye* (1951) partly takes place here, as does Thomas Pynchon's *V* (1965). Truman Capote's 1958 novella *Breakfast at Tiffany's* is a special favorite of many New Yorkers.

More current New York models include *Bonfire of the Vanities*, by Tom Wolfe; *The Mambo Kings Play Songs of Love*, by Oscar Hijuelos; *The New York Trilogy*, by Paul Auster; *Glamorama*, by Jay McInerney and *People Like Us*, by Dominick Dunne. For portraits of gay life, try Larry Kramer's *Faggots*, David Leavitt's *The Lost Language of Cranes*, and Sarah Schulman's *After Delores* and *People in Trouble*.

The experience of black people in Harlem has been chronicled in Ralph Ellison's *Invisible Man*, James Baldwin's *Go Tell It on the Mountain*, and Claude Brown's *Manchild in the Promised Land*. For a portrait of Harlem during the 1920s, there is *When Harlem Was in Vogue*, by David Levering Lewis.

The history of New York's Jewish population can be traced through such books as *World of Our Fathers*, by Irving Howe; *Call It Sleep*, by Henry Roth; *The Promise*, by Chaim Potok; *Enemies, A Love Story*, by Isaac Bashevis Singer; and *Our Crowd*, by Stephen Birmingham.

Greenwich Village and How It Got That Way is a fascinating study of that neighborhood by Terry Miller. Francine Prose's *Household Saints* is a fictional portrait of life in Little Italy. *The New Chinatown*, by Peter Kwong, is a recent study of the community across Canal Street. Kate Simon's *Bronx Primitive*, Laura Cunningham's autobiographical *Sleeping Arrangements*, and E.L. Doctorow's novel *World's Fair* are set in the Bronx.

Brooklyn's history is beautifully illustrated in *Brooklyn: People and Places, Past and Present*, by Grace Glueck and Paul Gardner. Anna Quindlen's *Object Lessons* is set in the Westchester suburbs; while Susan Isaac's *Compromising Positions* takes place on Long Island.

Mysteries set in New York City range from Dashiell Hammett's urbane 1933 novel *The Thin Man*, to Rex Stout's series of Nero Wolfe mysteries (continued by Robert Goldsborough) to more recent picks: *While My Pretty One Sleeps*, by Mary Higgins Clark; *Greenwich Killing Time*, by Kinky Friedman; *Dead Air*, by Mike Lupica, and *Unorthodox Practices*, by Marissa Piesman.

Beneath Brooklyn Bridge

Accommodations & Restaurants

Accommodations and Restaurants

The following recommended hotels and restaurants have been divided into three price categories:
($) = budget
($) = moderate
($) = expensive

Prices do not include taxes (see page 213). Note also that telephone numbers prefixed 800 are free outside the 212 code area when dialed within the United States (dial "1" first); local toll numbers follow the toll-free number, the code for Manhattan being 212 (see also page 255).

ACCOMMODATIONS

CHINATOWN

Holiday Inn Downtown ($$)
138 Lafayette Street, at corner of Howard Street tel: 800/HOLIDAY; 966-8898
The only hotel in Chinatown, with very small rooms offering two telephones, in-room movies, and individual climate control. Eat in the Pacifica restaurant, or head for the many cheaper alternatives in the busy streets around the neighborhood.

FINANCIAL DISTRICT

Cosmopolitan Hotel ($)
95 West Broadway
tel: 888/895-9400; 566-1900
The Cosmopolitan has comfortable and well-equipped rooms at a very tempting price. It is located inside an historic building almost in the shadow of the World Trade Center and on the edge of TriBeCa.

Millenium Hilton ($$$)
55 Church Street
tel: 800/752-0014; 693-2001
This black-glass tower rising 55 stories is situated opposite the World Trade Center. The Millenium was designed for the downtown business executive, with room rates to match. In return, you get an impressive array of services including a sky-lit swimming pool and choice of two restaurants—the Taliesin and the rather less formal Grille, both offering 24-hour full-menu room service. If possible, try to reserve an upper-floor room—the view is unforgettable.

New York Marriott Financial Center ($$$)
85 West Street tel: 800/242-8685; 266-6145
A traditional hotel catering mainly to business people, the Marriott Financial Center exudes the confidence of knowing exactly what it is trying to do and doing it extremely well. Service is both speedy and professional, and public rooms have plenty of atmosphere. The Liberty Lounge serves snacks and cocktails, or you can dine in superstar Hawaiian chef Roy Yamaguchi's newest outpost. Rooms are small, with the compensation of generously sized bathrooms and spectacular views. Weekend rates are very reasonable and make this a good base for exploring southern Manhattan.

Marriott World Trade Center ($$$)
3 World Trade Center
tel: 800/228-9290; 938-9100
Another state-of-the-art shrine to the needs of the high-flying corporate business traveler, this hotel's facilities include a fitness center and an indoor swimming pool to hone the muscles before clinching those crucial Wall Street deals.

GREENWICH VILLAGE

Washington Square Hotel ($)
103 Waverly Place
tel: 800/222-0418; 777-9515
There is no better placed or better priced Greenwich Village base, this hotel being situated just opposite a corner of Washington Square Park. The rooms tend to be somewhat small but are clean and pleasantly furnished, and the staff are extremely helpful. In a previous life as the Hotel Earle, this was the first New York home of Bob Dylan and was also where a homesick John Phillips of the Mamas and the Papas penned the 1960s hit song "California Dreamin."

LITTLE ITALY AND SOHO

Mercer Hotel ($$$)
99 Prince Street tel: 888/918-6060, 966-6060
Small and sleek, this downtown hotel caters to an affluent insiders crowd. The rooms are luxurious in an urban way and the services and amenities match the overall cool feel of the place. If your interests lie predominantly in downtown Manhattan, there is no better perch. The Mercer Kitchen in the basement is superstar chef Jean-Georges Vongerichten's latest restaurant, and it is most definitely worth the wait to get in.

Off-SoHo Suites ($$)
11 Rivington Street
tel: 800/ OFF-SOHO; 979-9808
These mini-apartment-style suites are very good value if you want to be within walking distance of SoHo, Little Italy, and the Lower East Side. Rates are inexpensive, but the suites are tiny, and the area, just the wrong side of the Bowery, may not be to everyone's taste. For budget accommodations, however, this is certainly well worth considering. Each suite is supplied with cable T.V. and V.C.R., and there is also a laundry and fitness room on the premises. Make use of the hotel's 24-hour discount cab service.

SoHo Grand ($$)
310 West Broadway
tel: 800/965-3000, 965-3000
Many considered the arrival of the first full-scale hotel in SoHo the beginning of the end of the neighborhood's charm. However, the understatedly elegant design of this trendy hostel attracts a crowd that is in perfect keeping with its environment. The rooms are comfortable and the lounge and bar in the second-floor lobby are particularly popular on weekend nights.

MIDTOWN MANHATTAN

Algonquin ($$)
*44th Street between Fifth and Sixth avenues
tel: 800/548-0345; 840-6800*
It took a Japanese company to restore this
literary landmark (home of the Round Table,
presided over by Dorothy Parker and friends
from 1919) to its former glories. Above the
sumptuous lobby and bar areas, however, the
Algonquin's rooms are only adequate, and
there are plenty of better-value alternatives in
the area.

Allerton House ($)
*57th Street at Lexington Avenue
tel: 753-8841*
A women-only and largely residential hotel with
tiny but clean, tidy, and very low-priced rooms.
Private bathrooms are only a few dollars extra.

Ameritania ($)
*Broadway at 54th Street
tel: 800/922-0330; 247-5000*
A glitzy, inexpensive hotel next to the Ed
Sullivan Theater and six blocks from Central
Park. Everything is new, from the black marble
bathrooms to the neon-lit lobby with waterfall.
There is also an Italian restaurant and a busy
pizza parlor and café on the premises. The low
prices are a major attraction—book early.

Beekman Tower ($$$)
*3 Mitchell Place at First Avenue and 49th
Street tel: 800/ME-SUITE; 689-5200*
The 1928 Gothic-style Beekman Tower holds
an all-suite sensibly priced hotel, especially
good for long-term stays—which explains its
popularity with officials from the nearby United
Nations. All the suites have kitchenettes with
microwave ovens and coffee-makers, and there
is a fully equipped fitness center.

Best Western Manhattan ($)
*32nd Street between Fifth Avenue and
Broadway tel: 800/567-7720; 736-1600*
Now part of the Apple Core chain of reasonably
priced hotels, this property offers unelaborate
but functional rooms in the heart of the
compact Korean business district almost in the
shadow of the Empire State Building.

Beverly ($$)
*50th Street between Lexington and Second
avenues tel: 800/223-0945; 753-2700*
Some much-needed renovations are helping
The Beverly, whose spacious, one-bedroom
suites, equipped with handy kitchenettes, are
very good value. Also located on the premises
is a 24-hour pharmacy.

Box Tree ($$$)
49th Street at Second Avenue tel: 758-8320
The perfect choice for an indulgent weekend,
The Box Tree fills two (soon to be three) adjoining brownstones in the Turtle Bay area of
Midtown. Trompe-l'oeil decorations are on the
walls, and a Gaudiesque main staircase leads
upstairs from the restaurant to a series of tiny,
private dining rooms, most of which have
Versailles-like themes. The 13 bedrooms are
decorated in different styles—Chinese,
Egyptian and Japanese—and the bathrooms
are tiny but delightfully stylish.

Carlton Arms ($)
25th Street at Third Avenue tel: 679-0680
Each wacky, threadbare room has been
designed and decorated by a different
(unknown) artist, and what the Carlton Arms
lacks in cleanliness and creature comforts, it
makes up for through its sheer eccentricity.
Book well in advance for a room with a
bathroom. Many struggling artists make this
their New York home, so expect bizarre fellow
guests and exceptionally low prices. If you pay
for six nights, you get a seventh for free.

Chelsea Hotel ($$)
*23rd Street between Seventh and Eighth
avenues tel: 243-3700*
Arthur Miller reputedly relocated here from the
Plaza Hotel because he was fed up with having
to put on a tie to go down to the front desk to
collect his mail. The Chelsea still attracts
refugees from more formal establishments,
with its laid-back but solicitous service and the
atmosphere of a run-down but arty apartment
building. For more on writers and artists who
have stayed here see the feature on page 85.

Chelsea Inn ($)
46th West 17th Street tel: 645-8989
Good value rooms with kitchenettes in a 19th-
century townhouse; the least expensive have
bathrooms shared with one other room.

Chelsea Savoy ($)
202 W. 23rd Street tel: 929-9353)
A no-frills option in the heart of the increasingly
trendy Chelsea neighborhood, this moderately
priced hotel offers no amenities but puts you
near art galleries and nightclubs.

Crowne Plaza at the United Nations ($$$)
*42nd Street between First and Second
avenues tel: 800/879-8836; 986-8800*
This stylish hotel is in a Tudor-style residential
section of Midtown Manhattan, a few minutes'
walk from the Chrysler Building, Grand Central
Terminal and the U.N. Rooms are spacious and
furnished in deep rich colors. The hotel also
offers corporate discounts and dual-line
phones with data ports.

Comfort Inn Murray Hill ($$)
*35th Street between Fifth and Sixth avenues
tel: 800/228-5150; 947-0200*
This branch of the nationwide chain predictably
has higher rates than its far-flung counterparts
but nonetheless represents good value for New
York City, with tidy, comfortable rooms.

Drake Swissôtel ($$$)
*Park Avenue at 56th Street
tel: 800/DRAKENY; 421-0900*
The lobby's wood and brass fittings (and the
bowls of complimentary Swiss chocolates) set
a comfortable, low-key mood that continues
into the comfortable, airy rooms.

Edison ($$)
*47th Street at Eighth Avenue
tel: 800/637-7070; 840-5000*
A partial refurbishment has made some of the
rooms here bright, airy and welcoming, while
others remain rather shabby. The good rooms
come at a fair price, although the hotel's size
(1,000 rooms) and its theater-district site
make it very much a tourist hotel.

263

Accommodations and Restaurants

Elysée ($$)
*54th Street between Madison and Park
avenues tel: 753-1066*
Recent refurbishment has sadly obliterated the
highly individual "Lucy goes to Hollywood" older
rooms, but some of the original furnishings
have been kept and have been incorporated
into the brand-new, Regency-inspired rooms.
Most of the doubles are small—opt for a suite
if you want space. V.C.R.s are standard
features, as are marble bath-tubs and safes.

Essex House Hotel Nikko ($$$)
*Central Park South between Sixth and Seventh
avenues tel: 800/654-5687; 247-0300*
From the etched brass and black marble
features of the art deco lobby to the amply
proportioned and tastefully furnished rooms,
the Essex House is stylish and enjoys an enviable position facing Central Park. The
best views are from the luxurious suites.

Four Seasons ($$$)
*57th Street between Park and Madison
avenues tel: 800/332-3442; 758-5700*
The Four Seasons is not only the tallest hotel
in New York—designed by the celebrated I.M.
Pei, it rises 52 stories high—but also the most
opulent. On average, each room cost a million
dollars to deck out in stylish contemporary art
deco form and acquire amenities such as
enormous bathtubs that fill within 60 seconds.

Gorham New York ($$)
*55th Street between Sixth and Seventh
avenues tel: 245-1800*
An excellent location to enjoy the best features
of Midtown Manhattan. The staff is noted for
courtesy and friendliness, and the more costly
of the very comfortable rooms feature
whirlpools, kitchenettes with microwave ovens,
and the latest in temperature-controlled baths.

Gramercy Park ($$)
*21st Street and Lexington Avenue
tel: 800/221-4083; 475-4320*
Facing Gramercy Park (keys to this private park
are available from the hotel porter), this grace-
fully aging hotel may have slow elevators and
few recent furnishings, but it does have lots of
character, offers discounts at weekends and
for long stays, and is usefully placed on the
borders of Midtown and Lower Manhattan.

Helmsley Middletowne ($$)
*48th Street between Lexington and Third
avenues tel: 800/221-4982; 755-3000*
Owned by the controversial hotelier Leona
Helmsley (but not to be confused with the
Helmsley Palace), the Middletowne occupies a
17-story former residential apartment house
conviently near the United Nations. The property has a mellow, homey ambience, and the
pleasant rooms have kitchenettes and fridges.
Some rooms open on to terraces.

Herald Square ($)
*31st Street near Fifth Avenue
tel: 800/727-1888; 279-4017*
Occupying the 1893 *Life* magazine building,
the rooms here are small and spartan but with
clean, tiled bathrooms. Most rooms have T.V.
and phones, and prices are cheap. The
location is noisy and relatively uninteresting.

Holiday Inn on 57th Street ($$)
*440 West 57th Street
tel: 800/231-0405; 581-8100*
Unexciting but dependable branch of a
nationwide chain of hotels, this is near the
Midtown Manhattan sights but occupies a
lackluster location.

Howard Johnson's 34th Street ($)
*34th Street between Seventh and Eighth
avenues tel: 800/633-1911; 947-5050*
Small, functional rooms are adequate for a
night's rest if you don't mind the slightly sleazy
location, opposite Penn Station. Each room is
supplied with cable T.V. and has a private
bathroom, with the low prices being the
main attraction.

Iroquois ($)
*44th Street between Fifth and Sixth avenues
tel: 800/332-7220; 840-3080*
A much-needed refurbishment has made a
definite improvement to this always depend-
able but once very shabby hotel. The more
expensive rooms are equipped with
kitchenettes; almost all are nowadays
tastefully decorated in relaxing pastel shades.
People who have stayed here recently say
that the service sometimes leaves a lot to
be desired.

Lexington ($$)
*Lexington Avenue at 48th Street
tel: 800/448-4471; 755-4400*
Beyond the marble-floored lobby with its
rosewood pillars and beautiful flower
arrangements are two types of accommodations—the dated older rooms and the
newly decorated (and also more expensive)
Tower rooms. Although both types of rooms are
small, there is plenty of space in which to
spread out elsewhere. A coffee shop, a
northern Italian restaurant, a highly acclaimed
Chinese restaurant and the western-style nightclub, Denim and Diamonds, are on the
premises. The Winter Citysaver rates are by far
the best value.

Mansfield ($)
*44th Street between Fifth and Sixth avenues
tel: 800/255-5767; 944-6050*
A place with few pretensions, the Mansfield
offers very affordable accommodations in a
prime Midtown Manhattan location (the more
famous Algonquin Hotel is just across the
street). The turn-of-the-century building was
designed by noted New York architect
Stanford White.

Marriott East Side ($$$)
*Lexington Avenue at 49th Street
tel: 800/242-8684; 755-4000*
Erected as an apartment house slightly more
recently than the medieval-style gargoyles on
the facade might suggest, the 34-story Marriott
East Side has successfully molded spacious
1920s New York residential rooms into
comfortable hotel accommodations. Each room
contains useful extras such as an iron and a
filter-coffee machine, although if you prefer not
to do all this for yourself, the service is helpful
and for out-of-room relaxing there is a club-like
bar downstairs.

Martha Washington ($)
*30th Street between Park and Madison
avenues tel: 689-1900*
Spartan accommodations in a semi-residential
area. The rooms are gloomy and range from
small to comparatively spacious; should you
feel the need for a private bathroom and TV,
you can expect to pay extra for them. Bookable
by the night or at very tempting weekly rates;
additional discounts for longerstays (there is a
one month maximum).

Michelangelo ($$$)
*51st Street at Seventh Avenue
tel: 800/237-0990; 765-1900*
Genuine 18th- and 19th-century European art
and a wealth of marble and crystal help the
Michelangelo to rank among New York's most
luxurious hotels. The large rooms come in
art deco, Empire, or country French styles with
seemingly every possible amenity, including
T.V. in the bathroom. There is even a free
unpacking service if you have too much
luggage to tackle alone. The atmosphere here
is a bit hushed, but this deluxe, self-styled
palazzo is one of the fanciest places to stay
around Broadway.

Milford Plaza ($$)
*45th Street at Eighth Avenue
tel: 800/221-2690; 869-3600*
Not the most characterful or luxurious of hotels
(in fact it has been described as being reminiscent of an airport lounge), the Milford Plaza
has its share of cramped rooms, but a prime
location on Times Square makes it a hit with
money-conscious tourists and business
travelers alike. The immediate area can be
dangerous at night, but hotel security is good.

Millennium Broadway ($$$)
*44th Street between Sixth Avenue and
Broadway tel: 800/622-5568; 768-4400*
Though situated in the heart of the Times
Square theater district, this hotel is geared
more toward business travelers than
tourists.But if the price is affordable, there are
few better-appointed or more up-to-date
options in the vicinity.

Morgans ($$$)
*Madison Avenue between 37th and 38th
streets tel: 686-0300*
The brainchild of the former owners of the
extremely chic 1970s-1980s nighclub Studio
54, Morgans has a minimalist design and a
color scheme based on black, gray and white.
The bathrooms feature unique stainless steel
basins and fittings, and every room has a video
player as standard. The clientele is
predominantly young and fashionable—and not
short of a dollar or two.

Parker Meridien ($$$)
*56th Street between Sixth and Seventh
avenues
tel: 800/543-4300; 245-5000*
From the glitzy interior architecture to the
pricey amenities, everything about Le Parker
Meridien symbolizes conspicuous wealth. The
ideal guest must be rich, beautiful, and
inclined to pose for hours at the rooftop
swimming pool.

Pickwick Arms ($)
*51st Street between Second and Third
avenues tel: 800/PIC-KWIK; 355-0300*
A comfortable lobby, a cocktail lounge, and a
roof garden go some way toward compensating
for the small rooms. This is a well-priced option
for the area, just a few minutes' walk from the
heart of Midtown Manhattan.

Plaza ($$$)
*Fifth Avenue at Central Park South
tel: 800/759-3000; 759-3000*
New York's leading hotel since it opened in
1907, the Plaza's past guests have included
Teddy Roosevelt, F. Scott and Zelda Fitzgerald,
the Beatles, and Solomon Guggenheim, who
lived in one of the Plaza's suites and decorated its walls with the art that later became the
core of the Guggenheim Museum's collection.
Property tycoon Donald Trump snapped up the
Plaza for $400 million in 1988 and put his
then wife Ivana in control of a $100-million
face-lift. Still the epitome of class, the Plaza
has every possible facility. Some tiny viewless
rooms have been made into suites; the pricier
accommodations have unbelievable
panoramas of Fifth Avenue or Central Park.

Portland Square Hotel ($)
*47th Street between Sixth and Seventh
avenues tel: 800/382-0600*
An unknown James Cagney was just one
among many struggling actors who used this
long-established budget-priced hotel in the
heart of the Broadway theater district. The
rooms have a few more frills than the
Portland's sister hotel, Herald Square: there
are places to sit in the lobby, lockers, and a
drinks- and ice-machine. Parts of the immediate area can be intimidating after dark.

Quality Hotel ($$)
*40th Street between Fifth and Madison
avenues tel: 800/228-5151; 447-1500*
Unfancy but crisply decorated rooms here offer
all the usual amenities in a good location at a
very fair price.

Remington ($)
*46th Street between Broadway and Sixth
Avenue tel: 221-2600*
Clean, no-frills accommodations in the theater
district. The cheapest rooms lack private bath-
rooms, but all are fair value for their low price.
Located very close to Times Square.

Regal U.N. Plaza ($$$)
*First Avenue at 44th Street
tel: 800/233-1234; 758-1234*
The rooms in this modern, architectural award-
winning structure do not begin until the 28th
floor, the lower levels being U.N. office space.
Chrome, marble, and mirrors are prevalent
throughout, and every room has a fine view.
The excellent sports facilities include indoor
tennis courts, swimming pool, and sauna.

Roger Smith ($$)
*Lexington Avenue at 47th Street
tel: 800/445-0277; 755-1400*
Just north of Grand Central Terminal, the Roger
Smith offers attractively furnished rooms and
the intimate, personal atmosphere most
Midtown Manhattan hotels can only strive for.

265

Accommodations and Restaurants

Roger Williams ($)
31st Street between Madison and Park avenues tel: 800/637-9773; 684-7500
Located in a quiet semi-residential area of Midtown, this is one of the friendlier budget hotels. Every room has a kitchenette and cable T.V., and there is a good choice of suites for families. The furnishings may have seen better days, but the hotel is good value.

Roosevelt ($$)
*Madison Avenue at 45th Street
tel: 800/223-1870; 661-9600*
Once a preeminent New York hotel catering to the thousands of train travelers who poured into the city at nearby Grand Central Terminal, the Roosevelt has matured into a slightly down-at-the-heels but dependable hotel. Renovations are now in progress—one of the first areas to be spruced up was the beautiful, vast, neo-classical lobby. Many of the rooms have been upgraded too; with the very reasonable room rate, this is one of Midtown's better deals.

Royalton ($$$)
*44th Street between Fifth and Sixth avenues
tel: 800/635-9013; 869-4400*
Another ultra-trendy hotel from the team that created Morgans (see page 264), the Royalton is designed with a cool artistry throughout and finds favor with the young and good-looking. Rooms are small but attractive.

St. Moritz on the Park ($$)
*Central Park South at Sixth Avenue
tel: 800/221-4774; 755-5800*
You will pay the usual high rates for a park view, but in general this is one of the less exclusive and more affordable hotels facing Central Park (if a little tired and worn). A reno-vation scheduled to begin October 1999 will bring the hotel back to its former glory.

Salisbury ($$)
57th Street between Sixth and Seventh avenues tel: 800/223-0680; 246-1300
A welcoming, professionally run, small hotel across the road from the Russian Tea Room, it is convenient for shopping. Decor is frumpy, but rooms are spotless and comfortable, the most recently renovated ones offering new microwaves and fridges. If you want even more space, opt for an apartment sized suite.

San Carlos Hotel ($$)
50th Street between Lexington and Third avenues tel: 800/722-2012; 755-1800
Little sets it apart from other Midtown Manhattan hotels, but the San Carlos offers good quality rooms with ample cupboard space and adequately equipped kitchenettes.

Sherry Netherland ($$$)
Fifth Avenue at 59th Street tel: 355-2800
One of the grand French chateau-style buildings put up along Fifth Avenue across from Central Park during the 1920s, the Sherry Netherland offers soaring park views and impeccable service. Rooms are spacious, with V.C.R.s and microwaves, and plenty of personal touches. The sky-high rates are worth it if you have a huge range of hard-to-satisfy demands. Room service is by the acclaimed restaurant, Harry Cipriani, located at ground level.

Vanderbilt-Y.M.C.A. ($)
47th Street between Second and Third avenues tel: 755-9600
Make an early booking to stay at the most popular and best-located of New York's Y.M.C.A.s. Open to men and women, it has newly renovated small single and double rooms at very low prices plus extra facilities such as a brand-new restaurant, luggage lockers, a swimming pool, a gym, and a laundromat.

W New York ($$$)
*Lexington Avenue at 49th Street
tel: 877/946-8357, 755-1200*
The flagship of a new chain of urban spa hotels, this smart property in the formal Doral location is abuzz with trend-setters. The design is chic, the atmosphere comfortable, and the amenities—like an elegant day spa and fitness center—indulgent. Drew Nieporent's Heartbeat restaurant serves creatively healthy fare pre-pared by chef Michel Nischan.

Waldorf-Astoria ($$$)
*Park Avenue between 49th and 50th streets
tel: 800/WALDORF; 355-3000*
After the Plaza, the Waldorf-Astoria is New York's most famous hotel. It was the birthplace of the charity ball and the prime rendezvous for New York high society from the 1930s—although it has taken $150 million to restore its grandeur. A sense of opulence strikes as soon as you enter the art deco lobby, and all the rooms are stylishly appointed with marble bathrooms. Only in the top-price suites and the Tower rooms, however, will you encounter a level of luxury to match the hotel's rich history.

Warwick ($$$)
*65 West 54th Street
tel: 800/223-4099; 247-2700*
Built by William Randolph Hearst in 1927, the recently renovated Warwick is popular with business travelers. It has over 400 rooms (all with T.V. and telephone), plus a restaurant and fitness facilities, and it is convenient for all the main Midtown sights.

Wellington ($$)
*Seventh Avenue at 55th Street
tel: 800/652-1212; 247-3900*
Except perhaps for the lobby, there is nothing fancy about the sizeable Wellington, where the rooms are clean and simple and reasonably priced for their prized central location.

Wolcott ($)
31st Street at Fifth Avenue tel: 268-2900
For a remarkably low rate, the Wolcott offers smallish but well furnished, comfortable rooms complete with private bathrooms and cable T.V. The mirror-lined, baroque-style lobby is a surprise bonus in this impressive budget hotel.

Wyndham ($$)
*58th Street between Fifth and Sixth avenues
tel: 753-3500*
The Wyndham feels more like an apartment building than a hotel and is especially popular with Broadway performers who could easily afford to stay elsewhere. Such good-sized rooms in this area and price bracket are very unusual; all are individually and tastefully deco-rated. Early booking is essential.

UPPER EAST SIDE

Barbizon ($$)
63rd Street at Lexington Avenue
tel: 800/753-0360; 838-5700
By the standards of the high-priced Upper East Side, the Barbizon is good value for its small-ish but cozy rooms and the dozen terraced suites (some with good views) that occupy the red-brick building's Gothic tower. Until 1981, the Barbizon was a women's residential hotel, and famous former guests include Grace Kelly, Candice Bergen, and Liza Minnelli.

Carlyle ($$$)
76th Street at Madison Avenue
tel: 800/227-5737; 744-1600
For years, the understated elegance of the Carlyle has provided a home away from home for high-ranking international dignitaries and those so wealthy that they have no need to flaunt their affluence. Crystal chandeliers hang above the public spaces, and the guest rooms are decorated with antiques, tapestries, and fresh flowers. Most also have fax machines. Sink into the marble bathtub and you will find that you have a phone at your elbow.

Lowell ($$$)
63rd Street between Park and Madison avenues tel: 838-1400
A small, luxurious hotel, the Lowell occupies an art deco building in the landmark district of the Upper East Side. Chinese porcelain, 18th- and 19th-century prints, and wood-burning fireplaces decorate the rooms; service is personal and attentive. There is a fitness room for the use of all guests, but if you like your workouts to be private then go for the Gym Suite, said to be inspired by one-time guest Madonna.

Mark ($$$)
77th Street at Madison Avenue
tel: 800/843-6275; 744-4300
In-room whirlpools, video players (select films from a well-stocked library), and courteous staff help attract a fashionable, jet-setting clientele. When the rich and famous don't want to be noticed, this is where they stay.

Pierre ($$$)
Fifth Avenue at 61st Street
tel: 800/332-3442; 940-8101
There is absolutely nothing surreal about the mural-lined corridors or the enormous, well-furnished rooms of the Pierre, even though this was Salvador Dali's favorite New York hotel. Packed with antiques and lined by lush carpets, the hotel's somewhat tired but nevertheless aristocratic ambience is heightened by the afternoon tea served beneath the rotunda.

Plaza Athénée ($$$)
64th Street between Park and Madison avenues tel: 734-9100
With Louis XIV-style furniture filling every corner and marble and crystal fittings wherever you look, the Plaza Athénée is intended to evoke the grandeur of a European royal palace. Even though some find it pretentious, plenty of wealthy guests bask happily in the pre-revolutionary Versailles atmosphere, and standards of service are high.

Regency ($$$)
Park Avenue between 60th and 61st streets
tel: 800/23-LOEWS; 759-4100
The lobby may be stuffed with French antiques, but the Regency, while extremely stylish, is a lot less snooty than many of its Upper East Side rivals. Be they financial wheeler dealers or rock stars on the rise, the clientele appreciate the tastefully furnished, airy rooms and the efficient, attentive staff.

Stanhope ($$$)
Fifth Avenue at 81st Street
tel: 800/828-1123; 288-5800
With high-quality reproduction Louis XIV furniture filling the lobby and antique porcelain sitting beside state-of-the-art electronic gadgets in every guest room, the Stanhope is an interesting blend of old and new but has a rather hushed and hallowed atmosphere.

Surrey ($$$)
76th Street at Madison Avenue
tel: 800/ME-SUITE; 288-3700
A small, quiet, and welcoming hotel, where all the rooms include kitchenettes—though it is hard to imagine the tidily bank-rolled guests opting for self-made snacks when room service operates around the clock and the acclaimed Café Boulud is located on the premises.

Wales ($$)
Madison Avenue at 92nd Street
tel: 800/428-5252; 876-6000
One of New York's longest-serving hotels, the Wales has been in business since 1900, and the attractive rates reflect its location on the northern edge of the neighborhood—though public transportation links to Midtown and Lower Manhattan are swift. The price of the nicely but not opulently furnished rooms includes afternoon tea and a light breakfast.

Westbury ($$$)
Madison Avenue at 69th Street
tel: 800/321-1569; 535-2000
Elegance takes on an English appearance at the Westbury, where genuine Chippendale furniture decorates the lobby and a generous number of top-class reproductions fill the guest rooms. Splurge on a deluxe room and you can stretch out on a four-poster bed. Extras include a well-equipped gymnasium for guests' use.

UPPER WEST SIDE

Beacon ($$)
Broadway at 75th Street
tel: 800/572-4969; 787-1100
A bustling, professionally run, small hotel, 10 blocks north of Lincoln Center and within easy reach of most Upper West Side attractions. The large rooms all come with cable T.V. and kitchenette, and Zabar's, the city's best gourmet deli, is just up the street. A very good deal, especially the newly renovated rooms.

Broadway ($)
Broadway at 77th Street tel: 362-1100
Mid-sized hotel with competitive rates. All rooms come with color T.V. and fridges. A few dollars can be saved by opting for a shared rather than a private bathroom.

267

Accommodations and Restaurants

Esplanade ($)
West End Avenue at 74th Street tel: 874-5000
Filling a large, red-brick building in a residential part of the Upper West Side, the Esplanade is an attractively priced, mainly suite-oriented hotel. All rooms are well proportioned; those facing west get views of the sunset across the Hudson River. Be aware, however, that the area, while safe during daylight, can be empty and rather spooky at night.

Excelsior ($)
81st Street between Central Park West and Columbus Avenue
tel: 800/368-4575; 362-9200
Standard but entirely acceptable rooms with spotless, old-fashioned bathrooms make this a good bet, in a residential area of the Upper West Side. Central Park, the American Museum of Natural History, and Columbus Avenue bars and eateries nearby.

Hostelling International New York ($)
Amsterdam Avenue at 103rd Street
tel: 932-2300
The largest youth hostel in the U.S. occupies an architectural landmark—dating from 1883, the building was designed by the man responsible for the base of the Statue of Liberty. Very clean and welcoming, with small dormitory rooms and a host of additional services for the budget traveler.

Malibu Studio ($)
Broadway between 102nd and 103rd streets
tel: 800/647-2227; 222-2954
Bordering a district that can be intimidating at night, though close to Columbia University and the Cathedral Church of St. John the Divine, the Malibu offers student-residence-style accommodation at very low rates. Rooms are unelaborate but homey, and a few extra dollars bring a color T.V., kitchen facilities and private bathroom.

Mayflower on the Park ($$)
Central Park West at 61st Street
tel: 800/223-4164; 265-0060
On the border with Midtown Manhattan, and with some rooms overlooking Central Park, the Mayflower offers tidily appointed rooms a stone's throw from Lincoln Center. Stage and screen stars are sometimes among the guests.

Milburn ($)
76th Street near Broadway
tel: 800/833-9622; 362-1010
One of the Upper West Side's best budget choices, the Milburn offers not only a quiet, graceful lobby and rooms with brand-new kitchenettes (with microwaves), but also prompt, friendly service. The spacious suites make ideal family accommodations (children under 12 stay with their parents free); there is a self-service laundry on the premises.

Olcott ($)
72nd Street between Central Park West and Columbus Avenue tel: 877-4200
Worn furnishings and offhand service may be offputting, but many theatrical and musical performers stay here for the inexpensive weekly rates. Shorter stays are subject to availability; early booking is essential (no credit cards).

Radisson Empire ($$)
Broadway at 63rd Street
tel: 800/221-6509; 265-7400
A luxury chain hotel, recently refurbished to the tune of $30 million, it offers small, well-furnished rooms all with C.D. and tape deck as well as color T.V. and V.C.R. The grand, high-ceilinged lobby displays a beautiful collection of model stage sets—appropriate for a hotel a few steps from Lincoln Center.

Riverside Tower ($)
Riverside Drive at 80th Street
tel: 800/724-3136; 877-5200
Located in a dull residential section of the Upper West Side, its spartan and somewhat dreary rooms have phones, T.V.s and superb views over the Hudson. There are no other facilities—use as a low-cost place to sleep.

West Side Y.M.C.A. ($)
63rd Street near Central Park West
tel: 787-4400
Book well ahead for these simple but usefully situated and reasonably priced rooms, which are available as singles or doubles in a large, echoey building close to Lincoln Center. The price includes use of a well-equipped gym and a large swimming pool, safe-deposit boxes, coin-op laundromat and 24-hour security.

RESTAURANTS

FINANCIAL DISTRICT AND TRIBECA

Au Mandarin ($)
World Financial Center tel: 385-0313
A well-priced selection of Chinese meals is offered on the first floor of this bustling, architecturally innovative structure, notable for its indoor palm trees.

Bridge Café ($$)
Water Street at Dover Street tel: 227-3344
If you have just crossed the Brooklyn Bridge on foot, why not reward yourself with a delicious lunch in this cozy red-brick dining room sited just beneath the bridge itself? Along with the usual lunch and dinner favorites, there is an appetizing selection of well-prepared seafood dishes.

Bouley Bakery ($$$)
120 West Broadway, at Duane Street
tel: 964-2525
Under the direction of one of the city's best chefs, this tiny, elegant bakery/restaurant offers exquisite, deceivingly simple French food with an unmatched selection of breads.

City Hall ($$$)
131 Duane Street tel: 222-7777
The latest venue for Cub Room chef Henry Meer features large portions of updated classics like she-crab soup and prime rib.

Franklin Station ($$)
222 West Broadway tel: 274-8525
A creative mixture of French and Southeast Asian cooking finds many discerning locals making this their favorite neighborhood dinner spot.

Fraunces Tavern ($$)
54 Pearl Street tel: 269-0144
A reconstruction of a landmark 18th-century tavern (see page 107), the Fraunces Tavern is an atmospheric dining place, but the regular American fare is seldom above average.

Harry's at Hanover Square ($)
1 Hanover Square tel: 425-3412
Harry's is an essential stop for seekers of the ultimate burger: the hamburgers are lovingly grilled over charcoal and apple wood and come with a range of toppings from caviar to avocado.

Montrachet ($$$)
239 West Broadway, between Walker and White streets. tel: 219-2777
One of the first restaurants in TriBeCa, this cozy bistro features terrific French-inspired food, great service, and a reasonably priced wine list of hard-to-find selections.

Nobu ($$$)
105 Hudson Street, at Franklin Street tel: 219-0500
Sister to London's latest hotspot and L.A.'s movie-star hang out, this Japanese-inspired restaurant has won awards both for design and for food. **Nobu Next Door** operates on a first come, first served basis.

Odeon ($$$)
West Broadway at Thomas Street tel: 233-0507
A favorite for its contemporary American food and its art deco and neon-decorated setting.

TriBeCa Grill ($$)
Greenwich Street at Franklin Street tel: 941-3900
Co-owned by actor Robert de Niro and set in what is now a film company building, the TriBeCa Grill draws a star-spotting crowd, but its real attraction is the gourmet-pleasing food, especially the carefully crafted fish dishes.

Windows on the World ($$$)
1 World Trade Center, 107th Floor tel: 524-700
Michael Lomonaco has improved the food, but the view is still the main reason to come to this American classic. The more casual Wild Blue has replaced the Cellar in the Sky.

CHINATOWN

Bo Ky ($)
80 Bayard Street tel: 406-2292
Nothing fancy about the decor but nourishing bowls of noodle soup with seafood or duck served at rock-bottom prices.

Golden Unicorn ($$)
18 East Broadway tel: 941-0911
A favorite for large family banquets or big parties. Large selection, from savory appetizers through dim sum to duck, fresh fish, and tofu.

Grand Sichuan ($)
125 Canal Street tel: 625-9212
Unlike any of the Szechwan food you'll find around town, the fiery authentic cooking at this Chinatown is remarkable, as is the fact that they take (and honor) reservations and have a menu that's fully translated into English.

HSF ($$)
46 Bowery tel: 374-1319
This is a fair bet for lunchtime dim sum, especially for first-time western visitors who will not feel as left out here as they might in some Chinatown eateries, thanks to a picture chart showing some of the options.

Joe's Shanghai ($)
9 Pell Street, between Bowery and Mott streets tel: 233-8888
One of the best Chinese restaurants in the city, known for its rich and satisfying Shanghaiese cooking—soup, dumplings, braised pork shoulder, lion's head, handmade Shanghai noodles, and more. Worth the long wait. Cash only.

Mandarin Court ($)
61 Mott Street, near Canal Street tel: 608-3838
Wonderfully chaotic dim sum parlor, busiest on Sundays when the communal tables are packed.

Mueng Thai ($$)
23 Pell Street tel: 406-4259
A variety of tantalizing Thai dishes. Anyone who wants to keep the roof on their mouth should take care when venturing among the spicier items.

New Indonesia and Malaysia ($)
18 Doyers Street tel: 267-0088
Hundreds of Indonesian and Malaysian dishes to choose from in this tiny but cozy diner, where everything from gado gado to fish head curry is spiced to the customer's wishes.

New York Noodle Town ($)
28 Bowery tel: 349-0923
Providing plenty of what its name suggests in many more varieties than you ever imagined possible. Duck with flowering chives is a must.

Nha Trang ($)
87 Baxter Street, between Bayard and Canal streets tel: 233-5948
Excellent, inexpensive Vietnamese. BBQ pork chops, crispy squid, and other regional specialties never disappoint.

Nom Wah Tea Parlor ($)
13 Doyers Street tel: 962-6047
Long-established and immensely popular, it serves a wonderful selection of dim sum throughout the day. Plenty of filled dumplings and pastries on the passing trays, although regulars claim standards have dropped.

Oriental Garden ($)
14 Elizabeth Street tel: 619-0085
The seafood at this Cantonese restaurant is as fresh as you can find—it flops its way from the tanks in the window to the kitchen. The drunken shrimp are actually cooked live at your table.

Shanghai Cuisine House ($–$$)
89–91 Bayard Street tel: 732-8988
Small and unpretentious venue for enjoying the Chinese cuisine of the moment: Shanghai.

Sun Say Gay ($)
220 Canal Street tel: 964-7256
This hole-in-the-wall rice shop dispenses simple dishes—bits of meat, vegetables and pickles on generous piles of rice—at absurdly cheap prices.

Accommodations and Restaurants

Sweet 'n' Tart Café ($)
76 Mott Street, at Canal Street tel: 334-8088
The menu is arranged according to rules of traditional Chinese medicine. Expertly prepared, fast, and super-inexpensive.

Thailand Restaurant ($)
106 Bayard Street tel: 349-3132
Inexpensive Thai favorites, and some lesser-known dishes, fill a lengthy, delicious menu.

Triple 8 Palace ($$–$$$)
59 Division Street tel: 941-8886
On the top floor of a building beneath the Manhattan Bridge, this is wildly popular with locals who show up mostly for the lunchtime dim sum.

20 Mott Street ($$)
20 Mott Street tel: 964-0380
Spread over three floors and offering a massive and (to Westerners) largely indecipherable menu, this is one of Chinatown's most celebrated restaurants, although its reputation is definitely for the food rather than the service

Vegetarian's Paradise ($)
68 Mott Street tel: 406-6988
A vegetarian cubby hole does wondrous things re-creating regular Chinese dishes but using nothing that ever walked, crawled, or swam.

Viet-Nam ($)
11 Doyers Street tel: 693-0725
An unpretentious setting for some of the best and probably most authentic Vietnamese cuisine in New York.

Wong Kee ($)
113 Mott Street tel: 966-1160
Fine selection of Cantonese dishes at irresistible prices; deservedly crowded.

SOHO

Aquagrill ($$$)
210 Spring Street, at 6th Avenue tel: 274-0505
Fresh fish and seafood in a trendy SoHo setting. Creative entrées balance simple preparations. Try the signature snail snaps and roasted cod. Great desserts.

Ceci Cela ($)
55 Spring Street, at Lafayette Street tel: 274-9179
This tiny French bakery with six tables at the back has the best croissants and classic French pastries this side of the Atlantic.

Balthazar ($$$)
80 Spring Street, at Crosby Street tel: 965-1414
The closest you'll come to a Parisian brasserie. This white hot scene is where power-brokers enjoy chilled seafood platters, roasted chicken, braised short ribs, and other brasserie fare. Reservations necessary.

Bar 89 ($$)
89 Mercer Street, between Broome and Spring streets tel: 274-0989
Though competently prepared, the food isn't the draw here, the bathrooms are. Clear glass stall doors flood with opaque light before you expose yourself to the world. Don't leave without sipping a beautiful martini or cosmopolitan.

Honmura An ($$$)
170 Mercer Street, between Houston and Prince streets tel: 334-5253
Handmade soba is the highlight of this serene outpost of a Tokyo favorite

Lombardi's ($)
32 Spring Street, between Mott and Mulberry streets tel: 941-7994
The 1905 coal-fired oven gives the pizza at this parlor an unusually flavorful crust. Many consider it the best on the island.

Omen ($$)
Thompson Street between Spring and Prince streets tel: 925-8923
This relaxed Japanese restaurant's house specialty is indeed Omen—a spicy soup dish with vegetables and noodles.

Palacinka ($)
28 Grand Street tel: 625-0362
The pancake's the thing at this pan-European crêperie which produces unusual variations on a familiar theme.

Quilty's ($$$)
177 Prince Street, between Thompson and Sullivan streets tel: 254-1260
Named for a character in Nabokov's Lolita, this elegant bistro serves creative modern fare.

Raoul's ($$)
Prince Street between Sullivan and Thompson streets tel: 966-3518
A winning New York version of a French restaurant, with a tempting array of main courses and desserts; an impressive wine list.

Rialto ($$)
265 Elizabeth Street, between Houston and Prince streets tel: 334-7900
Reasonably priced, upscale American menu, charming garden, and hip atmosphere.

Soho Steak ($$)
90 Thompson Street, between Prince and Spring streets tel: 226-0602
Don't be put off by the wait or the sardine-like seating in this tiny bistro. The menu—which features more than just steak—is expertly prepared and exceptionally well priced.

LITTLE ITALY

Assaggio ($$)
178 Hester Street tel: 226-2686
Not as rowdy as some Little Italy establishments, it has much that is good among its southern Italian staples.

Bellato's ($$)
55 E Houston Street tel: 274-8881
While there might be better Neapolitan food at other restaurants, few can match this one for Little Italy atmosphere.

Benito's ($)
163 and 174 Mulberry Street tel: 226-9012 and 226-9171
Two branches of the same trattoria, each with dependable, fairly priced dishes.

Caffè Biondo ($)
141 Mulberry Street tel: 226-9285
At this popular spot, arty, dressed-in-black SoHo types choose from a wide selection of coffees and pose by the front window.

Caffè Roma ($)
385 Broome Street tel: 226-8413
In business since the 1890s, Caffè Roma offers excellent coffee and superb freshly baked pastries and cakes to indulge in.

Ferrara ($)
195 Grand Street tel: 226-6150
Lacks the atmosphere of Caffè Roma (see above), but a nice place to sip a cappuccino and nibble your selection from a tempting array of baked goods.

Taormina ($$)
147 Mulberry Street tel: 219-1007
A touch pricier and classier than its neighbors. Serves Neapolitan dishes in a sedate setting.

EAST VILLAGE AND LOWER EAST SIDE

Acme Bar and Grill ($$)
9 Great Jones Street tel: 420-1934
Cajun cooking and lots of it—gumbo, jambalaya, and deep fried oyster.

Angelica Kitchen ($)
12th Street between First and Second avenues tel: 228-2909
Tasty and very inexpensive natural foods.

Benny's Burritos ($)
Avenue A at 6th Street tel: 254-2054
Burritos with a host of inventive fillings are dispensed here to a lively East Village crowd.

Caffè della Pace ($)
7th Street between First and Second avenues tel: 529-8024
This low-key spot is worth seeking out for its stylishly presented Italian food at very reasonable prices.

Christine's ($$)
Lexington Avenue at 40th Street tel: 953-1920
Christine's serves omelets, salads, and sandwiches, but knowing regulars choose the Polish dishes—tripe, homemade pirogi or blintzes—and leave room for babka dessert.

Dojo ($)
24 St. Mark's tel: 674-9821
An intriguingly combined Japanese and health-food restaurant, with a predominantly youthful and trendy clientele.

Emerald Planet ($)
2 Great Jones Street tel: 353-9727
Exotic variations on the Mexican burrito with a range of creative fillings and garnishing such as jasmine rice and mango salsa.

First ($)
87 First Avenue, between 5th and 6th streets tel: 674-3823
This clubby East Village bistro serves an intriguing menu of whimsically updated American favorites until 4 AM. Everything is cooked on the premises and brought to your table by waiters wearing black vinyl aprons.

Great Jones Café ($$)
54 Great Jones Street tel: 674-9304
This is where you will find the cutting-edge East Village faces selecting their late-afternoon breakfasts from the daily specials—homely American fare—chalked on a blackboard.

Il Bagatto ($)
192 East 2nd Street, between Avenues A and B tel: 228-0977
Surprisingly authentic homemade pastas and entrées at bargain prices in a lively setting. Always busy; always good.

Indochine ($$)
Lafayette Street between Astor Place and 4th Street tel: 505-5111
Dine amid palm fronds on a tremendous mix of Vietnamese, Thai, and Cambodian fare; open for dinner only.

Katz's Delicatessen ($)
East Houston Street near Orchard Street tel: 254-2246
Legendary for providing pastrami and corned beef sandwiches for over a century, Katz's found more fame in the 1989 film *When Harry Met Sally.*

Kiev ($)
Second Avenue at 7th Street tel: 674-4040
Eastern European specialties such as pirogi and generously filled blintze are served around the clock.

Miracle Grill ($)
112 First Avenue, between 6th and 7th streets tel: 254-2353
Among the first in the wave of ambitious, inexpensive restaurants in the area, the Southwestern food at this trendy restaurant still satisfies. Lovely garden.

Mitali ($)
6th Street between First and Second avenues tel: 533-2508
The quality Indian cuisine brings adventurous diners from all over New York.

Pommes Frites ($)
123 Second Avenue, between 7th and 8th streets tel: 674-1234
The smell of Belgian-style French fries crisping in peanut oil and the wide selection of homemade mayonnaises attracts lines to this new East Village take-out store.

Radio Perfecto ($)
190 Avenue B tel: 477-3366
Come for the roast chicken (available with a variety of sauces) and the comfortable environment. A collection of antique radios adorn the walls.

Ratner's Dairy Restaurant ($)
Delancey Street between Norfolk and Suffolk streets tel: 677-5588
Established in 1905, Ratner's is well past its prime for kosher Jewish dairy specialties, but the Lansky Lounge in the back room attracts a beautiful East-Village crowd for specialty cock-tails and definitively New York scene.

Second Avenue Kosher Deli ($$)
Second Avenue at 10th Street tel: 677-0606
This family-run Jewish deli is one of the last remaining places where you can sample kasha, kugel, knishes, and knaidels in authentic forms. The back room features memorabilia from the Lower East Side's Yiddish Theater.

Two Boots ($)
Avenue A at 2nd Street tel: 505-2276
Enterprising mixing of Italian and Cajun-style cookery: shrimp pizza is just one example.

271

Accommodations and Restaurants

Veselka ($)
Second Avenue at 9th Street tel: 228-9682
Earthy, filling Ukrainian and Polish fare is
served around the clock and in large quantities
to a surprisingly diverse East Village crowd.
For something light, stick to the blintzes.

Yaffa Café ($)
97 St. Marks Place tel: 674-9302
This is a hangout for East Village characters,
happily grazing on croissants or burgers inside
or out in the garden.

GREENWICH VILLAGE

Anglers and Writers ($)
*Hudson Street at St. Luke's Place
tel: 675-0810*
Plays up the neighborhood literary links and
serves snacks, tea, and coffee amid antiques
and rows of frequently thumbed books.

Artepasta ($)
*81 Greenwich Avenue, at Bank Street
tel: 229-0234*
Inexpensive pastas with the traditional accompaniments in a cozy setting. Lunch bargains.

Babbo ($$$)
110 Waverly Place tel: 777-0303
The food is robust and flavorful, the service
friendly and attentive, the atmosphere welcom-
ing. Try the five-course pasta tasting menu.

Benny's Burritos ($)
113 Greenwich Avenue tel: 727-0584
Like the branch in the East Village (see above),
its burritos are stuffed with as much cheese,
beans, meat, or vegetables as they will hold.

Blue Ribbon Bakery ($$)
33 Downing Street tel: 337-0404
A 100-year-old oven inspired this bistro-cum-
bakery, owned by the Bromberg Brothers of
Blue Ribbon fame. The menu offers small and
large plates of classic French fare. Sit downstairs for more ambience.

Caffè Lure ($$)
*169 Sullivan Street, between Bleecker and
West Houston streets tel: 473-2642*
This small, French bistro has real French flare.
Hip crowd and high-value.

Caffè Rafaella ($)
*134 Seventh Avenue, between Charles and
10th streets tel: 929-7247*
Sandwiches, salads, and desserts tempt in
this living-room setting, where people-watching
is as good as it gets.

Caffè Reggio ($)
119 MacDougal Street tel: 475-9557
Claimed to be the country's oldest coffee
shop, it has a dark, atmospheric interior and a
selection of pleasing coffees and cakes.

Chumley's ($$)
86 Bedford Street tel: 675-4449
A one-time speakeasy, Chumley's is
atmospheric for either a drink or a meal of
dependable American fare.

Clementine ($$$)
1 Fifth Avenue, at 8th Street tel: 253-0003
Contemporary American food distinguishes this
bar-restaurant from being just another scene.
The cocktails are exceptional.

Corner Bistro ($)
331 West 4th Street tel: 242-9502
Late-night, busy, no-frills stop for bistro burgers
(served on paper plates), and chilled beer.

Cowgirl Hall of Fame ($)
519 Hudson Street tel: 633-1133
Photos of famous cowgirls grin down at you
from the walls and country music plays on the
jukebox as plaid–shirted staff dispense
substantial helpings of Tex-Mex fare—and
potent margaritas.

Cucina Stagionale ($)
264 Bleecker Street tel: 924-2707
Simple, inexpensive and very pleasing Italian
food; be prepared to wait in line and make sure
you bring your own alcohol.

Drover's Tap Room ($$)
*9 Jones Street, between Bleecker and West
4th streets tel: 627-1233*
Home-style American menu features meatloaf,
fried chicken, mashed potatoes, crispy fries,
and satisfying desserts.

Florent ($$)
69 Gansevoort Street tel: 989-5779
Bistro specializing in, but not limited to,
delectable meat dishes. Being open around the
clock with breakfast available from midnight
finds an intriguing assortment of club-going
New Yorkers arriving through the small hours.

Gotham Bar and Grill ($$$)
12th Street at Fifth Avenue tel: 620-4020
From the perfect architecture to the perfectly
presented food, the Gotham Bar and Grill is an
impeccably stylish New York classic.

Home ($$)
*20 Cornelia Street, between Bleecker and
West 4th streets tel: 243-9579*
The reasonably priced food is surprisingly
elegant and delicious. Accompaniments such
as homemade relishes and sausages.

Il Cantinori ($$$)
*32 East 10th Street, between Broadway and
University Place tel: 673-6044*
Upscale Italian with fine pasta and Tuscan
specialties. Although the service can throw
attitude, the overall experience is lovely, if
slightly overpriced.

Indigo ($$)
*142 West 10th Street, between Greenwich
Avenue and Waverly Place tel: 691-7757*
Contemporary American bistro offering creative
food at very reasonable prices.

Japonica ($)
100 University Place tel: 243-7752
Spartan setting for substantial helpings of
sushi and other Japanese fare.

John's Pizzeria ($)
278 Bleecker Street tel: 243-1680
Long popular—not least with Woody Allen—it
serves perfect oven-baked pizzas in more than
50 varieties. The various outposts around town
are also reliable.

Le Gigot ($$)
*18 Cornelia Street, between Beecker and West
4th streets tel: 627-3737*
Tiny French bistro with excellent food and reasonable prices. Le GIgot also offers an
inexpensive wine list and friendly service.

Mama Buddha ($)
57 Hudson Street tel: 924-2762
Meat, seafood, and vegetarian options make up a tempting menu of Chinese dishes.

Marquet Patisserie ($)
15 East 12th Street, between 5th Avenue and University Place tel: 229-9313
Charming French bakery and cafe with fresh salads, soups, pastries, and cafe au lait served in bowls. Breakfast and lunch only.

Minetta Tavern ($$)
Minetta Lane and MacDougal Street tel: 475-3850
A historic Greenwich Village saloon decorated with 1930s artworks and memorabilia; very satisfying Italian lunches and dinners.

Moustache ($)
90 Bedford Street, between Barrow and Grove streets tel: 229-2220
There's always a wait for one of the 10 tables at this Middle Eastern restaurant, with freshly baked pittas straight from the oven.

Pearl Oyster Bar ($$)
128 Cornelia Street tel: 691-8211
This tiny counter of a seafood restaurant has recently expanded. The buckets of steamers, the lobster rolls, and other New England seafood preparations remain superb.

Petite Abeille ($-$$)
466 Hudson Street tel: 741-6479
This tiny restaurant (now a mini chain of three) started the recent Belgian craze. Salads, entrées, sandwiches, and omelets issued from the miniscule short-order kitchen are top notch.

Ray's Original Pizza ($)
Sixth Avenue at 11th Street tel: 243-2253
Ray's Pizza outlets are all over New York, but this is the first and best. It serves pizza by the slice to go or to eat at one of the few tables.

Sammy's Noodle Shop ($)
453 Sixth Avenue, at 11th Street tel: 924-6688
Bustling Chinese restaurant where everything is made from scratch, including the noodles, baked buns, and barbecued duck.

Taka ($$)
61 Grove Street, between Bleecker Street and 7th Avenue tel: 242-3699
Unusual because the sushi chef is a woman, this Japanese restaurant is extremely popular.

Tanti Baci Caffè ($)
163 West 10th Street, between 7th Avenue and Waverly Place tel: 647-9651
Inexpensive Italian trattoria with the feel of a grotto. Combine your favorite pasta and sauce or choose from one of the daily specials.

Tea and Sympathy ($)
108 Greenwich Avenue tel: 807-8329
As well as the traditional high tea, they also serve shepherd's pie, fish cakes, and stodgy "school dinner" desserts.

Tortilla Flats ($)
Washington Street at 12th Street tel: 243-1053
Tex-Mex eatery where the emphasis is on rowdy good times as much as on consuming fiery food and alcohol in very large amounts. Bingo night guarantees fun.

MURRAY HILL, GRAMERCY, CHELSEA, AND FLATIRON DISTRICT

11 Madison Park ($$$)
11 Madison Avenue tel: 889-0905
Union Square Cafe and Gramercy Tavern owner Danny Meyer owns this bustling American eatery (along with **Tabla** next door). Elegant, almost retro art deco decor and Kerry Heffernan's contemporary American cuisine.

Alva ($$)
36 East 22nd Street, between Broadway and Park Avenue tel: 228-4399
American bistro at its best; roast chicken, lamb, fish, mashed potatoes, and a neighborhood atmosphere.

Bendix Diner ($)
219 Eighth Avenue, at 21st Street tel: 366-0560
The menu has a little of everything—American, Thai, Italian, you name it—and it's all good and inexpensive. A hot brunch spot.

Bolo ($$$)
23 East 22nd Street, between Broadway and Park Avenue South tel: 228-2200
Creative Spanish food, deftly flavored and skillfully prepared.

Bottino ($$)
246 Tenth Avenue tel: 206-6766
Most restaurants that are this trendy and this jam-packed with beautiful people don't take the food very seriously. But this Chelsea hotspot features reasonably priced Italian fare of exceptional quality.

Bright Food Shop ($)
216 Eighth Avenue, between 21st and 22nd streets tel: 243-4433
Unusual Asian/Southwestern food in a 1930s coffee-shop. Odd-sounding menu selections turn out to be delicious.

Chat 'n' Chew ($)
10 East 16th Street, between Fifth Avenue and Union Square West tel: 243-1616
Huge helpings of American classics in a comfortable setting. Sandwiches, entrées, and desserts are tops. Late-night dining.

Chelsea Bistro & Bar ($$$)
358 West 23rd Street, between Eighth and Ninth avenues tel: 727-2026
A neighborhood French bistro that attracts gourmets from around the city. Foie gras ravioli and other equally innovative dishes are not to be missed.

The City Bakery ($)
22 East 17th Street, between Fifth Avenue and Union Square West tel: 366-1414
The architecturally urban setting of stainless steel and cement showcases beautiful sandwiches, salads, soups, cookies, tarts, and other luncheon items.

Coffee Shop ($$)
16th Street and Union Square West tel: 243-7969
Despite its name, this is actually a lively and fashionable spot for consuming American-Brazilian food and generally being seen by the right faces.

273

Accommodations and Restaurants

Ess-a-Bagel ($)
359 First Avenue, at 21st Street
tel: 260-2252
Contender for the city's best bagels. Smoked salmon, cream cheese, and other accompaniments are worth lining up for.

Follonico ($$)
6 West 24th Street, between Fifth and Sixth avenues tel: 691-6359
Among the most authentic-feeling trattorias in town. A wood-fired oven gives the Tuscan fare a welcome rustic flavor.

Frank's ($$)
14th Street between Ninth and Tenth avenues
tel: 243-1349
Operating in the so-called "meat-packing district" since 1912, this honest-to-goodness steak and seafood spot offers food of far higher quality than the sawdust-on-the-floor decor might suggest.

Gramercy Tavern ($$$)
42 East 20th Street, between Broadway and Park Avenue South tel: 477-0777
They set out to redefine four-star dining and succeeded with prix fixe, multicourse menus of inspired modern French cooking. There is a lighter menu available in the bar.

I Trulli ($$$)
122 E. 27th Street tel: 481-7372
An authentic trattoria with a beautiful garden in season, I Trulli offers homemade pasta and other sophisticated Italian fare. The diminutive **Enoteca** next door has a selective menu and a huge wine list.

Live Bait ($$)
23rd Street between Madison and Fifth avenues tel: 353-2400
Styled as a rustic southern fishing shack, Live Bait is a busy bar and also dispenses filling southern-style sandwiches, burgers, and fresh salads.

Lola ($$)
22nd Street between Fifth and Sixth avenues
tel: 675-6700
American food bearing a West Indian influence, and some genuine Caribbean and South American dishes, prepared to an exceptional standard. A "Gospel brunch" is served on Sundays.

Merchants, NY ($)
112 Seventh Avenue, at 17th Street
tel: 366-7267
Pub-like atmosphere with good bar food and outdoor seating.

Mesa Grill ($$)
102 Fiftht Avenue, between 15th and 16th streets tel: 807-7400
Considered the city's best Southwestern. Hefty portions and friendly service make this a favorite among well-dressed Yuppies. Funky, award-winning design.

Negril ($$)
362 West 23rd Street, between Eighth and Ninth avenues tel: 212/807-6411
Traditional and innovative Jamaican food served in a bustling, noisy setting. Be warned, there is always a wait for a table on the weekends.

Newsbar Inc ($)
19th Street between Fifth and Sixth avenues
tel: 255-3996
Serves breakfast, lunch, and early dinner, but visit this minimalist-designed café to sip coffee, people-watch, and scan the racks of international newspapers.

Park Bistro ($$)
Park Avenue between 28th and 29th streets
tel: 689-1360
Among the better of New York's many French bistro-style restaurants, this is deservedly popular for providing lovely food in a lovely setting.

The Parlour Café at ABC ($)
38 East 19th Street, between Broadway and Park Avenue South tel: 677-2233
Charming spot for breakfast or lunch on the ground floor of the elegant ABC department store. If you like the table, you can buy it.

Patria ($$$)
250 Park Avenue South, at 20th Street
tel: 77- 6211
Inspired, boldly flavored and stunningly presented "Nuevo Latino" cooking keeps this trendy restaurant packed. Lunch is a bargain. Dinner is prix-fixe.

Periyali ($$$)
35 West 20th Street, between Fifth and Sixth avenues tel: 463-7890
As upscale as Greek gets. Simple food with a few creative touches served in a friendly Mediterranean setting.

Pongal ($$)
110 Lexington Avenue tel: 696-9458
Authentic southern Indian cooking (that happens to be vegetarian and kosher) is the bill of fare at this popular restaurant. Try one of the thalis to sample a variety of dishes.

Tabla ($$$)
11 Madison Avenue tel: 889-0667
Chef Floyd Cardoz's cooking shows heavy Indian influences, unlike other Danny Meyer eateries. The food is fragrant with spices and elegantly presented. A more casual bread bar on the first level has a less expensive menu.

Union Pacific ($$$)
111 E. 22nd Street tel: 995-8500
Chef Rocco Dispirito's prix fixe menu offers some of the most daring and delicious culinary creations in town. An interesting wine.

Union Square Café ($$)
16th Street and Union Square West
tel: 243-4020
Contemporary American cookery has made this restaurant a particular favorite.

Zen Palate ($)
34 Union Square East tel: 614-9291
Vegetarian food with an Asian accent presented in delicately arranged portions.

THEATER DISTRICT

Becco ($$)
355 West 46th Street, between 8th and 9th avenues tel: 397-7597
All-you-can-eat antipasti and homemade pasta arrive as soon as you sit down. If you have room for an entrée, you won't be disappointed.

Cabana Carioca ($$)
45th Street between Sixth and Seventh avenues tel: 581-8088
Hefty servings of Brazilian food, well-cooked meat, and black beans by the bowlful. The bar serves lethal cocktails, and the diners come in party mood.

Churrascaria Plataforma ($$)
316 West 49th Street, between Eighth and Ninth avenues tel: 245-0505
An authentic Brazilian barbecue, where one price gets you a lavish salad bar and an endless parade of marinated and grilled meats.

Firebird ($$$)
365 West 46th Street, between Eighth and Ninth avenues tel: 586-0244
Prerevolutionary, aristocratic Russian cooking in an ornate setting. Blini, caviar, kasha, and other delicacies haven't been so good since the rise and fall of Communism.

India Pavilion ($–$$)
56th Street between Broadway and Eighth Avenue tel: 489-0035
Very fairly priced and extremely good quality Indian and Pakistani food, served in an intimate setting.

Jezebel ($$)
Ninth Avenue at 45th Street tel: 582-1045
Soulfood favorites, such as fried chicken, catfish, and grits, feature in a setting themed as a Deep South bordello.

Joe Allen ($$)
46th Street between Eighth and Ninth avenues tel: 581-6464
Burgers, bowls of chili, and other simple American food served in large portions amid Broadway show posters.

Landmark Tavern ($$)
Eleventh Avenue at 46th Street tel: 757-8595
Hearty lunches and dinners—fish-and-chips, and shepherds' pie alongside the ubiquitous burgers and sandwiches—are served in wood-paneled rooms dating from 1856.

Little Saigon ($)
374 West 46th Street tel: 956-0639
A useful pre- or post-theater stop for very well-priced Vietnamese dishes.

Sardi's ($$)
44th Street between Broadway and Eighth Avenue tel: 221-8444
A noted theatrical hangout and gossip-columnists' lair, Sardi's is well past its prime, but the caricatures of Broadway stars still line its walls and the service is still as off-hand as ever. Choose from an Italian menu.

Stage Deli ($$)
Seventh Avenue at 54th Street tel: 245-7850
Long time rival of the Carnegie Deli (see above), the Stage Deli provides much the same staple New York deli fare in equally generous portions, though the staff can often be less than gracious.

Virgil's Real BBQ ($)
152 West 44th Street, between Broadway and Sixth Avenue tel: 921-9494
Casual American barbecue joint with tender, tasty ribs, chicken, shrimp, corn bread, and other favorites.

MIDTOWN MANHATTAN

East and West Midtown

Aquavit ($$$)
13 West 54th Street, between 5th and 6th avenues tel: 307-7311
It's not easy to make Swedish food alluring, but this elegant restaurant raises herring and smoked fish to new gastronomic heights.

Carnegie Delicatessen ($$)
854 Seventh Avenue, at 55th Street tel: 757-2245
Mile-high sandwiches and oversized portions are priced to match, but the food's still good at this perpetually busy deli.

Delegates' Dining Room ($$)
United Nations, First Avenue at 46th Street tel: 963-7626
Armed with a reservation and proper attire, the general public can rub shoulders with United Nations officials and delegates on any weekday lunchtime. Top value is the buffet.

Four Seasons ($$$)
52nd Street between Park and Lexington avenues tel: 754-9494
At the helm of contemporary American cuisine, the Four Seasons rarely fails to delight the true gourmet. Its entrance decorated by a Picasso tapestry, it is inside the Seagram Building.

Hangawi ($$)
12 East 32nd Street, between 5th and Madison avenues tel: 213-0077
If you don't know what "vegetarian mountain Korean food" is, order the Emperor's Menu. Some 12 courses later you will understand the allure of this unusual and enticing restaurant.

Harley Davidson Café ($–$$)
56th Street at Sixth Avenue tel: 245-6000
Very few genuine bikers are found at this theme restaurant devoted to the legendary motorcycle; serves American staples such as burgers, chicken wings, and sandwiches.

Jean George ($$–$$$)
1 Central Park West tel: 299-3900
The sleek decor and uncompromising service complement the neoclassic *haute* French menu at this hotspot where Jean-Georges Vongerichten presides. Even given the astronomical prices, nothing disappoints.

Judson Grill ($$$)
152 West 52nd Street, between Sixth and Seventh avenues tel: 582-5252
Somewhere between a casual American bar and a fancy French restaurant, the creative, contemporary fare at Judson Grill makes this popular for both lunch and dinner.

Kang Suh ($)
1250 Broadway, at 32nd Street tel: 564-6845
Skip the sushi bar and head straight upstairs for the Korean menu. Oyster and scallion pancakes, tableside barbecue, and *kim chee* are served into the wee small hours.

Kaplan's Deli ($$)
59th Street between Park and Madison avenues tel: 755-5959
An unexciting but reliable standby, it has sandwiches, soups, and the usual deli fare in an otherwise pricey area.

Accommodations and Restaurants

Keens Chophouse ($$)
36th Street between Fifth and Sixth avenues
tel: 947-3636
Keens has been providing no-fuss meat-and-potatoes fare since 1885; mutton chop with mint is what they do best, although there are some hearty seafood options.

Kuruma Zushi ($$$)
7 East 47th Street tel: 317-2802
This small, second-floor eatery only serves sushi. If you are feeling rich, sit at the sushi bar and order the omikase (chef's tasting). Some of the fish is so fresh, it moves on your plate. Beware, dinner can cost upward of $200 per person—but it's well worth every penny.

Le Bernardin ($$$)
155 West 51st Street, between Sixth and Seventh avenues tel: 489-1515
Recently tapped by a national magazine as the best restaurant in America, this midtown mecca elevates fish and seafood to the *hautest* level of cuisine. The impeccable, doting service and an exceptional wine list round out the package.

Le Cirque 2000 ($$$)
455 Madison Avenue tel: 794-9292
The futuristic setting at one of the city's best and most expensive restaurants is regularly packed with celebrities and well-heeled gourmets.

Lespinasse ($$$)
St. Regis Hotel, 2 East 55th Street, between Fifth and Madison avenues tel: 339-6719
Christian Delouvier produces inspired French cooking in a very formal setting.

Lou G. Siegel ($$)
38th Street between Seventh and Eighth avenues tel: 921-4433
Kosher deli established since 1917 and still serving classics such as chopped liver, gefilte fish, chicken soup. Kosher hotdog "specials",

Lutèce ($$$)
50th Street between Second and Third avenues tel: 752-2225
The classic French menu has been streamlined and updated. Service has an attitude, but some of the modern French innovations make the suffering worth it.

Maloney & Porcelli ($$$)
37 East 50th Street, between Madison and Park avenues tel: 750-2233
Bring a large appetite to this whimsical American eatery.

Marichu ($$)
342 East 46th Street, between First and Second avenues tel: 370-1866
Around the corner from the U.N., this charming restaurant offers authentic Basque cooking.

Molyvos ($$-$$$)
871 Seventh Avenue tel: 582-7500
Upscale Greek food is served in this large, friendly restaurant. The meze are superb, and pricey entrees do not disappoint.

Motown Café ($–$$)
104 West 57th Street tel: 581-8030
Another theme restaurant, this one styled around the 1960s Motown sound, with decor of the decade and a largely soulfood menu.

Oceana ($$$)
55 East 54th Street, between Madison and Park avenues tel: 759-5941
A dining room like a cruise ship, but the inspired cooking breaks the metaphor. Elegant seafood preparations. Warm service.

Osteria del Circo ($$$)
120 West 55th Street, between Sixth and Seventh avenues tel: 265-3636
This upscale Italian trattoria mixes contemporary with traditional Tuscan fare.

Secret Harbor Bistro ($$)
Lexington Avenue at 37th Street tel: 447-7400
Chic place to start the day, with pastries, yogurt, and fresh juices, or to end it with a choice of dishes, from vegetable lasagna to blackened tuna in lemon-leek sauce.

Sparks Steak House ($$$)
210 East 46th Street tel: 687-4855
This quintessential New York steak house features prime aged beef and "all the fixins" with magnums of fine Bordeaux to match.

Sushi Bar ($$)
256 East 49th Street, at.Second Avenue tel: 644- 8750
Traditional and innovative Japanese food. Sashimi is the highlight of the long menu.

"21" Club ($$$)
21 West 52nd Street, between Park and Fifth avenues tel: 582-7200
A new chef has updated the menu at this historic restaurant.

Vong ($$$)
200 East 54th Street tel: 486-9592
Brainchild of one of the city's most talented chefs, Jean-Georges Vongerichten. Reserve in advance to sample the French/Thai food.

Zarela ($$)
Second Avenue between 50th and 51st streets tel: 644-6740
Zarela's raises Mexican cuisine to lofty heights with exotic yet subtle creations.

UPPER EAST SIDE

Aureole ($$$)
34 East 61st Street, between Madison and Park avenues tel: 319-1660
The exquisite upscale American food and startling presentations make this one of the city's best restaurants.

Bolivar ($$-$$$)
206 East 60th Street tel: 838-0440
The vibrant cooking at this busy and loud restaurant emphasizes the bright bold flavors of Central and South America.

Brother Jimmy's ($)
1644 Third Avenue tel:426-2020
Substantial sandwiches, soups, barbecued ribs, and other accompaniments to beer drinking and watching sports TV.

Café Boulud ($$$)
20 East 76th Street tel: 772-2600
The ever-changing menu at this casual cousin to Daniel Boulud's more formal four-star restaurant is overseen by top chef Andrew Carmellini, and it is just as good.

Club Macanudo ($$)
26 East 63rd Street, between Madison and Park avenues tel: 752-8200
A cigar bar where the food is incidental, but the atmosphere is comfortable and the crowd is, of course, made up of cigar smokers.

Daniel ($$$)
60 East 65th Street tel: 288-0033
The regal setting of Daniel Boulud's new temple of gastronomy seems set for royalty (and they turn up). Food is better than ever.

E.A.T. ($)
Madison Avenue between 80th and 81st streets tel: 772-0022
Continental Jewish snacks and sinful desserts.

Felidia ($$$)
243 East 58th Street tel: 758-1479
A perennial favorite for regional Italian cooking with an emphasis on game and specialties of Friuli. Lidia Bastianich stands guard, ensuring an impeccable experience.

Fred's at Barneys ($$–$$$)
10 East 61st Street, at Madison Avenue tel: 833-2200
A favorite of the "ladies who lunch" (and shop) and Upper East Side socialites.

India Grill ($$)
240 East 81st Street tel: 988-4646
Well-priced menu of Indian fare, and often offering daily specials.

J.G. Melon ($)
Third Avenue at 74th Street tel: 744-0584
Its American diner fare is a cut above the average, served at low cost in the homey environment of a wood-paneled bar.

Jo Jo ($$)
160 East 64th Street, near Lexington Avenue tel: 223-5656
Superb French bistro fare with a modern twist. Choose between the loud and packed main dining area and the more serene rear room.

La Fourchette ($$$)
1608 First Avenue tel: 249-5924
Marc Murphy's pricey prix fixe menu at this toney *haute* French restaurant has created a buzz. You won't leave unsatisfied, only poorer.

Lenox Room ($$$)
1278 3rd Avenue, between 73rd and 74th streets tel: 772-0404
The smooth service and sophisticated cooking at this neighborhood favorite make it a perfect place to rest after a day of shopping.

Park Avenue Café ($$$)
100 East 63rd Street, at Park Avenue tel: 644-1900
You can't help but laugh at the witty and whimsical interpretations of modern American cooking. Everything tastes even better than it looks. A favorite for weekend brunch.

Payard Patisserie & Bistro ($$)
1032 Lexington Avenue tel: 717-5252
There is a terrific bistro at the back of this popular patisserie.

Pig Heaven ($$)
Second Avenue between 80th and 81st streets tel: 744-4333).
With a Pig-themed decor as well as intriguing pork dishes, this place is a local favorite.

Rosa Mexicano ($$–$$$)
1063 First Avenue, at 58th Street tel: 753-7407
The Mexican food at this venerable restaurant is painstakingly authentic. Tableside guacamole with fresh corn tortillas and braised lamb shank with three-pepper sauce are not to be missed. Downscale bar area in front with more formal restaurant in back.

7th Regiment Mess ($)
643 Park Avenue between 66th and 67th streets tel: 744-4107
American home-cooking in an old wood-paneled restaurant inside the Seventh Regiment Armory. This place is great for children; booking is advisable.

Trois Jean ($$)
154 East 79th Street, between Lexington and Third avenues tel: 988-4858
Classic French cooking in a classic French bistro setting. Lunch prix fixe is a bargain.

Vinegar Factory Restaurant ($$)
431 East 91st Street, between First and York avenues tel: 987-0885
While the market carries on below, enjoy a terrific brunch in this weekend-only restaurant. The bread basket alone is worth the schlep.

277

UPPER WEST SIDE

Alouette ($$)
2588 Broadway tel: 222-6808
This is the type of French bistro that you'd expect to find in Greenwich Village, not the Upper West Side. Sssh. Don't say anything, cooking is sophisticated and delicious.

Avenue ($$)
520 Columbus Avenue tel: 579-3194
Breakfast, lunch, and dinner are all terrific at this neighborhoody French bistro.

Baci ($$)
412 Amsterdam Avenue tel: 496-1550
Cramped and often crowded, but has some of the best Italian food in the area.

Barney Greengrass (The Sturgeon King) ($$)
Amsterdam Avenue between 86th and 87th streets tel: 724-4707
The epitome of a New York Jewish deli-diner and owned by the greengrass family since 1908. House specialties include sturgeon and salmon; breakfast and lunch only.

Blue Nile ($$)
77th Street at Columbus Avenue tel: 580-3232
One of New York's few Ethiopian restaurants. The food is scooped up and devoured with spongy chunks of injera bread.

Café des Artistes ($$$)
67th Street at Central Park West tel: 877-3500
The 1930s Howard Chandler Christy murals compensate for the mediocre food and curt service. Reserve for dinner and Sunday brunch.

Café La Fortuna ($)
71st Street between Central Park West and Columbus Avenue tel: 724-5846
Sip coffee and sample an excellent pastry to feel at home in this neighborhood favorite.

Accommodations and Restaurants

Café Lalo ($)
83rd Street at Amsterdam Avenue
tel: 496-6031
This café attracts would-be writers, artists, and media folk who drink cappuccino and gorge themselves on a selection of irresistible cakes.

Café Luxembourg ($$$)
70th Street between Amsterdam and Columbus avenues tel: 873-7411
This is an art deco bistro aiming for a 1930s Parisian ambience. The top-rated food draws fashionable faces from all New York.

Calle Ocho ($$-$$$)
446 Columbus Avenue tel: 873-5025
The menu at this striking restaurant features classic and contemporary dishes inspired by the cuisines of Latin America. The flavors are vibrant and bold.

E.J.'s Luncheonette ($)
Amsterdam Avenue between 80th and 81st streets tel: 873-3444
Retro diner complete with chrome fittings and historic Coke advertisements. The sandwiches (try the grilled Cajun chicken breast) are huge.

Gabriela's ($)
685 Amsterdam Avenue, at 93rd Street tel: 961-0574
Inexpensive Mexican eatery that's always packed. The posole is particularly good, but for the price, you can't go wrong with anything.

Gennaro ($-$$)
665 Amstersdam Avenue, at 92nd Street tel: 665-5348
What is such delicious, homemade Italian food doing up here? Don't ask, just enjoy.

Good Enough To Eat ($$)
Amsterdam Avenue between 83rd and 84th streets tel: 496-0163
Grand selection of American staples, from ham and eggs to strawberry waffles, for breakfast, lunch, or dinner in cozy surroundings.

Indian Café ($$)
Broadway at 108th Street tel: 749-9200
Competitively priced Indian food includes inventive vegetarian selections, such as chickpeas with spinach and tomato, and sauteed lentils with garlic and ginger. Alternatively, feast on a selection of appetizers.

Joe's Fish Shack ($-$$)
520 Columbus Avenue tel: 873-0341
Sophisticated decor is not a feature of this intentionally ramshackle dining room that specializes in clams, crab cakes, and fish.

John's Pizzeria ($)
48 West 65th Street, between Columbus Avenue and Central Park West tel: 721-7001
A cousin of the original Greenwich Village John's, it has pizzas that are every bit as good and the atmosphere is a little more pleasant.

Josie's ($-$$)
300 Amsterdam Avenue, at 74th Street tel: 769-1212
The health-food-inspired menu has a number of vegetarian options. Fresh salads.

La Caridad ($)
Broadway at 78th Street tel: 874-2780
Inventive Chinese-Cuban dishes are served without fuss in informal surroundings.

La Traviata ($)
101 West 68th Street tel: 721-1101
This hole-in-the-wall outlet is popular with locals and dispenses tasty pizza by the slice.

Museum Café ($$)
Columbus Avenue at 77th Street
tel: 799-0150
Facing the American Museum of Natural History, it offers a delicious assortment of generous salads and pasta dishes.

Ollie's Noodle Shop ($)
Broadway at 84th Street tel: 362-3712
Chinese fare prepared in full view of diners. The noodle soups are flavorful and very cheap.

Picholine ($$)
35 West 64th Street, between Broadway and Central Park West tel: 724-8585
Expertly prepared modern French food in a country setting with its own cheese cave.

Rain ($)
100 West 82nd Street, between Amsterdam and Columbus avenues tel: 501-0776
The Thai-inspired menu fills this bustling eatery with a young crowd. Long waits at weekends.

Rancho Mexican Café ($$)
Amsterdam Avenue between 82nd and 83rd streets tel: 362-1514
Potent margaritas accompany the Mexican fare—for a free one, order during happy hour. Sunday brunch is riotous.

Sarabeth'sWest ($$)
Amsterdam Avenue between 80th and 81st streets tel: 496-6280
A refined place for smoked salmon sandwiches and fluffy omelets. Has a scintillating selection of homemade cakes.

Savann ($$)
414 Amsterdam Avenue, between 79th and 80th streets tel: 580-0202
American bistro with a French accent. An imaginative, but often crowded, restaurant.

Shark Bar ($)
74th Street between Columbus Avenue and Broadway tel: 874-8500
Tallahassee grilled shrimp, Louisiana fried crab cakes, or pan-blackened catfish—the tastiest fare from all over the south.

Shun Lee ($$$)
43 West 65th Street, between Columbus Avenue and Central Park West tel: 595-8895
Upscale Chinese served by tuxedoed waiters. The chef is talented, but the bill can be high.

Spazzia ($$)
366 Columbus Avenue tel: 799-0150
The fresh and flavorful Mediterranean cooking of Stephen Kalt is a welcome addition to a neighborhood overrun by mediocre food.

Symposium ($)
113th Street at Amsterdam Avenue
tel: 865-1011
Authentic, inexpensive Greek fare popular with students from nearby Columbia University. In summer, you can dine in the garden.

Tavern on the Green ($$$)
67th Street at Central Park West tel: 873-3200
More famous as a New York landmark, the tavern serves erratic—but usually excellent—meals beneath Venetian chandeliers.

Vince and Eddie's ($$$)
*70 West 68th Street, between Columbus
Avenue and Central Park West tel: 721-0068*
A cozy, American bistro that's a favorite of
quiet celebrities and Lincoln Center regulars.

HARLEM

Copeland's ($$)
*145th Street between Broadway and
Amsterdam Avenue tel: 234-2356*
Where the high-flyers of Harlem don their finery
and dine on a creative mix of soul food and
nouvelle cuisine.

Sylvia's ($$)
*Lenox Avenue between 126th and 127th
streets tel: 996-0660*
A landmark soul-food restaurant, serving huge
helpings of southern favorites, like spicy
barbecued ribs and chicken.

BROOKLYN

Cucina ($)
*256 Fifth Avenue, between Carroll Street and
Garfield Place tel: 718/230-0711*
Even Manhattanites travel to this Park Slope
trattoria for the friendly atmosphere, flavorful
pastas, and large entrées.

Junior's ($)
*386 Flatbush Avenue Extension, at DeKalb
Avenue tel: 718/852-5257*
A Brooklyn institution known for its large break-
fasts, corned beef and pastrami sandwiches,
and award-winning cheesecakes. Near the
Brooklyn Academy of Music.

Lemongrass Grill ($)
*61A Seventh Avenue, between Berkeley and
Lincoln places tel: 718/399-7100*
Inexpensive Thai food that's flavorful, fresh,
and fast. Nice garden.

Mrs Stahl's Delicious Knishes ($)
*1001 Brighton Beach Avenue
tel: 718/648-0210*
Delivers exactly what its name suggests:
expertly made knishes available with a host of
fillings. Buy several.

New Prospect Café ($)
393 Flatbush Avenue tel: 718/ 638-2148
Lively locals' eating spot, situated near the
Brooklyn Museum.

Noodle Pudding ($$)
*38 Henry Street, Brooklyn Heights
tel: 718/625-3737*
Although the name conjures images of lokshen
kugel, it is actually a loose translation of the
owner's last name, which he shares with a
Neapolitan dessert. The food is Italian, not
Jewish, and if you had to eat one meal in
Brooklyn Heights, this is where it should be.
The chef excels at fish, usually generously
portioned and lightly grilled.

Odessa ($$)
*1113 Brighton Beach Avenue
tel: 718/253-1470*
Come with a group. One price buys a bottle of
vodka and all you can eat from the Russian–
Georgian buffet table. Be ready to dance.

Patsy Grimaldi's ($)
*19 Old Fulton Street, between Front and Water
streets tel: 718/858-4300*
Pizza aficionados consider Patsy's among the
city's best. Red-checkered tablecloths and
plenty of Sinatra provide the atmosphere to
enjoy thin-crust pies with myriad toppings.

Peter Luger Steak House ($$$)
*178 Broadway, at Driggs Avenue tel:
718/387-7400*
Considered by many to be the best steak
house in the country, what it lacks in its turn-of-
the-century German beer hall ambience it
makes up for in dry-aged porterhouse, buttery
home fries, and creamed spinach. Cash only.

Teresa's ($)
*80 Montague Street, Brooklyn Heights
tel: 718/797-3996*
Very filling, very well-priced Polish food.

THE BRONX

Dominick's ($$)
2335 Arthur Avenue tel: 718/733-2807
Strong on atmosphere, with southern Italian
food. The menu is recited by the waiters.

Mario's ($$)
2342 Arthur Avenue tel: 718/584-1188
Often as busy as Dominick's (above), but with
slightly better food, much of it Neapolitan.

QUEENS

Elias Corner ($)
*24-02 31st Street, at 24th Avenue, Satoria
tel: 718/932-1510*
Grilled fish and other traditional Greek fare.

Happy Dumpling ($)
*135–29 40th Road, Flushing
tel: 718/445-2163*
Chinese fare, and rarely bettered for stuffed
dumplings or noodles.

Jackson Diner ($)
*74th Street between Roosevelt and 37th
avenues tel: 718/672-1232*
Probably the best priced of a glut of Indian
restaurants in this section of the borough.

K.B. Garden ($)
*136-12 39th Avenue, Flushing
tel: 718/961-9088*
Come for the raucous weekend dim sum or for
the lengthy à la carte menut.

Penang Malaysian Cuisine ($)
*38-04 Prince Street, at Roosevelt Avenue,
Flushing tel: 718/321-2078*
An exotic menu of Malaysian specialties ranging from Indian curry to coconut shrimp.

Ping's ($$)
83-02 Queen's Boulevard (718/396-1238
Ping prepares classic Chinese dishes fit (and
priced) for a king—braised abalone, giant lob-
ster on ye-men noodles, shark's fin, and other
delicacies.

Yao Han ($)
*135–21 40th Road, Flushing
tel: 718/359-2828*
Chinese and Vietnamese food make another
great find for noodle-lovers.

279

Index

A

Abby Aldrich Rockefeller
    Sculpture Garden 159
Abigail Adams Smith
    Museum 60
abstract expressionist art
    128–129
accommodations
    bed and breakfast 215
    Chinatown 262
    Financial District 262
    Greenwich Village 262
    hostels 215
    hotels 212–214,
        262–268
    Little Italy and SoHo
        262
    Midtown Manhattan
        263–266
    rates and taxes 212,
        213
    reservations and
        payment 214
    seasonal factors 213
    special deals 213
    student halls of
        residence 215
    Upper East Side
        267
    Upper West Side
        267–268
    women travelers 213
Adams, Franklin P. 153
African-Americans 73
Agee, James 116
airports and air services
    54, 246, 250
    John F. Kennedy 170,
        246
    La Guardia 170, 246
    Newark 246
Akeley, Carl 63
Albany 200, 204, 205
    Albany Institute of
        History and Art 205
    Corning Tower 205
    Empire State Institute
        for the Performing
        Arts 204
    Empire State Plaza 205
    New York State Capitol
        205
    New York State
        Museum 205
    Schuyler Mansion 205
Algonquin Hotel 153
Alice Austin House 180
Alice Tully Hall 134, 235
Allen Street 138
Allen, Woody 14, 77, 188
Alphabet City 54, 60–61
American Academy and
    Institute of Arts &
    Letters 61
American Ballet Theater
    236
American Bible Society
    61, 244
American Craft Museum
    62
American Crafts Festival
    27
American Federation of
    the Arts 62
American Immigrant Wall
    of Honor 100
American Museum of the
    Moving Image 172
American Museum of
    Natural History 52,
    63–64, 189, 242

Akeley Gallery 63
    Hall of Human Biology
        and Evolution 64
    Hall of Minerals and
        Gems 64
    Hall of Ocean Life and
        Biology of Fishes 64
    Hayden Planetarium 64
    Highlights Tour 63
    Nature Max Cinema 64
American Numismatic
    Society 61, 65, 244
American Radiator
    Building 163
Amityville 207
Annex Antiques Fair and
    Flea Market 140
apartment buildings 10,
    24, 52, 123, 189
    Dakota Apartments 24,
        83, 96, 189
    Kenilworth Apartments
        189
Apollo Theater 126
Aquarium for Wildlife
    Conservation 75
architecture
    apartment buildings 24
    art deco 162–163
    Beaux-Arts style 25
    brownstones 24, 39,
        76, 77
    Federal style 24
    Greek revival style 24
    International style 25
    plazas 25
    skyscrapers 24–25
    zoning laws 24, 162
Arkville 198
Armory Show 128, 149
art galleries
    art gallery listings 176
    Chelsea 177
    DIA Center 84
    57th Street 176
    guided tours 177
    nonprofit galleries 177
    SoHo 176–177
    Upper East Side 176
art museums
    Alternative 175
    free admission 244
    Frick Collection 20, 36,
        52, 110, 187
    Guggenheim Museum
        21, 52, 122–124,
        129
    Metropolitan Museum
        of Art 20, 52, 92,
        142–148, 162
    Museum of Modern Art
        (M.o.M.A.) 21, 25,
        129, 158–160
    National Academy of
        Design 164, 244
    New Museum of
        Contemporary Art 175
    New-York Historical
        Society 20, 21
    SoHo Guggenheim 175
    Whitney Museum of
        American Art 20, 52,
        129, 187, 191
Asia Society 65, 187
Asian American Arts
    Center 86
Asimov, Isaac 100
Astor, John Jacob 36, 98,
    168
Astor Place 98, 99
Astoria 53, 172
A.T. & T. Building 25
Auden, W.H. 23
Audubon, John James 61

Audubon Terrace 61
Austin, Alice 180
Avery Fisher Hall 134,
    234

B

Bacall, Lauren 15, 96
Bainbridge 154
Balanchine, George 105
Balducci's 113, 118
Baldwin, James 23, 116
ballet and dance
    235–236
Barclay-Vesey Building
    163
Barnum, P.T. 66, 80
Barrymore, John 118
bars 114–115, 224–225
    All State Café 115
    Bar Six 115
    d.b.a. 114
    Cedar Tavern 114, 119,
        128
    Coffee Shop 114
    Conservatory Bar,
        Mayflower Hotel 115
    Costello's 115
    Fifty Seven Fifty Seven
        115
    Greatest Bar on Earth
        114
    happy hours 224
    hotel bars 115
    King Cole Bar 115
    Live Bait 115
    Marie's Crisis Café 115
    McSorley's Old Ale
        House 99, 114
    Peculier Pub 114
    SoHo Brewery 114
    sports bars 91
    Top of the Sixes 114
    Top of the Tower 114
    White Horse Tavern 114
Bartholdi, Frédéric
    Auguste 181
baseball 70, 90, 152
basketball 90–91
Battery Park 66
Battery Park City 18–19
    Esplanade 19
    World Financial Center
        19, 25
Beame, Abe 46–47
Beat Generation 119
Bedford Avenue 78
Bedford Street 118
Beecher, Henry Ward 76,
    78
Behan, Brendan 85
Belmont Park 91
Berlin, Irving 16, 100
Bernard, George Gray 92
Bernstein, Leonard 96
Big Apple nickname 11
bike hire 195
Black History Month 26
Blade 133
Bleecker Street 118, 136
boat trips 67
Bohemian National Hall
    131
bookstores 99, 140,
    227–228
Booth, Edwin 152
Bow, Clara 77
Bowery Savings Bank
    150
Bowling Green 33
Bowne House 170
Bowne, John 170

bridges
    Brooklyn 39, 59, 80
    Kosciuszko 105
    Pulaski Bridge 105
    Verrazano-Narrows 59
Brighton Beach 53, 75,
    139
Brill Building 16
Broadway 38, 68–69
Bronx 52, 53, 70–72
Bronx Community College
    71–72
Bronx Museum of the Arts
    70
Bronx Zoo (Bronx Wildlife
    Conservation Park) 53,
    70–71, 242
Brooklyn 53, 74–79
Brooklyn Academy of
    Music 236
Brooklyn Botanic Garden
    79
Brooklyn Bridge 39, 59,
    80
Brooklyn Heights 53, 59,
    74, 76, 79
Brooklyn Heights
    Promenade 59, 76
Brooklyn's Historical
    Museum 76, 244
Brooklyn Museum 53, 79
Brooklyn-Battery Tunnel
    66
Brown, James 126
brownstones 24, 39, 76,
    77
Bruno Hauptman House
    71
Bryant, William Cullen 82
Burgee, John 161
Burnham, Daniel H. 106
Burroughs, John 196, 199
Burroughs, William 23,
    85, 114, 118, 119
buses
    airport services 246
    city 252
    long-distance 247

C

Café des Artistes 108
Caffè Reggio 113
Canal Street 86, 87
Canal Street Flea Market
    140
Capote, Truman 22, 79
Carnegie, Andrew 36, 95,
    202
Carnegie Hall 80, 235
Carnegie Hall Museum 80
Carrère and Hastings 168
Carter, Betty 76
Castle Clinton 35, 66
Castro, Fidel 125
Cather, Willa 23, 116
Catskill Mountains 195,
    196–199
cemeteries
    Green-Wood Cemetery
        74
    St. Raymond's
        Cemetery 71
    Woodlawn Cemetery 72
Central Park 52, 54,
    82–84
    Belvedere Castle 84
    Bethesda Terrace 83
    carriage tours 84
    Central Park Wildlife
        Center 242–243
    Concert Ground 83

Dairy 82
Delacorte Theater 84
Great Lawn 84
Hans Christian
   Andersen statue 242
Lake 83
Literary Walk 83
Mall 82–83
Naumberg Bandshell 83
personal safety 84
The Ramble 84
Shakespeare Garden
   84
Shakespeare in the
   Park 233
Sheep Meadow 82
Strawberry Fields 83
Visitor Center 82
Central Synagogue 120
Chambellan, René 163
Chanin Building 150, 163
Charles A Dana Discovery
   Center 243
Chase Manhattan Bank
   104
Chelsea 51, 84-85,
   153
Chelsea Historical District
   84
Chelsea Hotel 85
children's entertainment
   American Museum of
      Natural History
      63–64, 242
   Bronx Zoo 53, 70–71,
      242
   Central Park Wildlife
      Center 242
   Charles A. Dana
      Discovery Center
      243
   Children's Museum,
      Brooklyn 242
   Children's Museum of
      Manhattan 242
   Enchanted Forest 243
   F.A.O. Schwarz 243
   New York Hall of
      Science 171, 242
   New York Transit
      Museum 76, 242
   Richmondtown Historic
      Restoration 179, 242
   South Street Seaport
      178, 242
   Staten Island Ferry 59,
      179, 242
   storytelling in Central
      Park 242
   World Trade Center 58,
      193, 242
Children's Museum of
   Manhattan 242
Chinatown 35, 50,
   86–87, 88, 218
Chinese community 88
Chinese New Year 26
Christopher Street 113,
   118
Christy, Howard Chandler
   108
Chrysler Building 25, 52,
   89, 150, 163
Church, Frederick 204
churches
   Abyssinian Baptist
      Church 121
   Calvary Church 121
   Cathedral of St.John
      the Divine 52, 81, 94
   Church of the
      Ascension 113
   Church of St. Vincent
      Ferrer 120

Church of the
   Transfiguration
   (Mott Street) 87
Church of the
   Transfiguration (29th
   Street) 153
Grace Church 68, 112,
   113
Greek Orthodox
   Cathedral of the Holy
   Trinity 120
Jan Hus Presbyterian
   Church 130–131
Judson Memorial
   Church 118
New York Buddhist
   Church 121
"Old" St. Patrick's
   Cathedral 135
Our Lady of Lourdes
   Church 164
Plymouth Church of the
   Pilgrims 76
Riverside Church 94
St. Bartholomew's
   Church 150
St. James' Episcopal
   Church 65, 187
St. Mark's-in-the-
   Bowery 98, 99
St. Nicholas Greek
   Orthodox Church
   120
St. Nicholas Orthodox
   Cathedral 120
St. Patrick's Cathedral
   52, 112, 150, 154
St. Paul's Chapel 103,
   104
St. Thomas' Episcopal
   Church 150
San Isidro y San
   Leandro Orthodox
   Catholic Church of
   the Hispanic Rite
   120
Trinity Church 103,
   104
cinema 234
   films set in New York
      14–15
   New York Film Festival
      28, 234
City Hall 24, 39, 89
Clark, Edward S 96
climate 248–249
The Cloisters 92–93
Collins, Judy 118
Colonnade Row 98
Colton, Calvin 50
Columbia Heights 79
Columbia University
   94–95
   Low Library 94–95
   St. Paul's Chapel 95
Columbus Day Parade
   28
Columbus Park 87
comedy clubs 237
concert halls
   Alice Tully Hall 134,
      235
   Avery Fisher Hall 134,
      234
   Carnegie Hall 80, 235
   Kaufmann Theater 235
   Merkin Concert Hall
      235
Coney Island 53, 75
Conference House 179
Consolidated Edison 149
Cooper, James Fenimore
   22, 116
Cooper, Peter 95, 98

Cooper Union Building 95,
   98, 99
Cooper-Hewitt Museum
   36, 95
Corso, Gregory 85, 118
Cotton Club 16, 125
Coutan, Jules-Félix 166
Crane, Hart 79, 116
crime and personal safety
   11, 54–55, 249
Critchlow, Ernest 76
cummings, e.e. 116
Czech-American
   community 130–131

D

Daily News 95, 133
Daily News Building 95,
   150, 163
Dakota Apartments 24,
   83, 96, 189
Dalai Lama 179
Davis, Alexander Jackson
   201, 204
de Kooning, Willem 128
Delaware & Ulster Rail
   Ride 198
Dinkins, David 16, 60, 73
   89
disabled visitors 256–257
Dongan, Thomas 154
Dos Passos, John 23, 79,
   116
Doyers Street 87
Dreiser, Theodore 23,
   116
driving
   breakdowns 247
   car rental 195, 248
   chauffeur-driven
      limousines 108
   motoring organizations
      249
   regulations 249
   speed limits 249
Duane Park 183
Duchamp, Marcel 116,
   128, 149
Duncan, John H 78
Dylan, Bob 85, 118

E

East 6th Street 99
East 7th Street 99
East 84th Street 123
East Durham 196, 199
   Durham Center
      Museum 199
   Zoom Flume
      Water Park 199
East Harlem 53, 125,
   126, 127
East River cable-car 58,
   174
The East Village 19, 21,
   23, 51, 98–99
Easter Day Parade 27
Eastern States Buddhist
   Temple 87
Edgar Allan Poe Cottage
   71
Edison, Thomas 14, 39,
   199
El Barrio (East Harlem)
   125, 126, 127
El Museo del Barrio 126,
   157
Eleanor Roosevelt

National Historic Site
   204
Ellington, Duke 16, 72
Ellis Island 35, 100
Ellis Island Immigration
   Museum 100
Ellison, Ralph 23
emergency telephone
   numbers 249
Empire State Building 25,
   40, 52, 58, 100–102,
   150, 163
Enchanted Forest 243
entry formalities 246
Equitable Building 104,
   162
Erie Canal 38, 44
Essex Street Market
   138

F

the Factory 15, 97
F.A.O. Schwarz 243
Farmers' Market 149
Feast of O-Bon 28
Feast of St. Anthony of
   Padua 27
Feast of St. Gennaro 28,
   135
Federal Hall 104, 244
Federal Hall National
   Memorial 102
Federal Reserve Bank
   104
festivals and events
   American Crafts Festival
      27
   Black History Month 26
   Chinese New Year 26
   Columbus Day Parade
      28
   Easter Day Parade 27
   Empire State Building
      Run-Up 26
   Feast of O-Bon 28
   Feast of St. Anthony of
      Padua 27
   Feast of St. Gennaro
      28, 135
   Gay Pride Day Parade
      27, 117
   Greek Independence
      Day Parade 26–27
   Hallowe'en 28
   Harlem Week 28
   Independence Day 28
   Japanese Cherry
      Blossom Festival 27
   Labor Day Parade 28
   Macy's Thanksgiving
      Day Parade 28
   Martin Luther King
      Memorial Day Parade
      27
   Mostly Mozart Festival
      28, 235
   Museum Mile
      Celebration 28
   New Year
      (Times Square) 28
   New York Film Festival
      28, 234
   New York is Book
      Country 28
   New York Marathon
      28, 90
   Ninth Avenue
      International Food
      Festival 27
   Parade of Circus
      Animals 27

281

Index

Puerto Rican Day
  Parade 27
Rockefeller Center
  Christmas Tree 28
St. Patrick's Day Parade
  26, 27, 154
Shakespeare in the
  Park 28, 233
Ukrainian Festival 27
Washington Square
  Outdoor Art Show 27,
  28
Welcome to Brooklyn
  Festival 27
Winter Antiques Fair
  26, 226
Fifth Avenue 44, 186
57th Street 176
Film Center Building 102,
  162
Financial District 50, 59,
  102–104
Fire Island 208
Flatiron Building 24, 106,
  152
flea markets 140
Floyd, William 208
Flushing 170
Flushing Meadows-Corona
  Park 91, 170–171
Fonthill Castle 72
food and drink
  alcohol laws 238
  bars and beers
    114–115, 224–225
  cocktails 225
  coffee shops 217–218,
    219
  coffee and tea 223
  delis 216–217
  eating out 218–223
  soft drinks 223–224
  street food 10–11, 216
  tea rooms 223
  wines and liquor 225
  see also restaurants
football 91
Forbes, Malcolm S. 107
Forbes Magazine
  Galleries 107, 244
Ford, Henry 199
Forrest, Edwin 72
Fort Greene 74, 76, 77
Fort Greene Park 77
Fort Tryon Park 58–59,
  92, 93
42nd Street 18
Four Seasons 108
Franklin D. Roosevelt
  Library and Museum
  204
Franklin D. Roosevelt
  National Historic Site
  204
Fraunces Tavern 107
free sightseeing 244
French, Daniel Chester
  94, 190
Frick, Henry Clay 20, 36,
  110
  Frick Collection 20, 36,
    52, 110, 187
Frost, Robert 23
Fulton Fish Market 110
Further reading 258–260

G

gardens and parks
  Battery Park 66
  Brooklyn Botanic
    Garden 79
Central Park 52, 54,
  82–84
Columbus Park 87
Duane Park 183
Fort Greene Park 77
Fort Tryon Park 58–59,
  92, 93
Gramercy Park 152
Marcus Garvey Park
  126
New York Botanical
  Garden 71
Prospect Park 78
Tompkins Square Park
  60
Van Cortlandt Park 72
Washington Square
  Park 24, 116
Garibaldi, Giuseppe 180
Garibaldi Meucci
  Museum 180
Garland, Judy 96
Garment District 153
Garvey, Marcus 126
gay and lesbian scene 13,
  117, 239
Gay Pride Day Parade
  27, 117
General Assembly
  Building 184
General Electric Building
  150
General Grant Memorial
  78, 110–111, 244
General Theological
  Seminary 84
Gershwin, George 77
Gilbert, Cass 25, 190,
  192
Ginsberg, Allen 23, 114,
  118, 119
Goodhue, Bertram 120
Goodwin, Philip 158
Gorky, Maxim 75
Gottlieb, Adolph 128
Gould, Jay 36–37, 201
Governors Island 59
Grace Court 79
Gracie, Archibald 111
Gracie Mansion 24, 111
Gramercy 152
Gramercy Park 152
Grand Army Plaza 77
Grand Central Terminal
  11, 45, 52, 150,
  166–167
Grand Concourse 70
Grand Street 138
Grant, Cary 118
Grant, Ulysses
  S.110–111
Greek community 172
Greek Independence Day
  Parade 26–27
Greek Orthodox
  Cathedral of the Holy
  Trinity 140
Green Flea Indoor/
  Outdoor Market 140
Green-Wood Cemetery
  74
Greene Street 175
Greenpoint 105
Greenwich Village 23, 51,
  54, 55, 112–113, 114,
  116, 118
Greenwich Village Flea
  Market 140
grid-style street plan 38
Gropius, Walter 183
Guggenheim, Solomon R.
  21, 122
Guggenheim Museum 21,
  52, 122–124, 129
guided tours
  architectural tours 56
  art galleries 177
  backstage on Broadway
    68
  boat trips 67
  Grand Central Terminal
    167
  Harlem 57
  historical walks 56
  Lincoln Center 134
  Lower East Side 138
  Metropolitan Opera
    House 134
Guthrie, Arlo 118

H

Haas, Richard 168, 175
Halcottsville 198
Hall of Fame for Great
  Americans 71–72
Hallowe'en 28
Hamilton, Alexander 103
Harlem 16–17, 23, 53,
  54, 57, 73, 125–126
Harlem Renaissance 23,
  73, 125
Harlem Week 28
Haughwout Building 175
Hayden Planetarium 64
helicopter flights 109
Helleu, Paul 166–167
Henderson Place Historic
  District 111
Hertz, John 10
Himes, Chester 23
Hispanic Society of
  America 61, 126, 244
history of New York
  American Revolution
    32–33
  bankruptcy crisis 46–47
  corruption 42–43
  the Depression 40–41
  entrepreneurs 36–37
  European settlement
    30–31
  expansion 38–39
  Great Fire of 1835 165
  immigration 34–35,
    100
  Native Americans
    30–31
  New Amsterdam 32
  port of New York 44–45
  Wall Street crash 40
  World's Fair 170–171
hockey 91
Hoffman, Abbie 182
Holiday, Billie 126
Holmes, John Clellon 119
Hood, Raymond 95, 123,
  163
Hopper, Edward 191, 202
horse-racing 91
hotels
  Algonquin Hotel 153
  Chelsea Hotel 85
  Chinatown 262
  Financial District 262
  Greenwich Village 262
  Little Italy and SoHo
    262
  Midtown Manhattan
    262–267
  Pierre Hotel 108
  Teresa Hotel 125
  Upper East Side
    266–267
  Upper West Side
    267–268
Waldorf-Astoria Hotel
  150
Hudson, Henry 30
Hudson Highlands 202
Hudson Valley 194,
  200–205
Hughes, Langston 23
Hunter 196, 198
Huntington, Anna Hyatt
  164
Huntington, Archer M.
  126
Hurley 197
Hurston, Zora Neale 23
Hurt, William 134
Hyde Park 204

I

Independence Day 28
International Center of
  Photography 130, 244
Intrepid Sea-Air-Space
  Museum 130
Irish community 154
Irving, Washington 22,
  194, 201, 202
Isaacs-Hendricks
  Residence 118, 130
Isamu Noguchi Garden
  Museum 172
Island Historical Museum,
  Staten Island 179
Italian community 136
itineraries
  one-week 56
  two-week 57
  weekend 56

J

Jacques Marchais Center
  of Tibetan Art 179
Jamaica Bay Wildlife
  Refuge 170
James, Henry 23, 116
Janowitz, Tama 22
Japanese Cherry Blossom
  Festival 27
Jefferson Market
  Courthouse 113, 118
Jewish community 78,
  139
Jewish Heritage Museum
  66
Jewish Museum 131
John Burroughs Memorial
  State Park 199
John F. Kennedy Airport
  170, 246, 247
Johns, Jasper 129
Johnson, Philip 25, 108,
  158, 161, 171
Juilliard School of Music
  and Performing Arts 13,
  134

K

Kahn, Ely Jacques 102,
  162
Katz's Deli 15
Kaufmann Theater 235
Kenilworth Apartments
  189
Kerouac, Jack 118, 119
Kingsland Homestead
  170

Kingston 197
  Hudson River Maritime
    Museum 197
  Old Dutch Church 197
  Senate House State
    Historic Site 197
  Stockade District 197
  Urban Culture Park
    Visitor Center 197
Koch, Ed 47
Kosciuszko Bridge 105

L

La Guardia Airport 170,
  246
La Guardia, Fiorello
  40–41, 136
La Marqueta 126
Labor Day Parade 28
LaFarge, John 118
Lafayette Street 98
Laning, Edward 168
Le Corbusier 53
Leary, Timothy 203
Lee, Spike 15, 77
Lee Avenue 78
Lehman Collection 147
Lehman, Robert 20, 147
Lennon, John 83, 96
libraries
  Low Library 94–95
  New York Public Library
    25, 81, 150, 168
  New York Public Library
    for the Performing
    Arts 134
  Pierpont Morgan Library
    37, 169
lifestyles 13
Lincoln, Abraham 98
Lincoln Center for the
  Performing Arts 52,
  134, 189
Lindbergh, Charles 71
Lindsay, John 46
literary heritage 22–23
Little Italy 50, 135, 136
Little Odessa 75
Little Singer Building 175
Little Ukraine 98
Locust Grove 204
Long Island 195,
  206–211
  Amityville 207
  Clinton Academy 209
  Cold Spring Harbor 206,
    210
  Custom House 209
  East Hampton 208–209
  Fire Island 208
  Halsey Homestead 208
  the Hamptons 195,
    208–209
  Home Sweet Home
    Museum 208–209
  Huntington 210
  Jones Beach 206, 208
  Montauk Point 209
  Museums at Stony
    Brook 211
  Old Bethpage Village
    207–208
  Old Westbury Gardens
    207
  Palmer Vineyards 210
  Patchogue 206
  Port Jefferson 211
  Riverhead 210
  Sag Harbor 209
  Sagamore Hill 206, 210
  Sailor's Haven 208

Sayville 206
Setauket 206, 211
Southampton 208
Stony Brook 206, 211
Suffolk County Museum
  210
Sunken Forest 208
Vanderbilt Mansion
  210–211
Walt Whitman
  Birthplace State
  Historic Site 210
Whaler's Church 209
Whaling and Historical
  Museum 209
Whaling Museum 210
William Floyd Estate
  208
Long Island City 172
lost property 249
Low Library 94–95
Low, Seth 94
Lower East Side 23, 39,
  51, 137–138, 139
Lower East Side
  Tenement Museum 138
Lower Manhattan 50–51
Lugosi, Bela 100
Lyndhurst 201

M

Macy, Richard H 72
Macy's 230
Macy's Thanksgiving Day
  Parade 28
Madison Avenue
  186–187
Madison Square 68
Madison Square Garden
  91, 153
Madison Square Park 152
Mailer, Norman 23, 79,
  133
Malcolm X 73
Manhattan 39, 50–53
Manship, Paul 163, 173
Marcus Garvey Park 126
markets
  Annex Antiques Fair and
    Flea Market 140
  Canal Street
    Flea Market 140
  Essex Street Market
    138
  Farmers' Market 149
  flea markets 140
  Fulton Fish Market 110
  Greenwich Village
    Flea Market 140
  La Marqueta 126
Marsh, Reginald 190
Martin Luther King
  Memorial Day Parade
  27
Masters, Edgar Lee 85
Matthau, Walter 139
McGraw-Hill Building 163
McKenney, Ruth 116
McKim, Charles F. 169
McKim, Mead and White
  25, 81, 153
media 132–133, 250
  newspapers and
    magazines 13,
    132–133
  radio 132
  television 132
Meir, Golda 100
Melcarth, Edward 108
Melville, Herman 23, 72,
  116

Melville, Ward 211
Merkin Concert Hall 235
Metropolitan Life Building
  152
Metropolitan Museum of
  Art 20, 52, 92,
  142–148, 162
  American art and design
    144
  Arms and Armor
    collection 148
  Asian Art 146
  Costume Institute 148
  Egyptian art 143
  European art 142
  Greek & Roman Art 146
  Islamic art 145
  Lehman Collection 147
  Lila Acheson Wallace
    Wing 146
  medieval art 144
  Michael C. Rockefeller
    Wing 146
  Musical Instruments
    galleries 148
  prints and photographs
    146
  Temple of Dendur 143
Metropolitan Opera House
  68, 134, 237
Meucci, Antonio 180
Midtown Manhattan 52,
  54, 149–153
Millay, Edna St. Vincent
  116, 118
Miller, Arthur 79
Miller, Henry 79
Minetta Tavern 118
Minuit, Peter 31, 66
money
  A.T.M.s 250
  cash advances 250
  credit cards 250
  travelers' checks 250
Monroe, Marilyn 15
Morgan, John Pierpont 37,
  40, 169
Morse, Samuel 164, 194,
  204
Moses, Robert 41, 185
Mosque of the Islamic
  Culture Center 121
Mostly Mozart Festival 28,
  235
Mott Street 87
Mould, Jacob Wrey 142
Mount, William Sydney
  211
Mulberry Street 135
Municipal Assistance
  Corporation (M.A.C.) 47
Murray Hill 152
museums
  Abigail Adams Smith
    Museum 60
  Alternative 175
  American Craft Museum
    62
  American Museum of
    the Moving Image
    53, 172
  American Museum of
    Natural History 52,
    63–64, 189, 242
  Bronx Museum of the
    Arts 70
  Brooklyn Museum 53,
    78–79
  Carnegie Hall Museum
    80
  Children's Museum,
    Brooklyn 242
  Children's Museum of
    Manhattan 242

Chinese in the Americas
  87
Cooper-Hewitt Museum
  36, 95
El Museo del Barrio
  126, 157
Ellis Island Immigration
  Museum 100
free admission 244
Garibaldi Meucci
  Museum 180
International Center of
  Photography 130,
  244
Intrepid Sea-Air-Space
  Museum 130
Isamu Noguchi Garden
  Museum 172
Island Historical
  Museum, Staten
  Island 179
Jewish Heritage 66
Jewish Museum 131
Lower East Side
  Tenement Museum
  138
Museum of American
  Folk Art 155
Museum of American
  Financial History 155
Museum of American
  Illustration 62
Museum for African Art
  155
Museum of the City of
  New York 126,
  156–157
Museum Gallery, South
  Street Seaport 178
Museum Mile 186
Museum Mile
  Celebration 28
Museum of Modern Art
  (MoMA) 21, 25, 52,
  129, 158–160
museum stores 228
Museum of Television
  and Radio 161
Neuseum 155
New York City Fire
  Museum 165
New York Transit
  Museum 56, 76, 242
Nicolas Roerich
  Museum 189
opening hours 251
Police Academy
  Museum 152
Queens Museum 171
Studio Museum in
  Harlem 126
Ukrainian Museum 98
see also art museums
music
  alternative 175
  classical 234–235
  country music 241
  folk and rock 16
  folk music 241
  free concerts 234–235,
    244
  hip-hop 16–17
  jazz and blues 240–241
  new wave 16
  rap 16–17
  rock 239–240
  tickets 236, 240

N

Nabokov, Vladimir 85
Nash, Ogden 52

Index

Nassau Coliseum 91
National Academy of Design 164, 244
National Museum of the American Indian 164
National Arts Club 152
Nature Max Cinema 64
N.B.C. Television 174
New Paltz 197
New Windsor Cantonment State Historic Site 203
New Year (Times Square) 28
New York Academy of Medicine 156
New York Botanical Garden 53, 71
New York Chamber Symphony 235
New York City Ballet 235
New York City Fire Museum 165
New York City Opera 237
New York Convention and Visitors' Bureau 212, 255
New York County Courthouse 89
New York Film Festival 28, 234
New York Hall of Science 171, 242
New-York Historical Society 20
New York is Book Country 28
New York Marathon 28, 90
New York Observer 133
New York Philharmonic 28, 134, 234
New York Post 133
New York Public Library 25, 81, 150, 168
New York Public Library for the Performing Arts 134
New York School 128, 160
New York State Pavilion Building 171
New York Studio School of Drawing, Painting and Sculpture 113
New York Telephone Company 163
New York Times 13, 133, 176
New York Transit Museum 56, 76,
New York University 116
Newark Airport 246, 247
Newburgh 203
Washington's HQ/ Jonathan Hasbrouck House 203
Newman, Barnett 129
newspapers and magazines 13, 133
Nicolas Roerich Museum 189
nightclubs 238–239
nightlife and entertainment
ballet and dance 235–236
cinema 234
classical music 234–235
comedy clubs 237
country music 241

folk music 241
gay and lesbian nightclubs 239
jazz and blues 240–241
nightclubs 238–239
opera 237
"Poet's Slam" 237
rock music 239–240
theater 232–233
Nin, Anaïs 116
Ninth Avenue International Food Festival 27
Noguchi, Isamu 172
Nolita 135
Nyack 202
Hopper House Arts Center 202

O

ocean crossings 45, 247
O'Dwyer, William 43
Olana 204
Old Chatham 204
Shaker Museum 204
Old Dutch Church, Hudson Valley 204
Old New York County Courthouse 42, 89
Old Police Headquarters 135
"Old" St. Patrick's Cathedral 135
Olmsted, Frederick 82, 83
O'Neill, Eugene 23, 116, 118
Ono, Yoko 83
opening hours
banks 251
museums 251
post offices 252
stores 251
opera 237
Orchard Street 138
orchestras
New York Chamber Orchestra 235
New York Philharmonic 28, 134, 234
Outer Boroughs 53
Ozone Park 91

P

Paine, Thomas 115
Pan Am Building 183
Papp, Joseph 98, 233
Parade of Circus Animals 27
Payne, John Howard 208
Peking 178
Pelli, Cesar 19
Penney, J.C. 72
Pennsylvania Railroad Station 247
Perlman, Itzhak 134
Peter Minuit Plaza 66
Philip Morris Building 150, 191
Philipsburg Manor 201
Philipse Manor 201
Phoenicia 198
Pierpont Morgan Library 37, 169
Pierre Hotel 108
Pierrepont, Henry 74
Pierrepont Street 79
places of worship 120–121, 251

Players Club 152
plaza sculptures 21
Poe, Edgar Allan 23, 53, 71, 116, 203
police 251–252
Police Academy Museum 152
Polish-Americans 105
Pollock, Jackson 85, 114, 128, 129
Port Authority Bus Terminal 54
Porter, William Sydney (O Henry) 22, 85
Post Office Auction 141
Post Office (Ninth Avenue) 153
post offices 252
Poughkeepsie 203
Vassar College 203
Powell, Adam Clayton 121
Prattsville 199
Pratt Rocks 199
Zadock Pratt Museum 199
Prospect Park 53, 78
Provincetown Playhouse 118
Public Theater (Joseph Papp) 36, 98, 233
public transportation 252
publishing 13, 22
Puck Building 135
Puerto Rican community 127
Puerto Rican Day Parade 27
Pulaski Bridge 105
Pulitzer, Joseph 181

Q

Queens 53, 170–172
National Tennis Center 171
Queens Historical Society 170
Queens Museum of Art 171
Queens Wildlife Conservation Center 171

R

radio 132
Radio City Music Hall 163, 174, 239
rail services 247
railroad stations
Grand Central Terminal 45, 52, 150, 166–167
Pennsylvania Railroad Station 247
Rainbow Room 109, 174
Randel, John 38
R.C.A. Building 173–174
Reed, John 23, 116
Remsen Street 79
Renwick, James 112, 121
restaurants
the Bronx 279
Brooklyn 279
Chinatown 218–219, 269–270
East Village and Lower East Side 271–272
Eastern European 221

eating out with children 217
Financial District and TriBeCa 268–269
gourmet food 222–223
Greenwich Village 272–273
Harlem 279
Italian 218
Japanese 219
Korean and Indian 220
Little Italy 270–271
lunch and dinner periods 219
Midtown East and West 275–276
Murray Hill, Gramercy and Chelsea 273–274
Queens 279
regional food 221
smoking in restaurants 222
SoHo 270
South American and Caribbean 221
Spanish and Greek 220
steak houses 222
Theater District 274–275
tipping 216, 259
Upper East Side 266–267
Upper West Side 277–278
vegetarian 222
rest rooms 254
Richmondtown Historic Restoration 179, 242
Riis, Jacob 138
Riverdale 72
Robinson, Edward G. 100, 139
Rockefeller, John D. 92, 93
Rockefeller Jr, John D. 173
Rockefeller, Nelson 185
Rockefeller Center 52, 58, 94, 109, 150, 163, 173–174
Rockefeller Center Christmas Tree 28
Roebling, John A. 80
Roerich, Nicolas 189
Rooney, Mickey 77
Roosevelt, Franklin D. 204
Roosevelt Island 174
Roosevelt, Theodore 152, 182, 199, 210
Rothko, Mark 129
The Row 116
Roxbury 198
Jay Gould Memorial Reform Church 198
Runyon, Damon 22
Russian community 75, 105, 139

S

Sailors' Snug Harbor 179
St. Luke's Place 118
St. Nicholas Historic District 126
St. Patrick's Day Parade 26, 154
St. Raymond's Cemetery 71
Salinger, J.D. 22
Salmagundi Club 107

Saugerties 196, 199
Schuyler, Philip 205
Seagram Building 25, 108
Secretariat Building 184, 185
Sedgwick, Edie 85
Serpico, Frank 15
Sert, José Maria 174
Seton, Elizabeth Ann 66
Seventh Regiment Armory 187
Shakers 204
Shakespeare in the Park 28, 233
Shandaken 198
Shea Stadium 90, 172
Shelter Island 209
shopping
  antiques 226–227
  bookstores 99, 140, 227–228
  C.D.s and records 141, 228
  clothes 140–141, 228–230
  department stores 230–231
  flea markets 140
  jewelry 231
  Macy's 230
  museum stores 228
  opening hours 251
  personal shoppers 231
  photographic and electrical goods 230
  Post Office Auction 141
  sales and special offers 229
  secondhand goods 140–141
  shoes 231
  thrift stores 140
  unusual stores 227
Shrine of Elizabeth Ann Seton 24, 66
69th Regiment Armory 149
skyscrapers 24–25
Slabsides 196, 199
Sloan, John 85, 191
Snug Harbor Cultural Center 179
social problems
  A.I.D.S. sufferers 17
  drugs 17
  homelessness 17
  racial tensions 16–17, 73
  urban decay 11, 70
SoHo 19, 21, 51, 175, 176–177
SoHo Guggenheim 175
Soldiers' and Sailors' Memorial Arch 78
Sony Wonder Technology Lab 242
South Bronx 70
South Street Seaport 178, 242
sport
  American football 91
  baseball 70, 90, 152
  basketball 90–91
  horse-racing 91
  ice-hockey 91
  New York Marathon 90
  tennis 91
  scalpers 91
  sports bars 91
Staten Island 53, 178–180
Staten Island Ferry 59, 179, 242

Statue of Liberty 59, 180–181
Stein, Gertrude 173
Steinway 172
Steinway, William 172
Stock Exchange 12, 40, 104, 182, 244
Stone, Edward Durrell 158
Stonewall Inn 117, 118
Stony Point Battlefield State Historic Site 202
Straight, Willard 130
Strawberry Fields 83
Streisand, Barbra 77
student and youth travel 254
Studio Museum in Harlem 126
Stuyvesant, Peter 32, 98, 103, 170
Styron, William 116
subway 55, 252–253
Sunnyside 201
synagogues
  Central Synagogue 120
  Temple Emanu-El 187
  Wall Street Synagogue 120

T

Tarrytown 201, 202
taxi-drivers 12
taxis 10, 12, 54, 246, 254
telephones 255
television networks 132
Temple Emanu-El 187
tenement life 35, 137
tennis 91
Teresa Hotel 125
theaters 232–233
  Apollo Theater 126
  backstage tours on Broadway 68
  Broadway theaters 232
  information 233
  Off-Broadway theaters 232–233
  Provincetown Playhouse 118
  Public Theater (Joseph Papp) 36, 98, 233
  Shakespeare in the Park 28, 85, 233
  SummerStage 28
  Theater District 68–69
  tickets 232
  Vivian Beaumont Theater 134
Theodore Roosevelt Birthplace 152, 182
Thomas, Dylan 85, 114
thrift stores 140
Tiffany, Louis Comfort 187
Tilden, Samuel 152
time 255
Times Square 11, 18–19, 28, 52, 68, 69, 153
Times Square Center 19
Times Square Visitors Center 153
Tin Pan Alley 16
tipping 216, 255
Tompkins Square Park 60
tourist information 155, 212, 255, 260
travel
  outside New York 194

public transportation 252–254
  to New York 246–248
travelers with disabilities 256–257
traveling with cameras, camcorders and laptops 257–258
TriBeCa 19, 51, 182–183
Trotsky, Leon 52, 105
Trumbull, Edward 150
Trump, Donald 183
Trump Tower 25, 183
Twain, Mark 85, 116
Tweed, William 42
21 Club 108–109

U

Ukrainian community 98, 105
Ukrainian Festival 27
Ukrainian Museum 98
Umberto's Clam House 135
Union Square 68, 149
United Nations 52, 150, 171, 184–185, 244
United States Military Academy 202–203
universities
  Columbia University 94–95
  New York University 116
Upjohn, Richard 74, 113
Upper East Side 39, 52, 176, 186–187
Upper Manhattan 52–53
Upper West Side 24, 52–53, 189
U.S. Coast Guard 59
U.S. Custom House 25, 190

V

Valentino, Rudolph 100
Van Cortlandt Mansion 72
Van Cortlandt Park 72
Vanderbilt, Cornelius 37, 166, 204
Vanderbilt, Frederick W. 204
Vanderbilt, William K. 210–211
Vanderbilt Mansion National Historic Site 204
van der Rohe, Mies 25
Vassar College 203
Vaux, Calvert 82, 142, 152
Verrazano, Giovanni da 30, 66
Verrazano-Narrows Bridge 59
Vicious, Sid 85
views of New York 58–59
Village Square 113
Village Voice 119, 133, 176
Villager, The 133

W

Waldorf-Astoria Hotel 150
Walker, Jimmy 40–41, 43

Walker, Ralph 163
Walking tours 56
Wallace, De Witt 168
Wall Street 40, 102, 103, 104
Wall Street Journal 13
Wall Street Synagogue 120
Warhol, Andy 85, 97
Washington, George 72, 89, 102, 103, 107, 203, 209, 211
Washington Memorial Arch 116
Washington Square 27
  Outdoor Art Show 28
Washington Square Park 24, 116
Water Street 178
Web sites 260
Wells, H.G. 51, 58
West End Café 119
West Harlem 125–126
West, Mae 77, 174
West Point 202–203
  Drill Ground 203
  Fort Putnam 203
  Museum 203
  United States Military Academy 202–203
Wharton, Edith 23
White, Stanford 116, 118, 152
Whitman, Walt 23, 80, 210
Whitney, Gertrude Vanderbilt 20, 113, 191
Whitney Museum of American Art 20, 52, 129, 187, 191
Williams, Tennessee 116
Williamsburg 19, 78
Willow Street 79
Wilson, Edmund 116
Winter Antiques Fair 26, 226
Wolfe, Thomas 23, 85, 116
Wolfe, Tom 22
women travelers 213
Wood, Fernando 43
Woodlawn Cemetery 72
Woodstock 195, 198
  Byrdcliffe Arts Colony 198
Woolworth, F.W. 72, 192
Woolworth Building 58, 192
World Financial Center 19, 25, 56
World Trade Center 58, 104, 193, 242
Wright, Frank Lloyd 122, 124

Y

Yamasaki, Minoru 193
Yankee Stadium 70, 90
Yonkers 200–201
  Hudson River Museum 200–201

Z

Zeckendorf, William 185

285

New York Subway

Main St Flushing **7**

BRONX

Willets Point

111 St

103 St Corona Plaza

Junc Blvd

90 St

Grand
Avenue
Newtown

Woodhaven
Blvd
Queens
Mall

82 St Elmhurst Av

63 Drive 67 Av

75 Av

G

71 Continental Av
Forest Hills

Roosevelt Av-Jackson Heights
74 St Broadway (line 7)

Union Turnpike
Kew Gardens

QUEENS

F R

179 St Jamaica

169 St

Parsons Blvd

Sutphin Blvd

Van Wyck Blvd

E J,Z
Jamaica Center
Parsons/Archer

Jamaica
Van Wyck

121 Street Sutphin Blvd

111 Street

104-102 Streets

Woodhaven Blvd

85 St-Forest Parkway

75 St-Elderts La

Cypress Hills

Crescent St

Norwood Av Rockaway Blvd

Cleveland St

Van Siclen Av

B'dway
Eastern
P'way

Alabama Av

Lefferts Blvd **A**

111 St

104 St

Aqueduct Racetrack

88 St

80 Street

Grant Av

Euclid Avenue **H**

Shepherd Av

Van Siclen Av

Aqueduct North
Conduit Av

Howard Beach
for JFK airport

A,H
Far Rockaway
Mott Avenue

Beach 25 St
Wavecrest

Beach 36 St
Edgemere

Beach 44 St
(Frank Av)

Beach 60 St
Straiton Av

Beach 67 St
Gaston

Metropolitan Av **M**

Fresh Pond Rd

Forest Av

Seneca Av

DeKalb Av Myrtle Av

Av

Jefferson St Wyckoff Av

Halsey St

Knickerbocker Av

Wilson Av

Central Av

Kosciusko St Halsey St

Bushwick Av

Flushing
Av

Myrtle
St

Gates Av Chauncey St

Broadway East New York

Liberty Av

Atlantic Av

Rockaway Av

Ralph Av

Sutter Av

New Lots Avenue

Broad Channel

3 4

Van Siclen Av

Pennsylvania Av

Junius St

Rockaway Av

Livonia Av

New Lots Av

East 105 St

Beach 90 St
Holland

Beach 98 St
Playland

Beach 105 St
Seaside

Rockaway Park
Beach 116 St

C,H

S
Franklin Av

on Av/
gton Av

Kingston Av/
Throop Av

Utica Av

Nostrand Av

Dean Street

Park Place

Botanic Gdn

lantic Av Bergen St

Grand
Army Plaza

Eastern P'way
Brooklyn Mus.

Prospect Park **S**

Saratoga Av

Sutter Av

4
Kingston Av
Nostrand
Av

Utica Av

Rockaway Parkway **L**

President St

Sterling St

Winthrop St

Church Av

Beverley Rd

Newkirk Av

Flatbush Avenue
Brooklyn College **2 5**

ntic Av

Parkside Av

Church Av

Beverly Rd

15 St
F H'ton P'way

Cortelyou Rd

Av
Slope

Church Av

Ditmas Av

18 Av

Av I

Newkirk Av

Av H

Av J

Av M

Hamilton P'way

Bay P'way

Av N

Av P

K H'way

Av U

Av X

Kings Highway

Av U

Neck Rd

Sheepshead Bay

New
Utrecht Av/62 St

18 Av

71 St

79 St

20 Av

Bay P'way

K H'way

Av U

Av U

86 St

Brighton Beach **Q**

Ocean Parkway

West 8 Street

BROOKLYN

18 Av
20 Av
Parkway

M 25 Av

Bay 50 St

Stillwell Avenue
Coney Island **B,D,F,N**

Acknowledgments

Picture credits

The Automobile Association would like to thank the following photographers, libraries and associations for their assistance in the preparation of this book:
J ALLAN CASH 127a Market. **ALLSPORT UK LTD** 90a American Football (S Dunn). **AMERICAN CRAFT MUSEUM** 62 Museum interior (Dan Cornish). **BETTMANN ARCHIVE** 22b Damon Runyon (UPI/BETTMAN NEWSPAPERS), 42b *The Brains* (THE BETTMAN ARCHIVE), 43a William O'Dwyer (THE BETTMAN ARCHIVE), 44b East River (THE BETTMAN ARCHIVE), 46 Ed Koch (UPI/BETTMAN), 119a P Orbvsky & A Ginsberg, 119b A Poole in our time (THE BETTMAN ARCHIVES). **BRIDGEMAN ART LIBRARY LTD** 29a Irish immigrants disembark at the Battery in New York, 1855 (Museum of the City of New York, 1855/Bridgeman Art Library, London), 32a New York after Independence, seen from East River by George Torino (18th C) (Private Collection/Bridgeman Art Library, London), 36a Cartoon depicting Andrew Carnegie, 1903 (Private Collection/Bridgeman Art Library, London), 97b *Campbell's Soup* by Warhol, Andy (1930–87) (Wolverhampton Art Gallery, Staffs/Bridgeman Art Library, London). **CORBIS/ROBERT HOLMES** 117a, **CORBIS/GAIL MOONEY** 228, **CORBIS/ BILL ROSS** 233, **CORBIS/CHARLES O'REAR** 234/5. **D CORRANCE** 92 The Cloisters, 110 Frick Museum, 123 Guggenheim Museum, 177 Soho Martin Lawrence Gallery, 179 Staten Island Ferry, 241 Greenwich Village Jazz. **J HENDERSON** 127b Puerto Rican. **HULTON GETTY** 16a,16b. **HULTON DEUTSCH COLLECTION LTD** 46a,b Labour Strikes, 47a New York Strike, 73b Malcolm X. ©1999 **KELLY/MOONEY PHOTOGRAPHY** 18, 117b, 118, 166, 167, 256. **KOBAL** 15a King Kong. **MAGNUM PHOTOS LTD** 97a Eyes Warhol (Philipe Halsam), 188a Woody Allen (Ernst Haas). **MARY EVANS PICTURE LIBRARY** 22a Manhattan Transfer, 23 Henry James,(Mary Evans/ J Morgan) 30a Dutch Land on Staten Island, 33 Declaration of Independence, 34–5 Immigration, 41a,b Wall St Crash, 105a Immigrants at Ellis Island. **METROPOLITAN MUSEUM OF ART** 143a Egyptian Funerary Customs – Coffins (Rogers Fund 1915 (15.2.2), 145a Islamic Eastern Mediterranean Glass (Rogers Bequest of Edward C Moore 1891 (91.1.1530), 147a Henri Matisse painting (Robert Lehman Coll. 1975 (1975.1.194), 147b Jacopo Bellini painting (Gift of Irma N Straus 1959 (59.187). **MUSEUM OF MODERN ART NEW YORK** 129 Jackson Pollock painting, 158b *The Starry Night* Van Gogh. **MUSEUM OF TV & RADIO** 161 Int Lonsdale Room. **PICTURES COLOUR LIBRARY** 24–5 East 47th Street. **REX FEATURES LTD** 17a, 17b, 18. **ROBERT HARDING** 238. **RONALD GRANT ARCHIVES** 15b *Saturday Night Fever*, 188b *Manhattan* Woody Allen. **P SLATTERY** 8b Mick Sinclair. **SPECTRUM COLOUR LIBRARY** Spine Statue of Liberty, 26b Chinese New Year, 27 Flute Player, 154a St Patrick's Day, 154b Pipe Band, 240 Birdland Jazz Club. **THE MANSELL COLLECTION** 30/1 New Amsterdam, 31 Landing of Hendrick Hudson, 32 P Stuyvesant, 34b Entering a New World, 36 Andrew Carnegie, 37 Pierpont Morgan, 38b Brooklyn Bridge, 38–9 New York 1851, 45 SS *Queen Mary*. **TONY STONE IMAGES** 221. **UNITED NATIONS** 184 Int, UN Building. **ZEFA PICTURE LIBRARY (UK) LTD** Cover Park Avenue at night, 11 Tompkins Sq Park, 14 Times Sq, 18 Times Sq, 39 Harlem, 40 Wall St, 73a Boy & Water, 138 Delancey St, 155 Folk Art Mus, 173 Rockefeller Plaza, 176 Soho Gallery, 185a U N Building,189 Central Park, 203 West Point Parade, 205 Albany, 237 Musician & bike, 255 St Paul's Chapel.
All remaining pictures are from the Association's own picture library (AA PHOTO LIBRARY) with contributions from:
P BAKER 127c. **D CORRANCE** 4, 6–7, 13, 20, 25, 55, 58–9, 67a, 72, 76, 78, 79, 87, 89, 96, 101, 106, 126, 128–9, 135, 137, 146, 148, 159, 160a, 162a, 171c, 175, 181b, 182, 185b, 192, 214, 215, 217, 225, 229, 232, 233, 234–5, 242, 246, 257, 259b, 263, 266, 280.
R ELLIOTT 3, 5a, 7, 10a, b, 12–3, 17b, 19, 20a, 21, 24, 28, 43, 44, 45, 50, 51, 52, 53, 54b, 56, 60, 61a, 63, 64, 66a, 68, 70, 74, 80, 81a, b, 83, 86, 88a, b, 90b, 94, 99, 100, 112, 113, 114a, 115, 116, 124a, b, 125, 131, 139a, b, 140, 141a, b, 142, 143b, 144, 149, 150, 151, 153, 156, 157, 158a, 160b, 163, 164, 165a, b, 168, 169, 171a, b, 172, 174b, 178, 180, 183a, b, 187, 190, 191, 193a, b, 194, 195, 196, 197, 198, 199a, b, 200, 201, 202, 206–7, 208, 209, 210, 211, 212, 216, 220, 223a, 226, 227, 228, 238b, 239, 244, 247a, 250, 253, 254, 256a, 258. **P KENWARD** 2, 5b, 5c, 6c, 9, 12, 23, 26, 54a, 57, 66b, 71a, b, 75a, b, 84a, b, 91, 93, 102, 103, 104, 120a, 132a, 134, 136a, b, 152, 162b, 166a, 170, 174a, 181a, 186, 213, 218, 219, 221, 224, 231a, b, 235, 243a, b, c, 245a,b, 247b, 248, 252, 259a, 260, 261b, 279. **D.POLLACK** 65, 85a, b, 108, 111, 120b, 121a, b, 261, 275. **E ROONEY** 9b, 29b, 49b, 83, 222. **C SAWYER** 8a, 69, 105b.

Contributors

Revision copy editor: Grapevine Publishing Services
Original copy editor: Donna Dailey
Revision verifier: Mick Sinclair